Praise for *Pen Men*

"One of the few places where old-fashioned ball players still reside is in the bullpen, far from the stern gaze of the manager. Bob Cairns deserves a vote of thanks for letting us spend time with some of the game's most independent and enjoyable characters. A wonderful read."
    —Lawrence S. Ritter, author of *The Glory of Their Times*

"The book is hysterical. I read whole pages to my wife, and we had tears in our eyes. I especially enjoyed the new perspective of the players looking back on that special time in their lives of twenty to thirty years ago."
    —Jim Bouton, author of *Ball Four*

"*Pen Men* gives the bullpen a chance to tell its best stories."
    —*USA Today*

"Over the last thirty years, baseball's most important development has been the increasing importance of the bullpen. Bob Cairns in *Pen Men* does a top-notch treatment of this subject. His interviews with the star relievers and his own insights make rewarding reading."
    —Ernie Harwell, Hall of Fame Broadcaster

"Beautifully done. I read it in one sitting."
    —Jerome Holtzman, *The Chicago Tribune*

"Like I've always said, the bullpen is the game. And Cairns's *Pen Men* is like sitting out there with old friends, going over the great moments, talking about the players and the strategy and the situations that make the whole thing all so special."
    —Sparky Anderson, Manager of the Detroit Tigers

"Pen men are the backbone of every club. They deserve this recognition and more."
    —Tommy Lasorda, Manager of the Los Angeles Dodgers

"Great stuff."
    —Roy Blount, Jr.

"Bob Cairns's history of relief is much more than just a recital of the accomplishments of Sparky, Goose, Tug, Turk, Moe, and the Mad Hungarian—it is a portrait of a special breed of ballplayer. You'll wish the book were twice as long."
    —*The Dallas Morning News*

PENMEN

Previous Books by Bob Cairns
The Comeback Kids

BOB CAIRNS

PEN MEN

BASEBALL'S GREATEST BULLPEN STORIES TOLD BY THE MEN WHO BROUGHT THE GAME RELIEF

A THOMAS·DUNNE BOOK

ST. MARTIN'S PRESS   NEW YORK

Photo on title page courtesy of Sportschrome East/West

Library of Congress Cataloging-in-Publication Data

Cairns, Bob.
   Pen men / Bob Cairns.
      p.   cm.
   "A Thomas Dunne book."
   ISBN 0-312-08873-6
   1. Baseball players—United States—Biography. 2. Pitching (Baseball) I. Title.
GV865.A1C3   1993
796.357'092'2—dc20
[B]   91-37987
                                                                                CIP

First Paperback Edition: March 1993

10 9 8 7 6 5 4 3 2 1

For Alyce

"The bullpen welcomed me with cutting remarks and well-sharpened needles, which they inserted into my wisecracks. Above anything else, a sense of humor is necessary for life in the bullpen. Once admitted and accepted in camaraderie, a relief pitcher may even suggest a serious topic for conversation. Like baseball."
—Jim Brosnan, *The Long Season*

Contents

THE GOLDEN YEARS OF RELIEF 259

VOICES FROM THE PEN

TOP GUNS
Mach III With Their Hair on Fire 336

VOICES FROM THE PEN

EPILOGUE

Acknowledgments

My thanks to Alyce, who lovingly reads, spells, checks, and double-checks; to Stan Grosshandler for his encouragement, expertise, and numerous contributions; to Bob Milks for his consultation; to Tony Outhwaite for being there from concept to publication; and to Tom Dunne and Pete Wolverton for all that they did to make this a better book.

Lawrence S. Ritter's classic, *The Glory of Their Times*, and Donald Honig's *Baseball When the Grass Was Real* certainly had an influence on *Pen Men*. And I'd like to express my appreciation to John Thorn for his fine book, *The Relief Pitcher*, a must-read for anyone interested in a detailed history of relief.

Thank-yous are in order for Bill Gilbert and Dan Foster, Major League Baseball Players Alumni Association; Bill Deane, National Baseball Hall of Fame and Museum, Inc.; Ruth Ruiz, Los Angeles Dodgers; Bob Miller and Helen Conklin, Baltimore Orioles; Stephanie Schmidt, Milwaukee Brewers; Larry Shenk, Philadelphia Phillies; Dick Bresciani and Mary Jane Ryan, Boston Red Sox; Joe Kelley, Cincinnati Reds; Bill Brown and Jeff Odenwald, Detroit Tigers; and Jeff Wehling of the St. Louis Cardinals.

Many thanks go to the broadcasters and writers whose insights, expertise, and remembrances will (I hope) help the essays read more like talk than writing. My collaborators here are, along with the pen men: Ernie Harwell, Red Barber, Monte Moore, Mel Allen, Jon Miller, Harry Caray, Jack Buck, and Jerry Holtzman. The major league managers whose two cents proved worth a million are: Al Lopez, Earl Weaver, Sparky Anderson, and Whitey Herzog.

And finally my gratitude to the bullpenners, the men who have by far the greatest ownership in this book: Sam Narron, Mace Brown, Broadway Charlie Wagner, Ace Adams, Johnny Sain, Rex Barney, Joe Nuxhall, Clyde King, Joe Ginsberg, Smoky Burgess, Sam Esposito, Hoyt Wilhelm, Dick Hall, Elroy Face, Red Johnson, Ryne Duren, Roger Craig, Moe Drabowsky, Larry Sherry, Tim McCarver, Ron Perranoski, Bob Uecker, Jim Bouton, Dick Radatz, Tug McGraw, Rollie Fingers, Elrod Hendricks, Tom House, Goose Gossage, Bruce Sutter, Dennis Eckersley, Dave Righetti, Mark Cresse, Kevin Hickey, Dan Plesac, Mitch Williams, Gregg Olson, Roger McDowell, Jeff Reardon, Dave Smith, Phil Roof, Dave LaPoint, Carroll Beringer, Lee Smith, Barry Foote, Charlie Silvera, Don Mossi, Larry Haney, Tommy Byrne, Les Moss, Norm Sherry, Gerry Moses, Stan Williams, and Bryan Harvey.

Preface

If the hands on the old square Longines clock on the Gunther's scoreboard in Baltimore's Memorial Stadium could be trusted, then I know the precise moment that the dream changed.

Time: 1:35 P.M., September 9, 1956.

It was a Sunday afternoon, following batting practice, before an Orioles–Red Sox game. A scorcher, temperature up in the 90s, one of those dead-air, Maryland summer days. As I hung over the Birds' dugout, waving a scorecard and pen, doing my damnedest to break up a conversation between Tito Francona and Bob Nieman, I noticed a parade heading my way.

Pitchers and a catcher marching toward the bullpen. Three guys in front, two tall and tanned, the other with flaming red hair. A bandy-legged catcher trailed along behind carrying a mask and a bag of baseballs. They had their gloves rolled up and tucked in interesting places—Spaldings and Rawlings under armpits, jammed in back pockets. A big black Nokona was wedged under a broad black uniform belt. The men's cheeks were pooched out, their mouths packed with Beechnut and Red Man tobacco. One suntanned cheek appeared ready to burst from a bulging mixture of a brown and pinkish substance. A tobacco–bubble gum combo, I thought.

I checked my scorecard. Hal "Skinny" Brown and Billy Loes were in the lead. The redhead was Zuverink. The man bringing up the rear had a face that any gum card collector worth a flip would know. "Joe Ginsberg!" Ginsberg, a journeyman catcher, had bounced from Detroit to Cleveland to Kansas City before landing with my beloved Baltimore

Birds that fall. It seemed like every time I opened a pack of Topps or Fleers that summer I found myself staring into the face of Myron "Joe" Ginsberg.

And Joe, would that I could say it ain't so. But it was the common practice of some of us to throw you away. At the time my behavior seemed inexplicable. Why would I treasure Joe Ginsbergs, rescue my buddies' discards, and keep this rather unlikely collection (several dozen) rubber-banded together and stashed in the back of my bureau drawer?

In a matter of seconds on that steamy September day in the year of 1956 I would have my answer. Here he came, Joe Ginsberg, anti-hero, throwaway catcher, and world's worst gum card, trailing the bullpen procession. Joe had a couple of catcher's mitts wedged under one arm, an old oily black Spalding and a stiff new Rawlings with a bright red label. Billy Loes turned suddenly, spat and uttered something which I strained to hear but couldn't make out. Ginsberg threw a line into Miranda and Gardner's game of catch, punctuating their laughter by slapping a series of bongo beats into the pocket of his worn black glove. I felt something soft and warm at my back, a brush of a breast, a girl in a pink sun dress pressing past. Waving a piece of blue stationery, she dipped low over the box seat railing and called to the players by name.

Parade rest!

A little laughing, a little innuendo, a few golden moments of flirty "Do you have a couple of friends?" conversation from the players. And as I looked on with envy she folded the paper and deposited it into the outstretched glove of Billy Loes. The long fingers flexed, the note popped up. The grateful recipient held it aloft like a hymnal for the others to read. Smiles and nods all around. Brown laughed. Ginsberg spat. Loes offered a knowing look and dialed an imaginary phone.

That was it. The magic moment. As precise as the hands on that Longines center field clock. 1:35 P.M., September 9, 1956.

While the crew trudged down the third base line, spitting and chewing their way into a fresh conversation, I offered up a little prayer. "Dear God, if what I've just witnessed is the kind of stuff that goes on in a bullpen, then take me to where my man Ginsberg is headed!"

Forget the "Little League Dream" of major league stardom. Heck, I wasn't a hitter, never had been. I didn't run that good, couldn't throw that well. I was a young Joe Ginsberg. A conversational catcher, a guy with a nice pair of hands, good sturdy legs, and a constitution that could deal with what my Little League coach called "the pitcher's mentality." I was a lock for a pen job. A kid who loved to shoot the bull, pester women, and play practical jokes. A legitimate pen prospect at the age of thirteen.

In the coming weeks, as the Birds flopped around in sixth place, I sat by the old floor-model Philco in my parents' living room and listened to Ernie Harwell's play-by-play of the games from a perspective which I suspect differed greatly from other Baltimore fans. I let my mind's eye drift past the team's inadequacies, over the game's distant fences and into the activity of the Birds' bullpen. I'd conjure up all sorts of pictures—I'd see my friends Brown and Loes laughing and chewing, telling some outrageous story, then I would make up my own joke and supply the punch line. A frown, a red neck, a right-handed glove thrown to the ground meant Bill Wight didn't have good stuff tonight. Playing the role of Ginsberg, I'd ease myself up off the couch and walk to our kitchen phone. "Paul! Joe here! Bill doesn't have it tonight, the breaking ball's hanging. There's no movement on the fast one. What say we tune up Ferrarese?"

Crazy, is what my sister thought. A thirteen-year-old kid mumbling baseball gibberish into the kitchen phone. But I'd be with them some day. Robin Cairns, bullpen catcher. Just a matter of time. Another pen man was on his way.

VERO BEACH, FLORIDA, MARCH 23, 1989

My wife and I were well-situated that day, behind the Dodgertown clubhouse, pressed up against a long yellow rope, savoring a special moment. Fastballs and sliders cracked and popped in the warm morning air as Mark Cresse, L.A.'s bullpen coach, hunkered down behind a bullpen plate, sixty feet, six inches away from a silver-haired legend.

"Sandy Koufax," I said. "And still bringing the heat."

A sweet moment or two passed and I continued my thought. "Alyce, you're watching what your husband wanted to do with his life."

"Pitch? I thought you wanted to catch!"

My eyes were riveted on Cresse as he duckwalked left and short-hopped a Koufax slider. "Be a bullpen catcher," I said.

"A bullpen catcher? You wanted to hunker, squat, and sweat for a living?" she said, and laughed.

Holed up in a nice secure area, trading stories with major league pitchers and catchers, watching the American pastime played at your feet—if there is a better life I'd like to know where.

"Boring," said she.

"Exciting," said I.

And with that exchange came the inspiration for the following pages. After all, I was a writer, wasn't I? Why not go out and bag some evidence to back up my argument? If I could convince Alyce Cairns that anything even mildly interesting had occurred in the more than 100 years of the bullpen's existence then I'd have a story worth telling. So spurred by the challenge and armed with dozens of questions about the career that had passed me by, I began my quest. I'd find the game's great pen men—pitchers, catchers, and coaches—guys who saw the game in the ways that only the pen men see it, men whom I'd like to have spent a career shooting the bull with. I'd go for the big names, of course, pitchers like Drabowsky, Perranoski, Gossage, McGraw, Radatz, and Bouton. For catchers I'd want Uecker, Burgess, and my man Ginsberg, of course. And a book on the men of the pen wouldn't be complete without the great coaches, the Sains, Kings, and Houses. But names alone don't make a book. Over the next several years I'd make hundreds of phone calls, buttonhole dozens of scouts, complete an exhaustive, page-by-page inventory of the *Baseball Encyclopedia* to find the men who would ultimately make this the pen's *Who's Who*. Only a few said no to my request.

I learned of Sam Narron, the Brooklyn Dodgers' first bullpen catcher, at a Durham Bulls game from Red Hayworth, a New York Yankees scout. Carroll Beringer, a man who worked in the pen for years in Los Angeles and Philadelphia, came on a tip from Tug McGraw. And without exception, everyone insisted that I had to talk with the king of the pen, the great Moe Drabowsky. And there were all of Moe's subjects, of course. From Mace Brown and Ace Adams in the 1930s and 1940s, to the great 1950s and 1960s firemen like Duren, Sain, and Face, to the guys from the Golden Age—Fingers, Gossage, Sutter, and McGraw. And finally today's top guns—Eckersley, Reardon, Righetti, and Olson.

Early on, Stan Grosshandler, a friend who writes often for *Baseball Digest*, asked, "So what is it? The bullpen's answer to *The Glory of Their Times* . . . or what?"

I didn't have a good answer. The project was young and I was still tracking down ballplayers and arranging interviews. I wanted it to be a look at baseball—from World War II to the present—told by a series of anecdotal interviews. The book would be about the game's last fifty years as seen through the eyes of the men in the pen. And now that I've logged thousands of miles on the project, completed hundreds of interviews in major league dugouts from Candlestick to Fenway, in family rooms, on back-porch swings and yes, even chatted on the phone with the great Ryne Duren while he was immersed in a bathtub, I had Grosshandler's answer.

I wanted to experience, albeit vicariously, what that career in the pen might have been like. And while I sat and talked with the pen men, my recorder would capture their lives, catch anecdotes and reminiscences that would give a reader a view of the game as it was played, and do it from a unique perspective. How dark was it when Mace Brown threw that "Homer in the Gloamin'" pitch to Gabby Hartnett? What were Clyde King's thoughts knowing that it was he and not Branca who should be coming in to face Bobby Thomson on that October afternoon in 1951. Did Bouton's teammates know what he was up to when he slipped into bullpen johns and furiously wrote notes on those popcorn boxes? Did Sam Narron have a clue the day he caught Koufax at the Pirates' tryout that if the Bucs didn't come up with $15,000 they'd be losing one of baseball's greatest pitchers? Did Goose grab Brett's bat during the Pine Tar Incident? Did Joe Nuxhall sense history at all when at the age of fifteen he was called in to face guys like Kurowski, Hopp, and Musial? Did Ryne Duren purposely fire warm-up pitches into the backstop to intimidate hitters when he came in from the pen for his warm-ups? Or was the man actually that far out of control? Has anybody ever tried to get even with Moe Drabowsky, baseball's most notorious practical joker? And how about "Captain Hook?" Did Sparky ever have second thoughts about the way he went out there and yanked all those starters?

Baseball players are reputedly the best talkers in all of sport. So it stands to reason that the guys in the pen would take this talent to a higher level. They've made careers of perfecting the art of storytelling. And I owe a tremendous debt of gratitude to the men who agreed to share their lives and bullpen stories. As the pen men called up five decades of highs and lows, I found myself living the triumphs, suffering the defeats, and saddened by misspent youths. Most of all, these pen men made me laugh more times than the written word can convey.

When the interviews had been transcribed and the pieces written, Alyce—loving wife and spell-checker—crossed the T's and dotted the I's of every piece.

"Well, what did you think?" I said.

"You still can't spell," she said.

"About the pen? My career out there?"

"Quite a menagerie. Yes, I'm afraid you missed your calling. You would have fit right in," she said.

PROLOGUE

The Land of Odds

Sparky, Goose, Ratso, Tug, Turk, and Moe—sounds like the cast of an *Our Gang* comedy. The temptation is to come right out and say it: "Bullpenners are just a bit off-center, probably the guys who got dropped on their heads by their Little League coaches!" In the pen's hundred-plus years of existence, there's been one certified psychologist out there, Dr. Thomas Ross House, pitching coach, Texas Rangers. His diagnosis:

Are they different? I like to say Mach III with their hair on fire. No matter what their personality appears to be, these are the guys who seek out the adrenaline situations. They thrive on it, they have to be on the dance floor. Bullpen men are totally unembarrassable. They could give a flying crap what anybody thinks of them. They can look at a pile of horseshit in the road and as long as they're not stepping in it, they can work with it. In the psychological profession this is called positive denial. They will make a game out of anything, they have to have action all the time. There's a need to get the adrenaline up. From creating bets—*I'll bet you that that woman sits in that section in that row of seats*—to shooting moons and putting atomic balm in each other's jocks. Look, when God started making bullpenners, He said, "Give me all the hyperactive guys, left-handers first!"

This certainly brings a number of questions to mind. Who came up with the pen's first funny nicknames? Who fired up the first hotfoot? When did relief men begin stalking to the mound with that better-hang-loose-I'm-a-little-bit-different look in their eye, then back it up with a heater under a hitter's chin? What were the beginnings of this persona that Dr. House describes? How did this man and his pen evolve?

First, a word about the asylum. There's a common misconception. The Bull Durham tobacco signs posted on outfield walls in the early 1900s were not the inspiration for the name bullpen. Baseball historian Lee Allen directs us to the words of an indignant writer as the probable source of the name. On May 4, 1877, the *Cincinnati Enquirer* let the Red Stockings' management hold it for offering late arrivals a price break. "For ten cents or three-for-a-quarter, herding them in like bulls within a rope area in foul territory, adjoining the outfield," the admonishment said. As to construction, best guesses report hammers ringing along major league sidelines some time during the early 1900s.

The penners' funny nicknames have been around even longer. In *The Relief Pitcher*, baseball historian John Thorn lists monickers belonging to substitute pitchers from the "pre-relief" era prior to 1900: "Oyster" Burns, "Phenomenal" Smith, "Bones" Ely, "Stump" Weidman and "Silver" King. As the century turned, there were others—"Doc" Crandall, "Iron Man" McGinnity and "Three Finger" Brown.

The first great relief pitcher, the man who took the Washington Senators to their first-ever World Championship in 1924, had a penworthy nickname himself. Fred "Firpo" Marberry's teammates saw an uncanny resemblance in their fireman to Luis Firpo, "the Wild Bull of the Pampas," the Argentine heavyweight who knocked Jack Dempsey into the expensive seats in a 1923 heavyweight match.

The early relievers were oddly named but as yet no signs were evident that the personality of these men had begun to stray off-center. The suspicion here is that this was with good reason. Until Marberry's breakthrough—in his first three full years (1924–1926) he led the American league in appearances, games finished, and the then-unofficial categories of saves and relief points—relief was still an undefined profession. Most men who performed in these substitute roles were starters by trade, and many were older, mature, seasoned veterans, men who had little or no taste for the new specialty.

The birthplace of this pen pensona that Dr. House describes is arguably New York City. When Hugh Casey and Joe Page, two very different but dynamic individuals, took the mound in the 1940s, the press suddenly looked up from their Underwoods. Both men made great copy. Casey, a rotund Brooklyn Dodger right-handed spitballer, known for his drinking and ill temper, liked nothing more than to put one of his pitches under the chin of a hitter who dared to dig in at the plate.

2

Page, a handsome, curly-haired lefty who fired fastballs and forkballs at the opposition, consumed the city—especially the women, the bars, the bright lights. New York Yankees announcer Mel Allen watched Page walk into the spotlight.

You know, I believe that Joe Page really started it. He was the beginning of relief pitchers being stars rather than just guys who couldn't start. And there are so many stories about Joe. And of course, the lasting memory, the one that I'll never forget, is seeing him come out of that bullpen in Yankee Stadium. He'd sling his jacket over his shoulder and jump over the right field fence.

Dodger penmate Rex Barney remembers Hugh Casey as the man who made hitters jump.

Hugh Casey? I can just see him waddling out to the bullpen, making his slow trek about the seventh inning. He had been a mediocre pitcher all of his life and when he got to be about thirty-three or thirty-four he was a rotund guy, out of shape, heavy drinker, cheated a lot . . . spitter, he threw that a lot. But he was mean. And he would set you up and then he would knock you down. And he'd look you right in the eye when he did it too. And yes, he'd actually throw at guys in the on-deck circle. I saw him do it in Brooklyn.

Ernie Harwell, a young broadcaster with the Dodgers in 1948, recalls an earlier Casey, a competitor who wouldn't give in on land or sea.

I liked Casey. He was a competitor. I remember one occasion, we had played a night game in Philadelphia and got home very late. And Casey had asked several of us on the train if we'd like to go fishing . . . George Shuba and Carl Erskine and myself. We met at daybreak at Sheepshead Bay out on Long Island and had little or no sleep. And there was Casey with this big cigar, drinking whiskey. And we took off in this little boat. I'd been in the Marines and had never been seasick in my life. I got deathly ill and so did the rest of the guys. But not Hugh. He kept us out there all day. Nobody had guts enough to ask Casey to take us back.

Rex Barney remembers Page's off-the-field exploits.

And I remember Joe Page, do I ever! He was probably the biggest dissipater in the history of baseball—drinker, women . . . They'd send

3

detectives out to follow him and he'd end up getting the detectives drunk. Well the Yankees were on a road trip, and in those days we used to be on the road, three, three and a half weeks. So Page gets off the train at Grand Central Station and he's with a writer, Bill Roeder, a friend of mine who wrote for the [New York] *Telegram*. He's with Bill and now here comes Page's wife. Joe isn't expecting to see her there so when he goes to introduce Roeder he says, "Bill, I want you to meet my wife . . . uh, Mrs. Page." He forgot her first name! That's a true story, that was Joe Page.

Personalities like Casey and Page led the pen men into the 1950s but had they glanced over their shoulders, they would have seen someone gaining on them. Leroy "Satchel" Paige, a victim of the color line, spent his early days playing in the Negro leagues and barnstorming against major league teams. But once in the majors he enjoyed some excellent years, first with Cleveland in 1948 and 1949 and then with the St. Louis Browns from 1951 to 1953. Paige's career was short-lived but he'd remain a topic of bullpen conversations for years to come. Typical of the stories told about Satch and his command of the strike zone is one from his rocking chair days with the Browns. The Brownies, playing in Washington, D.C., were on a tight train schedule. The secretary of the club called from above the dugout to Satch as he ambled out to protect a one-run lead in extra innings. "Make it quick! We've got a train to catch!" "How about nine pitches?" was Satchel's response. Paige then proceeded to strike out the Senators on ten quick pitches. And as the Browns hustled to the station to make their train Paige was heard to say, "I can't understand how that man coulda called that one a ball!"

Following this paragon of control, the pen was blessed with three legitimate wild men, two in the personal sense and the third, Ryne Duren, a double threat. Ellis Kinder and Broadway Billy Loes both had the stuff of which good penners are made. Nocturnal by nature, they knew the pulse of the cities they played in by heart. Kinder, a starter who switched to relief late in his career with the Boston Red Sox, led the league in 1951, with sixty-three appearances and fourteen saves. But as good as "Old Folks" was on the mound, he was better with the bottle. In David Halberstam's *Summer of '49* we learn from broadcaster Curt Gowdy's eyewitness account of an all-night drinkathon on a train between Chicago and Cleveland. The bout ends in the dawn of a Cleveland morning with Kinder being pushed through the train station in a wheel chair, ". . . unconscious, his head rolling back and forth like a rag doll's." That afternoon in a doubleheader against Cleveland, "on a brutally hot day," Kinder frisked out of the pen to retire nine men in a row.

As for the joy pensters take from a well-placed wager, no one appreciated the action more than journeyman reliever Broadway Billy Loes. Penner Joe Ginsberg had the pleasure of rooming with Loes.

I roomed with his luggage. This was in Baltimore. And yes, Billy was a gambler, he loved to gamble and this [story] goes back to when he was with the Dodgers before the 1953 World Series. And the newspaper guys had asked all the Yankees—Mantle, Berra, all of them—what they thought the outcome would be. And the Yankees said, "Well, Brooklyn has a real good ball club, I think that we'll win it in seven." They asked the Dodgers and Campanella and he said, "I think it might go the limit and we'll hang in there and beat them in seven." So now they come to Billy Loes, a gambler, and a Dodgers pitcher, he says, "If you've got any money, you'll bet on the Yankees in six, because that's what's going to happen." And sure enough, the Yankees won it in six.

Third, and the pen man who pushed wildness to its limits, was Ryne Duren. Up with Baltimore briefly in 1954 and again in 1957 with Kansas City, Duren landed in Yankee Stadium in 1958. There in the pen in the South Bronx, Duren took a pair of dark, Coke-bottle-thick glasses, a drinking problem, and an oft-misdirected 100-mile-an-hour fastball and wove them into yet another bullpen legend. Duren was the fearsome mound presence who influenced Gossage, Hrabosky, and Dibble. Mel Allen remembers Duren.

Ryne Duren, he could throw so dadgum hard, almost a Nolan Ryan type, but he was just so wild. And the Yankees were going to see if they could harness him a bit, this was 1958 that he came over, but he didn't have the best of eyesight. His glasses were so thick that you'd have called them Coca-Cola bottle types. Joe Page had that habit of hopping over the bullpen gate when he was called in. Well a batter on-deck, he'd see that and he'd say, "Damn, that guy can't wait to start pitching." So Casey Stengel decided to try to get Duren to jump the fence like Page. And Ryne said, "Case, I can't see well enough to hop over the gate and if I miss, it's really going to defeat our purpose."

Here's my favorite Ryne Duren story. Now here's a man who has a reputation for having really weak eyesight. The Yankees are playing an exhibition game against Baltimore in Miami, a night game in 1959, I think. Duren is pitching and I can't remember who the batter was, but all of a sudden the plate umpire calls time out. Then all we could see

5

was Berra and the umpire looking down at the ground. And then everybody's out there digging around in the dirt around home plate, they're down on their hands and knees scratching around. I thought false tooth, then it occurred to me, damn, I didn't know that guy wore contact lenses. And that's what it was. All the time Duren is waiting patiently out on the mound, sixty feet, six inches away. Then all of a sudden here he comes marching in like a soldier, very quick steps, he stops, stoops over, picks up the lens and hands it to the hitter. Now this is the guy who is supposed to be blind. Well you talk about laughter. Both benches, the whole ball park was in hysterics. Of course it was the reflection off the glass that allowed him to see it. But Ryne almost destroyed his own legend that day.

By the mid-fifties many of the sixteen major league clubs had added drinking fountains and protective awnings to their pens. As many or more had been visited by Ma Bell, allowing managers and pitching coaches to communicate with these distant outposts more directly. No longer did managers have to stand on the dugout steps and pat their bellies to summon the fat reliever or make the circle sign in front of their eyes when they wanted the man with the specs to get up. But the best of these outposts would never be described as a room with a view. Some of the worst were in Philadelphia's Connie Mack Stadium. Penners watched the game through chicken wire. And it was the habit of some to fly to the coop. Bob Uecker recalls:

In Philadelphia we used to go out on the street in our uniforms, me, Turk Farrell, all of us. There was a little place, the Phillies Bar, across the street from the bullpen. We'd all go over there and get sandwiches and bring them back. A couple of times Gene Mauch [the Phillies manager] called for a pitcher and we'd have to put him on hold because the guy was out to lunch.

Out to lunch perhaps, but the noon meal was hardly Turk Farrell's favorite repast. Farrell liked to do his consuming at night. He and his penmates, Jim Owens and Jack Meyer, were called the Dalton Gang, and a blazing headline, "The Dalton Gang Rides Again," in the June 13, 1960, issue of *Sports Illustrated* led to an incident they're re-counting around major league bullpens.

The *SI* piece compared the Dalton Gang (named by Phillies pitching coach Tom Ferrick) to "hellraisers of old, the McGraws, Cobbs, Ruths and Alexanders." Harmless enough. But several quotes suggested that one of the players had come from a drinking family. The Dalton Boys didn't take kindly to the story.

How the spin-off is told depends on the pen man who's telling it. Here's a popular version told by a deep-throated voice from the pen.

After this story comes out in *Sports Illustrated*, Farrell and a couple of the Dalton Gang are in a bar in Philadelphia. An attorney approaches Turk and says, "Turk, did you know that the Dalton Gang was made up of a bunch of murderers and rapists, it's slandering your characters. You know you could sue the magazine." "Go for it," said Farrell. The attorney negotiates a fair settlement with the magazine. Each player is awarded one thousand dollars. The Gang takes their windfall, rents a suite in a posh Philadelphia hotel, brings in some hookers, ices down the booze and rides again!

Everybody has a Turk Farrell story. Larry Sherry remembers Farrell from his days in Houston. "We weren't on the radio then and Farrell would stay out all night, then steal the newspaper out of his driveway and tell his wife that we'd gone eighteen innings." Carroll Beringer, who coached in the bullpen of the Los Angeles Dodgers during the early 1960s, recalls the night when Walter Alston gave him an offer that he couldn't refuse. The Dodger skipper asked Beringer to room with Farrell for the sake of the entire Los Angeles pitching staff.

Turk had trouble finding his room at night. But room with Farrell? Now you talk about being sentenced! I'm a pretty straight-arrow guy and rooming with Farrell had very damned little appeal to me. But Walt said, "You know he's rooming with Stan Williams and heck, Turk's going to be Turk, but if he takes Stan down with him, he's going to hurt our staff." And I'll never forget, Drysdale is standing there listening to this and he's got the biggest grin on his face. And he says, "Now Carroll, you look like this is going to be very unpleasant, but this could be a big break for you!" And of course I ask how. "Just get you a little notebook, write down everything you see and you'll have yourself a best seller!"
You know he was unreal, he told me a story about a roommate he had in the minor leagues who wouldn't come out of the bathroom, in there reading or something, and so Turk shot a .45 right through the door. Turk said, "He came out then." A fun-loving guy, I'll tell you!

But it wasn't just Farrell. By the early 1960s the Milwaukee Braves Triple-A franchise in Louisville, Kentucky, appeared to be into some kind of off-center player development. It was in fact incubating two of the pen's looniest birds. While a young Bob Uecker set off salvos of

7

fireworks to celebrate walks and base hits, Moe Drabowsky lit up shoe soles, greased toilet seats and perfected an act that would begin to define the bullpen's persona. Drabowsky recalls:

Bob and I had a lot of fun together in that pen in Louisville, this was 1961. You never knew about Bob, he was always interviewing people in airports, pretending he was *Candid Camera* and trying to get people to do crazy things. He'd come down for breakfast and when he ordered he'd say, "I'll take a glass of orange juice, a couple of scrambled eggs and sausage, and a half of grapefruit." And the waitress would write all that stuff down and as she got ready to walk away he'd say, "Now wait a minute on that half grapefruit, I don't want the top half, make sure that I get the bottom half." She'd scratch her head and he'd say, "Hey, that grapefruit could have been sitting there for five days, and there's more juice in the bottom."

Bob Uecker would go on to become the bullpen's most famous alumnus . . . Mr. Baseball, the movie *Major League*, "The Tonight Show," the Miller Lite commercials, star of "Mr. Belvedere," a genuine multi-media celebrity. But when asked to crown their king, the relief men remember the man who stayed behind and worked in the pen. During the 1960s Moe Drabowsky took baseball high jinks to new and exciting heights, engineering everything from ball park phone systems and the Great Bullpen Wars of 1969 to the stocking of bullpen water coolers with fresh fish. Newspaper headlines like "Snake in The Clubhouse Gift from Drabowsky," and "It's Fun Time If Moe Picks Up The Phone," sang his praises.

And these pen men, the Ueckers, Drabowskys, et al. have, over the years, led the league in kibitzing and in opinionizing. Nothing escapes their scrutiny—the view, seating, phones, fans, women, acoustics and stadium music, rest rooms, food. The distant pens of Yankee Stadium have long been the favorites for . . . well, bullpen activity. Ryne Duren remembers his first encounter with them.

This has been an inside joke with the Yankees for years now. The first time I walked out to the bullpen in Yankee Stadium there were these passageways and catacombs out there, and I walked in on a Yankee player and a girl in, let's just say it was a sexual encounter!

Charlie Silvera, along with his pen pal Ralph Houk, took turns heating up pitchers and keeping tabs on the Yankees pen during the late 1940s and early 1950s, and Charlie recalls one of the greatest occasions ever held in the pen's little back room. It was a formal dinner catered by an All-Star shortstop.

This was in 1956, Phil Rizzuto's last year. He came down there a lot and helped me out. And one day, a doubleheader, he said, "Charlie, I want you to join me for lunch between games today." Well, I walked into that little room and it was set up with candles, a checkered tablecloth, and somehow he'd brought in this nice little Italian lady to serve us. We had pasta, Italian bread, the works. It was something. I got a little spaghetti sauce on my pinstripes that day.

And according to Silvera, over on the visitors' side, pitchers fought an uphill battle.

They had the mounds built and the ground sloped so the visiting team was pitching slightly uphill. We warmed up downhill, they pitched uphill. Just the opposite. George Weiss had it all figured out. And a lot of times when it rained, they [the grounds crew] wouldn't put any tarps on the mounds in the visitors' pen, just little things. And there were times when they did have them covered that somebody would happen to step on them with their spikes, to let the water run through. And there were bullpen phones jammed and wires cut in the [opposition's] pens. I've done some wire cutting in my time. Just little tricks of the pen.

It's this creativity that sets the pen apart. For nearly a century the men have managed to top themselves in bullpen activity, coming up with better and more innovative ways to scope and communicate with women, snack, chew, use and abuse bugs and rodents, display fireworks, spin yarns, expectorate, grill out, call loved ones long distance, set fires, impersonate players, and criticize management. Games developed by bullpen staffers would, I suspect, make the Parker Brothers a bit envious. Joe Garagiola, for instance, created All-Ugly, All-Fighter, and All-Football teams. Jim Bouton and penmates broke pop bottles with BB rifles in their bullpen range. Roger McDowell and Jesse Orosco played car chase with remote-controlled vehicles under the stands. Bobby Thigpen and his mates play baseball with sesame seeds. Norm Charlton and Rob Dibble hold salad-plate tossing contests on hotel and stadium roofs. And along more intellectual lines it should be noted that over the past thirty-five years at least two books were written in major league pens. Jim Brosnan's *The Long Season*, baseball's first tell-it-like-it-is work, was crafted during "The Professor's" days in the St. Louis and Cincinnati pens in the late 1950s. Jim Bouton's *Ball Four*, which blew the whistle and the lid off of baseball's extracurricular activity, hit the bookstands a decade later.

Yes, I wrote a lot of *Ball Four* on popcorn boxes in johns and major league bullpens. I'd hear a great line and run in there and get it all down before I'd forget it.

With the publication of *Ball Four*, the word was on the street. We had major league baseball players, role models for our youth, peeping up ladies' dresses through holes drilled in dugout and bullpen walls. If the country was outraged, it certainly didn't hurt the recruiting of pen men. The line formed at the rear—McGraw, Lyle, LaRoche, Borbon, Hrabosky, Stanhouse, Tidrow, and Quisenberry—suddenly all the big league loopies were opting for careers in the pen. Consider Tug McGraw.

Everything about McGraw said "bullpen." Californian, left-hander, long shaggy hair. McGraw's tank sloshed and splashed with so much adrenaline that you could hear him coming from the upper deck. The Tugger put up tremendous numbers in relief and would take his famed screwball to six league championship series. But as is the lot of these men, he'll probably be more remembered for "Scroogie," his nationally syndicated cartoon strip, or his one-liners—when asked to describe the difference between artificial and real grass McGraw said, "I don't know, I've never smoked any artificial stuff." His war cry, "You gotta believe!" which he shouted on the mound, in locker rooms, in buses, and bullpens, became the rallying cry of the 1973 Mets.

And then there was Sparky Lyle, distinguished relief specialist and 1977 Cy Young Award winner who once stripped all the way down to his skivvies to the delight of a capacity crowd in Arlington, Texas. Broadway Charlie Wagner talks about Sparky's favorite indoor sport.

When I was the pitching coach for Boston we had Sparky Lyle, he was a great guy and a fun lover. But he was the kinda guy who when people would send us birthday cakes, he'd come right over [naked] and sit on them. And I'd say, "Oh, jeeze!" I'm a cake lover anyway and Sparky loved to kill cakes.

And we'd be remiss if we forgot Pedro Borbon. Joe Nuxhall recalls his eating habits.

Remember the Buddy Harrelson and Pete Rose fight in the 1973 play-offs? A hard slide by Pete into second, they came up swinging but the best part of that story was Borbon. All of a sudden all hell broke loose—benches emptied, the bullpens came in and it was war. Now Borbon, a real character. After the fight breaks up, Pedro tries to put his hat back on and it doesn't fit. Turns out he's got Cleon Jones's hat, but he's trying to put it on and finally he takes it off and looks and here it's a damned Mets hat and he got so mad he just bit the bill off the cap, chewed it all up. Pedro is a beaut. He used to open beer bottles with his teeth, and you know he got quite a reputation for biting, maybe it all started with the Mets cap thing. But we got into a fight in Pittsburgh and he bit a pitcher there, I think it was Daryl Patterson, I'm not sure but he bit him right under the arm and the guy had to have a tetanus shot. And now after that we had another deal in L.A., this was the same year—Rose and Rick Auerbach, and both benches emptied and Borbon was down in the bullpen, but this time he didn't come in. And after the game in the clubhouse they asked Pedro, "Where were you during the fight, why didn't you come in?" And Pedro said, "Me no hungry!"

While we're sorting through this table of irregulars, let's not forget Al Hrabosky, "The Mad Hungarian." This gypsy pitcher put together some pretty good years with the St. Louis Cardinals and Kansas City Royals in the 1970s and early 1980s. He wore a Fu Manchu mustache, hair that fell just short of his massive shoulders, and on the third finger of his glove hand he wore a silver anti-werewolf ring, honoring "The Gypsy Rose of Death." Hungo was the game's Attila. And when he tired of stomping the rubber and kicking dirt, he'd turn from the hitter and cast death stares into the white shirts in the center field bleachers. When the Mad Hungarian got his blood pressure up in the 200 over 130 range he'd pitch. Whitey Herzog recalls "Hungo's" first performance as an American League reliever.

The Mad Hungarian, he'd had maybe eight years in the National League with St. Louis and we got him in Kansas City in 1978, and the first time I brought Hungo into a game, he started walking people like crazy. It's the ninth inning and we've got the lead but it's close and I mean he was throwing high fastballs over everybody's head. John Wathan was catching and he'd been jumping up and catching balls all over the place. Hungo was really mad now and he finally loaded up the bases and with one man out and a 2–0 count on the hitter, I brought in Larry Gura. So the first pitch is a one-hopper back to the mound, Larry goes home to first for the double play and we win the ball game.

I'm in the bus after the game and I see Hungo coming and I jump up on the front seat of the bus so when he climbs on I'm up there in a hitter's stance pretending to hold a bat. Hungo says, "What's this?" I say, "This is where a guy has to get to hit off of you, up on a goddamned bench!" Hungo says, "Screw it, I thought this was supposed to be a high ball league," and walks back the aisle and takes his seat.

11

So Hrabosky had a little trouble identifying the American League strike zone but how about the brothers Sherry? As pitching coaches, Norm and Larry both went through major identity crises. Larry Sherry once did a double take when reliever Will McEnaney, unhappy with the Pittsburgh Pirates management, sent his non-roster, identical twin out to take his place in the pen. But in this category of mistaken identity, Norm Sherry tells a story that goes his brother one better.

When I was with the Angels, this was in 1970 or 1971, Lefty Phillips was managing the ball club and we had a kid that was a left-handed pitcher but he could throw right-handed, and did it for fun, you know. So we're in Baltimore and the pens are behind the fence. He was out there screwing around throwing right-handed. Now Phillips tells me to get him up and so I holler over at him and now he starts throwing left-handed. I didn't hear Phillips but evidently he wanted a right-hander up too. But he'd looked out there and seen one working so I guess he thought I had both of them going. Well, he'd seen this kid, of course. Phillips thinks I've got them both ready, a lefty and a righty. So now they make the call for a reliever and when Phillips sees him coming he's hot. "I don't want him, I want the righty." I had no right-hander ready of course. Oh my God, that got me in trouble.

If the pitchers are the crazies, then the pen catchers are the guys with the nets who wear the white suits. Barry Foote, a man who caught in and out of the pens of the Montreal Expos, the Chicago Cubs, the Philadelphia Phillies, and the New York Yankees during the 1970s and 1980s, admits to having had the pleasure of working with "some of the real, real zanies." There were Mike Marshall and Dave LaRoche, and then there were the guys with the nicknames that stood out like a WARNING: MAD DOG sign—Dick "Dirt" Tidrow, Don "Stan the Man Unusual" Stanhouse, and Rich Gossage, a.k.a. "The Goose."

Mike Marshall was in Montreal when I got there and Mike was a different type guy. Physically he was unbelievable, he was into kinesiology, knew all about muscles. But he had a real high regard for himself. He kept a book, like a diary on all situations that came up. And I won't say who, but somebody got into that book one time and read it. And it never had one note about Mike making a bad pitch. The players were either playing in the wrong position or the hitter hit a good pitch. It was always somebody else's fault, the manager, another player, but never Mike. He'd show you up, didn't mind showing his teammates up, so he wasn't the most popular guy in the world. But I didn't dislike him, and he was one hell of a pitcher, in many ways way ahead of his time.

12

Last year [1990] I worked as a coach in the pen with the Chicago White Sox. Dave LaRoche handles our pitchers. LaRoche is a beaut. Jeff Torborg [White Sox manager and former teammate of LaRoche] likes to tell about the time LaRoche set the pen on fire in Cleveland, smoke billowing out, it was like a three-alarmer for the grounds crew. Another time they were looking for Dave, this was in Cleveland, and found him sitting on top of the scoreboard watching the game. But the classic LaRoche is the one of those deals that, well it was probably the only time that two relief pitchers ever came into the game at once. This was in the early seventies and Rudy May is a starter who the Angels have out in the pen during the late innings of a game in Boston. Lefty Phillips is managing California and he gets Rudy up instead of LaRoche. Now this is LaRoche's role late in the game. He's the stopper. So Dave says, "If he calls Rudy into this game I'm going in there with him." Sure enough, they call Rudy and there they go. Rudy May and Dave LaRoche, walking side by side into the ball game. LaRoche walks right up on the mound with May, takes off his warm-up jacket and then stalks into the dugout and up the ramp to the clubhouse. And if you're Phillips you've got to be wondering what the hell is going on. But that was LaRoche, he was done for the day.

Don Stanhouse—the names "Stan the Man Unusual" and "Full Pack" came later when Stanhouse was pitching in relief with Baltimore. I caught Stanley in Montreal earlier in his career. Mike Flanagan named him "Full Pack" because he worked so slowly that Earl Weaver went through a full pack of cigarettes waiting for him to make a pitch. God, was he slow! I think he needed all that time for his brain to stimulate all these processes to figure out what he was doing out there.

One game, this was in Montreal, 1976, Gary Carter is catching and Tim Foli is playing shortstop. Stanhouse doesn't trust Carter to call the pitches, so he decides that Foli will call them from shortstop. Between every pitch he's off the mound looking back at Foli to find out what to throw. One of Stan's slower arrangements.

Now Gossage, with the Yankees, was this nice easy-going guy until about the eighth inning and then you'd see this metamorphosis occur. All of a sudden he looked like a wild man. I remember the first time I caught him in Yankee Stadium he'd gotten behind on the hitter and they had a runner on first, so I step out in front of the plate to say something and he yells, "Get your ass back there and catch." He's screaming, I'm screaming, the umpire wonders what the hell is going on. Finally I go back, Goose throws three straight strikes and we're out of the inning. But that was Gossage, normally a very easy-going guy, but when the game was on, look out!

By the mid-eighties, though, the zanies began to thin out a bit. No more "Dirt" Tidrows, "Full Pack" Stanhouses, or "Spaceman" Lees.

13

Dan Quisenberry was now the pen's "personality." But as the decade wound down even the old Quismeister began to show signs of age, as this story by Whitey Herzog shows.

Quis is a very witty guy and he had more goddamned good quotes than anybody. And he was one relief pitcher that knew how to use his defense. After the game he always had some great line to describe what happened. Later when I was with St. Louis I ran into Quis and said, "Hey, I haven't read any of your one-liners in the paper lately." Quis said, "Whitey, when you're going horseshit, you're not as funny anymore!"

There were a few specialty items out there with the Quis—Joe Pignatano gardened, Charlie Kerfeld pigged out on barbecue ribs, Mark Grant imitated umpires, and Larry Anderson went for Guinness records by attaching hundreds of sesame seeds to his face—so the species wasn't really endangered, it had just leveled off a bit. The guys were still firing up shoes, ordering out for pizza and ribs, watching spiders eat bugs, and scoping the stands with their binoculars. The health-conscious had begun to replace the bulge in their jaws with seed, a substance equally as spittable as tobacco juice. There were more incidents of pie-facing with the increase of pre- and post-game TV interview shows. And then, in the spring of 1985, just as things appeared to be settling down, along came a kid carrying an attache case chock full of M-80s, stink bombs and cigarette loads. Roger McDowell swaggered into the pen of the New York Mets. The magic was back! McDowell was a man for the nineties. Brosnan's and Bouton's literary efforts, Drabowsky's newspaper headlines couldn't approach the big numbers that McDowell would put up through the power of Super Stations and cable TV. Millions of WGN viewers would watch Roger slide through a Wrigley Field snowstorm chasing fly balls while dressed up in shoulder pads and a catcher's mask. McDowell's Upside-Down Man, a bit in which Rog would suit up upside-down (shoes on his hands, gloves on his feet), and entertain TV viewers with what appeared to be one-handed pushups, delighted millions hooked up to WWOR from New York. And again it was McDowell and WWOR that gave America its first coast-to-coast hotfoot.

Bill Robinson, one of the Mets coaches, was one of my favorites to get with the hotfoot.* We're in Cincinnati and anyway, I get Robinson

---

*To make a hotfoot, a book of matches is taped to a cigarette which serves as the fuse. Then both are taped to the back of the shoe. When the cigarette burns down, the matches ignite, burning the unaware victim's foot.

taped up and he goes out to coach first base. And like he's talking to Pete Rose and Pete catches on, so now it's not just us. Pretty soon the whole Reds team is watching, waiting. The game was late in the second inning when I set the thing and now it's the third inning and Gary Carter is up and Tim McCarver who does TV for the Mets knows about it and they've got their camera on it waiting, so like half of New York City is watching. And about two strikes on Carter in the top of the third that thing fires up and Bill jumps, and at first Bill doesn't know that half the free world is tuned in. Then he turns around and everybody is laughing on the bench, the Reds and the fans. . . . It's a night game so it made a nice flash, with WOR and the TV cameras. And Bill came into the dugout with this shit-eating, I-can't-believe-you-got-me look on his face. I have a tape of this at home. And it was really neat the way WOR kept going back for updates. It had to be the best coverage of a hotfoot in major league history.

So with McDowell in place, the pen persona that Dr. House described—"Mach III with their hair on fire"; "unembarrassable"; and "adrenaline seeking"—appears to be progressing nicely. Life is edging further and further off-center, penned up out there . . . in the Land of Odds.

From the First Pitch to the Big War

So how did they spell relief?

In the 1860s, the baseball rulebook made no provisions for bench substitutions. There were occasions when a manager would walk to the mound, offer a few kind words, pat the pitcher on the rump, then snatch the ball from his starter's hand. When Cincinnati's Cherokee Fisher and Boston's Joe Borden were waved in to games from positions on the field on June 17, 1876, baseball had its first relief pitchers. But the early rule clearly stated that only an ill or injured moundsman warranted the substitution from the bench. There were no Dibbles, no Myerses, no "Nasty Boys" back then. So when line drives began to pin back a starter's ears, the skipper's options were limited. He could sit back and enjoy the fireworks or trudge to the mound, look to the strongest arm between the white lines (most often an outfielder), cup his hands and make the following pronouncement:

"Change pitcher!"

Then in 1891 came a rule change that would help pitching. For the first time, a manager was allowed to dip into the pitching talent perched on the dugout bench. But as historian John Thorn points out in *The Relief Pitcher*, the practice of substituting for the starter still wasn't widely accepted. Managers tended to dance with the one that brung them, and according to Thorn, by "1891 the complete game ratio had settled at eighty-five percent; by 1904, they were eighty-nine and ninety percent, up from the norm that seemed to be established." And it should also be noted that the early relief men, guys like Jack Manning, Kid Nichols, and Tony Mullane, went to their graves without so much as an official save to their credit. This statistic wouldn't be acknowledged until 1960. It would be another nine years before it would become an official entry in major league score books.

However, early on, Henry Chadwick, a noted baseball writer of the day, saw a trend in this thing called relief and expressed his displeasure in the *Spalding Baseball Guide*, circa 1902. Chadwick, it would appear, believed relief a sign of weakness and aimed this barb at the game's starting pitchers.

> The National League clubs in 1901 employed no less than seventy-five pitchers . . . and that in the face of the fact that the brunt of the pitching of every club is, year in and year out, done by a corps of four pitchers only. . . . The argument used by the pitchers, that most of them were "overworked," was little else than a bluff on their part to avoid their due share of box work during the season.

Major league managers John McGraw and Clark Griffith must have overlooked Chadwick's article regarding the work ethic of major league pitchers. In the early 1900s, Griffith's New York Highlanders and McGraw's New York Giants put relief pitching back into the game, and did so with gusto. By yanking starters and hustling fresh arms to the mound, they took teams to pennants and World Series play. The winning brought attention to relief and phrases like "the heroic saver" began to find their way into print.

In the years that followed, "saver" was consistently mentioned in association with the names of Claude Elliot, Rube Waddell, Cy Young, Jack Chesbro, Ed Walsh, Chief Bender, Allan Russell, and Mordecai "Three Finger" Brown. Three Finger, a Cubs ace (whose unique grip on the breaking ball was the result of a childhood run-in with a feed chopper), did double duty for the Chicago Cubs. From 1908 to 1910 Brown set major league work ethic records. He started an average of thirty-two games a year and got enough relief work in to lead the league in saves. In 1911 he topped himself with a record twenty-seven starts and twenty-six trips out of the pen.

The New York Giants' "Doc" Crandall led the National League in relief wins from 1910 to 1912 and brought attention to his late-inning specialty. Damon Runyon's tribute to Crandall in the *New York American* was certainly the finest bouquet ever tossed at a relief pitcher.

> Crandall is the Giants' ambulance corps. He is first aid to the injured. He is the physician of the pitching emergency . . . without an equal as an extinguisher of batting rallies and run riots. . . . He is the greatest relief pitcher in baseball.

One only had to read the revised 1920 rule book to see that pitching could use all the help it could get. The mound had long since been set (fifteen inches in 1903) and now the authorities were after the pitchers again. They took the spitters away and introduced a new ball, one that jumped over fences. More than ever, there was need for relief.

Ironically, it would be a spitball specialist who would lead relief pitching into the new decade. Allan Russell, the Washington Senators relief specialist, was one of seventeen pitchers who escaped the "no wet one" ruling. And Russell, not being one to look a gift commissioner in the mouth, took full advantage of the grandfather clause. He was, says Thorn, "the game's busiest saver, had a record forty-seven relief appearances in 1923 and was the first man to relieve 200 times."

But the big news came in 1924 when Fred "Firpo" Marberry went to work for Bucky Harris in D.C. Joining Russell in the Senators pen, Marberry contributed fifteen saves and helped Harris win his first major league pennant. The fireballing Marberry got the nod a record fifty times during Washington's pennant-winning year, then came back with a league-leading fifty-five appearances in 1925 to help nail down another flag.

And as important as the Crandalls, the Browns, the Russells and Marberrys were to the slow but steady acceptance of relief pitchers, much of the credit for its development lay with management. McGraw and Griffith believed in and won with their bullpens. But there is no better example than the management style exhibited in our nation's capital. For a four-year period, from 1923 to 1926, Donie Bush and Bucky Harris's Washington Senators would lead the American league in saves. Four of those five years the Senators pen led the league in relief points. Years later Calvin Griffith offered his educated opinion as to why Washington management believed in stockpiling reserve pitchers.

> The heat and humidity in Washington were always the worst in
> baseball and in the years the Senators were winning pennants [1924
> and 1925] they had great depth. I can remember my father saying that
> you had to have some people to fill in because of the intense heat.
> And of course, they played all the games in the daytime then. I'm sure
> it was one of the reasons why Washington used pitchers in relief more
> than any other team.

It would appear that Griffith's managers weren't the only weathermen in the American League. The records would lead us to believe that Miller Huggins had a thermometer in the dugout of the New York Yankees. In 1927 Wilcy Moore, an elderly rookie, got the call thirty-eight times and almost without fail effectively threw sinkerballs under the bats of the opposition. Moore, an Oklahoma farm boy, recorded a league-leading thirteen wins and thirteen still-unofficial saves while losing only three times in relief. He started twelve games and was 19-7 overall with an 2.28 ERA. The Yankees won a then-record 110 games that season and went on to sweep the Pittsburgh Pirates in the four-game World Series of 1927. Moore saved Game One and then went the distance as a starter to win Game Four. The men who caught Moore out of the pen that season were Pat Collins and Johnny Grabowski, but one of the best living sources on Wilcy Moore was the last man to catch that sinkerball. Monte Moore, broadcaster for the Oakland Athletics, remembers Wilcy Moore as a man who used to jump off his tractor and come into town [Hollis, Oklahoma] to throw batting practice to the local high school team.

When I was in high school, gosh Wilcy, he was pretty old, out of baseball. But oh, he'd toy with us, he'd throw the ball in there at batting practice speed and then all of a sudden he'd throw that sinker of his and we'd, well there was no way that we could touch it. He was probably sixty then, because he didn't get up to the majors until he was in his thirties. He was a character, I'll tell you that. And you know he beat Babe Ruth on that famous bet. [Ruth wagered that the weak-hitting Moore wouldn't get three hits during the entire 1927 season. When Moore won the bet he took his $500 in winnings back to Oklahoma, purchased two plow mules and named them Babe and Ruth.] Well, I never saw the mules, of course, but I grew up seeing that check that Ruth wrote. It was framed and hung on the wall in Wilcy's house and when I was a kid we used to go in there and look at it. George H. Ruth, that's the way the Babe signed it.

The New York Yankees weren't the only club in the 1930s and early 1940s spelling their starters. But they were the dominant team of the day and they owed their success, in part, to the big sweeping curveball of one of the bullpen's first legitimate aces. Johnny Murphy led the American League in relief wins six times and in saves another four. Called "Grandma" by his teammates for his rocking chair motion, Murphy pitched in six World Series, won two games, saved four and never suffered a loss. When Lefty Gomez, the Yankees great starter, was asked to what he owed his secret of success Gomez said, "Clean living, a fast outfield and Johnny Murphy."

For all Murphy's numbers and for all the attention that he brought to the bullpen, relief pitching of the 1930s was still far from the specialty as we know it today. Johnny Murphy with the Yankees, Firpo

Marberry and Jack Russell with the Senators, Clint Brown with the White Sox in the American League, Bob Bowman with St. Louis, Jack Quinn in Brooklyn, Mace Brown in Pittsburgh in the National League—also the first relief pitcher ever chosen to an All-Star team—that was basically it. There were few specialists. The pens of the day were stocked with guys who drank with the manager. In *The Relief Pitcher*, Thorn puts it a bit more politely. These men were, says Thorn, "veteran starters of suspect stamina, experienced starters down on their luck, or youngsters fresh from the farm looking for a chance to show their stuff."

Then came the war. Suddenly bullpens began to look a bit like the back porch at the old folks' home. Older players, many who had spent their careers pitching in the minor leagues, found themselves in big league uniforms. Red Barber, who called the Dodgers games from his catbird seat in Ebbets Field during this era, watched Leo Durocher work his war pen.

> A great realization of the importance of the bullpen pitcher came during World War II. There was a shortage of players, of course, and managers like Durocher in Brooklyn would have to dig down and come up with several pitchers who could fill in for a couple of innings.

Examples were found in every major league bullpen. But it was pitchers like Ace Adams of the New York Giants, a twenty-nine-year-old rookie in 1941, who would bring new-found attention to the pen. Adams topped the National League in saves in 1944 and lead the league in both saves and relief wins in 1945. He led the league in games pitched three consecutive years (1942–1944) and in games finished for four straight. Adams's seventy appearances in 1943 set a major league record, prompting Pittsburgh Pirates manager Pie Traynor to assess the worth of these specialty pitchers.

> It's not a question of how good [White Sox hurler Clint] Brown and Adams were or the caliber of the wartime competition. The point is that until they came along, most relief pitchers had been starting occasionally, and appearing only about thirty-five to forty times a season. Adams and Brown proved that real bullpen specialists could work sixty or more games without hurting their arms.

And it wasn't just the graybeards who made their mark during the war. Peach-fuzzed pen men like Joe Nuxhall distinguished themselves while the regulars were overseas. Nuxhall, a fireballing fifteen-year-old high school pitcher, became the major leagues' youngest player in June 1944, when he took a relief turn with the Cincinnati Reds.

So is that the 1940s story? War pens loaded down with old men and kids? No, there were teams that pitched the walking wounded. Bert Shepard, a one-legged war hero, spelled a Washington Senators pitcher successfully in a game in 1945. Shepard, who wore an artificial leg, ended his brief career pitching in the minor leagues several years later. But to say that the pens of that decade were nothing but old men, kids and the handicapped would be terribly misleading.

The bullpen was merely a reflection of what had happened to the rest of the game. Players pitched in to do the best they could. And the efforts from the men of the pen weren't ignored. Baseball offered the country diversion from the war—that was President Roosevelt's reasoning for refusing to close down the game. As the troops scoured their sports pages from home, they read of the heroics of America's pen men, guys like Ace Adams, Johnny Murphy, Jumbo Brown, Earl Johnson, Earl Caldwell, Howie Krist, Clyde Shoun, Xavier Rescigno, Harry Gumbert, and Ted Wilks.

When the war was won and the boys came home, they opened up their sports pages to stories about one of their own. Hugh Casey, a premier relief ace for the Dodgers in 1941 and 1942, not only survived the war, the Navy veteran survived the memory of one of the most infamous relief pitches in World Series history. With two outs and the Dodgers leading 4–3 in the top of the ninth inning, Casey's third strike got past Dodgers catcher Mickey Owen. The passed ball opened the doors to a Yankee comeback win in Game Four and ultimately to their winning the 1941 World Series. Following the war Casey led the National League in relief wins in 1946 and 1947. In the 1947 World Series he pitched well but not spectacularly, making appearances in six of the Series' seven games. But what was most important about that 1947 World Series was Game Seven.

New York's Joe Page stalked out of the bullpen on that sunny October 6 in Yankee Stadium, then proceeded to one-hit the Dodgers for the final five innings. He won the game and the Series, and in doing so took relief pitching into a new era. Names like Jim Konstanty, Hoyt Wilhelm, and Joe Black would soon headline every sports page in America. But before jumping too far ahead, let's listen to the penners of the time. Sam Narron, Mace Brown, Ace Adams, Johnny Sain, Clyde King, Rex Barney, Joe Nuxhall, Roger Craig, and Joe Ginsberg—these were the men who belonged to the fraternity when the Caseys and Pages gave relief its name.

VOICES FROM THE PEN

SAM NARRON
Catcher

ST. LOUIS CARDINALS, 1935, 1942, 1943

- Warmed Up Dizzy Dean In Hotel Lobbies
- Branch Rickey's First Bullpen Catcher
- Caught Harvey Haddix Before "The Perfect Game"
- On Base When Sammy Baugh Hit His First And Only Professional Home Run

I'm near Middlesex, North Carolina, on rural route 39 looking for Sam Narron's house. Finally I discover a brick ranch, Box 125. The screen door flies open, and a white-haired man dressed in a yellow golf shirt and khaki pants scurries down the back steps. Narron, one of baseball's original bullpen catchers, is built like his house, made of brick. Sam is a find. He's one of baseball's first pure pen men and the senior member of a clan of North Carolinians that sent seven of their men to play professional baseball. Sam's nephew Jerry, his youngest, played with Seattle, New York and California. Uncle Sam caught guys like the Deans, Walker, Hallahan and Haines in the St. Louis Cardinals bullpen in 1935, and after a stint in the minors served in the Redbirds pen again in 1942 and 1943. He worked the bullpen for Branch Rickey and the Brooklyn Dodgers in 1949 and 1950, then followed Rickey to Pittsburgh where he ran the Pirates pen until his retirement in 1963.

Narron shows me to his family room and a comfortable, overstuffed chair. He seats himself in a ladderback rocker and gestures to the framed picture on the wall behind him. "The 1935 Cardinals. Later you can try on these World Series rings if you like," he says, holding up his hands. "And oh yeah, I've still got my first uniform, the one I wore when I played for Martinsville back in 1934. You might be interested in that." I flip on my recorder. Too late. Sam's off and running, recalling his first encounter with "the Great Dizzy Dean."

Now the first baseball school that I knew of was in 1934 in Hot Springs, Arkansas. I read about it in *The Sporting News* and oh my, did I want to go! I was only nineteen but a pretty good country ball-player in this area and Miss Anna Rose Southern, a schoolteacher here, she wrote to Rogers Hornsby and told him about me. Hornsby was out there at that baseball school. I borrowed money, a little bit here and a little bit there and when I had me enough, off I went.

I couldn't believe that place. All my heroes were there. Rogers Hornsby, Dizzy Dean, Burleigh Grimes, Les Mann, and Joe Schultz, a Cardinal scout. Oh, and Babe Didrickson, the woman athlete was there, married to that wrestler George Zaharias, I believe. Anyway, that woman could throw like a man and when she got together with Diz there were some laughs, I'll tell you that.

My eyes was this big! Being around Dizzy Dean and them for a week. I'da stayed longer but my money run out. Anyway, towards the end of the week Joe Schultz, the scout, up and says, "Sam, would you like to sign a contract?" And then my eyes got even bigger. Here I was, all I'd ever wanted to do was meet people like Dean and Hornsby, and now I've got a scout asking me if I want to sign a Cardinal contract. Of course I say "yes indeed." Then he says, "Well, let's see you go up and hit one." Now I'm not braggin' or nothin' like that, but this got me so excited I could have snapped one of those tall pines in the back yard it felt so good, him asking me that.

I went up there to the plate and evidently the pitcher threw . . . it had to be a fastball . . . because I hit it out of the ball park. And that put me on cloud nine. I just went around those bases barely touching the ground.

Joe signed me. I was a Cardinal that night.

Well like I said, I was out of money. So I hitchhiked some, then caught a bus and pretty soon I was home in Zebulon [North Carolina]. I went to spring training that April in Greensboro with about 100 other boys who had signed Cardinal contracts. All of us with numbers on our backs and I was a third baseman then. I was there for about two weeks and we'd work out every day with Mr. Branch Rickey looking on. We all had the numbers on our backs and there was this great big bulletin board and every day we'd go in to see if our number was still up there or whether we'd been marked off to go home. Well I had a good spring training and Mr. Rickey sat right there and watched it with those little glasses perched on his nose. One of the smartest men I ever saw in baseball. People used to talk about him but even if you weren't on his team he'd try to get you a job. And that has never been printed, I don't think, but he was that kind of fellow.

I went to Martinsville, Virginia, that summer and had me a pretty good year. And the following spring I was sent up to Columbus, which was Triple-A ball and a pretty nice jump. Anyway, we were in Florida at spring training and Burt Shotton, that was Mr. Rickey's Sunday manager [Rickey didn't manage on Sunday for religious reasons when he was managing in the big leagues.] Course Mr. Rickey was the Cardinals general manager then. Anyway Mr. Rickey said, "Sam, have you ever caught before?" And I said that I never caught in my life. He said, "Do you want to go to the big leagues?"

My eyes got big again. I said, "Yeah." I was ready to go right then. And he said, "Well you can try." And he gave me a glove and I stood there like this, with it tucked under my arm. I reckon I thought I was Gabby Hartnett or somebody. Well that made me feel good. And from that time on I caught batting practice two hours every morning and two hours every afternoon. I'd close my eyes and I'd get hit in the leg and then I'd take one on the shoulder. And all of them, Mr. Rickey and Burt, would be standing out there laughing. Anyway I never caught an inning, just batting practice. Mr. Rickey would say, "Batting practice, batting practice, batting practice!" We were playing the Cardinals one day and I was still assigned to the Columbus Triple-A team at the time, Ray Blades was managing and for some reason he had sent all the catchers out but one that day. I was in the bullpen, of course, and late in the game the starting catcher got hit on the hand by a foul tip. There wasn't another catcher and when they had to take him out of the game Mr. Rickey stood up in the dugout and shouted, "Where's Narron!"

I jumps up in the bullpen and shouts back, "Here I am!" He hollers, "Are you ready, Sam?" and I come right back at him with, "Mr. Rickey, I stay ready!" And do you know, I think that helped me. Because later when he made speeches he would mention that. "Sam Narron, the man who stays ready," he'd say. Yes, I think it helped. Because he never forgot me saying that.

Well they sent me back to D-ball to learn to catch. I played for Albany, Georgia, and led the Georgia/Florida league in hitting that year. At the end of the season when the Cardinals were fightin' the Cubs for the pennant, they called me up to the big leagues. The Cubs eventually won twenty-one straight and beat us out but I'll tell you that was quite a thrill just being there. Those big crowds and all, well it was kinda like a kid goin' to the fair, all them people.

One day we was playing the Giants and Dizzy Dean was pitching and they wore old Diz out. I'm down in the bullpen, a young catcher who hasn't played a second of big league ball, and they decide to pinch hit for Diz and call for me. I come trottin' up there in front of 30,000 people and the bats weren't in a rack back then, they were all spread

27

out in a fan shape on the ground. I couldn't find a bat, didn't have one I guess. Durocher picks one up and hands it to me and says, "Hell, Sam, you can hit with anything." And I says, "Yeah," and I walked up there to the plate and there's "King Carl" Hubbell staring in at me. They announce my name. Now I'm shaking. Then I hear Diz shout from the dugout step. "Hey Sam, don't mess up, you're hittin' for a good man now!"

I was so nervous that I reckon that if he'd a throwed to first base I'd a swung. Hubbell throwed me one and I don't reckon that I ever hit one back any harder than I hit that pitch. Right back at him. Bang! Bang! He knocks it down about as far away as from here to that chair over there, pounces on it and throws me out. And I want to tell you that was a thrill. I came back into the dugout and I said, "Diz, you devilish rascal, you liked to scared me to death when you hollered like that." And Diz just laid back and laughed. If you knew Diz, what a great guy, just great. And I liked my fun too. We had us some times, me and Diz.

Now let me tell you something about Dizzy Dean. They always said that his brother Paul was the serious one, and he was. But when Diz took that mound and got the ball in his hand, he was as serious as a man can get. He knew what he was going to do with it. I only ever caught him once, in an exhibition game and believe me, he was great. And ever'thing you ever heard about him was true. He'd give you the shirt off his back. And you know he hurt his arm when Averill hit a line drive back at him and caught him on the toe, this caused him to start throwing unnatural, and eventually ended his career. But when Diz was Diz, oh how he could throw. And what an entertainer. He'd come down to the bullpen and carry on with the fans, holler at the outfielders and of course he had the run of the place. He was our breadwinner and we all knew it.

I used to like to get him worked up when we were playing on the road. We'd be sitting in a hotel lobby talkin' baseball. There'd always be a bunch of fans hanging around listening in. And pretty soon I'd steer the conversation to which of the opposition's batters he might be knockin' down in the next game he pitched. Diz would make me get across the lobby, squat down like I was catchin' him, and he'd start going into his wind-up, all the while regaling the fans with what he was going to do to some poor batter. "Sam," he'd shout, "why I'm gonna' bale 'em up and throw 'em on the wagon like a wet bale o' hay." He was a great guy alright. He used to tell us about hollerin' over at Hank Greenberg during the 1934 Series, tellin' Mickey Cochrane, the Tigers manager, he might as well send out a batboy to hit as

Greenberg, because the Great Diz was pitchin' that day. Diz claimed it made Hank so mad you could see sawdust he'd be squeezing the bat so hard. Later when Diz was broadcastin' the *Game of the Week* he used to say, "Hey, there's my friend Sam Narron out thar warmin' up Preacher Roe, best bullpen catcher in the National League."

That "gas house gang" was somethin' else—Collins, Durocher, Martin, Moore, Medwick, the Dean boys—and they always said that Frankie Frisch didn't like young ballplayers but he evidently liked me. Anyway, the reason I say that is in spring training one year, I believe it was 1936, Frisch calls this meetin' and tells us young players that he wants us to pick out an older player to copy, do what he does and you might make it, he says. Well the next day at batting practice I'm playing pepper with Rip Collins, Pepper Martin—boy there was a fireball!—Terry Moore and Leo Durocher is hittin'. Leo says, "Sam, have you picked out a ballplayer to model yourself after?" Now Frisch was a playin' manager, played second base. I says, "Yes I have. I'm modeling myself after the great Frankie Frisch." Leo says, "Well I bet you won't do what he's doin' now." I look up and there's Frisch leaning on the battin' cage with his chin restin' on his arm watchin' Medwick hit. So I walk over there right next to him and assume the same position. The chin restin' on the arm, just like Frisch. He wheels around and says, "Narron, what in the hell do you think you're doin'?" "I picked me my ballplayer to model myself after and you're it," I says. "Well I like to run," Frisch says, "so you can start out by running yourself around this field." He ran me good for that one.

Now in 1938 or 1939 I was in Rochester, that was the Cardinals top minor league club, Triple-A, and I won't say for sure, but I think that the Cardinals came through to play us a game. And Sammy Baugh, the great Redskin quarterback, was playing with me on that Rochester team. He played the outfield and when the Cardinals came in we had a throwin' contest, catchers throwing from behind home plate at a wooden barrel out on second base. And Sammy Baugh, he threw the football at the barrel, and he could throw that football just as well as we did the baseball. This was after his football career, Mr. Rickey signed him. He was a good athlete, he could run.

Now the day before the exhibition I was on second base—I forget who we were playing but I was on second base—and Sammy Baugh hit what I believe was his only professional home run. I had doubled and he came up next and hit that home run of his to right field, he was a right-handed hitter. And I hit one to left field later that same day. Sammy Baugh was a nice fellow, he could run and he could steal a base, just an all-around athlete but not as good a hitter as he was a quarterback, of course. I think he's got a farm out in Texas now.

I enjoyed working in the bullpen. I learned fast. In 1942 and 1943 the Cardinals had darned good teams. We won pennants those years. And I was out there workin' the pitchers both seasons. It was fun and we had a lot of laughs but you had to be serious. See, you're down there and it's all in that pen. You have to judge how they're throwin'. When I was with the Cardinals Billy Southworth would call and tell me who to get up. But I pretty much knew. You had your long man and your short man, and then of course in the eighth or ninth inning it was always the guy who could shut 'em down fast.

And another thing about a pen man, staying down there with the players. It was my job to keep the morale up, keep them from gettin' their daubers down. Because they all want to pitch. And I'd say, "Look here now. There can't be but nine men on the field and the manager, he likes us," I'd always put myself in there with them, "he likes us or we wouldn't be wearin' this uniform. We wouldn't be here. Don't get your daubers down. You'll get your chance and when you do, go out there give it all you got."

How did I get to be a full-time bullpen catcher? After I played in the big leagues I came home. The Cardinals let me go and Mr. Rickey had gone on to Brooklyn as part owner and general manager. Oh, I played a little ball here in Smithfield [North Carolina] but I didn't have a job and I told my wife, I said, "Sue, I'm going to St. Paul to the winter baseball meetings and see if I can land me a job." The meetings were in Minneapolis and it was zero degrees up there, I'll never forget that. Anyway I went straight to the hotel where I knew Mr. Rickey would be, took the elevator up to his room and beat on the door. Now Branch Jr. opened the door and I looked in there and what do you think? There was Burt Shotton, the Dodgers manager, he must have been almost seventy years old. There was Burt and Mr. Rickey, who was I don't know how old, chasing each other around the room popping each other with wet towels. They looks at me and didn't miss a pop, kept right on fightin'. Finally Mr. Rickey says, "Sam, what in the heck are you doin' here?" And I says, "I'm after a job." He says, "I don't have one." I says, "You need somebody in your bullpen." And he comes right back at me. "Never hired one in my life," he says. "I don't have a job." Well that sort of flopped my ears. But I says, "Mr. Rickey, there's always a first time." He says, "Nope," and looked down through those little glasses the way he did when he meant business.

Like I said Branch Jr. was there. Let me tell you about Branch Jr. and me, then I'll get back to Mr. Rickey and how I landed the pen man job. Branch Jr. and I went way back. He had been general manager of a couple of the clubs that I played for and so we had kind of gone up to the Cardinals together. Now Branch Jr. had been a wrestler in college and I was pretty strong so I'd wrestle with him, but we had an understandin' he wasn't allowed to use any of those professional holds. I'd say, "Now I'm nothin' but an old cotton field man but if you stay away from them holds I'll stay with you." I'll never forget the last time we wrestled. He came at me and got my legs and somehow I picked him up and lifted him over my head and fell backwards with him. Liked to killed us both. He come at me with every hold he'd ever learned. And that was it. I said no more. You're liable to break my legs and arms. And that was the end of the wrestlin' for this old cotton field man.

We were friends, me and Branch Jr., and when Mr. Rickey said "I don't have a job for you," Branch Jr. and Burt Shotton called me over and Burt said, "Sam, come to spring training." That was all I wanted to hear. I went to Dodgertown down in Vero Beach and that's when I sort of became Mr. Rickey's personal catcher. I don't know, there was something about him. He knew baseball, he'd show you how to grip the ball, how to make it spin, how to make the rotation and then he'd sit there and watch. Didn't miss a trick, that man. He had these strings stretched across in front of home plate. They ran crossways and up and down forming a strike zone for the pitchers to throw the ball through. Now I sat back there and caught those pitchers every day for Mr. Rickey. Me catchin' and him sittin' back there behind me watching guys like Preacher Roe and Rex Barney. And I'd be working back there thirty minutes to an hour, behind those strings and Mr. Rickey would say, all of a sudden, "Sam, what you doin' here, anyway? I don't have nothing to do with you!" I'd say, "Mr. Rickey, I'm earnin' my keep, payin' for my board and room." That's all he'd say, never once admitting that a job even existed.

Then the night before we broke camp we was havin' a coaches' meeting. And Burt Shotton makes an announcement. "Boys," he says, "I got me another ballplayer." The scouts and coaches say, "Who?" "Sam, here," he says. And they all applauded, which made me feel real good. Of course, Mr. Rickey wasn't at that meeting. But the next day we get on the plane headed north and there he is, Mr. Rickey is sittin' back there in the back waiting for the team to get on—Hodges, Reese, Snider, Robinson, Furillo, Campy—all file on and then he sees me. "Sam Narron, what are you doin' here? I don't have anything to do with you!" "Mr. Rickey, I'm follerin' the crowd," I says. Oh he knew he was goin' to take me all along. Probably made up his mind

31

back when he and Shotton were towel fightin' in that hotel room. Oh we had some fun, I stayed with him until he left Brooklyn in 1951 then went with him and caught pitchers in the Pittsburgh bullpen until 1963.

I loved Brooklyn, that was some club. We had us a club. Had a lot of fun in that bullpen too. It was along the right field line in Ebbets, and Roe, Palica, Branca, Newcombe and Rex Barney used to come down there and they were characters alright. I'll tell you what I started when I was in Brooklyn. To my knowledge there was no bullpen in the majors that had a water fountain. And I asked Burt Shotton if he'd mind if I carried a couple of water jugs down there, the kind we used to take in the fields when we was pickin' cotton. He said, "Go ahead, Sam," and from that day on the Dodgers bullpen had water for its pitchers and catchers.

I guess the most exciting phone call I ever got in the pen was the one I got in Brooklyn. I'm sittin' down there mindin' my own business when Barney, or somebody says, "Sam, it's for you." I sidle over and it's Burt Shotton, and he says, "Sam, come in here, Mr. Rickey wants you to go to Montreal to catch a ball game tonight." I says, "What? I haven't caught a game in two or three years. I'm a pen man." But it was a fact, Mr. Rickey had his private pilot waitin', somebody had gotten hurt or something and they needed a catcher. I had to borrow a coat from somebody, it was chilly up there. So off I went. Anyway I had me a time. Chuck Connors, you know "The Rifleman," he was playin' first base and Montreal had Sam Jethroe, one of the fastest men I've ever seen run, playin'. That man could outrun the ball, I've seen him do it. I caught that game. Claude Williams was pitchin' and boy, did I have some fun. When I got back I strutted up to Campy. "How'd you do, Sam?" he said. "Well I caught me a one-hitter and got me a base hit," I said. Edwards, our other catcher, had hurt his arm so I goes up to him and rubs my arm against his and says, "Yep, Williams's arm and my brains, what a great combination. I wouldn't be surprised if you see it here in Brooklyn someday." Campy laughs that high laugh of his and just called me all kinds of names.

The pen in Forbes Field was out there in what we used to call Greenberg's Garden, the area Hank Greenberg made famous for hittin' home runs. That was when I first went there in 1951. Later they moved it to along first base. Now we had us some guys in Pittsburgh that like to throw a lot. Vernon Law was one of them. A great guy and a real good pitcher but you can throw too much and on a hot day you don't need to overthrow. But I never had trouble with them. Law and Friend both, they'd come down there and I'd have to protect them from overthrowin' or gettin' upset when they didn't get the call.

Now that little [Elroy] Face, when the game was in the late innings you knew that little rascal was going to get the call. Had that terrific forkball, took it up himself. And when he had that great year in 1959 you had to wonder how he did it, but he did, had that great forkball and I don't think he weighed more than 145 pounds.

We had some bad teams there in the early fifties but it was fun. Joe Garagiola was there and he used to come down to the pen when we were warming up two pitchers. He was great, never a dull moment when Joe was around. I guess one of the longest home runs I ever saw hit flew right over my head there in Greenberg's Garden.

Ron Necciai, boy could he throw hard. Fred Haney was managing then and he put him in one night and Andy Pafko lit into one of his fastballs, and there was this statue of Honus Wagner in a park behind Greenberg's Garden. I don't know where that ball landed but it looked like it was still climbing when it went over our heads. The next night Necciai comes down to the bullpen and he says, "Sam, where did that ball go?" And I says, "Son, I reckon that was the longest throw you ever made. That ball hit Honus Wagner in the head."

There were some great moments out there in the pen. Some that I saw, some that I was in on firsthand. I remember the day one of our scouts brought Sandy Koufax into Pittsburgh for Mr. Rickey to take a look. I caught him and Mr. Rickey got down behind me and watched. Like I said, he always wanted to see how the ball jumped. I caught him for a while and he was wild. Good gracious! But yes, you could see that he had it. He wanted $15,000 to sign if my memory serves me correctly. But I think that his heart was with the Dodgers. We only won about forty games that year, had a bunch of high school kids back then. The Dodgers could spot pitch him. And believe me, when he came in with that stuff, he was right. So we didn't sign him but Mr. Rickey asked my opinion, and I said it before but I'll say it again, Mr. Rickey always asked. He was like that.

When it comes to big moments I saw from the pen I can think of three, right off. One bad one and two great ones. On the last day of the season in 1950 we're [Brooklyn] playin' the Phils, the year they called 'em the Whiz Kids. If we win we force them into a play-off. It's a 0–0 game until the sixth inning. They score a run. Then Pee Wee comes back in the bottom of the inning, hits a home run to right to tie it up. In the ninth inning with nobody out and Reese on first and Abrams on second, Snider slaps a single to center and Richie Ashburn, who was playin' shallow, charges the ball and throws a perfect strike to get Abrams sliding home. Well that was it. Furillo popped up and Hodges flew deep to Ennis in right. You probably know the rest. With two on in the tenth Dick Sisler hit a three-run homer and that was it. We failed to score and it was "Wait Till Next Year" again.

There were some great moments out there too you know. I saw some great ones sittin' out there. I watched the great Roberto Clemente play right field. Saw Kiner hit, watched Groat play short. I was in the pen in Milwaukee in 1959 when Harvey Haddix threw those twelve perfect innings. That was a sight to see. I warmed him up before that game. And yes, he warmed up good and he was throwin' as hard as he'd ever thrown but you never know. He went into that game and hit all the right spots at just the right time. We didn't mention no-hitter of course, everybody's superstitious about that. We just sat and watched and when Adcock got the hit in the thirteenth, that was a terrible ending to one beautiful baseball game.

I guess the best sight I ever saw from the pen was Yogi Berra, the Yanks left fielder, turning and looking up at Maz's ball clearing the left field fence in Forbes in the 1960 World Series. I knew it was gone. That ball got me this ring on my right hand and that World Series trophy over there on the table. I had a sayin' when I was in the pen for moments like that one. I'd slap the players on the back and say, "Boys, take me along with you. This here's better than pickin' cotton!"

MACE BROWN
Right-Handed Pitcher

PITTSBURGH PIRATES, 1935–1941
BROOKLYN DODGERS, 1941
BOSTON RED SOX, 1942, 1943, 1946

- First Relief Pitcher Ever Chosen To A Major
  League All-Star Team
- Threw The "Homer In The Gloamin'" Pitch To
  Gabby Hartnett During The Final Days Of The 1938
  Pirates Pennant Chase
- Led National League In Relief Points In 1937–1938
  And The American League In Relief Points In 1942

Mace Brown had the dubious distinction of being the guy on the wrong end of one of those historic pitches. He threw the "Homer in the Gloamin'" pitch, the ball Gabby Hartnett hit into the dark of a Chicago evening to knock the Pirates out of the 1938 pennant chase.

He was also one of the National League's first great relief pitchers, led the league in saves in 1937 and in relief wins in 1938. In 1938 when the National League All-Stars bested the American League 4–1 Brown made bullpen history. He was the first pure relief man ever selected to a major league All-Star team and the first to get a save.

The dark knotty pine walls of the den in Brown's Greensboro, North Carolina, home are covered with framed mementos: Ted Williams dressed in fishing gear, Tony Conigliaro kneeling with a bat, Bobby Doerr, Yaz, Rico Petrocelli taking a ground ball. Brown—player, coach and scout—has been in baseball for most of his eighty-two years. And if the inscriptions on the photos are any indication—("To one of the best guys I know, in or out of baseball": Joe Cronin)—he's made some friends along the way.

The term fireman that you hear today started with me in Pittsburgh. We had a sportswriter name of Les Biederman, and he was the one that gave us that name. He had me go down to a firehouse right near our house on Bellfield Avenue. I used to go down there and pitch horseshoes with the firemen there. I was just a small-town boy and I could pitch those horseshoes. Les came up with this idea of going down there and taking a picture of me with one of those fireman hats on and that's the way it all started—the fireman. Murphy in the American League was the reliever and me in the National League, we were the firemen during those years and I know that that's where that started.

Of course I played a lot of ball before I got to Pittsburgh. In fact when I was a kid all I ever wanted to do was play baseball and I remember when I was in the ninth or tenth grade the teacher asked us to write what our professional ambitions were, what we wanted to be, and I wrote a professional baseball player and everybody thought that was crazy back then.

We didn't have a high school baseball team. I played with what we called a little town team. This town was only about 800 people—North English, Iowa—and I was a catcher. I had a scholarship offered to me to the University of Iowa. Now the freshmen couldn't play back then so my sophomore year another fellow and me both had the catchin' duties. I didn't hit too good. I had a pretty good arm but wasn't much of a hitter. I got a job playing summer baseball up in a little town called Corwith, Iowa, catchin' and I always kinda wanted to pitch. So one day someone from another team came over to our manager and wanted a pitcher. I said, "Well I can pitch." And I did real good in this little game they had. Then the next year I went back down to school. We always took a spring training trip into Texas, Alabama and Mississippi, about a ten-day trip, and we were working out in a big field house there. I called the coach over and told him, "Come here." I was playin' catch with our other catcher and I said, "I want you to see my curve." I had a good one. I surprised him and he said that when we took our southern trip that he'd pitch me some. So we played Rice, and he pitched me four innings. I did pretty good and so from that day on I never was a catcher again.

I played ball for money that summer, the end of my junior year, and I was reported. Another pitcher from the University of Iowa and I, he was captain-elect of the basketball team, we were both reported. They investigated and made us ineligible. You couldn't play summer ball and get paid, so that made us both ineligible. So both of us signed contracts.

The coach got me a contract with the Cardinals and my buddy signed with Cincinnati. I signed for $700. The deal was this: They took me to spring training with the Cardinals and Branch Rickey was, of course, the big shot of the Cardinals. My contract was that if I stayed with the club for thirty days I was to get $700.

On the twenty-fifth day, somewhere around there, they pitched me three innings against the Athletics and I did alright. It was 1930 and the Athletics had just won the World Championship in 1929, so it was quite an audition. They had Jimmie Foxx and Al Simmons, Jimmy Dykes, Bing Miller, Maxie Bishop, Mickey Cochrane. Lefty Grove was one of their pitchers. I was scared to death, but I did good. But Rickey wasn't there. Then on the thirtieth day they pitched me against the Boston Braves, and Rickey was there. I did alright and so he called me in and I signed for $700.

After spring trainin' they sent us [Brown and pitcher Bill Lee] to St. Louis to meet with Rickey. He sent us both to St. Joe. Neither one of us stayed too long. That was Dizzy Dean's first year there too. Now he was crazy but he could pitch.

I know that year I pitched the opening game for St. Joe and we played Pueblo. They had an Indian named Chief Wano who played first base and he was a good one. I lost 4–3 and Dizzy pitched the second game and won something like 4–3. From then on, we had the worst club in baseball. Nobody could win except Diz and he won I think seventeen games that year, and I know that club didn't win nearly fifty. From there it was up and down. Mostly down. Pittsburgh bought my contract in 1934. Then I went off to Pittsburgh to play major league ball in 1935.

Now 1938 was certainly one of my best seasons in the majors and everything I did in the first part of that year was right. When you win fifteen games relieving like I did, you're darned lucky. Your club's coming from behind and scoring for you or you go in when the game's tied and they score. I started two games that year early and then they started relieving with me and I was 12–2 at the All-Star game. I just had a good year and then I was like 15–9 or something and we were leading the league by five and a half games on Labor Day as I remember. And why I'm saying this is because it has a bearing later on.

On Labor Day we played the Cubs in Pittsburgh and we had something like a two-game lead. We had a pitcher by the name of Russ Bauers who started the game and he had the Cubs shut out going into the ninth inning 2–0. In the ninth inning, he got the bases loaded, I don't just recall how. Walk, hit one and walked another or something, nobody out and Pie Traynor, the manager, put me in. Carl Reynolds was the first hitter up and he hit a little pop fly between third and home and we got it. Then Gabby Hartnett was the next hitter and I threw him a curve and he hit into a double play and we won the game. From then on the Cubs won ten straight, something like twenty-one out of twenty-two or twenty-three games. We won fourteen and lost eight but they still gained all that on us. And we had played good enough with that kind of a lead to win. Then we went into Chicago.

When we went into Chicago, we had a game and a half lead and three games to play. Dizzy was with Chicago then and he couldn't have knocked over that picture off that table over there. His arm was gone. He couldn't throw at all, hardly, and the Cubs were hurting for pitching at that time. They pitched Dizzy against us and he beat us. And I think the score was something like 2–1. We hit line drives here and there and they were right at someone, and we had the hitters too, Arky Vaughan, the Waner brothers, Rizzo. Anyway, Diz beat us and that left us a half a game up and then this game that everybody talks about. The "Homer in the Gloamin'" thing.

We were leading the Cubs by two runs going into the bottom of the eighth inning and Bob Klinger was pitching. The first guy up in the eighth got a hit off of Bob. Bill Swift and I were both warming up in the bullpen. This might sound egotistical, but why Traynor put in Bill Swift to pitch instead of me I'll never know and none of our players will ever know. But he did and they scored two runs on Bill. They still had the bases loaded and one out. The way they got the one out, Paul Waner threw a guy out at home plate. That was the only out and the bases were still loaded. And so now it was tied 5–5. And then he put me in to pitch and still only one out and the first hitter up was Frank Demaree. He hit a ground ball to Arky Vaughan, our shortstop. Double play! We're out of the inning. Still tied 5–5.

Then before the ninth started, that's when they had the meetin' at home plate to decide if it was too dark to play or not, and it was pretty dark. They shouldn't have played. It really didn't make that much difference to me. We had one inning to play and a chance to score, so I was ready to pitch. But of course we didn't score in the ninth and then in the bottom of the inning I got the first two hitters out. Cavarretta hit a fly to center, and Carl Reynolds grounded out. Up comes Hartnett and I got him strike one, then a foul ball for strike two, both curves. I had a good curve. When he was swinging at one of them he just looked like a schoolboy and I said to myself, "I'll just throw him a better one and strike him out." Well, I just made a lousy pitch! Instead of a strikeout pitch it was just a strike pitch which he knew was coming, I'm sure. He hit it to left center up into the seats up there. And no, I didn't follow it into the darkness. I knew it was gone. I didn't even have to look to see whether I could see it or couldn't because you just know when somebody hits one on you. But I think the "Homer in the Gloamin'" business is exaggerated a little bit. I'm sure that you could see the ball or they'd have had to call it because an outfielder couldn't have seen the ball. That just wasn't the case.

That put us a half a game back. The next day we pitched Russ Bauers and he had a real good curve and anyway we got beat. I think it was ten to nothing. But if I'da got Hartnett out that woulda been a tied game and we'da had to have played the Cubs two the next day.

I'm convinced that they'da beat us [in] a doubleheader. Of course, you don't know that, but our pitching was gone. When they beat us that next day, that put them a game and a half ahead. They had three games at St. Louis and we had four at Cincinnati, or maybe it was the other way around, but anyway they just went on and won. Our pitching just gave out.

As to when relief pitching came into its own, I guess in the thirties, it was me in the National League and Johnny Murphy in the American League. They never did get too much publicity at that time. I got some good write-ups in Pittsburgh, but they started recognizing the relief pitchers in about 1937. I won seven and lost two and led the league in saves with seven. Saves weren't like they are today, they were hard to come by. I think Cliff Melton had seven saves with the Giants that year too. Then the next year I was in fifty some games and 15–9. The record shows five saves but I saved more than five. That was the year I pitched in the All-Star game.

Yes, I was the first what you'd call relief man to be chosen to an All-Star team. That was 1938 and my memory of that game is this. I faced quite a few outstanding hitters, a bunch of Hall-of-Famers—Gehringer, Averill, York, Foxx, Greenberg, DiMaggio, Dickey, Cronin, and Gehrig—so many good hitters that it was scary. And yes, I got hit some but not as hard as the record might indicate, because some of those hits were infield hits. They didn't throw them out. But that was the best lineup I ever saw. I wasn't nervous but . . .

Bill Terry was the manager and we played at Crosley Field, left field there was short. Behind the left field wall was a great big laundry and it had a flat roof on it. We were sittin' watchin' hittin' practice, and they were using what we called a 97 ball, a batting practice ball which was as lively as it could be. It was a ball that wasn't used for regular play. The American League used it for batting practice that day and they were just flying balls off of that building.

Vander Meer started and shut them out three innings and then Bill Lee came in and shut them out for the middle three and then I pitched the seventh inning and they had, like I said, two of those hits in the seventh that were infield hits. They loaded the bases but I didn't think that I was hit that hard. In the seventh they brought in Rudy York to pinch-hit. Back then they just played nine men in an All-Star game, only changes were the pinch hitters. So I struck Rudy out to end the seventh. And then I got them out in the eighth inning one, two, three. I don't recall who they were, but I sure remember who I faced in the ninth. They scored a run in the ninth. I don't know which order but Joe Cronin hit a double and I believe there was one out at the time. DiMaggio got a single and scored Cronin and then Bob Johnson pinch-hit, a big home run hitter with the Athletics, and I struck him out and that ended the game. We won 4–1. The only time I was hit was those two hits in the ninth inning. The others were just ground balls. Back then we played our regular lineup except pitchers and pinch hitters, you faced the best [in] the whole game. There wasn't a lot of changing around.

I guess striking out Rudy York in the 1938 All-Star game was the high point. I got a kick outta Rudy. I had him three balls and two strikes and the only thing I could throw was a fastball. He barely fouled it and just barely ticked it and the catcher held it for strike three. And then you don't aim for nothin', you just throw with all you got and hope. That's what I threw him. Rudy later joined the Red Sox. Rudy drank a little bit and one day, I never will forget, I was sleeping, and we were playing Washington, staying in a new hotel and Rudy—I was sleeping sound and I forget who I was rooming with—but here come Rudy in and he had a bottle of beer in his hand and he poured some in my ear and it woke me up. And there he was staring at me and he said, "If I hadn't a had a brand new bat that day I wouldn't a fouled that ball, I'd a hit it." But I never will forget that and neither did Rudy. He remembered that 1938 All-Star at-bat till the day he died.

In 1946 when I was with Boston we played the Cardinals in the World Series. I was just out of the service and had a bad arm all that year. I came home out of shape and got off to a bad start and just sat on the bench all year. In fact I remember my wife meeting me at the train station in Washington, D.C., when I came home to be discharged. She didn't say "hello, how are you," what she said was, "my god, you're fat!" [laughs]. So anyway that wasn't much of a year. And it ended up with us losing the World Series to St. Louis. I pitched in Game Four, the one where we got the fool beat out of us. I think that game was twelve to three or something, but I really don't remember much about it. Now of course I do remember Slaughter's run from first base. That's something that you don't forget. It was Game Seven of the 1946 World Series, the deciding game. I wasn't in the bullpen because I'd hurt my arm. Bob Klinger was pitching when Slaughter scored from first base. But I still say to this day, and I know Slaughter probably wouldn't agree, but if Dom DiMaggio had been playin' center field. . . .

40

He was hurt and Leon Culberson was playing center. Then this ball that Harry Walker hit, it was hit to left center. Culberson run over and it was hit pretty good. He fielded the ball and it wasn't that deep. In fact it wasn't too deep that you couldn't throw a man out at home. Instead he threw the ball to Pesky which was the thing to do. But Pesky had no idea that the guy coulda scored and he turned around and took two hitches and threw it home. Slaughter slid under it and beat it. Slaughter didn't even stop at third. He just kept going, but I still say if Dom DiMaggio had been in center field. . . . Of course we'll never know, but I don't think that he'd of ever scored. DiMaggio was a great one and as good as his brother Joe in the outfield. I never saw a better one. Terry Moore mighta been, but Dom was something.

One of the low points of my career was 1941—sold to the Dodgers for cash. Durocher and I didn't get along, let's leave it at that. The Dodgers kept me all that year and I think I won three and lost one, and they kept me. This was the lowest point in my baseball career. They kept me and then on Labor Day they usually carry extra people and Durocher called me in and said, "We're going to send you to Los Angeles," which was a Triple-A team. "They need a pitcher out there to help them." What could I say? I couldn't say nothing, and so they sent me out and I wouldn't report to Los Angeles for a couple of weeks. L.A. called me a couple of times and finally we settled on something. I knew the general manager of the Los Angeles club, Stewart was his name. They were on the bottom so that was a bunch of hooey about needing a pitcher. I told him, "Whatever you do, don't you buy me because I'm not going to play in the minor leagues. If I can't pitch in the big leagues I'm quittin'!" I had already gone up to see about an umpire's job in the Carolina League.

When the season was over they wanted to put me on the Montreal roster and I said, "Let me go make a deal for myself." That's when I discovered at the winter meetings that they'd put the word out that my arm was bad, which it was not. At the winter meetings we stayed at Hugh Casey's home with his wife, and Charlie Grimm was managing Milwaukee [Triple-A]. I knew him pretty well. He had been with the Cubs all those years. He asked me about my arm and my arm was sound, not a thing in the world wrong with it, and he wanted to know if I'd come to Milwaukee, that was his first year managing. He said, "We're going to have a good ball club, and if we sell you back to the major leagues we'll give you half of your sale price." I said, "Charlie, I still think I can pitch in the big leagues and if I can, I will!" And Jewel Ens, who was my coach at Pittsburgh all those years, and I got to talking and he said, "How's your arm?" I said, "Jewel, there's nothing wrong with my arm." He said, "Wait a minute, Boston's here. Joe Cronin and Eddie Collins, they're sittin' over here, let me go talk to them." And he said, "They want to talk to you." They asked the same thing and said, "If we sign you to a contract and you don't make our club, will you go to Louisville?" I said, "If you'll give me a fair look in spring training, yes, I'll go to Louisville."

So I went down to Florida with the Red Sox and the first game they pitched me, I'll never forget if I live to be a hundred. The wind was blowing in strong and we were playing Washington who didn't have much anyway. Joe Dobson pitched the first seven innings and had them shut out. Cronin was the playin' manager and Joe put me in. He took himself out—he'd been playing third—and I couldn't get them out. Everything they hit was between somebody, not long balls just singles, and they musta scored six or seven runs. The harder I threw, the harder they hit it. And Joe come over to me and he said, "Do you think you've had enough?" And I said, "I sure have." I thought, here I go. A week or so later we played the Yankees over in St. Petersburg. Joe had me down to pitch. The pitchers were going longer distances. Tex Hughson went seven innings, and as I remember the score was tied, not much because they didn't get much off of Tex. I came in that day, pitched five innings and shut them out. I had a real good day. When it was over Cronin told me, "I'll pitch you one more time before we open the season." And he did. I had a good inning or so and when the 1942 season opened I was in a Red Sox uniform in Fenway Park.

Here's what happened in Boston. This cartoon here [opens scrapbook] tells the story of the first game I pitched for the Red Sox. That's me in the center with the fireman's hat and hose. The day before this cartoon appeared in the Boston paper we had the Yankees beat going into the ninth inning and they put in, I think it was Mike Ryba, who'd relieved a lot for the Sox the year before. The Yanks scored I think five runs in the ninth inning and beat us. The very next day, we were playing the Yankees again and Joe Dobson—I think he had them shut out going into the ninth inning—got wild and had a little trouble in the ninth. The bases was loaded and nobody was out and so this time instead of Ryba, Cronin put me into pitch. That was my first appearance for the Red Sox. This cartoon shows me with a fire hose, putting out the fire. Here are the fans leaving the game on the day before my debut and they're saying, "I can't stand these Yankee ninth innings, this business is getting so bad that a lot of people are going home at the end of the eighth." And it says "To the air raid shelters! Just follow the arrows and stay under the stands for the duration of the inning. . . ."

42

They were making this over the fact that we'd had trouble before. Then in this particular game, there I am pictured there in the center with the hose, putting out the fire. That was the game that got me off on the right foot in Boston. I guess this cartoon in the newspaper the next day didn't hurt.

Joe Cronin was a manager who looked at the relief pitcher with a great deal of respect. In 1943 I had a commission to go into the service. It came on Opening Day in Philadelphia and Joe talked me out of taking it. He pitched me that day against the Athletics, the last three innings. I lost the game in extra innings. I remember we had a terrible ball club in 1943. Williams was gone, DiMaggio was gone, and then I started off and won six straight. I don't know how many I won, but I pitched in five games in seven days. We had a doubleheader in Chicago against the White Sox and Joe put me in in the seventh inning. I got them out in the seventh, eighth and ninth and we won the game. And before the next game he told me, "You go in the clubhouse and take your uniform off, you are done." So I went in the clubhouse and boy, I was hot. I took off my sweatshirt and clothes and had me a bottle of beer. So I sat around in the clubhouse until I'd cooled off and I guess till it must have been the third or fourth inning and I said, "Shoot, I might as well go out and sit on the bench, I don't have anything to do."

I just sat there without a sweatshirt or nothing on and Joe comes to me at the start of the ninth inning. We had a one-run lead, and he said, "Do you think that you could pitch to one man?" I said, "Sure," so he said, "Go on down to the bullpen." I started throwing and they got that one run back and had some men on base. He put me in and I got them out. That was the ninth inning and I got them out the tenth, the eleventh, and the twelfth, and the thirteenth. Between every inning Cronin would say, "How do you feel?" and I said, "I haven't got nothin' but I'm gettin' them out." Somebody got on base in the, I think it was the fourteenth or fifteenth inning, and Luke Appling hit a triple and scored him. The game was over, and I'll tell you that was one game that I didn't mind losing. As I was walking across the field Cronin came walking by me and he said, "Mace, as long as I got a job, you've got a job." And he said, "I don't even want you to come near the ball park tomorrow, don't come." Now that's what Cronin thought of relief pitchin'. He was a great man.

The best hitter? Well Paul Waner wasn't the best hitter I ever saw, Ted Williams was without a doubt. But Paul Waner was the best hitter, pound for pound. He was one of the few hitters that could say where he was going to hit and could do it. If he couldn't he'd foul pitches off. But Paul, I wouldn't take anything away from him because I saw him get an awful lot of his 3,000 hits. And Lloyd, his brother, was a little singles hitter. He had no power but he could run and he was a real good fielder. Arky Vaughan, he was a real good hitter and very sure hands, he was a good one.

Now I'm not going to comment on Paul Waner as a drinking man because I think a lot of that was just . . . well, I can think of an incident or two but my, he still hit good. There's one, I never will forget with Paul, that was the darndest thing. We were playin' in St. Louis. I've never seen anything like it. It was hot and of course all day ball. We had a doubleheader, and I don't know if we won or lost the first game but we got in the clubhouse. Here Paul was, he did a flip in the clubhouse and he said, "It's not hot out, you guys just think it's hot out," Then he went into the trainer's room, Doc Jurgenson's, and said, "Doc, my stomach don't feel too good. Do you have a little brandy?"

The second game started. In St. Louis they had a dugout that was under the stands a little bit. Right behind that there was a concession stand. So Paul, in between innings if he wasn't at bat, he'd go get him a bottle of beer. You didn't have a bunch of coaches watching like we do now. Traynor, the manager, was coaching first base and Jewel Ens coached third. They had Honus Wagner, he wouldn't say nothing anyway, he just never said anything. I bet Paul had five or six beers at least. Paul Dean was pitchin' and Paul could throw hard. It came up to the seventh inning and we had a player by the name of Bud Hafey. He never ever played. We used to call him Waner's caddy, never played except in a real lopsided game. Paul got up and he said, "Bud, I got one swing left in me, that's all I got left," and he said, "You get ready because you're gonna play next inning. I'm through. One swing left and that's all." Well he got out there and the derned fool hit a home run. Hit it to right field and it wasn't too far from foul, right down the line. But he come around the bases and when he got between third and home he was just a-wobbling. He touched home and he come over to the bench and he flopped himself down and said, "Well there, I'm done." That was Paul. He was something.

I saw a lot of great hitters—pitched to that American League lineup in the 1938 All-Star game—but I think that Ted Williams was the greatest hitter that ever lived. Certainly the greatest one I ever saw. I was in the bullpen and saw a lot of Ted Williams's hits coming my way. I recall one in 1942. I was pitchin' against the old St. Louis Browns in Fenway in another one of those games where I went in late, maybe about the seventh. They scored a run off of me and it was a tied game. Then in the top of the ninth inning we were behind one run and I go in and fall back on the bench. Williams comes over to get a bat and he says, "What the hell are you down about?" And I said, "I ain't down." And he said, "Well, if Pesky gets on I'm gonna hit one outta here." Then he says, "If he don't get on I'm gonna hit one outta here anyway." So lo and behold, Pesky got on and that Williams hit one nine miles, and when he come trotting down into the dugout he just looked at me and said, "I told you!"

Here's another one. We were playing in Chicago, this was 1942 at the tail end of the season. My sister and my mother, they were both in the ball park, they'd driven all the way in from Iowa to see the game. And the first time up in this ball game, it was the tail end of the season and we had second place cinched. The Yankees had first, and Williams, I think he won the Triple Crown that year and the first time up he said, "I'm gonna give them that ol' Mel Ott stance, the one with the front leg kicking, and see how high I can hit one." Well he hit one nine miles, right straight up the infield, right up the old elevator chute. And he comes into the bench kinda laughin' and he sat down on the bench beside me. And I said, "Ted, you oughta be ashamed of yourself, my mother and sister have been reading about you since you started and have never had a chance to see you play. They drove all the way in from Iowa today and think about the other fans that paid just to see you today. I'd be ashamed of myself!" So he just smiled and said, "I'll hit one," and so help me, he hit one in the upper deck at Comiskey Park. When he come into the bench he said, "Mace, tell your mother that one was for her." He sure did.

I never pitched against Babe Ruth. But in 1935, that was his last year and my first, there was a day at Forbes Field that a lot of people remember. It's one I'll never forget, one of my favorite baseball memories. I was sittin' on the bench there in Forbes Field, right at the doorway in the dugout where all the visitin' players had to pass through to get to their dressin' room. And I'm sittin' right there, and my wife, Sue, she was sittin' in the upper deck and she had a little movie camera, a cheap one that I'd bought. She was taking pictures and Ruth hit three home runs that day. And it was the next to the last series he ever played. The first time up he hit a ball nine miles and it was just inside the screen in right field for a home run. The next time up against a different pitcher, he hit them off of three different pitchers, he hit one to right center in the upper deck where it was 375. Then the third time, I think it was the seventh inning, he hit one that cleared the roof. Sue got it on film, and it was pretty good. We shoulda preserved it and given it to someone, because I bet you nobody else had that.

And he hit that clear over the stadium and he ran around the bases and didn't even bother to go into the Braves dugout, which was on the third base side. He come right into our dugout, heading for the dressing room. And all of a sudden he sat right down beside me in the dugout and he looked down our bench and said, "Boys, that last one felt good!" And that was the last home run Babe Ruth ever hit. I imagine that he knew it was his last one.

There were so many moments that you remember. But that's one I'll never forget. That was 1935, my rookie year. Of course the "Homer in the Gloamin'" thing is something that they don't let you forget. But I'll tell you what. I never let it affect me the next year or during the rest of my career. And even to this day when I think of it, I think of it as what it was. It was just a lousy pitch. If I had it to do over, well. . . . They forget, like I said earlier, about the Labor Day in Pittsburgh with Hartnett hittin' with one out. He hit that curveball into a double play. And that pitch was just as important as the one in the dark.

If you're looking for Ace Adams, just go to Albany, Georgia, and follow the signs. There's Ace's Liquors out on Route 77 and of course Ace's Oyster Bar, a popular eatery right next door. Ace holds several distinctions. He's not only one of Albany, Georgia's most prosperous businessmen, during the years 1944 and 1945 there was no better relief pitcher in the National League.

Ace is as solid an eighty-year-old as you'll find. And when I arrived I found him in the back of the liquor store stacking beer cases. "Just taking a little inventory," he said. He's a laugher and a talker and if you're in Albany and have a need for a six-pack or desire some excellent seafood, Ace is the place. "You should see the line in front of the restaurant on a Friday night," he said.

We repaired to the Oyster Bar for lunch. For openers I presented Ace with a new baseball and asked for his signature. "You better be careful, I'm likely to take my ring and cut this thing. Force of habit!" He laughed. "You know, we did a little of that back then."

I was born in Willows, California, and grew up in the northern part of the state around Red Bluff, north of San Francisco two or three hundred miles, up in the mountains. Ace is my real name and I played my first baseball in grammar school. I played every position, like we always did, and the same thing in high school. In high school we had these city leagues back in the thirties, a long time ago, and I played all kinds of positions. I went down to San Francisco when I was about twenty or so and I was playing with this distillery team—El Rey Brewery. I was union, and I guess you'd call me a clock-winder but I didn't even have to wind any clocks. I was getting a big salary, like all the drivers, $41.67 a week. My job was to give out the samples when the tours came through, just hang around the brewery and give away beer, and to pitch for El Rey. We had a capacity of about 250 barrels a day and we'd ship it as far as Los Angeles. I just sort of checked the barrels and filled the people up with beer when they'd come in. And I'll tell you something, it sure was good coming out of those kegs.

I won thirteen games straight for El Rey. We'd play one game a week on Saturday in an industrial league, other companies, other towns. It was a pretty good little class of ball. If they'd had larger pitching staffs it could have been almost as good as Class-D, back in those days. Not everybody was paid to play, some had other jobs. Then a Brooklyn scout found me and signed me up for a little bit of nothing, I went to Cordele, Georgia, in 1937 and I had a pretty good year there. I won twenty-six and I think I lost thirteen, pitched a lot of games. Relieved some, played the outfield and pinch-hit. I was a pretty fair hitter in the minor leagues, but they threw it too hard in the big leagues. I remember hitting against Feller in an exhibition game and all I could think was, "Look at him!"

That's the way I got started. It was hard to go up back then, but they moved me to Winston-Salem to B-ball where I played for Alvin Crowder, an old pitcher for Washington. He gave me a lot of pointers. I think that was a Brooklyn franchise. Then I moved over to Nashville in 1938 and stayed there in Nashville in 1938, 1939, and 1940. And then in 1940 I led the Sally League in strikeouts and it was a good league. We had a lot of major leaguers down there for seasoning.

I had an injury that year. Ball came back, a line drive, and hit me on the finger and I couldn't throw the curveball that well. But I was 13–5, had a good year and led the league in strikeouts. The fastball and change, I threw them all, used everything. Fastball, curve, slow curve, different speeds, that's the way I pitched. And then when I got to the big leagues I started practicing up on a slider, and there weren't many sliders in those days. Jelly Collier, a pitcher with Nashville, taught me the pitch. He was a pitcher, dead now, a good friend of mine. [It was] a good, good pitch. But I really didn't need it until I got to the big leagues. When I got there I needed all I could get. In fact, here's my formula.

I would mix the rosin and Beechnut tobacco juice. Chewing tobacco and rosin. You could lick your fingers like that and when you got those two together you could throw a good curveball. That was legal. You can't lick your fingers now unless you walk off the mound. These guys

48

now talk about spitballs. If an umpire gets a ball and starts looking for spit on it . . . well you ain't got to have that much. Just a touch is all you need, by the time it gets there it's dry.

I went up [to New York] in 1941 in spring training. The Giants bought my contract from Nashville. I didn't know about it, we [Nashville] played in the Dixie Series. And we won—I won two games in that series and I won the first game and then we went out to Houston and I pitched out there and they thought they were going to beat me out there. Not one man reached first base, shut them out.

Then the Giants bought my contract and I started the 1941 season, went to spring training, Bill Terry was the manager, Mel Ott took over the next year. In spring training I didn't get to pitch as much as I wanted. I needed to pitch a lot. When we got back to New York, we opened the season in Brooklyn in Ebbets Field. That was a thrill, and I was sittin' on the bench and Bill Terry said, "Ace, go down and warm up." Well everybody was ready. Cliff Melton and Bowman and I went down there and started foolin' around. They ain't gonna put me in this game. It was the first big league game I'd ever seen. So Cliff told me, "Ace, you better get ready, Bill's gonna put your tail in there." I said, "Oh, right," and I kept pitchin'. So I really got warm, and about the time I got warm, the pitcher—I think it was Hubbell, might have been Schumacher—got in trouble. I went in with a couple of men on and I got them out. I pitched the last four innings, and held them, got the win in the first major league game I'd ever seen.

So that was a thrill, of course. My wife was listening to it on the radio. She was over in Manhattan and she and another player's wife stayed over at the hotel because we were brand new in New York, didn't know how to get around. So we left them home. After a while they could make it around themselves.

The good part of that first game was that I was making about $3,500. That's what they started you out at back then, wasn't that something? Bill Terry, a great big ol' feller—he died a few years back—he picked me up on his shoulders, carried me off and gave me a thousand dollar raise before we got in the clubhouse. When we got in the clubhouse, he said, "Brannick," Eddie Brannick was the traveling secretary and when he came in Terry said, "Tear up Ace's contract and write him a new one for a thousand more." Wasn't that a hell of a raise though? But it was thrilling to me.

When I came up to the majors I didn't know that I was going to be a relief pitcher. I came up, got into that first game as a reliever, and never started one that year.

I always wanted to be a starter, that's where the money was. My first chance to start was going to be against Boston in the Polo Grounds. This was 1942. We had a doubleheader and I was scheduled to pitch. Cliff Melton was scheduled to pitch the first game and I was going to pitch the second. By golly, I pitched two innings in relief on Thursday before that Sunday and then four innings on Saturday against Boston, and I think I won that ball game. We got in the clubhouse and Mel Ott said, "Ace, you worked pretty hard this week, I don't think we can start you tomorrow." I said, "If I don't, you're gonna have one dern mad pitcher. I'm scheduled to start and I'm gonna start if I only pitch three innings." Ott said, "Okay, hardhead, go ahead." So I pitched the whole nine innings and had a one-hitter going into the ninth, and I won that one. Never had any relief because I was the relief pitcher, so there was no one there to come in for me. Read an old article I found at the house about that the other day. I've got them scattered all over the place. People come in and look at them. "Ace had to go all the way because they didn't have an Ace in the bullpen," it said.

I started a couple, two or three ball games, but not many. And like I said, my mission was to get out of the pen and to be a starter. The reason I kept raising heck about being kept in the pen was because, like I told them, "The money is what I'm after." And I knew that starting pitchers made more money.

After that Sunday game in the Polo Grounds, after I'd had that good week, Mel took me in the office and he said, "If we double your salary, will you stay in the bullpen?" And I said, "Yeah, and I'll tote bats too." So I stayed in the bullpen. And the sportswriters were on them pretty good about not starting me. The pitching staff was pretty thin.

Back then nobody thought that much of relief. That's why I wanted to be a starter. I had a strong arm, stayed in good condition and I was able to pitch nine innings. I don't know whether it was all that Bill Terry had in his mind, that I'd stay in relief. That's just the way they started me out. I thought, "Well, I'll do this for a while and then they'll make a starter of me." But then it kept on and on and I got tired of it. So I'd hold out every year. And they'd give me a little bit more, but not much. I was dealing with Bill Terry. He got to be general manager when Mel Ott took over for him as manager. He was tough. Anybody else I could have done better.

I hardly ever got into a game unless it was on the line. Seldom did I pitch to be pitching. Every time the game was on the line. I guess if I was nervous, I didn't show it. The sportswriters always said that I had ice water in my veins. But I looked at it this way. I never brooded over losing a ball game. I'd feel bad about it but I'd say, "Well, we'll beat them tomorrow." You can't win them all and I came to that conclusion. Even though you want to. It seemed like every game I went into was trouble. Like I told somebody who asked me what hitters gave me a fit, I said "all of them." But there were a few who were really tough. Musial, Lombardi . . . I never liked to face him when he was with Cincinnati. And there was a guy with Philadelphia, Ron Northey. He wasn't much of a fielder but I'll tell you he could hit and especially against me.

Now you talk about relief pitching. You know they've gone back and credited me with all those saves. I think the books show me leading the league with saves in 1944 and then with fifteen in 1945. I guess that was my best year. But we didn't know what a save was back then. It wasn't listed in the book. We couldn't bargain with saves when it came time to talk contract because there was just no such thing back then. That's why I didn't like the relief. Now they make as much as the starters do.

I set the record for most appearances—seventy in 1943—and the Hall of Fame asked for that ball. I sent it along to them, and they sent me a nice letter saying that they'd received it and I've got that letter framed at home. Most appearances . . .

Yes, I was very fortunate, had some good years. One year I had an earned run average of about 1.84. That was 1942, I believe. Then in 1943, I was 11–7 with a 2.82 ERA.

As a relief man it didn't take me long to get ready. They used to say that I could just shake hands and be ready. Now back in the forties, our pen was way out in right field in the Polo Grounds, way back in that corner. You could see the whole game but it was quite a ways out there. We had some fun, cut up a little bit, we had a good time. Ray Berres was our pen catcher and we really had good catchers. Ernie Lombardi, I loved to pitch to him. We liked each other and used to cut up all the time. And he was about 6'3" and weighed about 235 pounds.

One time I was pitching to him in Pittsburgh, and it's ninety feet from home plate back to the backstop. So if you made a bad pitch everybody scored. So ol' Ernie, who was slow anyways, one day I was pitching and I threw a fastball that was way outside. He just reached out there with that meat hand and he caught it, just like it was nothing, and tossed it back. And when we got into the dugout, I was hot. I said, "What the hell are you trying to pull, you big son of a gun? Showing me up like that!" He said, "What?" I said, "You catch my dashing fastball with your bare hand in front of 20,000 people and you don't even rub." Yeah, he could have at least rubbed and let the fans know that I had something.

I guess one of the most exciting games that sticks out in my memory took place in St. Louis. I had pitched the day before and Mel asked me, "Ace, could you pitch one inning for me if I need it? I want this game bad." So he said, "Well, keep loose in the bullpen, watch and kinda be ready. I'm not going to go too far with you." So I go down and the first thing I knew he called me in and I think it was the bottom of the eighth. I struck out five in a row [including] Kurowski, Walker, and Musial. And then the last one popped up and we won the ball game. Boy, that made him happy. That was 1943.

If there's one pitch that I'll always remember it was one I threw in 1942. Danning was catching, and I threw a slider and got Kurowski. I'll never forget it because Danning came running out, jumping up and down and shouting, "That's the best damned pitch you ever threw in your life." I don't know, but I think I was either the first or certainly one of the first to throw the slider. I don't know of anybody else that threw one.

About two or three years later—it's funny that I remember these things about Kurowski, but I do—he got an infield hit off of me and when he got to first base he acted like an idiot. I couldn't figure out what he was so excited about. And I looked over there and hollered, "What in the hell's wrong with you?" "I've been batting against you for three years and that's the first hit I ever got off of you." I didn't even know it, of course. But I guess the finest compliment that I ever got from a hitter came from Stan Musial, he said that I was the toughest right-handed pitcher that he'd ever faced. They asked him who the pitcher was that gave him the most trouble and he said, "Adams." That was in the newspaper. I never heard it but they wrote it.

And you know I was on the Mel Ott Giants team that finished last in 1943. That's the one that Durocher made that famous comment about—"Nice guys finish last." See, Durocher had that rowdy Brooklyn team and we were a pretty decent bunch on the Giants. I guess that's what he was referring to.

But I'll tell you one time when Durocher found out that Ace Adams wasn't always Mr. Nice, not when you catch a guy stealing your pitches. He'd be coaching third and always trying to steal your pitches. I'd be watching him and he'd whistle to the hitter if he thought he had my sign. I kept watching him and I wanted to see if he had my sign. So I wrapped up a curveball where he could see it pretty good and then I threw a fastball right at the batter. Here comes the whistle and he [the hitter] is looking for the breaking pitch. Man, he went down and turned about three flips in the dirt. The whistling stopped after that. Boy, I was mad. After the inning he had to walk to his dugout and I to mine and our paths crossed. And he had said something. I stopped right there and I said, "You so and so, you get up there and pinch-hit. I dare you." He walked off, didn't say anything. But he was a real . . . well I'm not going to say it. There was a lot of rivalry there in New York.

It's not like it used to be. We wanted to win as a team. We never heard of crack or dope, but I'll have to admit we had a few pretty good drinkers. Jim Tobin with the Boston Braves, nickname was Abba Dabba—I had a fan write me a letter the other day telling me about a game I'd pitched against Tobin—he was a pretty good red-nose. And of course Big Poison, Paul Waner, he had a reputation for enjoying a drink [laughs]. I remember we were eating breakfast one morning at the Travelers Restaurant across the street from the Hotel New Yorker, and we were going to play the Dodgers that day. Paul was with the Dodgers then and he said, "Ace, for Lord's sake, if you get in there, don't throw anything too close to me. The way I'm feelin' I won't be able to get out of the way of it today." And I sure enough got in there and I knew that he was kind of woozy. The first pitch I threw him, he nailed, cut up the outfield grass with the ball. And I hollered over at him, "The hell with you, you son of a . . ." Oh, he was a hitter. So was Lloyd. I pitched against him in Pittsburgh. I got a write-up about it at home, and I struck him out. And the paper said that Lloyd Waner hadn't been struck out in 284 times at bat. Adams struck him out. Waner must have been ailing. Can you believe that? Lloyd must have been ailing, gave me no credit at all.

I liked playing in New York. It was a little bit too big for me, but I enjoyed it very much. But it wasn't so big that they didn't know you at all. I'd go out sometimes and they'd find out that I was in the restaurant and people would come up for autographs. Somebody'd see you and it would get started and then you'd have people coming over to your table. And I never refused to sign one, I didn't consider myself all that great.

With the three teams in town there could be at one time as many as six teams in town, with teams coming in and going out. We used to go out to a steakhouse in the Bronx called The Dutchman—dirt floors—they wouldn't allow that today but a great place to eat. You'd walk in there and see celebrities like Babe Ruth, Al Jolson, Harry James, Tommy Dorsey and more major league ballplayers than you could count. Everybody went out there.

New York was something. The biggest crowd I think I ever played in front of was in New York in the early forties at the Bond Benefit game, raising money for war bonds. It was All-Stars from both leagues, and we played against hitters like Greenberg. We played in the Polo Grounds, the stands were full and then they roped off the field and let the overflow out there behind the ropes. We were pitching one inning each. We had Brooklyn pitchers, Giants, Boston, it was all mixed up. Van Mungo was there, so I pitched just before he did. And I'll never forget I struck out Hank Greenberg. Nobody got on base against me and Mungo was going in next. And when I came out he said, "You wouldn't make it tough on your old buddy, would you?" I said, "You'll get them," nobody wanted to be scored on—a matter of pride—and they didn't score on either of us. I think it was American League vs. National League. Yes New York—the fact that we had the three teams there, saw each other in the city from time to time, played against each other—that and the fans, the rivalries, made it special.

Here's another New York memory. Another bond game that I'll never forget. Here's Ace Adams's strongest memory of Babe Ruth. I was talking to him in the clubhouse before the game and he was chewin' tobacco on one side of his mouth and drinking beer on the other side. Amazing. I couldn't do that. I could sure drink the beer and I could chew. But Babe was a double threat.

I've had a lot of questions over the years as to why I jumped to the Mexican League in 1946. I couldn't get enough money. Like I said, I'd never had an opportunity to start. An American man came to me and offered me $50,000 to pitch for one year. That was pretty hard to turn down then, all expenses paid, an apartment. Fifty thousand in 1946 for five months work. That's all I can save in five years. I was about ready to retire anyway, why not take it? I had a good time down there, pitched good ball, got to start. And I had no idea how many games I won. I pitched for Mexico City. And I'll tell you, I gave it my all, but I wasn't worried about my record, so I can't recall what that was. My wife went along down there with me and we had a nice year. She'd fly with me to different places. The crowds were well-behaved, they took it seriously and were good fans. And we were considered pretty big heroes. Nineteen of us all together went down there. In Mexico City we'd be recognized. I remember one time my wife was crossing the street and a man took her by the arm and held up traffic and helped her across the street. Scared her to death, but he was just being nice. Knew who she was, I guess.

We played Tampico, Córdoba, Monterrey, San Luis Potosí. We did some traveling but we went first class, train and plane. No buses and it wasn't bad at all. Mickey Owen was my catcher. We had [Harry] Feldman. Lou Klein came from the Cardinals. The crowds down there were very good, knowledgeable, and for the most part not too rowdy.

I remember the time that Babe Ruth came in for an exhibition and he asked me to pitch to him. He liked them about belt high, but three-quarter speed. He didn't want them too slow, but he could hit that ball. So I stood out there and grooved them and boy, he put on a show. He wanted me because he knew I had good control. And he hit a bunch out and those parks were big. It was 480 feet to center field. But the elevation was high, 7,500 feet, and the air was light and the ball would travel. But I'll tell you the curveball wouldn't break right down there. Even Max Lanier—his curveball just wouldn't work. He had a hell of a curve but he couldn't make it work down there.

I just played one year down there and I got my chance to finally start. They wanted me back when the season was over but I said "that's enough." I had my farm down here in Georgia. I had offers in the Pacific Coast League and offers up there to coach in Atlanta. But I was ready to go. The way it was, because we went and jumped, they barred us from major league baseball. They were wrong, and I'll tell you how bad it was. When I came back, I was coaching a little semi-pro team down in Florida and they sent somebody out on the field and said that I couldn't coach, took me off the field. I sued them and collected from the court. Major league baseball banned us and a lot of us got settlements.

Ace's secret of success? I just figured that I'd go out there and do my day's work and get it over with. And the fans, I never recall them getting on me. I just had good years all the time. If I had a secret I guess it would be that I just kept my ears open and my mouth shut—of course, having a good arm and that slider, and maybe a little rosin and Beechnut from time to time, well that didn't hurt me either.

JOHNNY SAIN
Right-Handed Pitcher

BOSTON BRAVES, 1942, 1946–1951
NEW YORK YANKEES, 1951–1955
KANSAS CITY ATHLETICS, 1955

- Won Twenty Games Four Times
- Led The American League In Saves With Twenty-Two In 1954
- Coached Sixteen Twenty-Game Winners
- Threw Baseball's Most Historic First And Last Pitch

Spahn and Sain and pray for . . . well there's more here than just a name that rhymes with rain—great starter, great relief man and a coach renowned for doing it his way. Sain was inventive, innovative, and by his own admission, controversial. As he talked from his home in Oak Brook, Illinois, I learned something else about Johnny Sain. He's forthright, as candid as they come.

"Yes, I do have a reputation for handling pitchers differently than some. And yes, I've heard it before. Johnny Sain never ran his pitchers, didn't believe in it. Well, let me tell you how that story got started," he said.

I guess most baseball fans have heard the controversy over my philosophy as a pitching coach. Johnny Sain doesn't make his pitchers run. Where that really got the publicity and got started was when I was [pitching coach] with Detroit. This was in the 1960s. We were in the White Sox park in spring training in Sarasota and the White Sox pitchers were running from foul line to foul line. We were just sittin' up there on the bench before the game. Lolich and McLain and them were sittin' there and talkin' about the Sox guys runnin' and I said, "Go down there and see what they're doin'." And of course we knew what they were doing. Lolich and McLain, they told the Sox pitchers, "Hey, we don't ever run over here." Lolich and McLain kinda liked that, got a big kick out of that. Of course, we did our running in the spring and all. But now, let's say you pitch nine innings one day. There's nothing that takes more out of you than that. When you come in from pitching a full game you can't get enough water. You're pooped so let's say you go out the next day and run yourself real hard, and then the next day. Would that be getting you ready to pitch?

Now here's a story that happened in Detroit, it was funny. You know I had that Chevrolet dealership back down South so I was flying back and forth. I went home when I had a day off and when I got back to Detroit the guys were laughing. Mayo Smith [the manager] got the pitchers out and worked them pretty hard, run them pretty good. So I went into Mayo's office and I said, "Mayo, I think that you need to know what's been going on. Everybody got a big kick out of you running the pitchers and I'm sure you didn't hurt them, in fact it was probably good." But I said, "Do you know who led the league last year in complete ball games?" He said, "Sure, we did." I said, "That's enough said, isn't it?"

I've heard and read some quotes from some players and managers criticizing my ideas on [not] running, getting in shape. But look, here's what I tried to do. I tried to explain to each pitcher what they should do to be ready to pitch and to be ready to pitch as often as they could. I don't think you can whip people into shape. They have to get themselves into shape and they have to be willing to keep themselves in shape. I never told anybody to do anything. I probably spent more time thinking about an individual and what I thought he needed to do and how I thought he could help himself than they did themselves. Then if I could come up with an idea, I would present it to them. In most cases they would try it and if it looked like they might be able to do it, I would encourage it. And if they didn't, I would discourage them and then try to get them to do it later. You know there's two important things in coaching: instruction and encouragement. And which is the most important? Which can be overdone? You can't over-encourage, that's for sure.

I grew up in a real small town, Havana, Arkansas. My dad ran an automobile dealership and garage, just a small-town garage. We lived around it in houses that we rented. Then finally we cut off four rooms in the building and we lived in the garage. From the time I was very small, I'd be out there helping him, handing him the wrenches. The reason I'm telling this is because this garage gave me access to the community. When kids would come in from the country they'd come by the garage. And I'd usually have a ball, glove, a mitt, and I'd catch with them and we would play pepper. So that any time anybody would come by to play, I'd drop the wrenches and go out and play with them.

Back to the encouragement. The one thing that really stands out in my mind is that my dad was a left-handed pitcher. I never saw him play but he showed me how to throw a curveball, I guess what you'd call an old schoolhouse out. He was a left-handed pitcher and I was a right-handed pitcher. So I don't know whether most people are familiar with that pitch or not, but the thumb is sticking up. You hold it with your index finger and your middle finger and the thumb is off the ball and you just kind of hook it out. You get the feel of controlling the ball without being behind the ball. That may have been the reason that I was eventually able to throw my breaking ball. I wasn't blessed with velocity, a fastball that you'd say "Here it is, hit it." I realized that I had to make sure that I didn't let the count dictate when I threw my pitches. And I knew that I had to vary my motions and speeds and variations of breaking balls and sinkers and things like that. When I was younger, I never had the burning fastball. I relied more on the breaking stuff and I think that is the reason that I had a rather difficult time catching on early with some of the minor league clubs.

Later my dad was in poor health and we sold the garage and we moved to Belleville [Arkansas]. I stayed with my grandmother and finished high school. I was eighteen, I guess, when I finished high school but I pitched a game in Belleville right after I moved down there. A fellow walked home with me that had grown up in Belleville. His name was Rube Thomas and Rube said, "Do you think that you'd like to play professional baseball?" And I said, "Well sure!" And he said, "Do you know that I know Bill Dickey and I'm going to ask Bill whether he'll talk to you." So I saw Rube several days later and he said, "You know I saw Bill and he said that, yeah, that he'd talk to you but that he'd try to discourage you." And he said, "I asked him, 'Well why would you do that?' and Dickey said, 'Well if I can discourage him, then he won't make it anyway.'" So that's been kicked around a little, that story, to where it's come out that Bill Dickey tried to keep me from playing professional baseball. And that just isn't true. That turned out to be one of the greatest driving forces that kept me going, because I always remembered that. I just couldn't be discouraged.

This fellow Rube Thomas made arrangements for me to go to Knoxville, Tennessee, in the Southern league, they called that an A-league back then. That was the beginning of a lot of bus rides and what you might call the heartbreaks of minor league baseball. A lot of releases and disappointments. But finally, in 1942 I went to spring training with the Boston Braves. Here's what happened.

I'd been playing for Larry Gilbert in Nashville, Tennessee. Larry was a super person and he had contacts with all the major league clubs.

Whatever he said, they'd believe him. They didn't have the scouting then. And he arranged for me to go to spring training with the Braves and Casey Stengel was the manager. That turned out to be one of the greatest things that ever happened to me because Casey liked me. And the Braves were short on players, the war and all. This guy Elton Walker in my home town told me, he said if I had an opportunity to go to spring training that I should get into the best shape I could before I went down there. And I shouldn't tell anybody. And I'd just come a little faster [than the rest] and that's exactly what I tried to do.

The first game I pitched, I pitched against the Washington Senators. In three innings I pitched to nine men, got them all. That was 1942. I noticed that they started taking me seriously. The fastball was still a little short but they liked that curve. I stayed with the club and started north. And Casey told me later that they bought my contract there on the train between New York and Boston. I found out that they paid Larry Gilbert $6,500 for me. In Boston that first year I was in forty ball games. I won four and lost seven. The first game I pitched in, I came in in relief and pitched to Johnny Mize and struck him out. I got him with a fastball.

That was 1942 and the draft board called me in the middle of that first year. I had a roommate, a guy named Jimmy Wallace, and he tried to get into the Navy Air Corps. I was familiar with the Corps because he'd briefed me. So when the draft board called me, I volunteered for the Navy. They had a waiting list and didn't call me until the season was over. Ted Williams joined and Buddy Gremp and Joe Coleman and Johnny Pesky. In November we went to Amherst College, took academics and learned to fly Cubs and Wacos and those twin-engined planes. Then we went to Chapel Hill, North Carolina, for more training and we had a heck of a fine baseball team there. That was probably one of the better clubs that I was ever on. We had Ted Williams in left and Harry Craft in center and Dusty Cooke in right. Pesky was at short, Buddy Hassett, Joe Coleman, some really fine players.

I remember we played a war relief game in New York. They wanted to see Ted Williams. It was called a Navy all-star team. And as it turns out, this for me was a historic moment because during that game I threw the last pitch in baseball to Babe Ruth. The Yankees played Cleveland in a regular scheduled game and then they took some players from the Yankees and Cleveland and formed a team to play us. Babe Ruth managed the club. He pinch-hit in maybe the fifth inning. Buddy Hassett came over and said, "Now don't throw him any curveballs." My curveball was my best pitch. I was ahead—I won the

59

game something like five to three—but I didn't want him to hit the ball. So I threw the ball hard. And if he didn't swing at it they called it a ball. So he walked and he got out on first base and jumped up and clicked his heels together which was a tradition, I guess. I didn't realize it but later when I was with the Yankees I saw this thing in *The Sporting News*, a picture of some famous souvenir baseballs. One of them said *Last Ball Thrown to Babe Ruth, Thrown by Johnny Sain* and then the date of the bond game. That's the only stats that I have on that but I'll never forget seeing Ruth clicking those heels together.

As it turned out, I made two of the most important decisions of my life in the service, one at Chapel Hill and another one later when I was teaching flying at Corpus Christi, Texas. When we were in training in Chapel Hill they came around one day and gave us a choice of the Marines or Navy. So Ted and Joe Coleman went to the Marines. Buddy Gremp, myself and Johnny Pesky went to the Navy. My only reasoning was that it's a bigger outfit and if I was going to go to war I wanted to be in the biggest outfit. So what happened when the war was over and we got out on points? The points didn't make any difference. The Navy had so many pilots I was able to get completely out of the reserves. Ted had to go to Korea and Joe Coleman had to go to Korea. Now Corpus Christi, that's where I got my wings. I did some test flying and some instructing and I was ready to ship out just when the war ended.

A real interesting thing happened to me down there. This was the second decision. One time we were going to play down where Ted Williams was stationed and we had five Beechcrafts, twin-engine small Beechcrafts. And I went up to one of the officers and said, "You know, I'd like to fly an airplane over there to that game." An advanced trainer and he said, "Well, you've got plenty of transportation," and I said, "Yeah, but it's a party by the time you leave and by the time you get back and I want to do all of the flying." So he let me do that. I flew myself over there and they did have a party. The next morning I got up early and flew back to Corpus. The next day I went down to the squadron and this fellow named Carr was taxiing out. He said, "Hey, do you want to take this flight for me?" and I said, "Why?" He said, "I've got to go look for one of those airplanes from yesterday, they didn't make it back." They found that plane scattered out by Galveston and that was the plane that I was supposed to be on. I wouldn't have been flying it. There were seven people on board and of course none of them made it back. My roommate was copilot. So those were two of the greatest decisions I ever made in or out of baseball. I chose the Navy and I didn't stay for that other flight.

After the war I put together some pretty good years with Boston. Four out of my first five seasons I won twenty games, and with nice earned run averages. It goes without saying that there's always a lot of great moments but at the time they don't necessarily make any great impression on you. Here's one.

I threw the first pitch to a black player in major league history but you know, nobody hardly knows it. Jackie Robinson, of course, Opening Day, Ebbets Field, 1947. The Dodgers didn't announce that Jackie was going to play until the game started. Hatten pitched for the Dodgers, and I don't know what the score was, 5–3 I believe. But Jackie didn't get any base hits. I didn't realize this but somebody told me later that he hit a ground ball to Bob Elliott at third his first time up. Jackie played first base and there were no incidents in that game. But a couple of years ago there was an anniversary game of some kind in Florida and the reporters got on the subject of Jackie's first game. They were trying to drag some dirt out of me or something. I said, "Hey look, that was 1947, the second time that I pitched an Opening Day game. And pitching Opening Day is a real thrill. I was excited about pitching Opening Day and as far as who I pitched against, I wasn't concerned about that. But there were no incidents, nothing at all. That's the reason nobody knows who pitched against Jackie in his very first game.

Everybody asks about the 1948 World Series. Billy Southworth [Boston manager] told me that I was going to pitch the first game. At the end of the season he gave me a choice. Five days off and miss my last start at the end of the season or pitch that game and start in the Series with only two days rest. I was going to start in the Series regardless. But I had to make up my mind about that last season start. The pennant was wrapped up but. . . .

I was better mentally prepared with two days rest so that made the decision easy for me. I took two days and pitched the last day of the 1948 season at the Polo Grounds. I pitched five innings and Bill Voiselle pitched two and they called the game on account of darkness. I got credit for that win. This will tell you something about relief pitching back then. That was my sixty-fifth win since I'd come out of the service and the first game that I didn't throw the last pitch of the game. After the war I finished every game I won until the last game of the 1948 season. I pitched 314 innings in a 154-game schedule in 1948.

The Series? We lost to Cleveland four games to two. I shut out Feller in Game One, 1–0, and was at the plate when a play that's gotten a lot attention occurred. But to me it was just another play.

There are a lot of plays in a game and that was just one of them. [Phil Masi, the Braves catcher, appeared to have been picked off second base by Bob Feller. He was called safe and eventually scored the winning run in the one-run game.] Sure, that was a play that has gotten a lot of attention. Maybe Masi was out, I don't know. I look at that a lot differently than most people. Everybody talks about that being such a big thing. Okay, let's say now that was one point in the game and he did score and it was the winning run. All right, in the last of the ninth I had a one-run lead and there were two men out. Ken Keltner was at bat and he hit a slow ground ball to Bob Elliott at third base. Elliott was known for throwing strikes to first base, but he came up and threw that ball ten feet over the first baseman's head. Now I've got the tying run on second base and two men out, exactly the same position that Bob Feller was in. Walt Judnich, a left-handed hitter, was up and it's 315 feet to right field in Boston. Here's my point. If Judnich can hit that ball out of the park, you woulda heard a lot about Bob Elliott's error. But I struck Judnich out and that was the ball game.

If Bob Feller had gotten Tommy Holmes out you wouldn't have ever heard anything about that play at second base. But Holmes hit a little quail over second base, I mean just a little inside-out swing. He was a left-handed hitter. So Masi scored. In the bottom of the ninth I struck Judnich out and we won the ball game. I've got the ball bronzed. The glove is bronzed too. It's not every day that you beat Bob Feller in a World Series, in a 1–0 shutout. It's like I said, there are a lot of plays in a game. Sometimes a lot is made of just one or two, especially in a World Series.

The question as to who said "Spahn and Sain and pray for rain" comes up from time to time. I asked Warren that once and he forgot. I'd heard that Southworth was talking about winning a pennant and some writer said, "Who's going to pitch after Spahn and Sain?" and Billy said, "Yes and then we'll pray for rain," but I think that could have been after the writers had said that. That just happened that way in 1948. It just really happened that way that season. We did get a break with the weather.

You know it's funny. But the next year, 1949 when I won ten games and lost seventeen, they gave me a lot of flack. [Sain went 20–14, 21–12, and 24–15 in the years 1946–1948. In 1950, he finished 20–13.] Even Grantland Rice wrote an article that said I was laying down on Southworth, that I wasn't "giving it enough bone and muscle." I chose not to tell anybody this but I had a sore arm. I'd never seen anybody helped by doctors. I'd watched it real close. I could do everything up to putting action on the ball. I think the reason that I had the sore arm was because I didn't have an exercise program during the winter after the Series. It was the only time in my career that I didn't. If I'd a barnstormed, if I'd a done some throwing, I don't think I would have had the sore arm.

As a relief pitcher with the Yankees in 1954, I had I think twenty-two saves. Twenty-two saves then was different than it is today. Back then, the only time you got a chance to get a save was when they needed you. It's not like today. When you're one run ahead they give the relief man the ball. Why did the Yankees trade for me when they had Allie Reynolds, who had been very effective in relief? Reynolds was a great starter too, just one heck of a pitcher. But Casey wanted to get Allie back in the starting rotation. So that's why they brought me over from the Braves. I'd played for Stengel before and he knew that I could relieve. Casey was just great. I told him that I'd do anything that he wanted me to do.

Casey and me, we·went way back. In fact my first year, in 1942, he brought me into a game in Philadelphia. The bases were loaded and nobody out. And he walked off the mound and then he run back out there and he said, "John, this guy is going to try to steal home. Throw the hitter a curveball but if you see him runnin' switch to a fastball. But don't hit the batter." He went back to the bench. I started to wind up and I'm lookin' at the runner. He's breaking and I hesitate a little and they call a balk and the game's over. And I come in and Casey says, "Son, you have a one-track mind!"

Casey was just great with me, he never got on me about anything. He liked the fact that I was serious about the game. After he'd retired I was in St. Petersburg for an exhibition game and I went over to him and he was sittin' up behind home plate and I walked up and acknowledged him. We started talking and he stood up in the stands and started telling all these people how great I was. If you'd a heard Casey, you'd a thought that I carried that whole Yankee club. He had the ability to do this. But you see, I could always communicate with Casey, we didn't even have to talk. He made me feel ten feet tall.

This will tell you what Stengel was like. I found an article that told me something that I didn't know. A writer said that the Yankees got me over there in 1951 just to help out and that in 1952 that they'd be giving me my walking papers. The writer asked Casey and Casey said, "Well, he's going to win several games for us. In fact, he's going to win some games for us with his bat! He's my number two pinch hitter behind Johnny Mize." But that was Casey. Not that I was his number two pinch hitter, that was just Casey handling the press. Well he pinch-hit me for Joe Collins once in Yankee Stadium against Billy

Pierce. The score was tied 5–5 and I hit a ball over Minnie Minoso's head in left field. We won the game and the nice thing is that even though he was just throwing the bull to that writer, I did win him that one game with my bat.

As a coach I've had some really fine pitchers and I hate to start naming names because you always might forget one. But relief pitchers? Mike Marshall, I had him at Detroit. I liked Marshall. He was stimulating. He was stimulating to anybody that would listen to him. He had a mind of his own. For example when he was talking about throwing the screwball—learning to throw that pitch takes a lot of dedication and a lot of time. And a lot of learning how. I wondered if he could do it. But he had that ability and he was persistent. That's the part that you can't see in an individual. You just have to let them show you. You can't see what's inside of them. And I'll tell you this, if you can't think, you can't play. You can't see whether a guy can think or not. He has to show you. And Marshall could think and of course he could play.

Arroyo with the Yankees, he was something, great under pressure. I only saw Luis nervous once. Never in a game. He reminds me of it every time I see him. This was in 1961 when he was doing all that outstanding pitching. [In 1961 Arroyo led American League relievers. He pitched sixty-five games, won fifteen, twelve of them in a row, and saved twenty-nine.] We were flying into Kansas City. We'd just eaten and the plane was getting ready to land. Luis came over to me and said, "John, I think I've got some problems with my stomach!" And I just started laughing. I said, "Oh, you got cancer, huh? You're getting all nerved up, aren't you?"

There are a lot of nerves in the bullpen, a lot of nerves in pitching. When you win pennants and championships in sports, you do a lot of it with your nervous system. In my case, people never thought anything about me being nervous. But before a big game I'd be wound up as tight as a fiddle. I had to try to minimize the importance of it. That's how I handled it. "I don't care, ah the hell with it!" Occasionally I'd just say, just see how far you can get today. When you magnify the importance, if you don't watch out. . . .

You know what takes more people out of this game than anything else? Over-exertion. Try to walk faster than you can! Try to hit the ball harder than you can and see if it doesn't show. There is a maximum exertion that each person can make. You have to control yourself the best you can. That's what "pitch within yourself" means. You hear that a lot. That's what it means.

Throwing made me sharper, better. I couldn't imagine going to the ball park and sitting on your duff and not throwing. Once you're ready, what you do is you train your subconscious mind to do a job and then you do it. You can't just turn it over to the subconscious but you can train your instincts. As a coach can you teach this? You don't talk in these terms. You just brainstorm and come up with solutions to problems. I enjoyed working more with the pitchers when they were in trouble. That's when you learn more about the individual and the individual learns more about himself. Who did I help? I never like to say that I helped anybody. It doesn't sound good when you say I did this and I did that.

But let me tell you this. My third year with Detroit I was sitting on the bench and Earl Wilson sat down by me. He was pitching that day. I looked at him and said something and he looked at me and he said, "You know, John, that's the first time you ever said anything to me during a ball game!" I never talked to a pitcher during a ball game. I never went to the mound and talked to them. I guess they were about ready to run me off at Atlanta because I wouldn't go out there. But I would recap a game the day after. By me not talking to them, they'd usually come and sit next to me. Then when they asked, that was different. But I always thought that there were more people hurt by coaching than helped. When I was a player if somebody was buzzing in my ear I'd stay away from them. You've got things on your mind and you can only do what you can think. Somebody else can't think for you. There are a lot of coaches and managers that think they can, but they can't. If a guy like Wilson asked for my opinion, then sure, I'd respond. But most of my response would be encouragement, very little instruction.

I've had some great experiences playing this game, so many that it's hard to single out one as the greatest thrill or biggest moment. But there's one thing that I'm convinced of. The greatest statement ever made in baseball history is the one that was made by Lou Gehrig when they had the day for him and he knew that he had ALS (amyotropic lateral sclerosis). He said, "I'm the luckiest person on the face of the earth." I didn't hear him say it, I wasn't there, but that made a great impression on me. Ever since then, and I've thought about it a lot as I've looked back on my career, I've thought the same thing. That I'm the luckiest guy on the face of the earth. I have no second thoughts because I know that I gave it my best.

There's a lot of ability wasted in sports. But if you find a person with a lot of physical ability and he is mentally sharp, then you're talking about your Ted Williamses and your Warren Spahns. And I'll name another one. Whitey Ford. He was serious as he could be about

65

the game. A smart baseball player and as a coach I'd use his mind. Here's what Whitey and I would do. If I'd think of something for another pitcher that I'd like him to try, I'd talk to Whitey about it and then maybe the next day, he'd say something to the guy. Or maybe I'd make the suggestion and Whitey'd come along and back me up. That's the way I liked to coach. I wasn't hung up on the credit or how the message got through. I just wanted to get the idea across, give them something to think about.

REX BARNEY
Right-Handed Pitcher

BROOKLYN DODGERS, 1943, 1946–1950

- **Feller's And Ryan's Fastballs Are Compared To Barney's**
- **No-Hit The Giants In 1948**
- **Branch Rickey Created String Strike Zone In Vero Beach To Cure Barney's Wildness**

To thousands of Baltimore Orioles fans Rex Barney is just a famous voice. He's merely the public address guy at the stadium who says, "Give that fan a contract!" when there's a decent grab in the stands. But when you ask baseball insiders about Rex Barney, the public address business never comes up. "Rex Barney? One of the fastest in baseball history!"

"They'll tell you I was wild as hell too," Barney laughs. Barney is seated just above the screen, behind home plate in the Memorial Stadium press box. He pulls his metal chair in behind his microphone, slips on some reading glasses and begins to pencil in his lineup for tonight's Orioles-Brewers game. He is tall, handsome, and sports a shock of white hair. In an hour or so he'll be talking to the Baltimore fans over the stadium P.A.

Barney is one of those blessed individuals. "There have been," he says, "several wonderful careers in baseball." Barney has been a player, play-by-play man, talk show host, and P.A. announcer. He has been in baseball for "most of my life and I'm still getting paid. It's unbelievable. I don't know of anyone who is more fortunate than I am." He laughs and lowers his voice, "Don't tell anybody, but I've got the world by the ass!"

I'm sixty-five now and I think the most disappointing thing in my life happened in 1934, so I had to be what, ten years old? In the Midwest in those days our only connection to big league baseball was the newspaper. The players used to barnstorm. You didn't even hear them on the radio. We had to read about them. We just didn't get to see the game. In Omaha, Nebraska, which is where I lived, the signs started going up in town. Babe Ruth and Lou Gehrig were coming in on one of those barnstorming tours. My parents were very strict and I went to a very strict Catholic school. And I just begged my father to go to that game and as it turned out, the game was on a weekday so I'd have to get out of school. But my father said, "If your grades reach a certain height you can go." Well needless to say, my grades were at that height. I saw to that. And my mother said, "Son, you deserve it. You get the day off and you get to go to the game." It rained all that day. They never played the game. I cried harder than it rained. I thought life was over for me. I thought that was the end of my life that day.

But lo and behold, in 1947 I pitched in my first World Series and Babe Ruth was there. And that winter he came back to Boys Town in Omaha. I had served Mass there for Father Flanagan as a kid. After that 1947 Series I ended up at the head table there at Boys Town sitting right next to the great Babe Ruth. And he said, "Oh, son, I saw you pitch, you throw very hard." That was nice. I ended up meeting Babe Ruth after all.

The first scout to look at me was from Larry MacPhail's group. Tom Greenwade was a famous scout in the Oklahoma area. He signed Hank Bauer, Mickey Mantle, Elston Howard, and he signed me for the Brooklyn Dodgers. He worked for Mr. MacPhail. Mr. MacPhail sold the club to Mr. Rickey about the time I signed so I was one of Rickey's boys. We were all called that.

I remember Mr. Rickey came to sign me himself. After I signed he took me to New York. We had to train inside during the war so I got to show up in the winter of, I guess, 1942. We were in upstate New York and he wanted to see me throw. They claim that he was the only genius in baseball history and I almost have to believe them. He said, "Son, let me see how you hold the ball." I showed him, he said, "Good, hold it out there again." I held it and he took it out of my fingers and he said, "Where did you learn that?" I'm dumb, so I say, "What?" He says, "To hold the ball that way?" I told him my high school coach had showed me. It was the proper way to hold the fastball, very loose. Then he explained something. He said, "If you get a guy who can throw as hard as you can and the ball doesn't do any-thing, then you're holding it too tight." I've told a few guys that and it's worked for them. He said, "If you hold it loose like that and hold it against the big seams . . . because you've got four seams going into there. . . ." All of this was so far-fetched to me. I was a kid. But it made sense later. He said, "If you hold it with the seams, the ball will sink. But you just keep doing what you're doing. Mr. Barney, I want you to spin the ball for a curveball." I didn't know what the hell that meant but I learned it pretty quickly. You've gotta have them all, all the pitches. You just can't get by on that one.

When I signed and went off to play my first season of professional ball, I went to Durham, North Carolina, and played for the Durham Bulls. That was 1943. I was on that club for a couple of weeks and when you're a pitcher getting paid to pitch you think that's the greatest thing in the world. The Bulls, of Bull Durham fame, was a Dodgers farm club then. Quite a few big stars played for that team. Duke Snider played there, Carl Erskine played there. Gene Mauch and I roomed together in a rooming house, paid $12.50 each a month. I sat around for a week waiting to play and then they finally pitched me in relief one night. My name was announced, and I came in and warmed up. And then I heard, "Now batting for the Norfolk Tars, Larry Berra!" And up comes Yogi, a left-handed, squat little hitter. That was my first batter. I got him out, he flied out. Yogi and I still laugh about that. And then I pitched against him again in Norfolk one night, threw a one-hitter, which was probably the game that got me up to Montreal in the International League. That time Yogi went 0–4. An old historian, a man who I know in Washington, I told him about that and he said, "I'm going to look that up for you." Yogi always claimed I was lying. So my friend in Washington got me a newspaper, a copy of the box score. And boy, I showed that to Yogi and you should have heard him then. Yogi is one of my favorites, one of the nicest guys alive.

That one-hitter got me to Montreal. I only stayed there a matter of weeks and before I knew it, I was in the major leagues. It was too fast, it really was. Hal Gregg, another Montreal pitcher, and I were called up to Brooklyn. And Mr. Rickey calls me into his office. Here I am, this innocent kid. "Mr. Barney, you've showed a lot of progress. . . ." He always called us "mister." That's why we called him mister, I guess. And he said, "You're only here because we know that you're going into the service as soon as the season's over. We want you to look around and get acquainted. Maybe when you get out of the service you'll be able to play for us. You probably won't pitch unless we're ahead 15–0 or behind 15–0." And I thought, boy, this is good. I'm going to get paid $500 a month to sit in with the great Brooklyn Dodgers for July, August and September.

So we go out to Ebbets Field. They had 1:30 P.M. games there in Brooklyn and Durocher is the manager. I get there about ten-thirty or eleven in the morning. Durocher calls me in and he says, "Kid, when did you pitch last?" I said, "Oh, about five days ago." And he said, "All right, you're starting today's game." Talk about scared to death! I was scared to death. But I pitched. When they took me out in the sixth or seventh inning, the score was tied 2–2. No decision. I started four days later and I won my first game against the Pittsburgh Pirates and Johnny Gee. He was the first tall, and for the want of a better word, freakish ballplayer, about 6'9". I'm ahead 5–4 in about the fifth inning. Vince DiMaggio hit a home run off of me with the bases loaded. So Durocher comes out to the mound and I think that I'm out of the game. But Leo says, "Kid, you're doing okay, stay in there." I ended up pitching nine innings and winning the game. In those days you pitched nine innings. They didn't take you out like they do now. And that was my baptism to the major leagues. I ended up winning two and losing two games that year.

I had a taste of the big leagues and one of my favorite memories of that first year is from Pittsburgh. Now I'm eighteen years old, this was my rookie year, 1943, and I remember coming through the Pirates dugout. You had to come through there to get to the visitors' bench. Right there as you'd step out, sitting there on the bench would be Honus Wagner. He sat right there every day. He'd just be sitting there in a Pittsburgh uniform. I don't know, maybe they suited him up just to keep the old man alive. He always had the same thing to say, "How's the weather, boys?" And I used to try to talk to him because I was a history buff in baseball. There was Honus, me talking to the great Honus Wagner, quite a thrill I'll tell you. That year really flew by. Hell, on October 2 I was in the Army. Good-bye Dodgers!

I played very little ball in the Army. I was overseas almost two and a half years. Got the Purple Heart twice, got shot in the leg, some shrapnel in the leg. But I survived. Mr. Rickey was going to give me the biggest bonus in the history of baseball. He was going to give me $5,000. And you know, getting that $5,000 just coming out of high school. That was a fortune. I didn't think anybody had as much money. I was so dumb, I didn't know anything. But two days after the season is over, I'm in the Army, making $21 a month. Mr. Rickey gives me this big bonus and then he says, "There's one thing, son. We're going to give you $2,500 now and if you come out of World War II in one piece . . ." This is the God's truth, this is the way he talked, ". . . in one piece and can still play, you'll get the other $2,500." And my father said, "Certainly he'll sign." I had to work out for about ten days when I came back from the war so they could see that I could run, walk, and throw, or I'd have never gotten the money.

Mr. Rickey was a businessman. But he wasn't as cheap as a lot of people thought. You know in 1946 we were picked to finish last in the National League. And we ended up in a flat out tie with the St. Louis Cardinals. The Cardinals beat us in a play-off. But a week before that play-off [was] the only time I'd ever seen Mr. Rickey in a clubhouse of any kind. He never did that. That was Durocher's team and he ran the clubhouse. But Mr. Rickey came in the clubhouse and said, "Gentlemen, I have to tell you something. This has been such a magnificent year for all of us that if we win this, I'm giving everyone of you a car." And he said, "Now I've checked with all the car manufacturers and there's only one that can supply us with this many new cars and that's Studebaker. I'd like to get you something else but that's it." We're thinking, "Gee, everybody that gets a full share gets a car." Here's what happened. We lost the play-off but he came down again after that last game and said, "Gentlemen, you played so well that you still get the cars." And there were thirty-five of them. I guess all of us were home about a month. I was in Omaha and I get this call from the local Studebaker dealer. And he said, "There are several cars here and you're allowed to pick out any one of them. The Brooklyn Dodgers are going to take care of it." Now you see, nobody knows that about Mr. Rickey.

And Mr. Rickey on marriage. Do you know what he called you if you didn't get married? "A devout coward." You were a devout coward. That's a true story. He wanted everybody married. Do you know what he used to say? "A major league baseball player on the road who has a game rained out can get into more trouble on that day than most people can in a lifetime." And he's right. A devout coward, that's what you were.

For the most part I was a starter. But I was out there in the pen a lot. And the bullpen with the Dodgers, during our heyday, which was 1946 through . . . Jeeze, it's never let up, really. But I was there from 1946 to 1950 and it was just a magnificent experience. Hugh Casey was the big guy. Uh! One tough son of a . . . . What a guy! He was tough. He'd knock you down just looking at you. Of course, so would a lot of other people in those days. He didn't have exclusive rights on that. But I can remember coming back from the war. You had to kind of work your way back into the rotation again. and Ralph Branca and I'd be out there in the pen together. We'd warm up for maybe five, six innings while a guy was pitching. This was a common thing. We just warmed up automatically, we were the middle men. But come the seventh inning we'd sit down because here came big fat Casey waddling down to the bullpen. He owned the seventh, eighth and ninth. They talk about closers today, one inning. The seventh, eighth and ninth, he owned them. If we were tied or there was one-run difference, Hugh Casey took over.

He'd actually throw at guys in the on-deck circle. I saw him do it at Ebbets Field. That ball park was altogether different. Everything was right on top of everything else. A guy would be that far in front of the batting circle and he'd throw at them and say, "Get the hell back in the batting circle!" Casey'd see a guy dig in and he'd holler in, "Are you ready?" The guy would say, "Yeah!" And *foom!* Casey would put one right under his chin. He'd say, "Do you think you can get up there a little quicker?" Casey would yell right in there at them, "You lousy cocksucker you." He didn't care. Oh, he would knock you down, but that's the way it was then.

I saw [Orioles first baseman] Randy Milligan hit three home runs the other evening here in Baltimore and he never once got a pitch in on his hands that night. I asked him, "Didn't you think you'd be going down?" He said he never really thought about it. Boy, I knew guys that would have killed him. You didn't have to hit all three off of them. Just hit one off a guy and that guy would not be living. I told him, "Maglie!" Listen, when I was playing we'd see Pee Wee go down, hit the dirt, Maglie pitching for the Giants and Durocher would just look at me and say, "Did you see that?" I'd be sitting there on the bench. I'd say, "Yes, sir." And I knew what it meant. I had to get somebody.

The trouble with the Ebbets Field bullpen was that it was so tiny. There was hardly room enough for two pitchers to warm up at the same time. We were right on that right field foul line and we'd be interrupted by foul balls. The other one was on the left field line. But all bullpens were like that back then—nothing, it was disgraceful, an afterthought. Just throw them down there in some damned corner, nobody cares about them. I was in that bullpen with Casey, Branca, Sam Narron, Bobby Bragan. Gil Hodges, he used to catch in the bullpen. But there were some great stories down there. Durocher tells this one.

The catcher in the bullpen in Ebbets Field sat right up against a wooden fence and we threw towards him. and Durocher would say, "When that wild man Rex Barney was warming up, I could tell when he had something because I could hear the ball beating up against that old wooden fence. I knew he had it because he was popping that sideboard. They didn't catch much of it out there but he had the stuff because I could hear him popping that fence board." You know I've gone through life with that wild tag and it wasn't unjustified. I *was* wild. But there were a couple of years that I wasn't so wild, 1948 and 1949. But when we would have meetings Durocher would say, "Rex, just get the ball over the plate, don't worry about inside, outside, just get it over." So I knew I could throw hard. I knew that.

There's a lot of funny stories. When Charlie Grimm was managing the Cubs, he was a comic. In those days the manager coached third base. One day I go out to warm up and I had great success in Chicago. I'd pitched a one-hitter there. I'd pitched a lot of good games there. So I'm warming up and I look over and there's Charlie, third-base side. He takes out his lineup card and he looks at me, shakes his head, and proceeds to dig a little hole in the ground along third there and bury the lineup card, like they were already dead. Then he starts praying over the dead. Now he was trying to shake me up, but I was laughing so hard. That day I did pitch a very low hit ball game but that's respect.

Story—Dizzy Dean! I'm eighteen years old, pitching a game in St. Louis. Diz was broadcasting and he came into the clubhouse. He came over to me and he said, "Son, let me tell you something, you can throw plenty hard. Not as hard as ol' Diz could throw." And I say, "Well I'm sure of that, Mr. Dean." I'm scared just talkin' to someone like Dizzy Dean. And then he said, "I'm going to tell you my philosophy on pitching. You know that little fucker that hits .220 or .230?" I said, "Yes sir!" And Diz said, "Well work your ass off gettin' him out. Because that son of a bitch hittin' .330 is gonna hit you, me and anybody else. No matter who you are or how hard you throw!" And I never forgot that. That makes a lot of sense. Jim Palmer, who I've been with here in Baltimore ever since he threw his first pitch, I told Jim that story one day not too long ago and he said, "That's the way I pitched all my life."

I've been asked a lot about velocity, was I in the nineties? I was faster than that. Bob Feller and I talk about it. They had Feller and me throw through a kind of a sound barrier thing, because they had no radar guns as we know them. This was in Cleveland at an exhibition. They said that we both threw it over 100-miles-an-hour that day but whether we did or not, you don't know with those devices.

I've got a story about my friend Yogi along these lines. When Yogi was managing the Yankees I'd pick him up at the hotel every day at two o'clock and take him to the ball park and we'd sit in the locker room until I had to go do my radio work. So Nolan Ryan pitched his fifth no-hitter and we were in Yankee Stadium. I was doing play-by-play for the Orioles then and the last couple of innings we're standing in the training room watching Ryan's game on television. Garagiola and Kubek are doing the play-by-play. Kubek says to Garagiola, "Have you ever seen anybody throw any harder than Ryan?" and Joe says, "Rex Barney, he threw harder." Kubek said, "How do you know?" And Joe said, "Well, I played against him a lot but I also caught him in the service. We were together a couple of years in the service," and that was a true story. That was the end of the conversation. A week later the Yankees are playing here in Baltimore, and Yogi and I are sitting in the locker room and Reggie Jackson comes in. Reggie says, "Rex, I gotta talk to you." And I said, "What is it, pal?" And he said, "I was watching that no-hitter last week and I heard Joe say that you threw harder than Nolan Ryan. Did ya?" And I said, "Well, I don't know, some people say that." Yogi is sitting there not saying a word. And Reggie said, "Well I'll tell you one thing, I'd have taken you downtown, I don't care how hard you threw!" And Yogi said, "You would like hell! When Rex got the ball over, nobody took him anywhere including me and I'm a better hitter than Reggie Jackson!" That was the end of Reggie. He just shook his head and walked away.

A lot of people still talk about my fastball and it's nice, you know. I heard it all the time when I was playing. Maybe it impressed me too much, because in the old days we warmed up right in front of the dugouts. I could make that glove sound like a cannon. And people would *ooh* and *aah*. It probably impressed me too. Control is the answer, I don't care how hard you throw. My problems with control never had anything to do with nerves. Here's what happened to me, last day of the 1950 season. I broke my leg severely, broke it in a couple of places and I never got back into the same motion. As a result I hurt my arm. There were spurts in 1948 and 1949 where I was throwing just as hard as I've ever thrown and had great stuff.

In the 1947 World Series I pitched in three games, relieved in two and started one. [The Yankees beat the Dodgers four games to three.] To play in a World Series like that was certainly a thrill. You have to understand, in 1947 I was really like the eleventh man on a ten-man pitching staff. I can remember going into Yankee Stadium and I just stood around looking at that place and thinking, Babe Ruth played here, Lou Gehrig, Tony Lazzeri, Red Ruffing, those great Yankee teams. Here you are, you might pitch in this ball park in a World Series. DiMaggio comes out and takes batting practice and he gets standing ovations from the vendors, just for batting practice.

Game Five. You see I had already had my dream, I'd pitched in Game Two in relief, played in a World Series. Before Game Five I'm in the outfield running with the other pitchers. Burt Shotton sends Clyde Sukeforth out and Suke yells, "Rex, come here a minute." I think this is strange—Rex, first name—all year I've been called "Hey you!" I said, "Yes sir, what do you want?" And he said, "How do you feel?" I thought, this is strange. And he said, "Well, I want you to go sit down, you're going to start today's game." I thought, "Oh dear God, how did I ever get into this mess?" I remember sitting on the bench waiting and Shea, the Yankee pitcher, gets up to warm up and Ebbets Field is carrying on. I walk out to warm up and they call me all those names that refer to your mother and father. Again, I wasn't the Dodgers number one guy. I was scared. But Bruce Edwards was the type of catcher who—usually some guy would warm you up the first five or ten minutes, but then Bruce would step in and take over the last because he wanted to see what you had. I remember him saying, "Boy, you've got great stuff." And I said, "Yeah, I do." And then I load the bases. Stirnweiss walks, Henrich doubles, Lindell walks. Great story—bases loaded and who's the next hitter? Joe DiMaggio! Nobody out. The guy who hit like what, .325 lifetime, struck out maybe ten times a year, he never struck out. And Bruce comes to the mound and he says to me, "Start him out with a curveball. It doesn't make any difference because you're not going to get it over anyway!" That's exactly what he said. And I did get it over. I struck him out.

One more relief story from that 1947 Series. They bring me in to Game Seven with runners at first and second and two outs. You walked in in those days and coming in from that bullpen in Yankee Stadium, it was like walking from here to downtown Baltimore. So I'm like only twenty-two years old, and here I am walking in. I've got two outs and two men on and I look at the hitter. DiMaggio *again!* At the mound [pitching coach] Sukeforth says to me, "Are you throwin' hard?" I say, "Very hard!" And he says, "Well, here's all you have to do." By the way, that's a famous line that relief pitchers hear when they get to the mound. *Here's all you have to do!* "Make this guy hit a lazy fly ball to center field." I said, "The guy is Joe DiMaggio. This guy's lazy fly balls are cannon shots." He says, "Don't be so damned smart. Just do what I tell you to do." And Bruce Edwards, my catcher, this is true stuff, says, "Rex, do you really have a good fastball?" And I said, "Yeah!" But of course in that situation you lie a lot. And he said, "This is what we're going to do. . . ." Both of us kids—mere mortals—and we're going to do this to DiMaggio. He said, "Start him off by throwing him a curveball. You won't get it over anyway." He gives me that same bullshit line. "And then throw the next one as hard as you can. He'll hit that lazy fly ball to center field. We've got Duke Snider out there, he'll catch it." It's like 484 [feet] to the monuments, something like that. And like five-something to the fence, the place where nobody'd ever hit one. The first pitch I threw I just bypassed the curveball, threw the heater, and threw it hard. The next thing I heard was *whack*, a shot, and all I could think was, "My God, you're going to be part of a record! This is going out where no ball has ever left Yankee Stadium!" I turn around and there's Snider dodging around the monuments. At the last second he reaches up and catches the ball between the monuments and the fence. Boy, I walk off the mound cocky as hell. Bruce catches up with me, and how's this for confidence? He says, "Boy, we sure fooled the hell out of him, didn't we!" And I was convinced, God, I was a hot dog! I remember after that World Series Henrich said, "He pitches like he came down from another league." The first time I'd ever heard that statement. And then DiMaggio said, "He's the hardest thrower that I've ever faced in my life. I've looked at Feller, nobody throws as hard as this kid." And I went home that winter and started thinking about that. I thought, "Damn it, if they think I'm that good, I've got to get my act together."

I got it together in 1948 and 1949, had my better years. I threw a no-hitter and a couple of one-hitters. Here's what reminded me of that. I happen to have the article right here. Some guy was telling me the other day that someone had told him that they referred to the Brooklyn Dodgers not only as the Bums but as the Brooks. And I said, "Oh yes." And he said, "That can't be." So another friend of mine had this article and mimeographed it. I'm very proud of this article, and here's the proud thing. I pitched a no-hitter September 9, 1948. But here's a newspaper article on the one-hitter, see the headline: *Brooks Score on Wild Pitch*, on this one, August 19, 1948. In this one I beat the Phillies and Robin Roberts. I think Roberts gave up one hit. We won it on a wild pitch and I gave up one hit. And just about ten days later I pitch a no-hitter so I was really in a groove. When you get into a groove like that just everything is there. You can do just about anything that you want to do. I know enough about myself and I read enough about it and when you're a kid you do too. You can't help it. I heard hitters, "Jesus Christ, does he throw hard!" But it all dawned on me and as Mr. Rickey used to say, "It's how you finish that counts if you're going to be a complete pitcher." But I think I struck out the side in that Philadelphia game, the one-hitter. You can see their lineup—Hamner, Ennis, Ashburn, Sisler, Seminick, Walker—they had a tough lineup.

And that same season the year I pitched the no-hitter against the Giants. That team led major league baseball in home runs. They had Johnny Mize, Walker Cooper, Sid Gordon, Bobby Thomson, Whitey Lockman. They were tough. That game was played at eight o'clock in the Polo Grounds. That's another thing, Brooklyn playing in the Polo

Grounds. The fans hated us and it was the same for them when they came to Ebbets Field. There were 39,000 people there and a major rain delay. It rained for an hour and I didn't think that we were going to play. A couple of stories about that night. The bat boy came to me during the delay and said, "Rex, why don't you have a hot dog?" And I said, "Oh, I've gotta pitch." And he said, "Nah, we're not going to play." So I said, "All right, get me two hot dogs." I ate them and I was sitting in there a little bit later and I see that the ground crew is taking the tarp off the field. I thought, "I better get my fanny out there." I burped those hot dogs halfway through the ball game. I found out later that Horace Stoneham, the traveling secretary of the Giants, was on his way upstairs to call the game off when he looked down and saw the ground crew taking the tarp off and he thought, well, we'll wait and see what happens.

I'm warming up that night and Bruce Edwards is catching. I asked for Bruce to catch me. Before the game I'm sitting up in that club-house in center field at the Polo Grounds and I told Bruce, "I got Shotton to let you catch me tonight." And he said, "Oh great." Bruce was hurt, couldn't throw and Campanella was sick, had the flu or something. So Bruce said, "You've gotta hold them on. You know I can't throw." So I said, "Don't worry, we'll be all right." And after he'd warmed me up he said, "Dear God, you're throwing hard!" And I said, "There's no way we're going to get beat tonight!" And he said, "I believe you, the way you're throwing!" That's all I said, just that I wouldn't get beat, there sure weren't any predictions about a no-hitter. In the first inning I've got the bases loaded and only one out. I think there were two walks and then an out, then an error. And Willard Marshall, who was one of their big hitters, hit into a double play. Second inning, there was another error. And I think I walked two and struck out ten in that game, but there were two errors. The second inning was the last base runner. I just went through them like nothing. And people say, do you know when you're throwing a no-hitter? Sure you know. You know every hitter that's ever come up and you know they didn't do anything. I pitched a hell of a no-hitter. Nobody hit a ball that was questionable. There were no great catches in that game, that was what I was very proud of and, of course, it was against the Giants and it was against Durocher. That was the year he went over there. I was one of Durocher's pets. After the game, well you know what the Polo Grounds looked like. The clubhouse was out there in center field and you had to run out there. When I got the last man I must have jumped fifty feet in the air.

The first guy there when I came down was Jackie. He grabbed me and said, "I knew you were going to do it!" And I started running to center for that clubhouse and I'll be damned if I don't feel somebody's arm around me and it was Leo. And he said, "You know I was on you the whole game!" I said, "I heard you!" And he said, "But I'm still proud of you, you finally got it together." And I had heard him, boy, when Leo got on you it was, "You rat bastard, you're nothing, you never were nothing." And when I'd come up to the plate to hit, it was worse. I'd hear all that stuff and you know people think you don't know when you're throwing a no-hitter. When Durocher whispered you could hear it in center field. He had one of those unbelievable voices. "Stick it in his ear, the cocksucker, he's no good anyway, stick it in. . . ." And you could hear this all over the ball park. They almost made a rule about this, with that kind of stuff. But it wasn't just Leo that night. Hell, the fans let you know. We're in the Polo Grounds and when you're doing it to Leo, the whole world knew. But the last two innings they applauded every out. They were actually on my side. We only won that game two to nothing so there was no leeway to make any mistakes, you've gotta do it. Whitey Lockman was the last out of that game—an unbelievably tough out, but I had gotten him twice before. Last hitter, two outs, and Bruce Edwards comes out to the mound and says, "What do you want to do with him?" And I said, "I'll just do what I've been doing all night." I'd fed him about five curveballs. "Nobody is going to get me tonight!" And he said, "Well, this is your guy." And I said, "I'll get him, I'm going to get him!" And the second or third pitch he hit a pop fly. Remember the dugouts in the Polo Grounds were a long, long way. Bruce Edwards took off, my catcher, and just kind of slid in the mud. He didn't fall, he just kind of slid and he caught that ball right in front of our dugout. That was it, the last out. Yes, that was the moment.

And there was the other one-hitter, the one in Chicago. I was a cocky one but I learned a lesson there. I'm sitting on the bench, start of the eighth inning, and Ralph Branca was sitting next to me. And I said, "I'm going to pitch another no-hitter." Branca said, "What are you talking like that for?" I said, "I'm going to do it. They've only got one guy, in the eighth and ninth, Cavarretta. If I get him out they're dead." I was ahead about five to nothing and I'm flying. So Cavarretta comes up with two out in the bottom of the eighth. Campanella gives me the curveball sign. I'm figuring everybody's going to take the first pitch off of me, a little bit wild, they've gotta get runners on base. So I shook Campy off, threw the fastball and he hit the son of a bitch, a line shot into right field. That's all, that's all they got, that was the end of that. I'm walking off the mound and Campy comes up to me and he says, "Let me tell you something, don't ever shake me off again." He said, "You know I'm smarter than you are so don't be shaking me off!" So the next day I see Cavarretta and I say, "Phil, how in the hell do you swing at the first pitch off of me?" He said, "I just outguessed you. I figured that you were going to try to get ahead of me, a fastball down the middle for a strike, and I guessed right. I beat you on that one." And that's what major league baseball is all about. It's not just about speed and ability and guys who can throw 100 miles an hour, it's a thinking game!

There's another thing that I'm proud of. In Vero Beach, Florida, Dodgertown, the club's spring training headquarters, pitchers have a standard that they're judged by. You have a Rex Barney fastball, a Johnny Podres changeup and a Carl Erskine and Sandy Koufax curve, that's how they grade you. Sandy Koufax said, "Rex, I heard about you because I used to live in Brooklyn. My uncle would take me to the Dodgers games and I remember admiring you. Then years later I go to Vero Beach for the first time and Mr. Rickey is standing there and he says, 'This boy has got a Rex Barney fastball.'" And he said, "That was the first time that I knew what I had." To this day they still judge them that way. Everyone knows about Mr. Rickey's strings, the strike zone that the pitchers had to throw it into. They invented that for me. Roger Craig, managing San Francisco now, said to me, "Rex, I've always hated you," and I said, "Why?" and he said, "Because at eight o'clock in the morning in Dodgertown, Mr. Rickey would have you out there throwing through those strings, popping that damned glove, waking everybody up." So I go back to Dodgertown every year. This year I'm over at Holman Stadium [in Dodgertown]. Sandy and I are sitting there talking and he invites me to go over and have lunch with them in the clubhouse. And he says, "By the way, your monument is still here." And I say, "What the hell are you talking about, my monument?" He says, "Come here," and he shows me the exact same spot that he inherited from me. The place where Mr. Rickey made me throw. They used to tell Sandy that he was just as wild as Rex Barney. But there they were, the strings. He said, "They've added a couple of mounds but there they are, the Rex Barney strings."

JOE NUXHALL
Left-Handed Pitcher

CINCINNATI REDS, 1944, 1952–1960
KANSAS CITY ATHLETICS, 1961
LOS ANGELES ANGELS, 1962
CINCINNATI REDS, 1962–1966

- **Youngest Man Ever To Play Major League Baseball**
- **Gave Up His First Hit To Stan Musial**
- **Turned It Around Back In Cincinnati Late In His Career With Outstanding Years In 1963 And 1965**

Joe Nuxhall, the youngest man ever to play professional baseball, still has a bit of the kid in him. I find him perched behind the Cincinnati Reds winter training headquarters in Plant City, Florida, eyes riveted on an algae-covered pond, waiting for a friend of his to surface. "There's a big ol' gator out there," Nuxhall says, "saw him yesterday."

All of middle America and most of the rest of us know him as "Nuxie," Marty Brennaman's sidekick and the colorful voice of the Redlegs. To National League hitters for a day in 1944, and some fifteen summers (from 1952 to 1966) he was the hard-throwing, oft-wild left-hander, a man whose lifetime numbers (135 wins, 117 losses, 3.90 ERA) were a sight better than some Reds fans care to remember.

Nuxie looks like a poster boy for public links golf today—white club cap, banlon shirt, red plaid bermudas. Dozens of baseball diamonds dotted with the red and white uniforms of minor league Redlegs surround us. Nuxie's looking thoughtful, pulling at a cigarette, watching the pond, recalling a historic day: June 10, 1944.

I signed with the Redlegs when I was fifteen. I guess because I was still in school they let me stay around Cincinnati and didn't send me out to a minor league club. But I'd go down to Crosley Field on week-ends and for night games, suit up and sit on the bench. I just happened to be there one Saturday afternoon [June 10, 1944] when the Cardinals

were beating the Reds pretty good. Bill McKechnie [the Red.
said, "Well, maybe this is a good time to run the kid in the\
he did and now it's history.

What I remember most was just sitting on the bench and watch\
Musial and those guys hit. The way they could hit was amazing. An\
then all of a sudden I'm told to warm up and *bingo*! I'm in the game.
Suddenly baseball wasn't quite as much fun. Hell yes I was nervous.
But what I've always said, and it's a "what if?" What if I'd a retired
three batters in a row? They were looking for talent, and if I'd gotten
those hitters out and not shown any real sign of wildness, then you
never know, I might have hung around for my whole career. [Nux-
hall's next major league appearance came eight years later in 1952.]

I walked a hell of a lot of players, gave up a lot of runs, only two
hits and Musial got one of them. I don't remember who got the other
one. But Musial got the first hit—a line drive to right field. I remember it well. He knocked the heck out of it too. And later on when I
thought about it I was amazed. I'll never forget how he just dug in
and stood up there. I'm throwing fastballs all over the place, everywhere, and he stood right up there like I was a needle-threader. And
when I finally got that first pitch in there, *Wham!* If there was any
good of it from my perspective, well hell, a Hall-of-Famer got the first
hit off of me. I got to look at the entire St. Louis lineup. The Cooper
brothers were pitching and catching. Marty Marion, and Whitey
Kurowski, Johnny Hopp, Danny Litwhiler . . . that was a good
Cardinal club. That was the only year that two St. Louis teams played
in a World Series, 1944.

That first game was quite an experience for a fifteen-year-old kid.
Crosley Field didn't make me nervous because I'd been there before.
But when you think about it, standing out there on the mound facing
Stan Musial—I forget what the attendance was that day, probably
about 300—but it's like I tell people, I swear I've talked to 40,000 fans
who were there that day.

When I got back up to the majors, this was 1952, the dugouts were
kind of small. If I started the day before, I'd head on down to the
bullpen and sit with my buddies out there. We'd get out of the way.
And there would always be a couple of starters down there. There were
so many great guys and stories from bullpen guys. I remember an incident that happened with Jack Billingham. This was later, in Cincinnati
when I was in the broadcast booth. The most expensive sandwich
maybe ever served in a bullpen. This is a case where the starter goes
to the bullpen for a leisurely afternoon. Jack told the clubhouse kid,
he says, "About the fourth inning bring me a ham and cheese sand-

81

wich out to the bullpen." And about the fourth the kid makes up a nice ham and cheese, wraps foil around it. Sparky sees it and says, "Son, who are you taking that to?" and the kid says, "I'm taking it to Mr. Billingham in the bullpen." He says, "Oh, you are?" and Sparky took it and just squeezed it up into a dough ball, wadded it all up and said, "Now you take it down there and you tell Mr. Billingham that our ham-and-cheeses are $50 today!"

We had a guy by the name of Marshall Bridges, a left-handed pitcher, he was a pen guy. There was this one time that Marshall fell asleep in the dugout, dozed off on the bench before a game. You could plug up the drain in the floor, so we took a hose and filled up the dugout with water. He woke up on the bench and the place was flooded, he liked to drown in there.

Here's a pen story. We had a deal in New York one time. Willie Mays was playing center field for the Giants and the bullpen in the Polo Grounds was in left center on the playing field. You sat right there on a bench up against the wall with a little canopy that hung down over you to protect you from the fans up above from throwing stuff on you. Mays hit a ball out there that went right through the canopy and it landed in Smoky Burgess's lap. He was sitting there on the [bullpen] bench. And then Frank Robinson, our left fielder was standing right there. Smoky says, "What should I do with it?" And I said, "Hell, give it to Frank!" So he goes like that and flips it to Frank. Frank wheels, makes a perfect throw to McMillan, the cut-off man, and he fires it to home. They hold Mays to a triple. Well, when you check the home run records Willie should have one more [than 660] because that ball was definitely an inside-the-park home run. And the next day I pitched. Leo Durocher was married to Laraine Day at the time and she had a post-game show. As the winning pitcher I was asked to be on it. So one of the first questions she asked was—I wouldn't be surprised if Leo put her up to it—"Joe, were you in the bullpen yesterday?" I said, "Yes ma'am!" and she said, "What happened to that ball Willie hit out there yesterday?" I said, "Well it was the strangest thing, it hit the fence and took one hop right to Robinson!" She said, "You know it looked like somebody threw that ball out of the bullpen!"

Here's one that isn't so funny. One time in Philadelphia I pitched the night before, a Friday night, and we were playing a day game in Connie Mack the next day so I went down to the pen. They had a cage around their pen and you couldn't see the game very well from in there so we sat out along the right field foul line. I went inside the pen and had a newspaper, and reading the newspaper, dadburn if I didn't fall asleep. Somehow I turned over, and all of a sudden I smell smoke in the bullpen. I'm still in the twilight zone, not really aware of what's going on, and I can kind of feel the heat underneath me. I reach under the bench and go to swipe this stuff out of there. When I come up, my hand's on fire. Somebody—and I still don't know who did it—had taken foam rubber out of the padding they used to protect along the fence and threw it under there and lit me up. And that's what it was and my hand was totally black—fingers, thumb, the palm of my hand were just one big blister. Now I've gotta go into the dugout and when I get there of course, Birdie [Tebbetts] wants to know what happened. And so I say, "Aw, I was lighting a cigarette and the matches blew up in my hand." But he had to know better because my hand was a mess. The only plus was it was my right hand.

Art Fowler story . . . a real character. A game in Philadelphia that I recall, about 1954, somewhere in there, I was starting and we got four runs in the first inning and three in the third, one of those pitcher's dreams. Again, I was just struggling like the dickens, but I had this tremendous lead and I could smell an easy win. In about the fourth I'm still having problems. I always hated early runs, because it affected my concentration. I couldn't get into the ball game. You get four or five runs early and you say well, all I've gotta do is throw strikes and you just screw everything up, which I was doing that day. So Art Fowler, one of our [relief] pitchers and a real character, was in the dugout and he's watching this. Birdie tells him to go on down to the bullpen and warm up and when he's ready to lift his cap. Fowler sees an opportunity here, a chance to steal an easy win. So he goes out there and doesn't throw a pitch. He's about halfway to the bullpen and I happen to look over there and he's taking his hat off, he's ready. It's the fourth inning and we're still ahead and here comes Birdie out to hook me. Fowler takes over and steals my win. Needless to say, I had a case of the pinkie over that one, wasn't too happy!

The pen was fun but jeeze, when you're out there, boy, you face some tough hitters. I guess one of the toughest for me, nobody ever believes me, but it was Granny Hamner of the Phillies. It didn't make any difference where or how I threw the ball, he could hit it. He just had a whammy on me, he could hit it. And then there were the Musials, the Mayses, the Aarons, Ennis. Ken Boyer was tough. Hell, those guys are going to get a hit about every three times at the plate. I saw a program listing not too long ago and it had all of Aaron's home runs and who he'd hit them against. I was surprised I pitched against him all those years and he only hit one home run off of me. Hell, I expected to see at least four or five. Of course, that list didn't count the nicks he took out of the outfield walls with those line drives of his.

There have been some nice memories and great breaks for me in this game but if I had to pick out one thing it would be coming back to the Reds in 1962. When I left, got sent down, I never dreamed that I'd be back here. So when I got the call from the Reds, it was very special. When I'd left it wasn't under the best circumstances or conditions. I was terrible and I admitted it. I did keep my cool and didn't yell at fans because it wasn't their fault that I was horseshit! Had I come back and gotten the same treatment that I was getting before, I mean, oh man, they were on me. Adolf Hitler could have walked out there and gotten a better reception than I did in 1960. And I was bad, what am I going to say?

And that game, the first one after I came back in 1962, Fred Hutchinson was the manager and he put me in in relief. We were playing the Braves and when I went down to the bullpen to warm up I was concerned, thinking, "Oh jeeze, I wonder how they're going to accept me if I get in the game?" When Fred called me in and I walked out there and the announcer said, "Now pitching . . ." the fans cheered. That really took a big load off of me, relaxed me and consequently I did well. I worked about five innings and did well . . . Mathews, Aaron. And I always thought that Waite Hoyte, who broadcast our games, was a big part of my gaining acceptance with the fans again. He talked on the air about me coming back and set it up pretty good with the fans from what I understand. Hell, a little help never hurts anyone. And I've always tried to do that for players since I've been in the booth. Hell, look what it did for me. I got off to a nice start that day and, well, let's just say things worked out nicely. I've been with the Reds ever since.

CLYDE KING
Right-Handed Pitcher

BROOKLYN DODGERS, 1944–1945, 1947–1948, 1951–1952
CINCINNATI REDS, 1953

- Should Have Been The Man To Face Bobby Thomson When Ralph Branca Threw The "Shot Heard Round The World" Pitch
- Led National League In Relief Points And Relief Wins In 1951
- Received A Sports Coat From Leo "The Lip" Durocher For Extraordinary Relief Work

Clyde King can talk the game of baseball. He's worked at every level—pitcher, bullpen coach, pitching coach, manager, general manager, superscout. He started his career with Branch Rickey and the Dodgers and ended it with the Yankees as a survivor of the Steinbrenner years.

King's Goldsboro, North Carolina, home looks like a page out of *Southern Living*. It's late November and Clyde has the wood popping and cracking in the living room fireplace. He sees me eyeing a large framed color photo on the wall. "Don Mattingly, Yogi Berra, and me, celebrating Mattingly's batting championship in 1984. I have a lot of my souvenirs upstairs in a special room. I'll give you the grand tour later," he says. We move into a spacious dining area off the kitchen. Through rear windows we can see the sunlight playing on a well-manicured lawn. I suggest that he must have a pretty good grounds crew. "You're talking to him. Compliment accepted," King laughs. I click on the tape recorder. "Let me tell you about the first lesson I ever learned in this game," King says. "And this was before I ever met Branch Rickey or played a game with the Brooklyn Dodgers."

I was born and raised here in the Goldsboro area. And heck, I was playing for a men's team when I was fifteen. We'd play on weekends and I remember the first home run that I ever hit that went over a fence. We played in a lot of open fields. We called them cow pastures in those days. They'd have a corn field beyond the outfield. I'd hit some home runs in those fields where they couldn't find the ball. But the first home run that I hit over the fence was in Lucama, a little town not too far from Raleigh. It was a Saturday afternoon and in those days baseball was big in the communities. They had about 2,000 people at the game and I was pitchin' and we were leading 2–1. I hit the home run in the seventh inning with a man on to knock in our two runs. Then in the bottom of the ninth, with two outs, a guy named Harvey Pittman, he was forty-two years old and I was fifteen playing with men. Harvey had played in the minor leagues for twelve or thirteen years and he was a good hitter, a first baseman, a left-handed hitter. He comes up in the bottom of the ninth with two out and nobody on, and he hits a ball down the left field line, a Texas Leaguer. In those days they only had one umpire and he stood behind the pitcher. So Harvey Pittman, wise and smart and all, hits this blooper down there and he knows that the umpire has to leave the pitcher's mound, race over there and look down the third base line because he has to call it fair or foul. And I'm standing there looking too, and all of a sudden I hear this rumpety-bumpety-bump sound coming towards the mound. And it's Harvey. He comes running right through the pitcher's mound, and I just look and he goes right by like a freight train to second base and then just stands there. The ump's still looking out into left field and he's calling it a fair ball. Well, everybody in the stands saw what happened. But Lucama was Harvey's home town. We're all hollering, "Hey, he didn't touch first!" Now the umpire says, "Well, I can't do anything about it, I didn't see him." And when I tell that story people always say, "Is that the truth?" Well it is, the Gospel. That's exactly how it happened. I was fortunate, because I got the next guy out and we won the ball game. But Harvey Pittman didn't help me any. Except that lesson he taught. You've gotta watch the runners, make sure they touch every base.

I went on and played American Legion ball here in Goldsboro. We had city league ball, the "Bombardiers" and the "Tigers," team names like that. I played high school ball and then went on to the University of North Carolina at Chapel Hill and played baseball for them. I signed with a Brooklyn scout there, Howie Haak. I didn't notice it but every time I pitched, Howie umpired, to make some extra money, I guess. I didn't get the connection until he approached me. Howie would umpire behind the pitcher and I'd throw a pitch that might be four or five inches outside the strike zone and he'd say, "Strike!" I'd throw another one that was a little low and he'd say, "Strike!" So finally, when we were all finished with a game, he approached. "I'm a scout for the Dodgers. I work for Mr. Branch Rickey and I'd like you to go to Brooklyn for a tryout," he said, "Mr. Rickey called me and asked me if there was a pitcher in this area"—in what we called the Ration League, it was during the war—"that might be able to pitch in the big leagues." He was looking for a guy who could throw, had good control, wouldn't scare and wouldn't panic. And then he said, "Clyde, you're the guy! Would you be willing to go up for a workout?" And I said, "Howie, I'm thinking of signing with the Red Sox." Coach Bunn Hearn was our coach at Carolina and he wanted me to go to Roanoke, Virginia. A-ball I think it was then. I was going to get a bonus of like $3,500 and I thought that was great. And that was a lot of money, especially when I hadn't been any further west than Chapel Hill. Howie told me that all I had to do was go up there and try it and if I didn't like it or it didn't work out, then I could come on back and sign with the Red Sox.

I wasn't committed to the Red Sox, so he put me on a train in Raleigh. And I borrowed my roommate's suitcase and we'd played Duke the week before. The suitcase had BEAT DOOK, D-O-O-K, written on it. So I went up there and Mr. Rickey called me in the office and he said, "Mr. King, I have some good reports on you from Howie Haak, our scout down in North Carolina." Then he proceeded to give me the Rickey treatment. Later he became like my second father, took me under his wing, and I just sat at his feet.

The first game I pitched in Brooklyn was against the Giants. That was June of 1944. It was late June because I didn't go up until the session was over at Carolina. My best friend, Ralph Branca, broke in at the same time. It was June of 1944 and he was out of NYU. It's kind of ironic because Ralph and I were best friends. Then in 1951 when he pitched to Bobby Thomson I normally would have been the guy to come in for a situation like that. I'll get to that later. But my first appearance in Ebbets was against the Giants. And this was the first game that Mr. Rickey saw me pitch in person. The bases were loaded and Mel Ott was the hitter. I remember I threw twelve pitches to him and he fouled all of them off. Finally he hit a ball off the scoreboard, a two-run double to right field, out there by the Abe Stark "Win a Suit" sign. I threw Ott nothing but fastballs. And here's why I did it. Mickey Owen was the catcher and he came out and I guess he thought, "Here's a young college pitcher, probably wild and everything," so he said, "Son, don't pay any attention to my fingers. Whatever I put down you just throw all fastballs. Let's get out of here and go home." Because we were six runs behind. They [the front office] were testing me, never playing pro ball and all. They wanted to have a look at how I'd conduct myself. I threw the twelve fastballs until Ott got one he liked. That was it—a bases-loaded double.

The next morning there was a note in my mailbox from Mr. Rickey telling me come over to 215 Montague Street after breakfast. The boss wanted to talk to me. This was just five or six days after I'd signed. And I wasn't really nervous. I thought maybe they were going to send me down. In fact I kind of expected it. So I went over and Mr. Rickey started talking. "What kinds of pitches do you throw?" he said. Now I knew he knew what kind of pitches I threw because he'd just worked me out five or six days before. And I knew there was a purpose to his question. I said, "Well, Mr. Rickey, I throw a fastball and a curve." "Oh, you've got a curve?" he said. "Yeah, I've got a curve!" He, of course, knows all this. This is vintage Mr. Rickey. Then he wanted to know how many I'd thrown in the game the night before and I told him that I hadn't thrown any. "Well, what did you throw?" "Fastballs!" I said. Then he wants to know how many. "Twelve," was my answer. "Yes, you threw twelve and you threw them all to a fastball hitter. Now, why didn't you throw your curve?" Mr. Rickey said. And then I told him the story about how Mickey had come out and said, "Nothing but fastballs!" He said, "Young man, that's your first lesson. You're the boss on the mound. The catcher does not dictate! He suggests. If you agree, fine. If you don't, just shake your head. You shouldn't have thrown all fastballs. I'm not blaming you, I'm blaming Mickey Owen. I'll have a talk with Mr. Owen." He called him Mr. Owen. Mickey came up later and told me that I got him in trouble. He said, "The boss got after me for calling all fastballs. I didn't know that you had a curve." That's the way Mr. Rickey was. He didn't miss a thing.

The only time Mr. Rickey ever got mad with me was well. . . . He had written an article for *The Sporting News* about the base-stealing angle of the game. He loved base stealing. Mr. Rickey would have loved Curt Flood, and Maury Wills and Brock and Rickey Henderson. They would have been geniuses with him. They could have hit .200 and he'd have called them geniuses. He thought stealing a base was one of the most exciting things, besides an inside-the-park home run. He thought that was the most thrilling. I was there when Jackie stole home in the Series and I was there that time in Boston when he stole home. We were like seven or eight runs ahead and he stole home in the ninth inning and they told us, "We'll get you tomorrow," walking off the field. And they did. Sometimes a stolen base. . . .

But Mr. Rickey was writing a story and he had me when I was still in the minor leagues—this was later when I hurt my finger—he had me instructing the Dodger pitchers in Vero on how to hold runners on base because I had a pretty good move to first. He had me proofread this article and said, "I want to know what you think of this." Imagine Mr. Rickey saying that to me. And I said sure, and I read it and as always, I had to tell him what I thought. I said, "Mr. Rickey, you're just discriminating against the pitcher and I don't like it. I don't like it!" That's the only time he ever got angry at me. He said, "Aren't you interested in the overall picture of the game?" and I said, "Yes, but everything in recent years has been against the pitcher. They've shortened the strike zone." This is before what they've done to it now. And I said, "Everything is geared to the hitters and I'm just going to have to stand up and defend the pitchers. I hope they don't accept this." And I said it jokingly but he didn't take it as a joke. He said, "I thought you were going to be some help to me." I said, "Mr. Rickey, I thought I was being helpful!"

Mr. Rickey was something, but when it came to field managers, Leo Durocher was the best, the best I ever had. I don't hesitate to say that because it's true. The best at everything, getting the most out of his players. I played for other good managers—Walt Alston, Rogers Hornsby, Chuck Dressen and Burt Shotton—quite a few of them, but Leo was a fighter. You knew that he would take up for you with the umpires or with the opposition or whatever. He was my first manager and he wasn't really a kids' manager. He was a veterans' manager but for some reason he took a liking to me and he pitched me quite a bit. And I remember in later years, when I was more established, a time when I had pitched three days in a row in Chicago, all three days in relief. We were going to St. Louis for the weekend and Leo said, "Now you're tired and we're playing the Giants when we get back home. So when we get to St. Louis I want you to rest!" We were playing the Cardinals on Friday, Saturday and Sunday and were in a pennant race with the Giants. He made it clear that he wanted me to be strong for the Giants when we got back home. "Don't even take your glove out," he said. So I didn't, and don't you know—Preacher Roe is pitching the first night and the temperature is 106 degrees.

We were playing in old Sportsman's Park and Preacher was forty or forty-one years old. You know he wouldn't admit to his age. He was a left-hander, of course, skinny thin, not very strong in the upper body. He had real strong hands, could crush a beer can. And that was back before they were aluminum. But he wasn't a strong-bodied person. I'll get back to my story but it's hard to talk about Preacher without mentioning the spitter. Everybody said he threw it. And he may have. But we never caught him. Erskine and I used to sit on the bench and watch. I'd say, "He's still getting the sign," Erskine would watch his mouth and his hands and then I'd say, "He's ready to pitch." But we never caught him. If he was loading them we never saw it. We heard that he used to get it when he'd take off his cap. He'd spit there [heel of his hand] and the umpire would say, "Wipe it off!" And then he'd make him wipe and touch there where it was still wet. But Preacher was pitching and Leo had told me to leave my glove in the equipment bag because I wasn't going to pitch in St. Louis. Well, Preacher got into trouble. He really didn't get in trouble. He'd pitched six great innings and just came in and told Leo that he couldn't go anymore. It was incredibly hot. Now we're leading 2–1 with three innings to go and we've got to face Musial and those guys—a tough club. Leo came down into the dugout, it was a double-tiered dugout in Sportsman's Park. He came down and stopped right in front of my nose and put both hands on the wall above my head, looked down at me and said, "Can you do it?" I mean just out of the clear blue sky. I wasn't about to say no. So I took Branca's glove and I went to the bullpen. And I remember on the way to the bullpen I said a little prayer. I said I'd like to protect this lead for Preacher, it was his nineteenth win, 1951 I believe, and we knew that he might retire soon. And don't you know that I didn't have anything when I went out there. But I retired nine men in a row. And you never saw so many line drives in your life. Infielders took off diving. Billy Cox was diving, Snider made a catch in left center field—a thing of beauty I'll tell you, I've never seen a greater one, Willie Mays included. I made stars out of all of them that night.

Then we went home, back to New York. We played the Giants in the Polo Grounds then came back to Ebbets to play Philadelphia. Danny Comerfort, the clubhouse man, comes up to me before the game and says that Leo wants to see me in his office. When I get there Leo says, "Clyde, I had a coat made while we were on the road and it's too big for me." Ben Dillon, a Brooklyn tailor who made coats, fitted us and measured us. I never will forget that coat. It was blue, sort of a plaid and it was beautiful. Something like Leo would wear and something I couldn't have afforded. So Leo says, "Try it on. See if it fits." Well I did and it was a perfect fit. Then he said, "It's yours." At the time it didn't dawn on me. I said, "Are you sure?" And he said, "Yes, I am. You did a job for me in Chicago and St. Louis and this thing's too big for me so you take it." I took it back to the locker room and was tickled to death. Ben Dillon, the tailor, comes in to deliver some other clothes to the players and he says, "Clyde, did that coat fit you?" I said, "What coat?" And he said, "The one Leo had made for you." I said, "He didn't." "Yes," he said, "Leo called me and asked me to make a coat for you." Now that was Leo Durocher!

And another time, it was during the war, because Howie Schultz was playing. Howie, Ralph and I were the only college men on that Brooklyn team. We were playing the Giants again and I'd pitched two innings of relief already and we were in the bottom of the thirteenth, and it was tied 3–3. The bases were loaded with two outs and Howie's up. Leo calls him back to the dugout and tells him—by the way this is illegal now, you can't do it—Leo says, "Howie, if you get a base hit, get hit in the fanny, just get on and I'll give you $100." Well, $100 was a lot of money so the first pitch Howie hits back through the box and we win the game 4–3. We go into the clubhouse and Danny Comerfort comes over and gives me a package with some money in it. It had one of those wrappers around it and I looked and it was $100. I said, "What?" He said, "Leo sent this to you." Later when I asked Durocher why, he said, "Well, Clyde, you held them for three innings." Yes, Leo knew how to do it. Leo Durocher was always at least three innings ahead, all the time. Yes, he was quite a manager and a man who knew how to instill confidence in his players.

When it comes to great bullpen men or relief pitchers from the forties, Hugh Casey, on our club, was a great one. He liked to throw at them. And after he did he'd walk right down there, halfway to home plate, hoping they'd say something about it. Yes, he was mean. He'd knock you on your backside in a hurry. And that's where I learned it. I had the reputation of doing that and I learned it from Casey.

I would throw at them but I wasn't really that keen on knocking people down. It had some effect. But back then the guys took it. If somebody hit a two-run homer you just knew that he was going down the next time around. And they did. They went down, then got up and dusted themselves off and that was it. Now today if you come that much inside, the umpire wants to kick you out of the game and the batter wants to fight you. Oh, there was another time. This was in 1953, when I was with Cincinnati. Rogers Hornsby was the manager. I'd been traded in 1952, after the World Series. I had a sore arm and couldn't throw much at all. Rogers knew that I would do that, brush people back, and the Cardinals were just stomping us in St. Louis. So Rogers came out and he said, "I want you to knock Musial down." I said, "Rogers, over the years I've gotten Musial out, I guess as good as anybody, and there's no point in knocking him down." And he said, "No, I'm telling you, I'm not asking. You knock him down." Sure enough, I knocked him down. The ball went right up here [under the

91

chin] and the bat went one way and his body went another way. And he hit the next pitch on the roof in right field. Home run! He killed it. And that's the only time in my whole career that I ever said anything to the manager, negative or bad. I went back into the dugout and I said, "That knockdown was for you, Hornsby." It really aggravated me.

I recall an amusing incident that occurred when I came in to relieve. It was in Brooklyn. Chuck Dressen was the manager, in 1951, I believe. Our infield then was Hodges, Robinson, Reese and Cox and Campanella. While I was on my way in from the pen Chuck called Pee Wee over and said, "Now Clyde hasn't had time enough to warm up, so when he finishes you pretend that you've got something in your eye. Get Jackie to help you get it out. And while you're working on it he'll get in some extra pitches." I didn't know what Chuck had told them and what made matters worse is the fact that Dressen had forgotten that I had warmed up three times already that night before I got the call. I was more than warm. I appreciated that Dressen was trying to give me more time but I didn't appreciate the fact that he wasn't paying attention. So I finish my warm-ups and look and there's Jackie trying to get something out of Pee Wee's eye. I walked back to the mound and began looking for my stocking. I always tore a white sanitary stocking in half and kept it in my pocket to wipe my glasses with because it didn't leave any lint. So I walked over to Pee Wee and said, "Hey, Jackie, take this!" Pee Wee says, "Get back there. You're supposed to be warming up. We're giving you extra time." I said, "Pee Wee, I am warm!" He said, "Oh!" and the eye cleared up in one quick hurry.

I guess the Lavagetto double in the 1947 Series is something that I'll never forget, the one that broke up the no-hitter. I was sitting in the bullpen at Ebbets Field and the pen is right up against the right field wall because there's not much room between the foul line and the stands in Ebbets. I was a reliever then and I sat in that first seat and home plate was right there and the right field wall was as close as that table over there. And the fence went around like this. My right foot was either on the foul line or in fair territory most of the game. And we're sitting there and most people think that Cookie batted for someone else but he batted for Eddie Stanky. I think that the reason a lot of people don't realize that is because they were both the same type of hitters—line-drive guys, not home run hitters. And here Bevens was, with a no-hitter going and two outs and Leo sends in Miksis to run. Lavagetto hit that ball down the right field line and it was coming right at me, it started curving and curving and that thing just did hit fair. I'll never forget that, just watching that thing. Then I turned my eyes back and there goes Miksis running like crazy. He scored all the way from first base. That was such a thrill. And it meant something then, but years later, after it had been played up so as one of baseball's greatest moments, I really realized how significant it was. I was the closest guy to that ball, closer than Henrich, the Yankees right fielder, or anybody else. One of the big hits in baseball history and I could have almost reached out and touched it.

I was right there again, there in the bullpen in the same series, when Gionfriddo made that catch on DiMaggio, the one you see in the films where DiMaggio kicked the dirt at second base. That was the only time I ever saw him show emotion. The fence at Yankee Stadium was only waist high and that was right at the gate that you opened to let in parades and cars and things. It was a long gate and the bullpen was right there. A truly great catch and it was right there in front of me. Had the ball not been caught it would have landed several feet from my head. But I'll tell you what's interesting. I got a letter a year or so ago from a lawyer doing some research on the forties and fifties and he said that his father had been at the Series game the next day, the day after the catch. He had remembered that I was the guy who had thrown balls to Gionfriddo so the movie people could get it on film because they'd missed it the day before. And I said, how in the world did he know that? It was the first time I'd thought about that since it happened. The man was right. That was exactly what happened. They evidently missed the actual catch because they came out with a movie crew and asked me to help them and so I did. I must have thrown forty or fifty baseballs to him until they got what they wanted. I'd throw a ball and G.I.—we called him G.I.—he'd run over and catch it and they filmed maybe forty or fifty shots of it. And now when we see the catch on TV in the films, I always wonder. I don't know if that's my ball he's catching or the real one. I've looked carefully, but I'll tell you why I think it might be one of the ones I threw. There's nobody in the bullpen (in the film), so it makes me think that it's one of the ones I threw. We were all right there, standing there watching it come in. Take a look at that film and you'll see. There's no one in the pen. They knew that I was in the bullpen. And they said, "Would you mind throwing some balls while we get this shot of Gionfriddo?" and I said, "No, I'll be glad to." They did it during batting practice, and I remember Ralph Branca was one of the guys we had in front of the photographers to protect them from batting practice line drives. I really hadn't thought about that until that guy mentioned that in his letter.

On the Thomson home run, the "Shot Heard Round the World," I don't think that there is any doubt that when Branca was walking in that day that I had the thought, this might have been me. But my arm was hurt. I'd been 13–4 at one time during the season, maybe 13–5, and I started getting some pain in my arm and that was the beginning of my arm problems. At one point I couldn't even comb my hair with my right hand. For the previous couple of weeks of the season I just couldn't throw at all, and I didn't get into that last game in Philadelphia until late. It was a fourteen-inning game, I think, the one where Jackie won it with a home run, the one that got us into the play-off game with the Giants. There's no doubt that I would have been the guy if I'd been healthy, and ironically my best friend, Ralph Branca, was the guy that was called in to face Thomson. He and Ann got married after that, October 20. They came to Goldsboro. They stayed with us and while they were here, Ed Sullivan called and asked Ralph to be on the show with Bobby Thomson. I drove Ralph back to Raleigh-Durham airport and he flew back to New York and was on the show. I drove up the next morning, picked him up and brought him back to Goldsboro.

We all felt confident because Newcombe got Monte Irvin out, and Newcombe did a great job. He got a lot of criticism but Newcombe pitched an awful lot down the stretch and he had to be awfully tired. We were leading at the time in the bottom of the ninth inning. He couldn't have been pitching too poorly, not in the Polo Grounds. I mean we're leading, 4–2, and I was thinking, "This could be me," when Ralph was walking in, but Ralph was a heck of a pitcher. And yes, this was a big moment in relief. Ralph was one of the youngest pitchers in history to win more than twenty games. He was 21–12 in 1947. He had a great curve and if he hadn't had back trouble and some knee problems, he would be in the Hall of Fame because he had that kind of stuff. But he had a bad back then, his back was out of line by an inch and nobody even knew it. He didn't complain. But the first pitch he threw, you could tell, he threw it right by Bobby. And the next pitch looked like it was in the same spot, and in Ebbets Field it would have been a foul ball because in Ebbets it was 348 down the left field line. It was only about 257 in the Polo Grounds. I mean there's quite a difference there. And when people talk about it, a lot of them think that it went in the upper deck. But it didn't. It fell in the lower deck and I can still see Pafko with his hands up, reaching like that. And when it happened, at that moment, all that I could see was those thousand dollar bills flying away with that ball, just waving good-bye. Over the years, Ralph has been a wonderful sport about that but enough is enough. "The Giants win the pennant, the Giants win the pennant." I can hear that in my sleep.

JOE GINSBERG
Catcher

**DETROIT TIGERS, 1948, 1950–1953
CLEVELAND INDIANS, 1953–1954
KANSAS CITY ATHLETICS, 1956
BALTIMORE ORIOLES, 1956–1960
CHICAGO WHITE SOX, 1960–1961
BOSTON RED SOX, 1961
NEW YORK METS, 1962**

- **Caught New York Mets First Home Game In The Polo Grounds**
- **Holds AL Passed Ball Record With An Assist From Hoyt Wilhelm**
- **Caught Steve Dalkowski In Famous Aberdeen Proving Grounds Test**
- **Watched Maris's Sixty-First Home Run From Best Seat In The House**

Joe Ginsberg, my inspiration to follow a career path that would lead me to a major league pen, is alive and well in Punta Gorda, Florida. He's busy playing golf, working at the Detroit Tigers Fantasy Camps, doing an occasional gum card show and enjoying life, he says, "like never before." We met at Port Charlotte at Joe's country club. We sat in the sunshine overlooking the lush eighteenth green and discussed a thirteen-year career that found him in the pens of seven major league clubs. I wasn't disappointed. Joe Ginsberg is the pen man I longed to be.

You know I had thirteen years in the major leagues but 1962 was very special. I caught the first game that the Mets ever played in New York, the Mets home opener in the Polo Grounds that year. What had happened was the Mets were just getting organized and they didn't know which way to go. They'd either get a lot of young players or go get a bunch of guys who had just about had it in their careers with pretty good names. Names that people would recognize. And they settled on that. So they signed Gil Hodges, Don Zimmer, Rod Kanehl, Charlie Neal, Gene Woodling, Marv Throneberry, Gus Bell, Frank Thomas. There was quite a crew and when they got all of us together, I think the average age was about thirty-five. Stengel was the manager. I caught the opening game in the Polo Grounds. We played Pittsburgh and I think Friend was pitching, a great game, I think that we lost 2–1 and then we went on to lose about nine in a row. And I'm not even going to say what that season was like. Opening Day was a big kick and you can't believe how those fans supported the Mets. We outdrew the Yankees that year and we lost something like 120 games. They were there, screaming, holding up signs, they'd meet us in the airport and we were losing like crazy.

Some great names on that team. Roger Craig was an excellent pitcher and he lost twenty-four games for the Mets that year. Opening Day, as I said, we lost a close one and then we go on to lose about nine more in a row, and then on the tenth day we come to the ball park and it had started to rain. It looked like we weren't going to play that day, and we come into the clubhouse and Casey has a big banquet set up—first class—with ribs and chicken and champagne bottles and everybody is wondering what in the hell is going on. And the guys are looking at each other thinking this is it, this time the old man really has gone nuts. And finally they called the game off on account of rain. Out comes Casey and he stands in front of the banquet table and says, "Okay, fellas, go ahead and get into that spread, eat up and drink up. This is a victory party. No son of a bitch is going to beat the New York Mets today!"

Casey could never remember my name. I was a Detroit boy, so he just called me the left-handed hitter from Detroit. And that's where I played my first baseball. Detroit was a big haven for major league baseball and major league baseball players. And at that time, when I signed, which was in the forties, there was a gentleman by the name of Wish Egan who was the head Detroit Tiger scout. I guess his name was Aloysius. He was the head scout for the Tigers for years and years when Mr. Walter O. Briggs owned the Detroit Tigers and they called it Briggs Stadium at the time. And Wish really signed everybody. He signed Hal Newhouser, Hoot Evers, Johnny Lipon, Neil Berry, myself, everybody that ever played ball around Detroit. And consequently, one year we had about seven of us that played on the ball club who were from Detroit. So it was really a haven for local boys. Art Houtteman was there, Ted Gray, Billy Pierce, and these were all major league baseball players.

We grew up playing for the city high schools. Gray, Pierce, Houtteman, we all played against one another. I went to Cooley High School, Art went to Catholic Central, Ted Gray and Billy Pierce went to Highland Park, so we all played against one another. And then we ended up playing for the same ball club, the Detroit Tigers, in the fifties.

I signed with the Tigers in 1944 and I had just turned seventeen years old, I was in the eleventh grade and going into the twelfth grade, and I thought it's time to quit high school and go play baseball for $100 a month. They sent me to Jamestown, New York, which was Class-D, that was the lowest rung of professional ball back then. If you don't make that ball club then you go home. I had a pretty good year, wound up hitting .275 there and I was only seventeen years old. We lived at the YMCA for three dollars a week, had a nice room and it was quite an experience for a young fellow. Right after the season I turned eighteen and I got drafted and went in the service for two years. They sent us overseas and we went to the Philippines. And the first thing I heard over there was the crack of the bat and I knew that there was some kind of ball game. I ran into Early Wynn, Max Macon, and met Joe Garagiola. There were a lot of ex-major league ballplayers, ex because they were in the service. And we started a baseball team over there and called ourselves the Manila Dodgers. The reason for that was because Kirby Higbe, a pitcher for the Brooklyn Dodgers at the time, was sort of the head guy, the oldest, and he said, "We're going to call this team the Manila Dodgers." And we drew like thirty and forty thousand GIs every single night. And the war was still going on. That was 1945. We were all in the special service and our job was to entertain the GIs and sailors that came into Manila. We played all the teams that were overseas, and we played every single night, under the lights in Manila stadium, Rizal Stadium. When we were there, Babe Ruth's name was on the wall. Every time that you hit a home run in Rizal they would paint your name on the wall. So there's Lou Gehrig, Babe Ruth, and then all of a sudden Garagiola's name was put up there. I finally got a hold of one when the wind was blowing out and so my name joined Ruth, Gehrig and the rest.

Joe Garagiola is about a year older than I am and that would make him nineteen. I was eighteen, see, and Joe was a catcher with St. Louis. I was with the Tigers, both catchers, but I used to like to play the outfield once in a while. So we traded off the catching duties. Joe said, "You catch one and then I'll catch one," and it worked out fine. And our pitchers, we had great pitchers, Early Wynn, Jim Hearn, Kent Peterson, who pitched for the Reds, a great prospect, who never really did live up to his potential. And we really did have a ball club over there and did that until we got discharged. When I came back I had some big league experience and the Detroit Tigers thought, "Well, he's been playing over there, he's not a Class-D player anymore." I skipped a couple of classes and went to Williamsport, Pennsylvania, to Class-A in the Eastern League. Scranton, Wilkes-Barre—it was like the New York and Pennsylvania league. And that was in 1947. Then Detroit brought me up at the end of 1948 and I had a real good end of the year. I wound up getting about thirteen hits in the short time that I was up there. Detroit took it all in and decided that they had found the guy who they wanted to be the catcher for their ball club.

There were some great names with that club, Dizzy Trout, Hal Newhouser, George Kell, Art Houtteman, Ted Gray, Johnny Lipon was our shortstop, and our outfield they called the Million Dollar Outfield—Wertz, Evers and Groth. That's when guys were making $5,000 a year. It was really a thrill to be playing major league ball in your home town. But in Detroit, unless you were a superstar the fans didn't really take to you. They didn't go as much for the average run-of-the-mill baseball player. They wanted you to be a superstar, and if you were a hometown boy and you weren't, they didn't like that. They were a little tough on guys like myself but they weren't on Newhouser. But he was a superstar. He won twenty-nine games one year, but if you were just a .250, .260 hitter and a pretty good catcher, they didn't really recognize that. They wanted you to be a big hitter. When I got traded it was much easier to play in the other towns.

In 1951 I caught 102 games and I think I hit around .260 and had about thirty-some RBIs. When I look at the newspaper and see guys playing today that are having that kind of year, they're making about $250,000 a year. At that time I was making $5,000. One day I'll never forget, this was when I was with the Tigers, 1949, we had a team meeting in Dizzy Trout's basement and we started to add up all the salaries that the guys were making. I was making $5,000 and another guy was making $16,000 and Newhouser was making $60,000, you know. And we wound up with a $600,000 team salary. That was the whole thing, that was all of us, the whole twenty-five of us. Now you see these million-dollar guys and they're making twice as much as all of us. We had some big money players, Newhouser, Trucks, Trout, and Evers.

I got traded to Baltimore in 1956. I went over to Baltimore because Paul Richards who caught for Detroit years and years back was the manager of the Orioles. So Paul thought, "Here's a Detroit boy and I'm going to catch him a lot." It was Gus Triandos and myself. We were the only two catchers there. One day there was a play at the plate and the ball almost slipped out of my hands but I caught it and the guy was out. Richards said, "Joe, you know you almost dropped that ball." And I said, "Yes, I know that but I didn't." And he said, "Well, we're going to work on a play. You know where the pitcher goes on a line drive to center field and a man on second, don't you?" I said, "Sure, he goes behind the plate to back me up in case there's an overthrow." So he says, "What's to keep the catcher from getting the pitcher's glove as he goes by and using it like an infielder would on a play. He could catch the short hop and take the high ball and tag the guy out. The pitcher doesn't need the glove back there in a back-up role." So I thought, "Well yes, that's a pretty good idea," and we worked on that all spring. About the third day of the season we're playing in Cleveland and Doby is on second base and I think it was Mitchell hit a line drive back through the box. Here comes the pitcher to back up behind home plate and I'm yelling for him to give me his glove. He threw me the glove and I threw the catcher's glove at him. But it didn't quite work out. The pitcher was Bill Wight, a left-hander, and here I am trying to get his glove on backwards, catch the ball and make a tag. Now I'll tell you that was the end of the glove-switch play and Joe Garagiola thinks that is the funniest story he's ever heard. Here are 40,000 people in their seats and I'm trying to put that left-hander's glove on and everybody scored. Joe thinks that one's a classic, every time I see him he asks me to tell the glove-switch story.

We had some good times in Baltimore. We had pitchers there like Milt Pappas, Jack Fisher, Chuck Estrada, and a guy that's the pitching coach for the A's, Wes Stock. When I was with the Orioles we got a guy by the name of Steve Dalkowski. Dalkowski was a left-hander that weighed about 178 pounds and he could throw the ball harder than probably anybody that's come along, harder than Feller and Barney. And I caught him, when he threw strikes, which he never did. If he could hit the backstop he was doing pretty good. The way I remember my introduction to Dalkowski, it was in spring training and here comes this kid, about 5'10", 178 pounds, not real big, but when we saw him throwing on the sidelines, some of us catchers were saying, "Jeeze, this kid can really hum it," harder than anybody we'd ever seen. And at that time they didn't have a gun where they could time the pitches like they do now. I know in my heart that Steve Dalkowski could throw the ball over 100 miles an hour. So one day, Richards comes to me in Baltimore and says, "We're going to take this kid to Aberdeen," up at the Aberdeen Proving Grounds, an Army installation where they worked with ballistics and missiles. And they had a little box where they timed bullets, and when the bullet went over the box they could time how fast it was going. So they were going to have Steve throw this ball over the box and Paul sent me up there with him to catch for the test. And I said, "I'm not going up there and catch that kid without my mask, he's liable to hit the box and break everything." So here we go and he threw, and this is the real story. He threw hard heat for twenty minutes and never got one over the box. So they couldn't time it, and all of a sudden he was tired and he fired one in and got it over the box. The thing was going ninety-three miles-an-hour, and that was after twenty minutes of hard throwing. And then about the third or fourth pitch after that he hit the box and broke the damned thing. It flew apart and that ended the day and the great Steve Dalkowski speed test. But Steve never did make the big leagues and I really believe that that kid could throw harder than anybody alive. If you'll talk to other players that played for Baltimore at the time, they'll say the same thing. He just couldn't get the ball over—not a matter of choking, I think, but just wild. One day in spring training he was going to start against Cincinnati and Richards said, "We'll start him against the Reds in a night game." I'll never forget, Birdie Tebbetts was the manager of the Reds and Tebbetts watched him warm up and said, "There's no way I'm putting my regulars in this game because this guy is going to kill someone." And he told his players, "Don't swing the bat, just make sure he doesn't hit you."

The toughest to catch was Hoyt Wilhelm. He put Gus Triandos and myself in the record books—three passed balls in a single game. Not only Gus and me, but I think Wes Westrum with the Giants as well. It was three or four passed balls, I'm not sure which. But I know one thing, Hoyt put a lot of us catchers in record books because of that knuckleball, I do know that. Oh my God, you know there were only two catchers in Baltimore at the time, Gus and myself, and if there was a left-handed pitcher going against us and Hoyt was going for us, then Gus was going to catch him. The next thing I know, I'd go in the clubhouse and here's Gussie throwing up. I'd say, "What the hell's the matter with you?" He'd say, "I don't feel well." Well, I know what the hell was the matter with him, Wilhelm was pitching that day. Richards would say, "Well, Gus doesn't feel well, get the big glove out, Joe, and go get him!"

The big glove, here's the story on that. Gus and I were the first in baseball to use it, one of Paul Richards's fantasy ideas. He said, "Why can't we make an oversized glove? There's no rule against it and we'll call it the elephant glove." And he said, "You'll use a regular glove for everybody else and then when Hoyt comes in, switch to the elephant glove," which we did. We broke it in and the darned thing really worked, except for one thing. When there was a man on first and he

100

went to steal and you caught the ball, you knew that it was in there somewhere but you didn't know exactly where. You'd be digging around in there looking for it, and sometimes the guys would be circling the bases while you were doing it.

That's the best knuckleball you'll ever see in your life and I'll say this, he knew what he was throwing but he didn't know what it was going to do. I know that for a fact because a lot of times I'd say, "Hoyt, anything that you can tell me that will help me be a better catcher with this thing?" It's embarrassing in front of fans to be hit and not even be able to catch the ball. And he'd say, "Well, when I come sidearm the ball will sink." So okay, we've got a man on first and second and here he comes sidearm and so I get down and it goes up and right over my shoulder. I never even laid a glove on that one. But I walked out and said, "You better let me figure it out for myself." Believe me, I know that he didn't know what it was going to do.

The only thing we ever figured out about catching the pitch was this. Keep your eye level above the ball. If you did that you had a chance. Eye level above the ball and body in front of it. So if you didn't catch it, you could go down and block it. If you let your eye level go below the ball you were dead, because if the ball should happen to go up, then there was no way you were going to catch it. Easier to go down and block than up, so that was the secret, such as it was, of catching the Wilhelm knuckler. And you're hearing that from the man whom the pitch put in the record books.

When you did a job catching the pitch it was a very good feeling. I recall catching him in Yankee Stadium and he beat the Yankees 3–2. I caught the whole ball game and if I say that he struck out Mantle three times, I mean, Mantle didn't even come close to hitting the ball. He'd swing and miss three feet. And that was really a thrill. And they asked Casey, "Casey, what do you think about Hoyt and this guy Ginsberg, he caught him pretty good today." Casey said, "Sure he caught him good today. The reason is that that guy Wilhelm, he cut down the break of the ball, so he could catch it!" Typical Casey Stengel and that was a funny thing because you know if you could cut it down, which of course you couldn't, well, if you did it so someone could catch it, they sure as hell could have hit it! But that was Casey, and they wrote it.

There are a million Casey stories. There's one that Bob Miller loves to tell. We had two Bob Millers in the bullpen with the Mets that first year, Lefty Bob and Righty Bob. And one day Casey calls the bullpen. The coach answers and Casey says, "Get Miller up." The coach says,

"We got two Millers, which one do you want?" "Bob Miller," Casey says. "We got two Bob Millers, which one do you want!" "Surprise me!" Stengel says and hangs up the phone.

He really was that funny. He could talk to the press all night long but he forgot guys' names and he'd forget who he was talking to. Hell, he was about seventy-four years old at the time. And again, he called me the left-handed hitter from Detroit. He'd say, "Hell, you never hit many home runs and now you're with me and all you want to do is hit home runs." He was something else. And I'll never forget, he fell asleep one day in the dugout, a hot day in New York and we're getting shellacked pretty good. About the fourth inning he hears the crack of the bat and wakes up and shouts, "That's the way to go, fellas!" And the guy sitting next to him says, "Nah, Case, you got the wrong club, we're in the field!" And of course he comes right back, stands up and says, "Well hell, we'll get 'em next inning then."

He'd call guys in to pinch-hit. He'd look at them and not know their name and he'd say, "Son, get a bat. Can you hit?" And they'd say, "I sure can, but I'm a pitcher. You took me out in the third inning." He didn't want his ballplayers to stay out late, but he would. He'd get the press to stay up with him and they'd go out drinking all night. I'll never forget one night, he caught four or five of us out late and he gave us this long dissertation about why we weren't winning. And so not too long after that a bunch of us were coming in past curfew and we got on the elevator. There was a midnight curfew and if you weren't in, you were supposed to be fined. Well Casey was never in so we never worried about it. And so this one night the elevator operator in the New Yorker Hotel had a baseball and he wanted it autographed by everybody. So a lot of us autographed it and the next day Casey had a pre-game meeting and he pulls out this baseball and starts reading our names off of it. He says, "So-and-so and so-and-so, I want to see you guys in my office." We walk in and he says, "You guys were out after curfew!" We, of course, were defensive, "How do you know?" And Casey tosses us the ball and says, "Because I told the goddamned elevator operator to get everybody who got on after twelve to sign this ball!" I was one of the guys on the ball—me, Clem Labine, a lot of us.

Being a part of that original Mets team, you can't believe what that has done for me in later years. And as I said before, the fans in New York just seemed to take the Mets to heart. Every day there were big articles in the paper, more so than there were on the Yankees. And there was this little balcony behind the clubhouse facing the street out there in center field in the Polo Grounds and the fans would come and cheer for the Player of the Day. We didn't have too many Players of the Day when you lose about ten or twelve in a row, but Craig lost twenty-four and never got traded. We had Richie Ashburn. The names were there but they were at the end of their careers.

I have a lot of good memories from a lot of good ball clubs. I was with Boston in 1961 when Roger Maris broke Babe Ruth's record. The catcher, I believe, was Russ Nixon, I was in the bullpen. The pitcher was Tracy Stallard. And I knew Tracy, we used to go out on the town together some. He was a little younger and a little crazy and he told me, "If I ever get a chance to slop up that one that Maris gets sixty-one on, I'm going to throw him a nice little fastball right down the middle. I'm just going to let him hit that son of a gun." And I'd say, "Trace, why are you going to do that?" He said, "Because he's going to break Babe Ruth's record and I'm going to be on that banquet tour all winter as the pitcher that did it!" But I don't think it worked out that way. I'm pretty sure not too many people ever heard Tracy speaking because he was the guy who threw Maris the pitch he hit for the sixty-first home run. But he did say that and he said, "Roger, here it comes, baby, right down the middle!" Did he groove it? I know he did!

The season was over, Boston wasn't going anywhere, I think the Yanks already had it won. And he just laid it in there. I was in the bullpen there in Yankee Stadium. And when Tracy threw that baby up there, there was no doubt in my mind, I knew Roger was going to get it. He hit it in the right field bleachers and I mean there was no doubt about it, that it was gone. He hit it upstairs and it was gone from the moment it left his bat. Pandemonium on the field after that. But the guys in the bullpen? We said, "There goes Ruth's record!" But ballplayers are very unassuming when it comes to things like that. The fans went nuts, cheered, it was like a ticker-tape parade in the stadium that day.

That was a big moment but there were others too. I caught Virgil Trucks's no-hitter, which was a big thrill for me. Virgil did not have a good breaking ball, he had a nice slider and a 100-mile-per-hour fastball. And that day against Washington, there was no doubt in my mind that from the seventh inning on that he was going to do it. He was just untouchable from that inning on. He went through those hitters like a knife through butter. With the last hitter there's always pressure—the fear of it all ending there, breaking up the no-hitter. Then he went to Yankee Stadium and pitched another one there. [Trucks threw two no-hitters in 1952, in Washington, D.C., on May 15 and in New York on August 25.] As a catcher I celebrated it with the pitcher, you are happy for that pitcher. Catchers don't get enough credit, but nevertheless, you're not going to catch a no-hitter unless the pitcher has great stuff. I mean, you're not going to catch a guy who can't get anybody out. I've always had the debate with the pitchers, them saying, "Hey you called the wrong pitch." But I say, "Hey, even a mule can shake his head." That's my answer and once there's a good rapport with the two, you've got something.

I guess my all-time favorite pitchers to catch were guys like Virgil Trucks who could throw so hard. They were easy to catch because they could throw it by the hitters. Guys like Newhouser had great stuff, a great curveball and a real good slider, good fastball, and those guys should be in the Hall of Fame and they're not. And then over in Cleveland guys like Lemon, Wynn—I'm sure there were no better pitchers in the world.

These guys were competitors too. I know in Detroit, Newhouser, you couldn't get the ball away from him, he hated to be pulled from a game. Steve O'Neill was the manager in 1948, and Newhouser was the ace of the staff, O'Neill would come out there and say, "Okay, Hal, it's time to give it up!" And he'd say, "No it isn't, I'm going to pitch to this guy." "Give me the ball." "No, goddamn it, you get back in the dugout, I'm going to pitch to this guy!" And often that's the way it ended, with Steve going back to the dugout and Hal staying out there. Sometimes he'd still be out there four or five innings later. That doesn't happen anymore, I don't believe.

The classic story along these lines was Broadway Billy Loes, who pitched with the Orioles when I was in Baltimore. I roomed with Billy Loes. Richards was the manager and one time he went out to the mound and said, "Billy, you're throwing too many fastballs, you've got to throw that curveball." I'm standing there and listening to this and Billy just looks at Paul and says, "Paul, how many games did you ever win in the big leagues?" And Richards says, "Well, what do you mean by that?" And Loes says, "Well, weren't you a catcher?" Paul says, "Sure." He says, "Well, you never won any games, so why don't you get out of here and let me pitch and you just manage. I'll show you what to do out here." Paul comes back and says, "Billy, don't forget, I am the manager." Billy says, "Yeah, but you never won a game in the big leagues." Those two really went at it. Paul would say, "Billy, I'm going to trade you." Loes would say, "No, you're not, I've got a sore arm, who the hell is going to take a sore-arm pitcher?"

You can't sit in the bullpen with a major league team and not have good memories. And I'd have to say one fact comes to mind that I think might surprise a number of people. Years and years ago, back in the late forties and early fifties in Briggs Stadium in Detroit, both teams sat in the same bullpen. Dead center field, both teams sat together, and, of course, that's unheard of now. We really got to know one another. And I'll never forget the first time I saw Satchel Paige. Here's Satchel Paige sitting in the bullpen—he was with Cleveland then—and it's a cold day in Detroit. We're sitting there with our jackets on and Satchel had built a little fire in the bullpen to keep his feet warm. He said they were freezing. So we got to talking and someone asked him how many strikes he thought he could throw in a row. Satchel says, "All of them. I could throw for ten minutes and not throw a ball!" And he said, "I'll tell you what. If you guys can get some money together, I'll not only throw ten strikes in a row, but I'll throw seven out of ten over this matchbox. You can put it on the plate." Now I'm in the bullpen and my job was to catch him on behalf of the Tigers involved in the bet and my job was to call balls and strikes. So the bet was $100 and I put the matchbox down there, Satchel got up and got ready to throw. And I'll guarantee you that he threw seven out of ten over the matchbox and there was $100 bet on it. There was some discrepancy over one pitch that our guys claimed was a ball, but it wasn't. It was right on the corner and seven of them went over the matches. I know because I caught them. All that was taking place right while the game was going on. He was an old man then, that had to be about 1948, and I was a kid and had heard so much about Satchel Paige. Here I was in the bullpen and catching him like that. It was a real big kick, I'll tell you that. I don't know how old he was, but he could throw hard then. He had thrown all those years in the Negro leagues and now here he was in the big leagues. They used to give him a rocking chair to sit in, Satchel was quite an individual. His age was always the subject of debate even out in the bullpen. But Satchel didn't look old. The guys who played with him claimed that he rubbed some sort of solution on his arm. They said it was goose grease and that it smelled terrible, and that Satch would take a shower and then rub all this stuff on his arm and come to the ball park. And that you could smell him coming with that stuff on his arm two blocks away.

One day we were out there with Satch and Harvey Kuenn had come into the league and Harvey was a real good hitter. Satchel said, "You see that fellow there, you've got to pitch him inside. If you throw him outside, he's going to hurt somebody." And the first time Harvey ever batted against Satchel, we're all watching now to see what he's going to do. Well, he threw the ball on the inside part of the plate and Harvey screamed it right back through the box, almost knocked Satchel off the mound. Back in the bullpen the next day, Satchel says, "Gentlemen, you cannot pitch that young fellow inside, if you do he's going to hurt somebody."

I guess if I had to recall one memory, one that I'll never forget, it was with the New York Mets, in the Polo Grounds, and the Pirates are beating us 1–0. The game was going into the eighth inning and the hitter that was up before me got on first base, I don't recall whether it was a walk or a hit, I can't remember, but there was a man on first and nobody out. And Casey called me back to the dugout and I thought, "Oh hell, he's going to pinch-hit for me." But Casey said, "Let's make them think that you're going to bunt, but you're not going to bunt. I want you to try to hit the ball through the hole. The first baseman will come in and just pull it into right and we'll have a man on first and third and nobody out. And we'll wind up winning this ball game." So I said, "Okay, that's fine." So they are expecting a bunt. Sure enough, here comes the first baseman charging and the third baseman charging, and they laid the ball right in there for me to hit. I swung the bat and I hit the god-darned ball right up in the air, popped it right up and, believe me, I still, for some reason, dream about that pitch. If I had hit that pitch hard enough, it would have been a single, double, or whatever and I'd have been the hero of the day. Hell, the way the Mets were going, who knows? I might have ended up managing that ball club. Casey wasn't going to last too long. And I dream about that pitch to this day, and you know that was 1962. I wake up and say, "God, why didn't I hit that pitch?"

The Game Gets Its First Save

Relief in the postwar forties? Again, World Series action showcased baseball's bullpens. "Dodgers Top Yanks As Casey Stars" and "Page Lauded By Manager Stengel For Brilliant Relief Work In Must Game" bannered U.S. sports pages. In the years that followed, other bullpenners would share the ink with Casey and Page. Jim Konstanty, Ray Narleski, Don Mossi, George Zuverink, and Joe Black—all of them had their day but none would enjoy Hugh Casey's longevity and with the exception of Jim Konstanty's numbers in 1950, none would approach the stats that Joe Page rang up during the summer of 1949. His twenty-seven saved games, thirteen wins and forty relief points during New York's championship season set a record that wouldn't be surpassed for a dozen years. So the game had another standard. Teams that won pennants knew how to pitch in relief.

The pen phones—in those ball parks that had them—rang off the hook, at the rate of fifty to sixty times a season by 1950. Eddie Sawyer, the Phillies manager, called for Jim Konstanty a league-leading seventy-four times that summer. And the results? Konstanty took Philadelphia to its first pennant in thirty-five years. And in doing so, the thirty-three-year-old retread starter became the first relief man ever to win the Most Valuable Player Award. The Phils big right-hander pitched 152 innings, finished sixty-two games, won sixteen, lost seven, saved twenty-two and compiled an ERA of 2.66.

Relievers were gaining more and more prestige with each passing season. Allie Reynolds, the outstanding Yankees starter, became one of the game's first great swing men, leading the team in saves in 1953. Stengel's ability to convert his "Chief" to "Fire Chief" helped take his team to more post-season paydays. During the summer of 1952 a couple of first-year pitchers in the National League excited all of baseball by going head-to-head for Rookie of the Year honors. Joe Black, a broad-shouldered Dodgers stopper, won out, besting Hoyt Wilhelm, Leo Durocher's newfound knuckleballer. Black won fifteen, lost four and saved fifteen games, while compiling an ERA of 2.15. Wilhelm won fifteen, lost three, saved eleven and finished the season with an ERA of 2.43. Black's career was short-lived. Never again would he enjoy the success of his rookie season. But Wilhelm would carry on the pen's award-winning tradition. Following a twenty-one-year career, he became the first relief man ever inducted into the Hall of Fame.

While the National League's two freshmen performed so brilliantly in 1952, a couple of sophomore managers in the junior circuit were working their pens in ways that harked back to the days of McGraw and Griffith. Chicago's Paul Richards, a natural teacher with a flair for the creative, knew the value of freak pitches and how to recycle old arms. Al Lopez, the Indians young skipper, had a feel for the pitcher's mentality. Lopez knew when to pull the plug on a starter.

I think that I had one of the best bullpens that I ever saw there in Cleveland in 1954. I had two young guys, Mossi and Narleski, a left-hander and a right-hander. And then I had Hal Newhouser who had had trouble with his arm but he was good enough to come in and fill in. I don't know if I was the first one to have the real good left-right combination out there, but I'm sure that winning the pennant that year brought a lot of attention to that situation.

Sam Esposito, a Chicago White Sox utility man, who went on to become a highly respected coach of the college game, learned relief by watching the moves of Paul Richards.

Richards was really creative with his bullpen. I remember one thing he used to do with Billy Pierce. If there was a right-handed hitter that Billy had trouble with—this would always be late in the game—he'd send Billy over to play first base and bring a right-hander in to face the hitter, maybe a guy like Dorish. Then when he got the guy, he'd yank Dorish, bring Billy back to the mound and run in a substitute first baseman. And this wasn't as risky as it sounds because Pierce was no shoemaker over there at first. He could play, and Richards knew this.

Everyone had his guy in the pen. In Flatbush Clem Labine bailed out guys for Walt Alston. Dick Farrell mopped up for Mayo Smith in the City of Brotherly Love. Later, Fred Hutchinson, remembering something he'd seen work well in Cleveland, put together a nice righty-lefty combination in Cincinnati in Jim Brosnan and Bill Henry. And in the American League, as games wound down, hitters began to find themselves facing formidable opposition. Stengel called on Ryne Duren; Lopez, Staley; and Richards, O'Dell. In 1958 even Cookie Lavagetto's last place Washington Senators had a strong arm in the pen. Dick Hyde won ten, lost three and saved eighteen games that summer while posting a lowly ERA of 1.75.

The specialty progressed throughout the 1950s and ended fittingly. The year 1959 was the year of relief. Lindy McDaniel, Don McMahon, Don Elston, Ryne Duren, Billy Loes, Mike Fornieles, and Bill Henry all had great success. Elroy Face won eighteen games in relief while only losing one, an unprecedented feat out of the pen. And Gerry Staley and Turk Lown, another Lopez mix-and-match creation, took one of the weakest hitting pennant winning teams in baseball history to a World Series on two pitches: an erratic fastball and a fall-off-the-table sinker. Al Lopez recalls:

> In Chicago with the White Sox I had the two right-handers, Staley and Lown. Lown could throw real hard. His problem was control. He'd scare you with his control, but Staley had great control and he could throw that sinkerball. If I needed a strikeout I'd call Lown, and if I needed the ground ball I'd call Staley in. And I guess one of the biggest games that we ever played was out in Cleveland, this was the end of the 1959 season, the pennant clincher. We had a 3–1 lead and the Indians had men on first and third with one out in the ninth inning. I brought Staley in, the sinkerball pitcher. Vic Power was the hitter. Staley threw him that sinker, a perfect double play ball to Aparicio. Looie took it, went to the bag at second and that was it, one outstanding relief pitch. It won us the pennant that day.

And when Lopez and specialists returned to the South Side's Comiskey Park to open the 1959 Fall Classic, they were greeted by a bullpen buzz saw. The Series had enjoyed its share of relief heroics over its fifty-six-year history but never had it seen anything quite like Larry Sherry of the Los Angeles Dodgers. Larry Sherry remembers his first season:

> My first year, my first World Series. The irony of that Series is that there wasn't one complete game pitched. I got the record of finishing with a win or a save in all four of the Dodgers wins. It's funny, the next year Elroy Face came very close to doing the same thing. But for me, in 1959, with a staff like Drysdale and Koufax you would never expect something like that to happen.

So 1959 was the year. The bullpen came of age that season in the form of the Face heroics, the Staley/Lown combination, and Sherry's remarkable Series accomplishments. But the big break for relief pitching didn't take place between the white lines. Earlier that summer while bouncing along on a bus from Chicago to St. Louis, Jerry Holtzman, a young *Chicago Sun-Times* reporter, came up with a formula that would finally give relief pitchers their just rewards.

I wasn't the first to use the term "save." But I came up with the formula. I got the idea during the year that Face was 18–1, 1959. I was traveling with the Cubs then, and it occurred to me that the Cubs had two outstanding relievers. They had Don Elston, a right-hander, and Billy Henry, a left-hander. And I thought that the two of them together were just as effective, possibly even more effective than Elroy Face with the Pirates. Face was compiling a sensational record, but my thinking was that a relief pitcher who wins games more often than not gives up the tying run. He comes in with the lead, gives up the tying run, then his team comes back and wins it, maybe in extra innings. So on a bus ride from Chicago to St. Louis I worked out the formula for the save. And when we left town I wrote a letter to J. G. Taylor Spink, who was then the publisher of *The Sporting News*. I was a correspondent for them then and soon thereafter he called me up and said that he thought my idea was a very good one and that he thought they'd adopt it.

The importance of the reliever was coming to baseball at that time, and so they [*The Sporting News*] gave me a bonus, a hundred dollars or maybe two hundred and from that day *The Sporting News* ran a weekly summary of who was leading in saves and I kept all the records. Every week I'd write a column or a short story about who the leaders were and what the standings were in both leagues. Then, the following year, 1960, *The Sporting News* started their Fireman of the Year Award.

THE SAVE RULE

The save became official for the first time in 1969. A save was recorded if a reliever was not the winning pitcher but protected a lead to the end of the game or until he was removed for a pinch hitter or pinch runner. If more than one pitcher qualified, the one judged by the official scorer to have been most effective got the save. An adjustment in the rule in 1973 required the reliever to work three innings or come in with the tying or winning run on base or at bat. A modification in 1975, which is still in force today, noted that the tying run could be on deck.

The temptation is to rip right through the sixties, jump to the days when the names get funny again—Rollie, Goose, The Monster, and Captain Hook. But relief pitching got just what it needed during this decade, a steady growth period that would prepare the bullpen for its golden age. With Jerry Holtzman's "save" formularized, complete games reached an all-time low and saves an all-time high in 1960. At the close of that season, *The Sporting News* named the Boston Red Sox' Mike Fornieles and Lindy McDaniel of the St. Louis Cardinals the game's first-ever Firemen of the Year. Others who could for the first time mention saves at contract time during this period were Elroy Face, Dick Radatz, Stu Miller, Al Worthington, Ron Perranoski and Luis Arroyo.

There was the matter of league expansion. The first expansion in sixty years took place in the American League in 1961, resulting in a league with ten teams instead of eight. The National League followed suit in 1962 and baseball found itself with a number of watered down starting rotations. This led to more creative use of the bullpens, more call for relief.

In 1961, the year Mantle and Maris made their historic runs on Babe Ruth's home run record, Whitey Ford, for the first time in his career, pitched every fourth day. And when Yankees manager Ralph Houk saw the slightest hint of fatigue in his little left-hander, he picked up the phone and dialed 9-100-LOUIE. Arroyo, a screwballing left-hander, went 15–5, saved a league-leading 29 games and posted a microscopic ERA of 2.19 that season. The call to rescue came so often that when asked about his own efforts that year, Ford said, "I'll have a good season as long as Louie's arm holds out." Mel Allen remembers Arroyo.

> The Yankees came up with Luis Arroyo, a great dresser, wealthy Latin, smoked those cigars. Nothing like Joe Page, but one hell of a pitcher. He had one wicked screwball. That's the way he became such a great relief pitcher. He'd set them up and then come in with the screwball and he saved a lot of games for Whitey Ford that year. Ralph Houk used them in combination a lot. So much so that when they had a day for Whitey, they brought Arroyo out wrapped up inside a great big role of Life Savers.

To say that the great relief pitching in World Series play came in pairs might be a stretch. There were Casey and Page in 1947 and 1949 and Sherry and Face in 1959 and 1960. No relief man dominated game after game of Series play the way it had been done by Casey,

Page, Sherry, and Face. But there were two individual outings by relief men in the 1960s that would go down in World Series history. In Game Four of the 1964 Series, Roger Craig and Ron Taylor threw eight and two-thirds innings of two-hit ball at the New York Yankees to help the Cardinals hold on to a 4–3 win. Roger Craig talks about that game:

Frankly I was disappointed that I didn't get to start that game. I thought that I had a chance to start it. Our manager, Johnny Keane, told me before the game, "I don't want you to run or throw, but as soon as this game starts, as soon as Ray Sadecki throws the first pitch, I want you to go down to the pen and start throwing." And so I thought, well, why don't you start me then? So Ray gets in trouble and I come in and I remember I had real good control that day, and I think the shadows of Yankee Stadium helped me. I struck out eight men in four and two-thirds innings and I picked Mickey Mantle off of second base. Then Ron Taylor relieved me, and he pitched the last four and I got the win. I was pretty dominating and it was just one of those days when everything I did was right.

And then there was Game One of the 1966 World Series. Moe Drabowsky, the Baltimore Orioles' long man, came to the aid of Dave McNally and pitched perhaps the best six and two-thirds innings ever in World Series play.

I came in in the third inning of that game. Brooks and Frank [the Robinsons] had homered in the first to put us ahead but then McNally got into trouble and I think I struck out eleven batters [six of them in a row], but I really had no idea of the impact of that at the time, or the impact that a World Series game would have. . . . It was such a blur that to tell you the truth, I don't even remember striking hitters out. I really don't. I know when the game was over and they started asking me about the row of strikeouts I was surprised. I would have thought that there would have been a pop up in there somewhere. But all that was was tremendous focus, fastball down-and-away, fastball up-and-in, slider down-and-away. Intense concentration on every pitch.

One only had to watch post-season games to get the line on relief. When big games were in jeopardy, managers went to their phones. Some skippers were more creative than others. For Dodgers manager, Walt Alston, relief came any time day or night during the season. Harry Caray, who called the play-by-play action for the St. Louis Cardinals, recalls the Alston flair for the unorthodox.

112

I think that Alston might have been one of the first to use the pen this way. He felt that if there was one inning in a ball game that he could get the other side out he'd have a chance to win. And he'd use his ace relief pitcher in the first inning at times. Bases loaded, maybe two on, and he'd bring in Perranoski, just to keep the other team from having a big inning.

There were a number of sages, men who understood relief, working in major league dugouts in the 1960s, managers like Lopez, Alston, Mauch, Durocher, and Houk. In 1965 Al Lopez put together what had to be the all-time knuckleball pen. Eddie Fisher and Hoyt Wilhelm with the help of their crewmates posted a record fifty-three saves in Chicago that year. Wilhelm saved twenty games while Fisher rang up twenty-four and led the league in relief wins with fifteen and relief points with thirty-nine. Of greater importance was the consistency with which these soft-tossers pitched. Fisher threw a record eighty-two games and 165 relief innings that year. Later the White Sox presented the league an opportunity to hit against yet another Wilhelm-trained knuckleballer. Like Fisher before him, Wilbur Wood spelled White Sox pitchers eighty-six times in 1968, picking up twelve relief wins and sixteen saves.

One of the best relief crews operating late in the decade was in Minneapolis/St. Paul, where the Twins' Al Worthington led all American League relief pitchers with eighteen saves in 1968 and Ron Perranoski carried on the grand tradition in 1969 and 1970 by saving thirty-one and thirty-four games respectively. However, as the decade wound down, attention centered on World Series play once again. Which of the game's great bullpens would control the 1969 World Series? The Baltimore relief corps, managed by sophomore manager Earl Weaver, had been superb that season—Watt, Hall, Leonhard, and Richert had a cumulative ERA of 2.09. Gil Hodges had a pretty well-stocked pen himself—Ron Taylor, Cal Koonce, and a young screwballer named Tug McGraw. But the great pen duel never materialized in this miracle year. Great hitting and spectacular catches dominated the Series, not the two pens. Nolan Ryan and Ron Taylor each notched a save. The Orioles pen picked up two losses and proved unable to save anything—not even the manager. (Earl Weaver earned the distinction of being only the third manager ever ejected from a World Series when he got the thumb for arguing balls and strikes in Game Four.)

So with the exception of the workman-like efforts of the Mets' Ryan and Taylor, 1969 proved a disappointing World Series for relief. And why not? Wasn't 1969 the season that started with a rather bad omen?

The rule makers were at work, attacking pitching again. It had been long in coming, of course. In 1968 earned run averages in both leagues fell below 3.00 and batting averages had slipped to embarrassingly low numbers. Carl Yastrzemski's paltry .301 average was good enough to lead all American League hitters. So the 15-inch mound—the pitchers' springboard and source of power which had been gradually sloped in 1950—was now cut to 10 inches. This time the slope would be "both gradual and uniform." And then just for a kicker, the Commissioner's office called in the umpires and suggested a new tighter strike zone.

It was an ominous time for pitching it would seem, save one notation in the rule book that year. The save, Scoring Rule 10.20, became official and relief men had a new topic to talk about at contract time. And there was expansion. Both the American and National leagues had become twelve-team leagues. More teams, more job opportunities. As hitters preyed on weakened starting rotations, the relief men found themselves being called early and often. The voices that follow are of the pen men who played the game in the "pre-save" days—from Smoky Burgess, one of the pen's great pinch hitters, to Moe Drabowsky, the quintessential pen man of the sixties. This place in time and the people of whom they speak—the pitchers, catchers, coaches and managers—all helped change how baseball has come to know this specialty that we call relief.

VOICES FROM THE PEN

SMOKY BURGESS
Catcher

**CHICAGO CUBS, 1949, 1951
PHILADELPHIA PHILLIES, 1952–1955
CINCINNATI REDS, 1955–1958
PITTSBURGH PIRATES, 1959–1964
CHICAGO WHITE SOX, 1964–1967**

- **Second On All-Time Pinch-Hit List With 145**
- **Caught Harvey Haddix In Twelve-Inning Perfect Game**
- **Lifetime .286 Pinch-Hitter**

Talk to a pen man and you're going to get some opinions on pitching and hitting. They are two of the pen's most popular topics. And in the course of my travels the names of several hitters were consistently ranked at the top—Ted Williams, Hank Aaron, Stan Musial, Joe DiMaggio, and Forrest Harrill "Smoky" Burgess.

Burgess's 145 career pinch-hits puts him second on the all-time list. Only Manny Mota has more. We talked in Smoky's club basement in Forest City, North Carolina. The walls display a bronzed bat and catcher's mitt and color photos of Smoky in uniform. A huge white shag baseball covers the tile floor of the comfortable room. Burgess is a scout for the Atlanta Braves. He's had a bout with lung cancer and is not the round man who once stroked fastballs past diving infielders. But with the tummy gone, my attention went to the broad shoulders and thick wrists, the physical gifts that generated those 145 pinch hits.

"Joe Nuxhall told me that Smoky Burgess could probably walk out there today and still get around on the fastball," I said. Burgess laughed. "Well, I don't know. But I'll tell you this, I've worked at some of the Pirates Fantasy Camps and a couple of years ago they got me up there looking at some decent fastballs and . . . well, I smoked them pretty good!"

They used me a little differently than they did a lot of pinch hitters. Manny Mota passed me as the [all-time] pinch-hit leader. He's a good guy and I'm glad to see him set a record, but he and I were two entirely different type hitters. He'd hit in the second or third inning to start a rally maybe, and I never did do that. I guess it was my last year that Eddie Stanky with the Sox had me hit in maybe the early innings but when Lopez was there he'd say, "There's no use in you even coming in from the pen until the seventh or eighth inning, I'm not going to use you until I've got the tying or winning run on base." And that's the way it is and I believe that if they'd go back and check, that there wouldn't be anybody even close to the RBIs that I got as a pinch hitter. Les Biederman, the writer for *The Pittsburgh Gazette*, told me that he didn't think that there was anybody close or with RBIs or winning [pinch] hits.

Because of the way I was used, I was a little different from most people in the pen. I knew that I might pinch-hit in the game so I was always trying to focus on the pitcher. Here's how I'd do it. I'd pick out a left-handed hitter on my team and I'd watch how he would pitch to him, paying attention to the situation in the game, of course. If there was nobody on he'd pitch to him one way, if there was a runner in scoring position maybe he'd pitch to him another way. I'd try to figure that out and then when I'd go up to hit, that's what I'd look for. I'd be ready for what I'd seen and that helped me a great deal. And I think that that's what helped give me the success that I had as a pinch hitter.

And I was always more relaxed when there were men on base and I guess the reason I was so relaxed was because I had it in mind that there were only two things that you could do. You could produce or you could make an out, and I wasn't going to get cheated, I was going to get my swings. Now you take Koufax, I loved hitting Koufax. And when he became an announcer on the "Game of the Week," he asked me one day, he said, "I've got to talk to you, you hit me so hard and I need to know why." And I told him, "Well, I never did look for your curveball. If you threw the curveball I'd take it and I'd just wait for the fastball, I was always just tuned in for it." But guys like him that really threw hard, I liked. Robin Roberts, I always had good luck with him. When I was with the Cubs I remember he pitched a four-hitter the first time we faced him and I had three of the hits and the next time we faced him he pitched a three-hitter and I had all three. So when I was traded to the Phillies he sent me this telegram saying something like "*Welcome to Philadelphia . . . Delighted . . . Won't have to pitch to you again!*"

And I always had good success on Warren Spahn. In the 1961 All-Star game Warren Spahn was the starting pitcher. And Warren refused to let anybody warm him up but me that day. Del Crandall, his own catcher, was there. He still talks about it today when I see him. He warmed up in the bullpen and I caught him. He was funny. He wouldn't tell me when he was throwing a slider, a fastball, curveball, anything, he'd just throw it. So after he got warmed up and I got the stuff on and ready to catch the game, he went to Crandall and he said, "Del, I got Smoky now. He won't hit me any more. I didn't tell him a pitch I was throwing and he didn't drop a one of them, caught them all." He said, "His confidence is built up now. If he can catch me like that he'll think that he can hit me. Now I'll get him." And sure enough the rest of that season I didn't get a single hit off him. But the next year we opened in Pittsburgh against Warren and I went right back at him. I said, "Okay, Warren, you know what happened last year?" He said, "Yeah, this is another year, all that's behind me." And sure enough the first time up I hit the ball and it hit right on home plate, bounded way up in the air like a fly ball and I beat it out. I tipped my cap to him from first base. I ended up getting two or three base hits off of him that day and was off to another good year with Warren.

It was the junk ball pitchers that I had my trouble with. Stu Miller, he'd throw changeup off of changeup. He'd give you a rough time. Dave Koslo, he didn't throw hard, he'd just throw sort of sidearm and threw that breaking pitch. And Konstanty was hard to hit when I played against him. The two pen guys that were really the toughest for me to hit were guys that most fairly young people aren't going to remember. When I first went up a guy by the name of Nels Potter pitched in relief, this was late in his career for the Boston Braves. And he was what they called a screwball pitcher, a right-hander, and I know he got me out so easily, it was pathetic. You couldn't believe it.

Here's one, how about Marcelino Lopez, with the Angels, ever hear of him? A big tall left-hander, the funny thing with him, I was out in the bullpen—this was with the White Sox—and I was warming up Wilhelm, fighting that knuckler of his. Al Lopez, the manager, called out there and wanted to speak to me, and he said, "Have you ever faced this Marcelino Lopez?" I said no. "Ever seen him pitch before?" I said no. He said, "Do you think you can hit him?" I said, "Is he going to throw the baseball? If he throws the baseball I'm going to have my rips at him." So Al said, "Well, come on in." And when I got in there the score was tied, the bases were loaded and there were two out. Al said, "Now you know who you were warming up in the bullpen!" I said Wilhelm. He said, "Well, if you don't get that runner in, you're going to have to catch him." So the first pitch Lopez threw was a high fastball and I hit it down the right field line for a double and the run scored and we won the game and I didn't have to catch Wilhelm's knuckleball. When I got into the dugout Lopez said, "Well, I didn't figure that you wanted to catch him."

There were a lot of funny things that happened with Wilhelm. We'd have to warm him up with that knuckleball of his and we had the big mitt then, the one that Paul Richards developed for him when he was with Baltimore, Big Bertha I think they called it. We were in Washington playing the Senators and we had a guy by the name of Walt [No-Neck] Williams, who was an outfielder. They called him down there and told him to warm up in case we tied the game up, because he was going in for defense. I was warming Williams up and I'd been imitating Hoyt and I got to fooling around with the knuckler and threw one. It so happened that I got one that really broke for me. It jumps up and hits Williams right between the eyes. He goes down like a rock and is just laying there on the ground and all I can think is, "Oh my gosh, what's going to happen now? Mr. Lopez calls back and wants Williams. I've got to tell him that I've hit him between the eyes with a knuckleball." Fortunately the call never came but. . . . We always had a lot of fun out there and a lot of it centered around the catchers trying to catch all those knuckleballers. In Chicago we had Hoyt, Eddie Fisher, and Wilbur Wood.

I was pretty relaxed with the knuckler, especially after they came up with the big glove. What I did when I was with the Phillies and we had Johnny Lindell—his knuckleball was a lot harder to catch than the rest of them simply because he threw it so much harder—all I'd try to do was just be in front of it and let it hit me. It would hit me and drop, I'd just knock it down. I'll never forget when we got him, Steve O'Neill wondered which one of the catchers was going to volunteer to catch him. I told him, "The only thing is, Steve, whoever's name you put down is going to catch him. If it's mine I'll do it, if it's Lopata he'll have to catch him." So he said, "Well, you're catching him then." So I caught him in Milwaukee and we had a one-run lead and I got thrown out of the game in the ninth inning. And Lopata had to come in and when he did we got four or five passed balls and they scored and beat us.

We go from there into St. Louis. The next time Johnny's pitching he goes along the same way and I get thrown out again on a ball that I hit and thought I had it beat out at first base. I argued with the umpire there and got thrown out of the game. Well I'll never forget Steve O'Neill, he came to me in the clubhouse where I was and he said if we lose this game because Lopata can't catch him, it's going to cost you. It so happened that they tied it up in the ninth but then we finally won it in the eleventh. So everything was alright, but we were on the train going from there to New York. He called me into his cabin and talked to me. He said, "From now on it's automatic. When Lindell's pitching with you catching, if you get thrown out of a game it's an automatic $1,000 [fine], it's as simple as that. I just can't stand to lose you."

So we went into Ebbets Field and we had five innings in. Lindell had been pitching good and we had a lead, and boy, his knuckleball was working. But the wind started blowing, right out to center field. Boy, it [the ball] would really cut up. We had a 5–4 lead with two outs and he threw a knuckleball to Carl Furillo. He swung at it and the ball broke and went behind him so the tying run scored. He came out there to take Lindell out and he said, "That's the first time I ever had to take a pitcher out because he had too good a stuff." I just told him I oughta been thrown out a couple of innings before.

There were some great games. But there's one day that was more memorable than any others, one in all my eighteen years in the big leagues. We had a doubleheader in Philadelphia, I was with the Phillies then and Robin Roberts was going in the first game. Lopata, our other catcher, was hurt. So I knew that I would be catching a doubleheader. It so happened that Roberts had to go extra innings. He wasn't throwing really good in the first two or three innings but he got better and better as the game went on and by the time he got into extra innings he was rolling right along. Roberts went eighteen innings that game and I finally got the winning hit to beat the Braves, got it in the eighteenth.

Like I said, Lopata was hurt and couldn't play but we had Ken Silvestri, who was like a coach-player, bullpen catcher, and I thought, well, I caught eighteen innings, surely he'll catch Ken in the second game. It was right in the heat of the summertime so I go in the clubhouse and get in the shower thinking, well, I won't play the second game, I'll just dress and go back out to the bench. About that time I hear the public address announcer calling the lineups for the second game, "And catching, Smoky Burgess!" So I had to rush and go back out there and darned if I didn't end up catching eight more innings. It mighta been more but the curfew caught us. I think Steve O'Neill was the manager, but the other guy, Silvestri, hadn't caught in about ten years, so I was it. And it's days like that you don't forget.

I also remember this, I remember Bob Prince, the Pirates announcer had a pre-game radio program. He had the fans in the stands asking them questions. One of the questions was, Who caught Harvey Haddix's perfect game? [Haddix pitched twelve perfect innings.] And very few people remembered. The answer of course is Smoky Burgess. Here's what I remember about that one.

In the bottom of the thirteenth [a scoreless tie] Don Hoak throws it low and I'm backing up first. Felix Mantilla rounds first and I run out and tag him and I think he's out. I get into it with the first base umpire. Now Matthews was the next hitter and he laid down a pretty good bunt and sacrifices Mantilla to second, then we decide to walk Aaron. And up comes Adcock. Well that game was one of the biggest thrills of my career. I was probably one of the only ones who knew all the time that he had a perfect no-hitter going because I go by the lineup, who's hitting, and I know what inning it is. You get three outs, so at the end of three innings there's only been nine up and at the end of six, eighteen, and we'd been around twice. But the thing that I remember about that game was this. Lew Burdette was pitching great for the Braves and Harvey is perfect for us. I didn't really feel any pressure in that game, because Harvey was throwing where he wanted to throw it and where I wanted to throw it and we were playing great defense and all. To me it was just a great game that you really enjoyed because of the way things were going. We were upset because we didn't score him a run. Perfect game through twelve innings. He had great stuff, great control, to me he was pinpointing every pitch. I remember a few really great plays. There was one ball that Virdon made a good catch on in left center field, I don't remember who hit it. And it seemed like one of the infielders, I don't recall whether it was Maz or Schofield, one of the two made a good play, and they were the only balls that were even close to hits.

So here we are into the thirteenth inning with Aaron on first and Mantilla on second. There's one away because Matthews has bunted Mantilla to second. So Adcock comes up. Now if Joe could get those arms out he could hit anybody, but Harvey was busting that fastball and the slider right in on his fists all night. And the only pitch that Harvey didn't get where he wanted . . . You see, we'd been pitching Adcock in, and in, and jamming him, and this one broke. But it broke over the outside part of the plate—a slider—and he got his arms out there and hit it over the right center field fence. The ball just barely got over the fence, so Virdon jumped into the fence like he was catching it. Aaron thought that he had caught the ball or that the ball had hit the fence, so he went down and tagged second instead of coming around. The one run, the winning one, came on in. That was Mantilla. So Hank, thinking that it had hit the fence, just walked across the pitcher's mound and into the locker room. When Aaron walked off, Adcock went over and tagged third. He was out for passing the runner. Nobody in the stands or on the field saw it. I got Frank Dascoli, the home plate umpire, by the belt and held him and pointed to Aaron. See, that would have been a 3–0 game if they'd a counted the home run. But I said, "Well, that will help Harvey's earned run average." So he called upstairs and told the official scorer that it was a 1–0 game, that Adcock was out for passing Aaron on the base path. Only one run was counted.

The Haddix perfect game and the 1960 World Series are, well the thing that I remember about the Series was that every game we got beat, we got beat bad and every one we won was close. But we had the pitching and Law won two and I think Haddix won the other two. We kept at them and we were a team that if you beat us, you beat us bad. But the biggest thrill I guess of all my baseball was the home run that Maz hit. Nobody realizes it but we were behind a couple of runs and I got a base hit that drove in a run and I was on second base. I hit a double off of Bobby Shantz. It was the tying run so Murtaugh put Christopher in to run for me. He scored to tie the game. Then we finally went ahead and then we got behind again. Hal Smith, who replaced me, hit the home run to tie it. Hal came in to replace my pinch runner, so just for fun I like to ask, if I'm speaking or something, I'll say, "Now which base hit was the most important in the 1960 World Series? Maz's?" No, Maz wouldn't have gotten up if Hal Smith hadn't hit the three-run homer that tied it up. But how did Smith get into the game? If I hadn't gotten the base hit off of Shantz and been a slow runner, I'd still been catching, so which hit was the most important?

And about the bullpen . . . mostly I remember it being a good place to be. We'd be sitting down there talking and carrying on. One time we were out there doing just that, playing the Cubs in Chicago. I was with Cincinnati then and Birdie Tebbetts called down to the pen and told me to come in, that I was going to pinch-hit. And when I got into the dugout he said, "Smoky, I want you to go up there for one reason and one reason only. I want you to hit a home run, a home run or nothing because we lack one home run of tying the record for most home runs hit by a National League team [221]." Sad Sam Jones was pitching for the Cubs and I came in and I went up to hit. We had quite a good lead anyway. This was the next to the last day of the season and Birdie tells me that we're going for the record. It was the top of the ninth inning. So the first pitch comes in and I'm ready. Sam threw a slow curveball that was real low and I golfed it over the right center field bleachers at Wrigley Field. And that's one I'll never forget. The only time in my life when I went up there and did exactly what I wanted to do. When I came in Birdie says, "Well, Smoky, that's what I sent you up there for." And it tied the record. That's one you can look up!

Smoky Burgess died on September 15, 1991.

SAM ESPOSITO
Infielder

CHICAGO WHITE SOX, 1952, 1955–1963
KANSAS CITY ATHLETICS, 1963

- **Star Of The Best Game Ever Played In Comiskey Park**
- **South Side Chicago's Favorite Son**
- **Father Of The Batting Glove**

It's Indian summer in Raleigh, North Carolina, and Sammy Esposito and I are sitting behind Doak Field's right field fence in metal folding chairs. North Carolina State's Wolfpack is at home today. And Esposito, the man who distinguished himself by backing up Luis Aparicio and Nellie Fox of the go-go White Sox for almost a decade, is enjoying the college game from a different angle these days. Before his recent move into administration here at N.C. State, Esposito spent some twenty-one years establishing himself as the winningest baseball coach (513 wins) in N.C. state history.

The game is full of lineup changes, coaches running pitchers in and out. It's fall ball, a meaningless practice game. Not so, says Esposito. "This is a learning experience for a lot of guys. Here comes the breaking ball, watch."

The N.C. State hitter chases a curveball into the dirt. "Keep your eye on the second baseman. The middle infielders are getting the signs from the catcher and passing them along. See, watch his hand. See the flashing, the two fingers behind the back? Another breaking pitch!" The batter lunges into the curveball and turns the hook into a weak fly ball. "This is the view from the bullpen. You learn to look for that kind of thing when you're sitting out here," Esposito says.

I was a utility infielder but I was what we used to call a pen rat. I liked to sneak down there and sit with the pen guys. When you do that you end up working out there. In the old days each club carried two catchers. When one got hurt, they needed a guy on the club who could go behind the plate for the second round of infield and a guy who could catch some BP, or go out to the pen and warm up the pitchers. And I'd do all that. In fact a lot of times I was the back-up catcher. I never got in the game as a catcher, thank God, but I was there in case of a real emergency. But of course if the second catcher went down they'd bring somebody up the next day or so. But I always lived with the chance of that happening. And so I spent a lot of time in the bullpen and believe me, what every team and at every level has in common, the one thing that doesn't change in baseball is bullpen behavior. Absolute wackos out there. All kinds, more things going on out there than you can imagine.

One pen story that I'll never forget, now this was later in Chicago, during the Lopez days, and it involved Ray Herbert, a right-handed pitcher who we called the Hawk. He was always hawking the broads. He was one of those hotel guys, used to sit around hotel lobbies checking out the women, kinda hawking them, you know. That's where he worked. Some of the guys worked in the bus stations, some worked in the bars. Everybody had their own territories. Hawk used to work in the lobby. Anyway we're playing the Yankees in Yankee Stadium, a doubleheader on Sunday. It's a holiday, maybe Columbus Day, and anyway it's a Catholic holiday and the day when they have St. Christopher parades in big cities. I was in the White Sox bullpen and in the stadium the bullpen is in left center, it's way the hell out there. Herbert was a starter, a very good pitcher—fastball, slider. And he did a lot of relief work between starts. A very valuable pitcher for you because you could use him a number of different ways. It was about the sixth inning and the phone rang, and a tight game, I think we're up one or two. It's Lopez and he tells Berres to get Herbert up. So Berres turns around and says, "Hawk! Get up! Sam, you catch him." So I walk down to one of the plates to catch him, turn around and he's not there. Berres starts going nuts because we can't find him anywhere. We're checking the john, under the stands. No Hawk. And now we start worrying. Did anybody see him today? Yeah, he was in the outfield. Saw him in the dressing room before the game. One of the guys remembered walking out with him to the pen. So we start running all over the place and for some reason I went running through the tunnel, in left field there. And there was a big double gate there that they used to bring in trucks, ground crew equipment and things into the stadium. And I noticed that the door was just a little open, where I could see a little daylight out there. And when I pushed the door open I heard the bands playing. Here comes this big parade right by the left field fence. And I start to turn around and all of a sudden I see this White

126

Sox uniform. Hawk is sitting there with his legs crossed in this folding chair, leaning against the wall of Yankee Stadium watching the parade go by.

And I said, "Hawk, you better get your ass back in the pen, Lopez is about ready to call you into the ball game." He scuffled back in there and he must have thrown two pitches and here goes the phone again. I mean he didn't even get past soft-toss and they're saying, "Come on, let's go, you're in there." He runs in. There was no cart or vehicle in those days. He threw his six or so warm-up pitches and proceeded to shut the Yankees down. We're all like this, with our fingers crossed but he got the job done. And to this day I don't know whether Lopez ever found out about that one.

I signed with Chicago as a college kid. I was attending Indiana University on a basketball scholarship when I tried out in Chicago, and I'll never forget this. I worked out with the White Sox and after the tryout they brought me up into Mr. Frank Lane's office and I signed with them. And a couple of weeks after that I went to Waterloo, Iowa, but before I left I called Branch McCracken, our basketball coach, and told him that I'd signed. Now my junior year was coming up, I was the captain and starting guard on the basketball team and this was the team that would go on that year to a National Championship. Of course McCracken didn't know at that time that he could win it without me. Branch went absolutely berserk over the phone. He told me that he knew Frank Lane, that he used to officiate with him and that he was going to call him and . . . I said, "Coach, I'm sorry, but I'm going to be getting on a bus in a few minutes and I'm going to Waterloo." And he wouldn't talk to me after that. I went back to school that winter to do some work on my degree at Indiana, and I had to watch that team play. McCracken wouldn't talk to me. Until they won the National Championship. Thank God. Because McCracken and I became great friends again.

That's how I broke in with the White Sox. Waterloo, Iowa, my first year and then I got drafted at the end of the summer. And I'll never forget that either. Zack Taylor, who was our manager, an old-time catcher, a great guy. He must have fined me about three or four times for missing curfew that year and he used to get on my butt a little bit. But let's see, where were we? We were playing on the road and I got drafted and had to leave the team to go into the Army. In fact I had to take a bus out that night after the ball game and Zack gave me a radio and the forty dollars that he'd fined me over the summer for breaking curfew. He said, "Son, there's two things you're going to need in the Army, money and a radio. You like to stay up late!"

I was in the Army for two years, came back and played in Memphis, Tennessee, for the Chicks, that was Double-A ball. We won the pennant there. Here's how I joined that team, and I'm proud of this. I took a train all night long, met the team in Mobile, Alabama. I walk into the ball park in my Army uniform, had to pay my way in. I go over to the Chicks dugout and I'm standing there watching them take infield. Jack Cassini, the manager, is playing second base and there's this little guy at short scooting around gobbling everything up. And he's throwing peas to first base. That turns out to be Aparicio. So when they're finished Cassini, the manager, comes over and I introduce myself. He says, "Oh good, what position do you play?" Now I've been watching, the manager is at second and they've got Louie at short so I say, "Third base!" I'd never played a day of third base in my life. Cassini says, "Great, go get yourself a uniform, you're starting at third today." And that's where I played. In fact later, when I went up to the White Sox, I ended up playing more games at third than any other position.

The Chicks were a great club that year. With Aparicio hitting first, me hitting second and Jack hitting third, we stole a hell of a lot of bases, a running ball club. Cassini got beaned with about six weeks to go in the season and the interesting thing about when Jack got hurt, the White Sox sent Ted Lyons down to manage the club. Ted was a Hall-of-Famer and he was quite old at the time, didn't see very well but he used to throw BP. And we worried about him because he had trouble seeing balls hit back at him. But the great thing about that was that all the years Ted was in the big leagues, and I think he was up there for more than twenty years, he played every game in the majors for the Chicago White Sox. A Hall-of-Famer, and he never played on a winner and here we win a pennant for him. He'd been a pitching troubleshooter for the Sox in their minor league system. And now this is his first shot at managing and we win the pennant in the Southern Association, a great league at that time. A lot of guys would jump from there right to the majors. We had like six guys on that team who were with the White Sox the following year. And after the pennant-clinching game Ted, Aparicio, myself and a catcher named Dutch Dotterer, who was owned by Cincinnati and eventually went up, well the four of us after about fifteen beers each, at about three in the morning, head home to our hotel which was about three blocks from the park. It's three A.M. and we're still in our baseball unis walking back to the hotel holding hands. Arms around each other, Ted's crying. Here's a great, great man, a Hall-of-Famer, who had never experienced that winning feeling before.

128

That was my two years in the minors and then I went up to the White Sox where I spent nine years as a utility infielder. My tenth year I ended up with Kansas City. One of the most frightening duties I had with the White Sox was getting caught in a situation out there where I had to warm Hoyt Wilhelm up. Ray Berres was our pitching coach and he was getting pretty old so sometimes my number would come up. The pen guys used to love that because when I'd warm him up I'd put on all the gear to do it—mask, chest protector, shin guards—the works. It looked a little strange out there, me in all that paraphernalia. They'd get on my ass pretty good about that. But I had to gear up. I didn't want to get killed out there. And I used to wave at those butterflies with my glove and think how fortunate I was to be playing for Chicago. At least I didn't have to try to hit against him.

Here's a bullpen story that probably kept me in a Chicago White Sox uniform for a few extra years. For a long time it was one of major league baseball's best-kept secrets. Frank Lane, our GM, got p.o.'d because we were going into ball parks around the league and getting our signs stolen. You know, guys in the bullpen with binocs stealing the catcher's signs and then signaling the hitters as to what was coming. So Lane and Lopez go them one better. Here's how it worked, and boy, it was a real beauty. We did this maybe three, maybe four years. And it was so good I really think that the Sox were afraid to trade anybody, it was really helping us that much. Lane comes back from a series in Cleveland after he's observed Lou Boudreau, the Indians manager, get signs from the bullpen. They had the binoculars and had a guy leaning over the bullpen fence. If his arms are crossed, it's a fastball. So when Lane comes back he's talking to George Kell and Bob Kennedy and he says, "You know those SOBs are stealing our signs." So George and Bob, here's what they came up with. Lane puts Del Wilber, a bullpen coach, in a little room in the scoreboard with a pair of high-powered binoculars. He had this little hole that he'd look through and for the first couple of innings he'd watch the catcher, get all his signs, fastball, breaking pitch, and all the switches, the decoys the catcher uses when there are men on base. Then he'd call into Lopez and say, "I got 'em." So there in the room he has this little contraption, something like a doorbell button which is wired to a light bulb which is tucked up under the stands in center field, left center but actually closer to center. The stands in Comiskey in left go out so far and then drop off and then there's dead center field. Now that's where the light is, tucked up there under the stands. There were other light bulbs around it but only one was wired up to Wilber's button. You could see the bulb from home plate and from our dugout at third, but you couldn't see it from the visitors' dugout along first. If it was a fastball Wilber would push the button and the light would come on and the hitters knew it was hump city. If it didn't come on, then you knew it was a breaking pitch. Did it work? Wilber once called something like seventy-two straight pitches correctly and we lost to Frank Lary 1–0 in extra innings. That's a hell of an outing. He shuts us out 1–0 in ten and we knew what was coming.

Another time Del called four consecutive curveballs on Herb Score. All four wound up as doubles. It was really funny, you'd be sitting in the bullpen or dugout, the pitcher would be winding up, in his motion, and our hitter would still be looking up at center field, waiting for the light to come on. Sherm Lollar loved the light, Walt Dropo loved it. Nellie Fox wouldn't use it. Nellie was a slap hitter and he was afraid if he knew it was fastball that he'd muscle up on the pitch and end up hitting a long fly ball, one of those warning track outs. Did I use it? Use it? Hell, I needed it. I got a couple of home runs in Comiskey and you can just about bet they came when Wilber's light was on. This lasted by the way until Al Worthington, a pitcher, came over in 1960 to the club. Al had a problem with the light, didn't think it was right and so he went to Lane and to Lopez about it. He left the club over it and pretty soon the word was out, and so was the light.

Another piece of Sox genius involved Early Wynn. Early came over to the White Sox in the late fifties and here's one that Early and Al Lopez cooked up. They decided that they'd communicate on pitches through this little radio headset hidden in Early's cap. Al would sit on the bench and say something like, "Curve his ass!" and then Early would deal him the hook. And I'm tellin' you this one was a riot. Early's got this little radio in his cap out there. And Early was a beaut anyway, a great guy, big heavy-set guy, we called him the Sea Lion. Now you'd see him standing there on the mound tiltin' his head trying to bring Lopez in on the headset. And one day a storm comes up and he's bobbing around out there, I don't know, maybe he's getting a lot of static, but all of a sudden there's a clap of thunder and lightening hits. The Sea Lion goes charging off the mound, runs into the dugout, throws the cap down and tells Lopez what he can do with it. I think that was the last time Wynn wore the radio hat.

I was in the pen a lot but when I played it was usually as an infielder. Like I said, I caught a lot of BP and worked second infield as a catcher, but I was an infielder, second base, short, third. And one thing that I always felt good about was the fact that the guys that kept me from playing on that White Sox team were Luis Aparicio and Nellie Fox. One's in the Hall of Fame [Aparicio] and the other one should be. Now Looie and I used to room together. He was moody, he'll tell you that himself, but a great guy. But sometimes when things weren't going right for him, maybe the wife got on his butt or the kids were sick, he'd get a bad stomach and wouldn't play. And always when we'd go to Cleveland, not always, but this was a running joke with the players, Looie would take a look at that starting rotation. They had Score, Lemon, Wynn, Garcia, and Feller. Bob was on his way out but a spot starter. Now in the bullpen you're looking at Narleski and Mossi, one of the best right-left relief combinations in baseball history. And so a lot of times Looie's belly wouldn't be feeling right and so old Espo would go in there and take his 0-for-4's, regularly. I think one week I went 0–16 before we got out of Cleveland. Of course, a lot of other guys did too. But this didn't help me because I never got a chance to get back in there after that. One Saturday evening we're playing a twi-nighter in Cleveland. The first game was a makeup, at six o'clock and Herb Score is cranking it up. And I still say that he, Ryne Duren, the Yankee reliever, and Koufax, whom I saw in spring training, were the fastest I ever played against. Just unhittable. Every once in a while they might hit your bat but as far as seeing the ball, forget it. And besides that fast one, Score had the great curveball and so did Koufax. I'm in there doing Looie duty and we're playing a twi-nighter. I'm leading off, and in Cleveland in Municipal, that big stadium there, the sun's coming right through center field, beaming in right on home plate. It's bad enough if you have to face Herb Score when you're playing every day, but here I am a sub looking into the sun. Now Joe Paparella is umpiring behind the plate and Jim Hegan is catching. And Score wound up and threw the first pitch and I didn't see it. I don't know how Hegan saw it to catch it. And Paparella says, "Ball one!" And Hegan threw it back. Score cranks up, next pitch, and of course I can't even see so I'm not swinging. Pappy calls it ball two. Jim sort of looked back at him but didn't say anything. And now Herb throws the next pitch and Hegan caught it right across the middle of the plate and Pappy says, "Ball three!" So now Hegan gets up and gives him some lip and when he's through Pappy takes his mask off and says, "Jim, you can't see it, I can't see it and I know Sam can't see it. Besides, he's Italian and the way he hits, the little bastard needs four strikes anyway. So get back in there and catch!" So the next pitch is ball four and I gladly run to first base. I'm telling you I didn't see any of the pitches. And I don't know how Hegan caught them. Nellie Fox comes up behind me and Score throws him a curveball and Fox lines a double down the right field line and I score from first. I think that was the only hit that we got. Score proceeded to strike out something like fifteen, sixteen guys, but we won the ball game one-zip. My blind walk and Nellie's double. But you know, I remember going out in the bottom of the first to take infield and we're around second base and I asked Nellie if he saw that pitch he hit. He said, "Yeah, he threw me a curveball and I hit it!" And I said, "Well, maybe that's why you hit .300 and I hit .200!"

Nellie was a great contact hitter—fastballs, breaking pitches—he had that big-barreled bat and he'd just move the ball around. Talking about hitting reminds me of a story about Hank Aaron. This was maybe his second or third year up and we're playing a Grapefruit League game at their place. We walk in by the batting cage and Aaron's hitting in there. He'd had the great year the season before. Sherm Lollar, our catcher, and I just stood there and watched him hit. And man, he was hanging ropes everywhere. Outside pitch, *Boom!* Line drive, right field. In and over the plate shots up into the palm trees, you know. So anyway we watch this little fireworks display for about five minutes and when he's finished he comes out of the cage and Sherm asks him . . . Now Sherm was a very astute baseball guy. Very smart. Sherm has passed away but I always thought that he'd have been a great manager. So anyway we've been watching Aaron hit and Sherm says, "Hank, what's your hitting philosophy. How do you do it? What do you think about up there?" Sherm was getting toward the twilight of his career and looking to get himself a little edge at the plate. And I'll never forget it, Hank just looked at him and said, "I take my stance and when that ball's about right here I take a good whack at it!" I mean I laughed like hell, but you know when you think about it, what Aaron said makes so much sense. There's great hitters and there's guys who don't hit as well. And it's mostly hand-eye coordination. Now taking the good whack. I think all of us do that but some have the ability to get that bat out there, the good swing, the perfect timing. Some are right there on the money and others of us were a day late and a dollar short!

One of my favorite stories, and Earl Torgeson told this one but it involves a kid, a rookie catcher who had been working in the bullpen, and in the late innings as the game's winding down he comes in and sits in like the back corner of the Detroit dugout. Detroit is hitting and Bucky Harris is the manager and he's leaning on the railing, up on the top step of the dugout, got his arms crossed contemplating a pinch-hitting move. It's church quiet and all of a sudden from the corner of the dugout comes this big *varoom!* A boomer of a fart, rattles the dugout wall. Harris wheels around and hollers, "Who did that?" And this little rookie catcher says, "I did, Skip!" And Harris says, "Get a bat and go hit for Garver, that was beautiful!"

I think every professional player dreams of playing in a World Series game or being in a World Series or an All-Star game. And my situation, a player of my caliber who never really lit it up or played every day, a guy who didn't experience a lot of great moments, just clinching a pennant and then playing in the World Series was maybe the happiest thing that ever happened to me. I remember that we clinched it in 1959 on the road and in Cleveland and then had to fly back to Chicago. And you know I'll never forget, Jim Rivera and I each got a bottle of champagne and we went in the crapper. There was press all over the place, and we just sat in there on two stools, still in our unis, slugging down the bubbly. Anyway we had to catch a plane back to Chicago. [When] we land there's like ten or fifteen thousand people there waiting for the team. You couldn't move. I did get into that World Series. I [went] 0–2 and played a little third base.

But I guess the biggest game for me was one that I was reminded of the other day. Hell, I'd forgotten it and I got this call from Bob Vanderberg of *The Chicago Tribune*. They're getting ready to turn out the lights in Comiskey for the final time and the newspaper had assigned Bob the job of writing a story about the most exciting game ever played there in its history. Well he calls and says that according to his research I'm the hero of this "greatest game" story. And I'll tell you what my response was, "Do you mean to say that in eighty years of Comiskey, you pick one game and Sam Esposito is the hero. Son, you need to go back to the files on this one!" But when he started to tell me the story, it all came back and it was a biggie, there's no doubt about that. It was a Friday night, June 22, 1956, my rookie year. Now I'm cheating a little bit here because Bob refreshed my memory on the thing the other day. But keep in mind I'm a Chicago kid, played my high school basketball, football and baseball right there on the South Side. Maybe that made it all a bigger deal. It's a Friday night, sell-out crowd, the first in a four-game series. We're in second place, a couple of games out, chasing the Yankees as usual. They had Mantle, Berra, Skowron, all those horses. But the game starts out . . . a beauty. Dick Donovan pitched no-hit ball for us for something like seven and a third innings. We took a one-run lead against Sturdivant. Then Doby homers in the eighth and it's two to zip. But Martin doubles—I believe it was Martin—and that scores a Yankee runner. Suddenly a one-run game. Are you still awake? I'm getting to the good part. In the top of the ninth McDougald singles, takes second on an infield ball, a ground ball. Now Mantle singles to right to tie the score. And that was it until the eleventh. You have to understand the thing that the city of Chicago had about the Yankees. I mean they hated them.

133

They score again in the eleventh and now we're trailing. There are two away. We've got guys on second and third. I remember the tone in Marty Marion's voice, he said something like, "Sammy, get a bat, kid!" like we can kiss this one good-bye. So anyway I'm hitting about .190 or something and Marty gives me the old, "Get a bat!" Well, I came around late on a fastball and hit it down the right field line and all of a sudden we've got two and tied the game. So now we get the Yanks in the twelfth, I think Howard doubled but we go to the bottom of the inning and Dave Philley singles off of Coleman. Stengel brings in Tom Morgan who promptly hits Sherm Lollar in the back. Two on and nobody out. Then Jim Delsing bunts and they throw Philley out at third. Bubba Phillips strikes out. Two away. Now two on and two out, tie game, twelfth inning and who's coming up for us? Round Ron Northey, a great left-handed pinch hitter who had just beaten the Yankees the week before with a home run. In the on-deck circle you've got me, a guy who isn't hitting Northey's weight. Stengel puts Northey on and with the bases loaded and two out I bloop a little flare into short left just out of the reach of Phil Rizzuto. We win it 5–4. Local boy makes good. The newspapers made quite a deal out of it, front page of all four Chicago dailies—"Rookie Beats Yanks In 12th"; "Rookie Hero Tames Yanks"—a picture of me and my mom and dad. We went on to sweep the Yankees four in a row. A big, big game I guess, when you consider how much Chicago hated the Yankees.

I mentioned Round Ron Northey, the guy Stengel walked to get to me. Let me tell you about Northey. Late in his career he mostly pinch-hit, a heck of a left-handed hitter. Hell, the guy had to be, he didn't own a glove. Earlier that spring, we're in Florida playing the Phillies, I think in Bradenton. Anyway, a lot of times in Grapefruit games, a lot of the time you take a split squad. The A-team will go somewhere and the B-team will stay at home. So consequently we're on a road game with three outfielders and one of our guys sprained an ankle so our skipper told Northey to go into left field for him. Now Ron was just a notorious left-handed pinch hitter and that's all he was. A very colorful character. Big, heavy-set guy. When this happened he was toward the end of his career. So Northey gets the call to go to left field and he says, "Skip, I'll be glad to go out there but I don't have a glove!" So he borrows mine, goes out there and proceeds to get hit in the head. I'm not exaggerating, he got nailed right between the eyes with the first thing hit at him. This one took stitches. That was Ron Northey—great bat, no glove. If the Sox could have put Ron and me together they'd have had themselves a heck of an all-around player.

And talking about those great Yankee teams, the guy who I think was maybe the best hitter, along with Williams, that I ever saw was Mickey Mantle. We called him Superman. To me, one of the great athletes to ever play the game. I haven't seen Bo [Jackson] in person, but that's how Mickey was in the old days—strength, power, speed. Just a great athlete and of course Mickey was hurt, had osteomyelitis, and was always taped from his neck to his ankles. He was a great guy, would always speak to everyone. As great a player as he was, he was friendly with everyone. And it just goes to show you about athletes and how they react. Some have got to have twelve hours sleep before they perform and some can stay up all night and when the bell rings they're out there ready to perform. The thing that hurts them over the long run is when they do it for a number of years, it shortens their careers. But one Saturday night in Chicago, one of the few times during my career that I was out on the streets, I run into Mickey, Billy Martin, the same crowd—Berra, Ford, Bauer. The five of them were inseparable. And it's early in the morning and let's just say everybody's having a good time. Now we've got a double dip with them the next day at Comiskey. I know that I'm not playing the next day. I won't go into all the details but I know that Mantle isn't going to get much sleep because I'm not blind and I'm pretty good at telling time. The next day I'm sitting in our dugout over by the water cooler, nursing my head. And in Comiskey, the Yankees have gotta come out of their locker room and through our dugout to get to the field. Mantle doesn't come out until maybe ten minutes before game time, and we look at each other and we both laugh. His eyes looked like two West Virginia road maps. Anyway he moseyed over to their dugout. I'm thinking we won't have to worry about him today. And if I'm not mistaken in that doubleheader he went like nine for ten with about three or four homers and nine or ten ribbies. Every time he'd circle the bases, he'd come by third, look in our dugout and wink at me. He amazed me how he could perform like that.

So many games over a career. Yankee Stadium. Late in the day it gets real bad in there. Hell, anybody who ever watched the World Series, all those Dodger-Yankee Series back in the fifties will remember how it looked on TV. Sun on the mound, and that creeping shadow between the pitcher and home plate, where it's dark as hell. I'm playing in a game there late in the afternoon, one of those games where I went in for defense. And they bring Ryne Duren on. Now we've got one or two on, I don't remember which. You know, two outs and we're up a run, a time that they might normally pinch-hit for me but they figure since we've got the run Lopez figures maybe we'll go out, catch the ball and get them out of there. Now Duren is throwin' peas as usual. Stuff you just can't see. I'm up there and take a cut, swing and miss, take another cut, swing and miss and now Lopez calls time out, and calls me over to the dugout. Lopez is a man whom I have the very most respect for, one of the great managers in baseball. You very seldom see this, calling a guy into the dugout with two strikes. So I'm pleased because I think he's going to pinch-hit for me. Any time something like that would happen Ron Northey would come in and hit for me. I'm delighted about the prospects of getting as far from those Duren heaters as I can. So I ran over there and Lopez is wearing this serious-as-hell look and he says, "Sam, go to right field on him!" I can't believe what I'm hearing. I say, "Skip, where the hell do you think the ball's going to go if I do make contact?" And it hit Lopez. He started laughing and I went back up there, took my third strike and got us out of the inning. But if Sammy ever pulled one on Duren, you'd have had yourself a little baseball history, you know what I mean?

Here's one that came later in my career. My last year in the majors I was with Kansas City and I didn't go out to the pen as much as I did with Chicago, but I did go out from time to time. This story is about Hawk Harrelson, and this took place in 1963, Hawk's rookie season with Kansas City. Harrelson and I made a little baseball history together. I was hanging on, my last year, and I hardly played at all. And Hawk was a rookie, so he didn't play that much but we used to play golf about every day. And in Kansas City you never had an afternoon game, unless it was a Sunday afternoon game, always night games because it was so hot there. So we'd go out and crank it up on the golf course and have like a $2 Nassau, something like that to keep the game interesting. Hawk was one of these great gimmicks guys, he could play anything. A great athlete, bet you a dollar on anything, a great game player and very hard to beat. And I'm sure that most people are aware that after Hawk got out of baseball he tried the professional golf tour for a while. He could play. I played to anywhere from a two to a five handicap. I could scramble a little bit and play a little better than that when I was playing a lot. But I never really learned how to play the game, took lessons or anything like that. I had a flat baseball swing and I sprayed it around a lot. I could get it up and down pretty good. But I could never beat Hawk. I mean he was just better than me. He outdrove me. I think if Hawk had taken up golf when he was young instead of baseball he could have made some money on the golf circuit. He was very competitive, thought a lot of himself, thought he looked like Tyrone Power. I used to say I hated everything about Harrelson—the hair, the jewelry, the clothes—except Hawk himself. I loved the guy, you know. He was just way ahead of my generation. Hawk should have been twenty-two years old today. I mean he had the flair, wore the jewelry, the whole package, and this is 1963. He just came a little too early. And one day we were playing and he beat me again. I was mad so I said, "Hell, let's double the bet and play nine more." We've got a game that evening but I talked him into another nine. And you've got to experience Kansas City in the summer to understand the heat. It's like an oven and after we'd played twenty-seven that day we get in the car and Hawk takes a look at his hands and they're nothing but blisters, I mean ugly, big blisters. So he says, "I don't think I'll take BP tonight, I'll tell Lopat"—Eddie Lopat was our manager—"I'll tell him I've got a headache or something."

Now we're running late and I'm telling him that it doesn't matter because he isn't going to be playing anyway. Neither of us played that often that year. So we come busting into the clubhouse, just in time to hit with the scrubinies. And Hawk glances up at the lineup posted on the wall and he's in there. The Yankees are pitching a right-hander. So he comes to me and says, "What am I going to do, look at my hands." So I suggested that he go out to the car and get his golf gloves and put them on. He always wore one on each hand when he played. So I said, "Get the gloves and try them in BP." Well, that would be considered bush by the other players, to wear golf gloves to hit in—to wear gloves for anything for that matter. But Hawk, he doesn't care what anybody thinks.

Hawk went to the car, got the golf gloves, wore them in BP. Our guys are on him, the Yankees are on him. This brash kid, hitting with golf gloves. Nobody had ever seen anything like this. Well, in the game Hawk proceeds to hit one or two home runs and did they get on him! Especially the next day. Because now Hawk's had success with them and so he isn't going to part with the gloves. Hell, he shows up with two brand-new ones on the next day. The Yankees are all over his ass around the batting cage. But he wore them from that day on and now we have something called the batting glove. That's how it happened, how the batting glove was invented. Maybe someone, somewhere, wore something like a golf glove but I don't think so. It was Hawk Harrelson who made them popular. Later he was all color coordinated and everything with them. Unfortunately, neither of us had enough sense to patent them. We'd be millionaires.

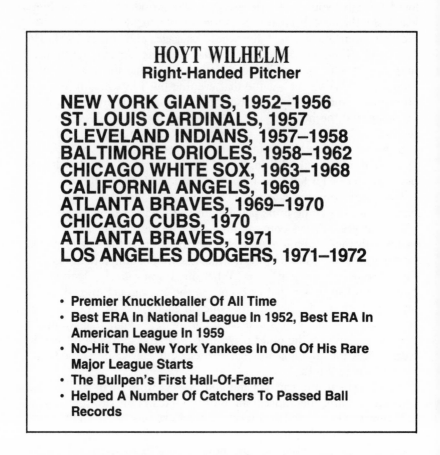

HOYT WILHELM
Right-Handed Pitcher

NEW YORK GIANTS, 1952–1956
ST. LOUIS CARDINALS, 1957
CLEVELAND INDIANS, 1957–1958
BALTIMORE ORIOLES, 1958–1962
CHICAGO WHITE SOX, 1963–1968
CALIFORNIA ANGELS, 1969
ATLANTA BRAVES, 1969–1970
CHICAGO CUBS, 1970
ATLANTA BRAVES, 1971
LOS ANGELES DODGERS, 1971–1972

- **Premier Knuckleballer Of All Time**
- **Best ERA In National League In 1952, Best ERA In American League In 1959**
- **No-Hit The New York Yankees In One Of His Rare Major League Starts**
- **The Bullpen's First Hall-Of-Famer**
- **Helped A Number Of Catchers To Passed Ball Records**

Hoyt Wilhelm was as hard to catch as . . . well, a knuckleball. I called, I wrote, I conversed with Mrs. Wilhelm, I got to be on a first-name basis with Hoyt's answering machine. Then, just when I was about to give up, I applied Bob Uecker's sage advice: "Here's how I used to handle the knuckleball. I'd just let the thing go right on by, let it hit the screen. When it had rolled to a stop I'd bend over and pick it up."

So one spring day in March I just showed up at the Yankees minor league training facility in Tampa, Florida. Wilhelm, the bullpen's only Hall-of-Famer, was busy working his pitchers, watching Yankee hopefuls sprint across the green Florida grass. But when the running session ended and Hoyt had finally "rolled to a stop," I found him to be gracious and free with his conversation. We walked to an outside eating area near the Yankee clubhouse, ducked under an awning and sat on a picnic table. Hoyt banged a bat in the dirt at his feet, smiled and said, "Okay, let's talk!"

A lot of people ask the question, "Why aren't there more great knuckleball pitchers?" A lot of people say, "Well, anybody can throw a knuckleball because you don't have to throw it hard." But that's not true, a knuckleball is really hard to throw. I'm not saying physically hard, but like my job [minor league pitching coach for the Yankees], I'm working with kids mostly. You take a pitcher, any pitcher that's never thrown a knuckleball, and you show him how to hold it, it's just so unorthodox that there aren't many guys who can pick it up. I'll say that a knuckleball pitcher, most of them are kind of born with the knack of throwing it. And that's about all I can say about it. Yes, I still throw a little batting practice but not much and (laughs) I still throw the pitch. I can't throw hard enough anymore to make it do anything.

I've worked with some other knuckleball pitchers, Charlie Hough was with Spokane with the Dodgers Triple-A club, and the year that I was released Tom Lasorda called me and asked me to go out. I went out there at the end of the season and Charlie Hough was there. He was already throwing a knuckleball. I worked with him. I don't know how much I helped him but I hope I did. He was there and then the next year I think he was with the Dodgers and, of course, he's had quite a bit of success. But you know I just talked to him and worked with him. If I helped him, great.

I came from North Carolina originally and at one time the old Washington Senators had about four knuckleball pitchers up there. Dutch Leonard was one of them, and I probably picked the pitch up from reading about one of those guys, but nobody ever taught me the pitch. I just worked on it myself until I got pretty consistent and decent control of it. When I pitched I didn't throw it to the middle of the plate. I picked a zone, I just imagined a zone and tried to throw the ball in there, and plus I pitched up most of the time.

Now 1952 was a great year. [Wilhelm's rookie year when he won fifteen, lost three and saved eleven.] No particular games come to mind. I remember some of the games but I was just happy to be in the big leagues. And as far as being a relief pitcher, I had never been a relief pitcher. Until then I was always a starter and had probably led every club I pitched on in the minor leagues in innings pitched. But Leo Durocher wanted to make a reliever out of me and I had the type of arm that could do it, pitch every day and it worked out good. I would have rather been a starter but like I said, in my case I was just happy to be there, happy to be in the big leagues. I really liked Durocher, I thought he was a good manager. He was the guy who gave me my first chance to play in the big leagues and we won a World Series with him in 1954.

Of course any time you're in a World Series you're going to have memories and so 1954 against the Indians, when we won four straight, that's something you don't forget. A lot has been said and was written about the Indians that year winning 111 games, or whatever and how we didn't have much of a chance, but the thing about that is this. Sure they won 111 games, but you know we played them in spring training every year—God, we must have played them twenty games—I know we were big underdogs in that Series, but it didn't turn out that way.

When Willie made the catch on Wertz I was sitting right out there in right center field in the bullpen. [The bullpens in the Polo Grounds were benches on the field covered by an awning to shade players from the sun and spilled beers.] That was a great catch Willie made, but the ball was hit high. He got a great jump and I had seen him make a lot of catches that good or better. I thought he had it. If the ball went up in the air out his way he caught it. You know everybody thought the ball was over his head and he catches the ball and turns around throwing to hold the runner at first. [Mays made the back-to-the-plate catch with Doby on second and Rosen on first. Doby took third on the catch but the throw held Rosen on first and the Giants held the Indians scoreless in the inning.]

I think I pitched in several of those games. [In Game Three of the Giants Series sweep Wilhelm relieved and shut down the Indians by retiring the last five batters in a row.] I don't recall how many. I think I struck out a couple [Wertz and Majeski] in one game. I know it was a great thrill to be playing in a World Series.

I had always had pretty good control of the knuckleball but there was a time in the mid-fifties when yes, I did have trouble getting it over. When I first got traded to St. Louis, well I had had a pretty good year the year before [1956]. They [the Giants] got in a situation where they needed a first baseman and they traded me for Whitey Lockman and the trade didn't bother me that much. At first it shook me a little bit then I figured as long as I was in the big leagues it didn't really matter, what the heck.

Then in 1958 I went to Baltimore and played for Paul Richards, and if you'll look at Paul Richards's record of rejuvenating older players, it was great. Paul Richards to my mind was one of the best pitching coaches around, the best that I ever saw and he helped me over there.

When I came in over there—let's see, I'd been pitching for quite a while and was in a period where I wasn't doing too much—and yes, he helped me. Richards is the one who said, "Anyone can start a game but it's important who finishes it!" That was the way he felt about relief pitching. Another big thing over there in Baltimore was that glove. Triandos never caught me too much but after we got that big glove, the knuckleball then wasn't the problem that it had been for catchers. [Paul Richards had a special glove made, called "Big Bertha" and or the "elephant glove," which enabled catchers to catch the knuckleball.] Clint Courtney caught me most of the time over there.

Now the no-hitter which I threw against the Yankees in September of that year, I think that was really only about the ninth or tenth game that I ever started in the big leagues. We were playing in Baltimore against the Yankees and it just rocked along and about the seventh inning I realized, hey I got a no-hitter. Nobody talking about it of course. I don't know, it just happened. I'm sure there were a lot of great plays, I just don't remember. I do recall that Tasby made a catch in center field that was one of those that you had to run a little ways to catch the ball and I guess you would consider it a good play. But other than that the main thing I remember about it was Hank Bauer was the last hitter and he tried to bunt twice. And the ball was just foul on the third base side and it had rained the whole game. If either one of those balls had been just fair, I probably would have fallen down making the throw. But after I got two strikes, he popped up to Billy Gardner at second base and that was the ball game. Triandos hit a home run off of Bobby Shantz for the only run of the game, I believe.

Atlanta was toward the end of my career. I came in there towards the end of the 1969 season and I pitched real good. I think I won a couple of games and had a couple of saves. But the game that I remember most was a three-team race, Cincinnati, San Francisco and Atlanta. I believe we were all still in the race right until the end. And the night the Braves clinched that thing we only had a couple more games to play, but the other teams still had a chance. So I remember that game because Niekro started and he pitched six innings. We had Cincinnati beat, I believe 3 to 1, and I came in and pitched the last three innings and cinched the Western Division title that night. That was the game that I remember most down there.

I guess the Hall of Fame is something that a lot of players don't think about until they play several years in the big leagues. I know that I didn't think about the Hall of Fame until I got about fifteen or sixteen years in the big leagues and then maybe I did start thinking about it a little bit. I didn't know if I'd ever be elected, but I'll tell you what, that was one of the greatest thrills of my life, being elected. Records, yes I've got a few of those too, but records are made to be broken. If you've got one that stands up, well you know that somebody might come along and break it. And then they might not, that's what baseball records are about. But the Hall of Fame, that will be there forever.

DICK HALL
Right-Handed Pitcher

**PITTSBURGH PIRATES, 1952–1957, 1959
KANSAS CITY ATHLETICS, 1960
BALTIMORE ORIOLES, 1961–1966
PHILADELPHIA PHILLIES, 1967–1968
BALTIMORE ORIOLES, 1969–1971**

- **Played In More Big League Ball Parks Than Anyone In Major League History**
- **First Pitcher Ever To Win A Championship Series Game**
- **Entertained Penmates By Eating Bugs**

I caught Dick Hall at his Timonium, Maryland, home on a Friday evening. It was the middle of tax season and he ducked through the front door carrying an overstuffed brief case. "Homework," he said. But major league baseball's tallest accountant (6'7") willingly delayed the drudgery of deductions and bottom-line math to retreat to his basement for baseball talk—pitching, hitting, and a nineteen-year major league career that took Hall from Mazatlán, Mexico, to Baltimore, Maryland.

The summer before my senior year in college at Swarthmore, I started to visit some clubs. I was getting some pretty big offers. But they were beginning to say, "Take it or leave it," so I got a little chicken, and I went out and spent a week at Pittsburgh and stayed in Branch Rickey's house. And he liked me. One of his daughters went to Swarthmore, and I think that he liked the fact that I had come from that college. And he was interested in me as an outfielder/pitcher and it was his theory that if you could play every day that you were more valuable.

Now Branch Rickey, to me he was the greatest baseball mind ever in the game, one of the great innovators. I got to know him because I stayed that week in his house and he took me down to Washington and Jefferson College where he was giving a speech. He was a tremendous speaker. If he'd been a politician, he'd of ended up being a senator. And just talking to him was like listening to the voice of God. He started coaching baseball as a graduate student at Michigan, and his star player was George Sisler. Rickey really kind of halfway rode Sisler's coattails to the major leagues. Rickey went with the Browns and got started that way and once he was in, the talent took over. He went with the Cardinals and that's where he opened up the huge camps where he'd bring all these kids in for tryouts. He'd sign maybe fifteen of them. The kids would all have numbers on their backs. Rickey was the one who started the farm system. And he had working agreements. He was the first one to set up all these minor league teams and put his own manager in there and he'd tell them, "I'm going to send you all these prospects and they're to be groomed to be big league players. Hopefully I'll send you enough good ones that the club does well." But the theory wasn't to have local heroes. This changed the role of just being a minor league club for that city to being a pipeline to the majors. He got a big jump on the rest of the teams and this is what built the Cardinals. Then he went to the Dodgers and this carried over.

Now Jackie Robinson. That was partly for business reasons, and—I know this from talking to him—partly because of [Rickey's] religious background. He said, "I thought I could get a jump on the rest of the teams. And besides it really should have been!" So he signed Jackie Robinson, and of course this gave him a big jump.

That of course is what he's best known for, but really he's the one who developed the farm system as we know it today. That is as big a change as there ever was in baseball. When he came over to Pittsburgh he was convinced that a lot of hitters were gun-shy and that all the hitters should wear batting helmets. When I played the outfield at Pittsburgh they still allowed you to leave your glove in the field. People don't realize this but this carried over to 1955 or 1956. So that was the reason that Rickey designed the kind of protection helmet that he did [Dodgers general manager Larry MacPhail designed a hard hat for Ducky Medwick following a beaning by Bob Bowman of the Cardinals in 1940.] If you'd have been wearing the hard helmet like we know today, you'd have had a problem. Because after you hit you always ran right out to your position where your glove was. What do you do with the hard helmet, where do you keep your soft cap? You'd go straight to your position, so he invented this [protective] helmet that you could wear in the field too. And the Pirates all wore this special batting helmet in the field. It was like a plastic, but it was formed a little differently. It didn't have the ear flaps and it wasn't quite as molded. The visor was kind of short like a Derby, almost plain-looking, but the Pittsburgh players had to wear it that year on offense and defense. Then they changed the glove rule, where now you had to take your glove to the dugout. So after you hit you didn't have to run right to your position, now you had to go back to the dugout. There was no reason for the funny Rickey helmet in the field. But he's the one. All the Pirate teams had to wear batting helmets, even the minor league teams. At first some of the guys did wear liners under their caps but because he enforced it, it became the thing to do then. But then it spread and snowballed throughout baseball. It really is a help to the hitter. Everyone wears batting helmets now and Branch Rickey is the one that put that in. If you ask about Rickey everyone will say, "He's the man who signed the first black ballplayer," but he's really responsible for the minor leagues as we know them today and the batting helmet, and believe me, they really changed the game.

After signing with Rickey I went to a fall camp and I signed before my senior year. They had the equivalent of an instruction league, De Land, Florida, and he had all his prospects come down there. I signed for $25,000 which was pretty good for 1951. Part of that was guaranteed salary, but still it was good. The first year I played in Burlington [North Carolina]. The club paid me something like $200 a month and then Pittsburgh picked up the rest. That was the type of salaries in those days. I went to spring training and I played mostly first base. This was in San Bernardino, California, and I was having a good time, hitting pretty well, batting against Maglie, Feller and Bob Lemon. And he brought in a lot of kids. The Pirates had a bad team, so he told me, "If you'll stay with the club instead of going back to school, you can open with Pittsburgh and play in the big leagues." Well I thought, I only have one semester left, even if I go in the Army, which I figured would happen as soon as I dropped out of school, but I thought I can finish any time.

The last exhibition game of spring training was against Washington. So Rickey says, "I bet you could play third base." He sticks me in there and Tuesday night we were going to open in St. Louis. I'm playing third base, the first time I ever played it and in my first real big league game. I'm hitting fifth for the Pittsburgh Pirates behind Ralph Kiner. And all of a sudden I said to myself, "Now I've gotta hit." And I was over my head. I played in like five games and struck out five times in a doubleheader on Sunday and then he sat me down.

But I remember the first time at bat on Opening Day like it was yesterday. Gerry Staley was the pitcher and my first time at the plate I really nailed the ball. And he had a real snake-looking motion.

Somehow I really crunched one, hit a line drive right at Stan Musial in left field, and he misjudged it. He started to come in on it but it was hit hard and at the last minute he went back and he caught it. And that was the only ball I hit hard in those first five games. I beat out a couple of ground balls to short, broke bats, but I was just too nervous. In those games they could carry a forty-man roster, keep that many for the first month and then when cut-down day came, they sent me down.

But I'd been on the bench so I was the logical one to go. I went to Burlington and I played mostly shortstop. I guess he figured I could play the infield and I led the league that year in one department—errors. I'd charge the ball and throw it in the dirt, back up and throw it over the first baseman's head. The field was bad, every time it rained a new crop of stones would come up. I think that I hit about .242 that year, B-ball, the lowest you could play with a big league contract. And I didn't go in the Army. I was 6'7", too tall.

The next year I go back to Burlington briefly. Then they send me to their other B-club which is Waco, Texas, except a tornado had just blown the ball park away and they moved the club to Longview, Texas. I played a lot of second base. Then the next winter I went down to winter ball in Mexico—Mazatlán—that's where I met my wife. I'd hit something like .249 in Texas, a little better but not much. In Mexico I started out pretty good. I hit a couple of home runs, for me I was doing well, but they expected their Americans to do really well. I didn't realize it but they were about to send me home and then the manager said, "Why don't you turn your wrists over a little bit, to pull?" Playing golf now I realized what happened. Anyway I did it and we always played like a four-game series each weekend. I think I hit like three home runs. *Boom! Boom!* and it ended up that I set a league home run record. And by the way, this is my favorite statistic. Luke Easter hit twenty the next year but nobody surpassed the twenty, so I set the Mexican Pacific Coast league all-time home run record.

After all those home runs Rickey gave me another shot. In 1952 he said, "I've got a bad team and we're going to finish eighth. I'm going to play the rookies." And they did consider me a prospect, so he said, "Okay, let's play these guys, Bobby Del Greco, Tony Bartirome." The O'Brien twins, John and Eddie, came somewhere in 1953 I think. And Garagiola was there. I met him in 1952 at that first fall camp in De Land, Florida. In fact, he gave me my nickname. He saw me eating one night and I had my head down over my plate and he said, "Ah, look at that turkey gobbler!" And they started calling me Turkey Gobbler and then it got shortened to Turkey. I kind of had a long neck so it stuck. That was my nickname in the majors. It was Garagiola that pinned it on me.

I ended up in Pittsburgh playing in the outfield in 1954 platooning with Jerry Lynch—hit .239 with two home runs and we didn't do very well and I didn't do very well. But then I went back to winter ball and I told the manager down there, "Look, I used to pitch in semi-pro ball and in college, so if we get behind. . . ." We only had four pitchers. The manager [was] Memo Garbey. He was like a legend in Mexican managers. He's one of the all-time great managers in Mexico and to my mind one of the best managers that I ever played for. They carried four pitchers. Your top four would be like Double-A or Triple-A pitchers and the fifth pitcher wouldn't make a D-club. So I told him I probably could pitch good enough to mop up and then we'd have nine hitters. So he relents and we're playing up in Hermosillo, the fourth game of a series and we're getting beat 6–3 in the fourth and I come in. *Boom! Boom! Boom!* All strikes, I pitch the rest of the game, we score like seven runs and win the ball game. A couple of weeks later the same thing happens, and Howie Haak, who was one of the super-scouts for Pittsburgh, saw me pitching down there. The next spring training they're saying, "Let's see if he can pitch and let's make a switch hitter out of him." And the switch hitting didn't work but fortunately the pitching idea did.

I came up then again at the end of the 1959 season, the year that Elroy Face had that wonderful 18–1 record in the bullpen. And then that December, they traded Kenny Hamlin and me to Kansas City for Hal Smith, the catcher who was such a big part of their 1960 season. That was an ideal trade. Kansas City came in last and Pittsburgh won the pennant. But that was a real shock. The first time you're traded it's a real shock, it really got to me. And then the Pirates win it all and that makes it even worse.

At Kansas City I started out all right, pitched six games and my arm was all right. I was like 4–2 and my ERA was like .230 or something like that. And then the arm gave out on me again. I basically started, eventually they put me in the bullpen. In 1961 Finley took over and I'd been like 8–13 with them. There were rumors that I was getting traded. Then like the third day of the season we were in Boston and I got traded to Baltimore.

I was happy. I had been primarily a starter but they had such a good pitching staff—Steve Barber, Hal "Skinny" Brown, Estrada, Pappas and Jack Fisher—and I pitched pretty well. I started mostly, something like thirteen games that year. But they had such a good pitching staff that gradually I began to be used more and more in relief. And I started having a little bit of arm trouble, so I became the long man in the bullpen. I began to pitch much better coming out of the pen than I did starting. McNally came along and then Palmer in 1965. And it was never a matter of fighting the idea of being a bullpen guy. My attitude was, if Rickey wants me to be an outfielder then I'll try to be the best outfielder that I can be. If the Orioles want me to be a long man, okay, I was glad to be there, and partly my personality. Whatever they wanted—mop up? Okay I'll do it. I'm not going to have a tantrum, even if I disagreed with the manager. If he thinks it's going to help the team, I'm in.

Now Wilhelm was there before I got there. And you know they had that big glove that Triandos used to catch the knuckler. Wilhelm was funny, he loved to throw that knuckleball and try to hit you. A lot of the time the pitchers go in the outfield—in those days you'd hit for about twenty minutes and then go in the outfield and shag. Normally you'd throw a little bit, play catch to get your arm loose. So you do some running and throwing out there and so you play catch. Well Wilhelm loved to play catch and he constantly threw the knuckleball, play catch and throw that floater. And you really had to pay attention. With a fielder's glove I probably missed ten percent of what he threw, and pretty soon you know you're going to miss one. He loved nothing better than to hit you. So what I'd do was I'd put my glove up and as soon as he'd throw it I'd jump out to the side and catch it over here. Finally I got so jumpy that I quit playing with him. Dave Nicholson and the bat boy were the only guys that would play catch with him. Nicholson was a big strong kid. The players were ragging him in the clubhouse when he was a rookie and he got so mad that he walked in and turned the showers off so hard that nobody could turn them on. That was in spring training, fortunately I'd already taken my shower. So anyway Dave would catch Wilhelm in the outfield, and I don't know, maybe it was because he was so big and strong that maybe they didn't hurt when they hit him. Another thing about Wilhelm, his nickname was Sarge, but we called him "Tilt." He had a bad eye, one eye rolled up on him, so to make his eyes level he had to tilt his head over.

Back to Wilhelm and the knuckler. He had a great one. He taught me how to throw it, that's one of the advantages of playing with people like that. The ideal changeup was Stu Miller's and when he was with the Orioles he taught me that one. So I learned the slip pitch from Paul Richards, the change from Stu Miller, and the knuckleball from Hoyt Wilhelm. I didn't use or perfect them all, but I certainly learned them from the masters.

148

Now years later [laughs], here's the Dick Hall secret. What I did was this. I threw fastballs on the outside corner, my fastball had a little ride to it and they tended to try to pull it. In fact, this is my theory of pitching. In the last seven or eight years being a relief pitcher I would pitch maybe only two or three innings at a time. So I'd only go through the lineup maybe once so they wouldn't see me again that game. They might not see me again for a couple of months. And because I didn't throw it that hard, and here I am this guy with a real funny motion. When I was young I threw harder, maybe in the eighty-five to ninety range. But then late in my career maybe eighty-five, but I threw a slip pitch. I had that funny motion, and threw kind of like a girl. The ball had backspin on it, and I think that they had trouble because I threw out of my shirt. I was all arms and legs and I think that they had trouble picking the ball up. It was a riding fastball, kind of uphill almost because I threw from down here. In fact I used to practice in the winter in a cramped basement. I had trouble standing up down there but I had no trouble throwing because of that crazy delivery. Short-armed is what they called it. The ball would ride and I'd go for the outside corner. I think that the hitters would think, "I can hit this guy," and here would come the pitch, a nice-looking fastball. They'd take the big cut and try to pull it and it would be right on the outside corner. When they tried to pull it, they'd end up just missing it and hitting a big high fly ball to center field. "Ah, just missed it!" and then two months later they see me again and it's the same thing, "Ah, just missed it!" For the left-handers I would take the slider and drop it on the outside corner. And they'd either give up on it or swing and hit a fly to left. Except for the left-handed power hitters, they gave me a fit. Mantle gave me trouble, again the big strong left-handers. I threw a lot of long fly balls and the left-handers like Mantle, a lot of those [fly] balls landed on the other side of the fence.

I think Ted Williams had a book and he had a diagram of the strike zone. You've got high-ball hitters, low-ball hitters, outside hitters but they all like it down the middle. They all hit .400 down the middle. Out there on those corners they hit .200. And with two strikes they have to swing at that pitch. With two balls and no strikes, they don't. So this is one of the key things.

I pitched against Ted Williams his last year, in 1960, and I thought that I had pretty good luck with him. He was one that I kept track of. I could almost tell you every time at bat what he did to every pitch. And one day I was saying, "Yeah, I had pretty good luck with Williams, let's see, he only got four for ten (laughs)." But it was funny, he was one of the guys who really thought up there. And right away

149

the first time I faced him there was a man on second and I threw him a low-and-away fastball. He hit a single over the shortstop's head and scored the run. The second time up I got two strikes on him or something, and I threw him the slider. He took it for a called third strike, and that was the first one I'd thrown him, and it dropped over the corner. That's because he hadn't seen it before from me. The first time I threw it, it fooled him. Then I pitched against him in three games that year. What I started doing was I'd bust him inside. He wasn't quite as quick with his bat and I'd start him with fastballs high and away and he was flying out on them. And then I get in a ball game up in Boston and it's the sixth inning and it's tied 2–2. He's famous, you know, for having the good strike zone. And I crank up and throw him a fastball. I could see him as soon as I let go of the pitch he just started cranking and it was up here, that far out of the strike zone. He was guessing fastball, and that's what I wanted because it was a bad pitch. I wanted him to chase it. He got up there and hit it in the bullpen in right center field.

You can't spend much time in the pen without meeting some characters. In Philadelphia we had John Boozer. John is dead now but he was from South Carolina and a big old country boy. He was a real pen character. He would bite grasshoppers in half, stick the back half under his tongue and let them hop out of his mouth. And he would eat moths and all kinds of insects. He was always spitting tobacco on the bullpen ceiling. He'd do lovely things.

Somewhere along there he taught me to eat bugs. He'd say "Grasshoppers, they've got something in them." He'd call it tobacco juice, but apparently it's to make them less palatable to birds. And I think I tried one or two grasshoppers. They'd really make you gag so I stuck pretty much to moths. Moths are nothing, they're just fluff. So then I get to Baltimore, this is like 1968, after Boozer has taught me to eat the bugs. This was pretty entertaining bullpen stuff. New players liked to see you eat them.

I come to Baltimore fresh out of Boozer's school of insect eating. Boozer was nuts, and then there was Turk Farrell . . . that Philadelphia pen was a disaster. But I get traded to Baltimore, a good team with a good bullpen, conscientious players. They tended to pay a lot more attention, occasionally word games like Twenty Questions. Richert was the leader of that game. But they'd get into stories and somewhere along in one of these games I started eating moths, and I'd just pop them in. Like I said, moths, there's nothing to them. This really entertained them and they'd bring me a bug to eat. Occasionally a new pitcher would come in the middle of the season and I'd have to eat a few for him. Sometimes they'd stage it and ask me what kind it was and I'd look at it then, pop it in and say, "Gee, I don't know, but good eating." So somewhere, and I think it was 1970, I could look this up because the seventeen-year locust came. We'd hear this high-pitched weird noise. They were out in force. We had a good team and were winning a lot in Baltimore. I think it was Eddie Watt who came to me with a locust and asked if I'd eat it. And they are the most ugly-looking things, big and I mean ugly. We're winning like eight to one so finally I said okay. I bit it in half, and it was real crunchy. I spit it out and I don't know whether it was the locust but at the end of the game I was kind of dizzy. I went into the clubhouse and all of a sudden I was having some eye problems. It was like a blind spot. I'm looking and almost in the middle of where I'm looking it's all blurred. So I go to Dr. Blaustein, one of the club doctors. I said I'm feeling dizzy and I'm having eye problems and I don't feel sick, and I didn't do anything out of the ordinary. He says, nothing? And I say, well the only thing that is possibly a little different is that I did eat a seventeen-year locust. He just shook his head and walked away. I didn't really think it was that but I didn't eat any more locusts, I stuck to moths after that. I decided I'd wait the seventeen years to try my luck again, when they came back.

Here's a Boozer and Mauch story. There's some baseball history here. We're [the Phillies] in Shea Stadium in 1967 or 1968. We pinch-hit for somebody and brought Boozer in. A right-hander, and this was the first year that they had the rule about going to the mouth. John had a habit of wiping the rubber off with his fingers to get it clean. Then there was mud all over his fingers so he has to get them clean. So he wipes the mound off and then goes to his mouth. Remember John's the guy who would eat anything. So Boozer goes to his mouth and the umpire is watching this and he says, "Ball one! You can't go to your mouth on the rubber." Now Mauch comes out screaming, "He hasn't even thrown a warm-up pitch! He's got five warm-up pitches! It's not a balk until he's ready to throw, you're misinterpreting the rule." And the umpire is "naaaing" him, shaking his head. So Mauch is getting really incensed. He then tells Boozer to go to his mouth again. The umpire says, "Go to your mouth and it's another ball." Well Boozer goes to his mouth. "Ball two!" Now Mauch is screaming, and he's cussing and carrying on. "Boozer, go to your mouth again!" And this time the umpire says, "He goes to his mouth again and he's outta here!" And Mauch says, "Boozer, if you don't go to your mouth it's a hundred dollar fine!" Well Boozer thinks this over for about a second. Not too tough a choice. He goes to his mouth. "Ball three and he's outta here!"

Now at the time I don't know this but he tells Mauch, "If this next guy of yours comes in here and even comes close to his mouth, you forfeit the game." So Mauch calls me in and I get out of the car and Gene says, "Dick, don't go to your mouth." I say, "Okay," because I see what's just happened to Boozer. What I don't know is there's a forfeit riding on the thing. I've got to warm up and I've got this uncontrollable urge to go to my mouth. It's kind of like, "Don't think of a pink elephant." Somebody tells you that and you're going to think of them, right? The next batter is Bud Harrelson, and he might just be the first guy in baseball history to be kneeling in the on-deck circle with a 3–0 count on him. Finally I get warmed up. First pitch, strike one. Then called strike two. The next pitch is a fastball right here at the knees and Harrelson hits a little dribbler back to the mound. And we've got them, ball game! But here's the ending, the historic part. Mauch protested the umpire's interpretation of the going-to-your-mouth-on-the-mound rule and the next day the league office changed the rule. They said, here's the interpretation. You can't go to your mouth when you're facing a hitter. During the warm-ups is a different story.

Great games? The first play-off game, 1969, the first in history. We beat Minnesota 4–3. I came in with runners on second and third and Zorro Versalles at bat. I think it was the twelfth inning and I walked the bases loaded to get the force. So I get a couple of strikes on him and it was funny, I threw him a slider and I really missed with it. I figured that he was probably kind of anxious. I tried to miss by four or five inches, but I missed really bad. It must have like two feet outside and he was so pumped up that he swung at it and missed. We won that play-off game in the twelfth inning when Blair dropped a two-out suicide squeeze bunt. It scored Belanger and I was the winning pitcher. The first pitcher in history of the world to win a play-off game. (Laughs.) Another record for the grandchildren, because our game was played before the Mets and Atlanta game that day.

I got into the fourth game of the 1969 Series, that was the infamous game where Buford lost the ball in the sun and the Mets beat us in extra innings. Weaver got ejected and then later we had the big argument over whether J.C. Martin ran outside the base path going to first. We just couldn't get it going in that one, lost to the Miracle Mets in five games. But the 1970 Series, that's the one that I pitched quite a bit in.

I used to have a story I told about that Series. What is the one outstanding moment that you remember in baseball? Nineteen Seventy, Game Two. Cuellar, Phoebus, Drabowsky, half of our pen had pitched. The Reds took an early lead. Moe is pitching and he's having arm trouble. And in the seventh I think Bench hit a home run to tie it up. And they got me up. Moe has one out and a man on first and Rose is up and he goes like two and two, starts fouling off pitch after pitch and then three and two and more pitches are fouled off and then he walks him. So I know Weaver, you can give up eighty-two home runs but if you walk somebody, you are out of there. So I say, uh oh, one switch hitter and seven right-handers, and who is it? I'm going in there. Weaver is going to be calling me in. And I've got mixed feelings, real nervous. And sure enough, out comes Weaver, signals to the pen and that was the moment that I got my greatest thrill in baseball. He called in Lopez.

Actually Lopez pitched to Tolan and got him and then Weaver yanked him and I came in to pitch to the right-handers. Perez was up and I threw him a high fastball and he somehow hits a ground ball. I'm the fly ball pitcher and somehow he got over that thing and hit it on the ground. That was luck. Then I kept going. I got Stewart, the last hitter of the game. He hit a nice fly ball. I started to walk off the mound thinking "Save, Hall!" then all of a sudden I look up and it was carrying and carrying. Then *boom*! Caught on the warning track. So I pitched to seven batters and protected a one-run lead and got a save in a Series game and that's a nice memory. It's on one of those World Series films. I still watch it from time to time.

Oh, one more Hall record. When I played in Philadelphia I was the oldest player in the National League. When Wilhelm retired I was the oldest player in the American League. The age leader in both leagues. I may spare my grandchildren that story.

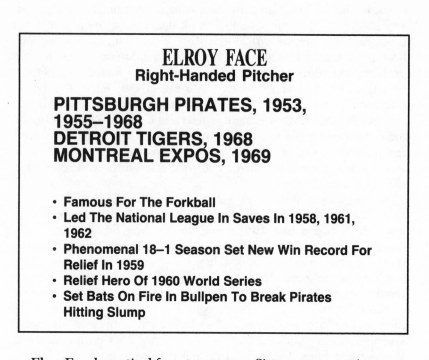

ELROY FACE
Right-Handed Pitcher

PITTSBURGH PIRATES, 1953, 1955–1968
DETROIT TIGERS, 1968
MONTREAL EXPOS, 1969

- **Famous For The Forkball**
- **Led The National League In Saves In 1958, 1961, 1962**
- **Phenomenal 18–1 Season Set New Win Record For Relief In 1959**
- **Relief Hero Of 1960 World Series**
- **Set Bats On Fire In Bullpen To Break Pirates Hitting Slump**

Elroy Face has retired from two careers. Sixteen years a major league pitcher, twenty-one years a finish carpenter. . . . The man has hung a few forkballs and one hell of a lot of doors in his life. Face and his wife are headed to Florida, driving their new motor home south for some sunshine and golf. I caught up with him at a Holiday Inn along Interstate 77 in the mountains of North Carolina. The carpentry work has served him well. Face is looking well, flat-stomached and healthy and as he begins to talk, one senses that he's enjoyed both careers.

Joe Page didn't teach me the forkball. I learned the pitch in 1953 in Pittsburgh. In spring training that year Branch Rickey told me he was going to send me to New Orleans, he wanted me to work on an off-speed pitch. And Joe Page was trying a comeback with the Pirates at the time and I saw him throwing the forkball in spring training and decided that that's the one that I'd work on when I got to New Orleans. But Page didn't teach me the pitch, I got the idea from watching him throw it. The pitch was self-taught. I went to New Orleans and spent half the season working on it in the bullpen, and then I started using it. And it made the other pitches better. Later on when I came back up to the majors I saw Page and we compared how we held the pitch. Basically it was the same but he would move his fingers on the ball, getting the first finger on the stitch to get pull on it this way. And put the second finger on the stitch to get pull the other way. But I just held it on the smooth part of the ball [like a fork between the first and second fingers] and let it do whatever it wanted to. I worked on it for quite a while, and yes it worked, it got me back to the big leagues. I just aimed it for the middle of the plate and it would break whichever way it wanted to, sometimes in, sometimes out, but usually down. I was accused of throwing a spitter sometimes because the ball really went down. I've seen them miss the ball two feet sometimes, over the top of the ball. Or I've had guys swing and the ball wasn't there yet.

How I used the forkball depended. If it was working I probably used it seventy-five, eighty percent of the time. If it wasn't, maybe thirty or forty percent of the time. It all depended, some days it worked better than others. The count didn't make any difference. I'd throw it three and two, two and 0. I think it is the forerunner to the split-finger fastball. I think that the split-finger, they spread their fingers on top of the ball. I put the ball in between the fingers. And my fingers would get sore, but no calluses or blisters. I used to get calluses in my first finger from applying pressure throwing the fastball and breaking ball. But no calluses with the forkball.

Carpentry was in my family long before baseball. In fact, my whole family are carpenters. My father, uncles . . . all from upstate New York, east of Albany. We didn't have anything like Little League when I was a kid, so I started playing ball when I was in high school when I was about fifteen or sixteen years old. I pitched a couple years in high school and we won a championship, the first time the school had ever won it. And then I quit high school when I was eighteen and joined the Army, played a little bit when I was in the service, but nothing organized, just teams that got together. I played second base, short and pitched. I threw pretty hard. About all I had was a fastball and curveball. And Labor Day, this was 1948, after I was out of the Army, we had a game near my home in New York and Fred Matthews, a Phillies scout, was on his way home from vacation. He'd read an article about a game I'd pitched. So he came to the ball game and called me over to his car in the seventh inning and signed me to a contract. I lost the game that day. I'd only lost one game in high school and the same guy that beat me that day did it again in front of the scout.

I think that I was the only guy that ever made it to the big leagues that Fred signed. I was twenty-one years old, small, and only weighed

151 pounds. He told me he didn't think that I'd make it but that he'd give me a chance because I had a good arm and threw good. So I went to Bradford in the Pony League in 1949, and I won fourteen and lost two, then went back to Bradford and was 18–5. The Phillies left me up for grabs and Branch Rickey drafted me for the Dodgers. The same year he drafted me he moved to Pittsburgh. I went to Pueblo and went 23–9 with a sixth-place ball club. Then I went to Fort Worth and was 14–11 and led the league in earned run average. Then Mr. Rickey drafted me again to the Pirates. He must have seen something.

The night I got drafted to Pittsburgh I was working for a fellow back home in New York on what they called hop-toad diggers. They mounted them on the back of a truck for backhoes. I'd gone to Hudson [New York] that night to pick up one of the trucks he'd bought and I'd had a lot of trouble getting home. It had frozen up, wintertime, and the winter baseball meetings were going on. I didn't get home until about, I guess ten o'clock that night, and I opened the door and my father was sitting there and he said, "Hold it." He looked at me for a minute or two and then he said, "I think you'll make it!" "Make what?" I said. He said, "You were drafted by Pittsburgh." So I wasn't there when the news came but he had the telegram and he was so pleased. He and my mom used to watch me play right through the minors. He used to come down to Bradford when I played there. They never came to Ft. Worth or Colorado but the two years I played at Bradford, they'd come down on weekends and see the ball games. Then after I got to Pittsburgh they were in Knoxville and I brought them up for the All-Star game and World Series. They were there in 1960 when we won it.

I guess the thing that I'll always remember about Branch Rickey is what I mentioned before. He drafted me twice, to the Dodgers and then later to the Pirates. And then in 1953 when I got married, one of the first places that I went was up to his office to introduce him to my wife. I never had too many dealings with him. Most of the contracts were worked out with Branch Jr. He intercepted us.

Rickey was shrewd. Dick Groat told us a story about Bob Friend. Bob wanted to get a raise and they sent him a contract with a $500 raise. He wanted a thousand or something like that. Friend said he wasn't going to sign his contract. So he had a meeting set up with Mr. Rickey in Pittsburgh and he had his contract in his pocket. He went in and started negotiating with Mr. Rickey. Through the negotiations the phone rings in Mr. Rickey's office. Mr. Rickey gets on, and it was probably Branch Jr. or somebody in another office, but he made believe that it was somebody from a minor league team. And Bob is sitting there listening to the conversation. And by Rickey's response, Bob is hearing someone ask, "What about this guy you got?"—gave a name and everything—and then Mr. Rickey says, "Well, we've got Bob Friend here that might be available, but I think he's already signed his contract, is that right, Bob?" And of course Bob says, "Yes, I've signed it." He thought he was going to the minor leagues somewhere. He agreed to terms.

Now I know one guy that beat Mr. Rickey on a contract deal. Al Leap, I played with him in 1951 in Pueblo, Colorado. He was a shortstop. I don't think Al ever made it up, maybe spring training with the Phillies. He was a Tennessee runaround, quite a free spirit. Mr. Rickey liked married guys because if you were a married guy you were home with the kids and all that. So he told Al Leap once, "You get married and I'll take you out and buy you a new car." So Al Leap went to him and told him that he was getting married. Mr. Rickey said, "That's fine, you're getting married. I promised you a new car, we'll go down and you pick out what you want." So they went down and Al picked out a new red Ford convertible. He got the car and he never got married. I played with this guy in Pueblo. He had the car there, I've ridden in it. That was the only guy that I know of that ever pulled anything over on Mr. Rickey.

Here's how I guess it all started, the relief thing. I was supposed to start in Chicago the day that Murtaugh took over for Bobby Bragan in 1957. He scratched me and put me in the bullpen. When we came off that road trip my wife met me at the ball park and he told her to make sure that I got my rest because I was going to be doing a whole lot of pitching from now on. So he had his mind made up that was what I was going to do. And I didn't mind it. I really enjoyed it because I enjoyed the challenge of coming in with a couple of guys on base, nobody out, maybe bases loaded. If you got out of it you accomplished something. If you go in with nobody on base and you get them out, you've done your job but you haven't really accomplished anything. You go in with a couple of guys on and nobody out and you get out of it without letting them score, then you've really accomplished something.

When I was in the bullpen I wanted to pitch all the time. There were times when I'd hope they'd get a hit so I could get in there. A lot of people have asked me how I could stand the pressure of relief pitching. Well, to me I didn't feel like I had pressure. I had eight guys to help me. The batter had nobody. He had the pressure. I didn't. Seven times out of ten you're going to get the guy out anyway. Even a .300 hitter. You're going to get him seven out of ten times. If he's already got two hits that day, the odds are with you. Make them hit the ball, you have eight guys out there behind you to help you. I never fought the manager when he'd come to get me. He was the boss. You never like to leave a ball game but I wouldn't argue with a manager about taking me out. There were times when my arm was tired that I'd tell him, "Get somebody ready!" Here's how I handled losses. I used to go home and my wife would have to say, "Who won?" And then I'd have to tell her if we won or lost. I never took the ball game from the ball park. I might stay in the locker room and talk them out after a game, but I never brought one home.

I was a bullpen pitcher but I really didn't spend too much time out there. I never went into the games until the seventh inning so I'd go into the clubhouse and lie down and then they'd come in and call me. I'd listen to Bob Prince on the radio and there were times when they had to wake me up. The bullpen in Forbes Field was relocated. For a while it was out in left field by the scoreboard, and we used to go into the scoreboard, and hang out there. We had a hot dog cooker, warm buns, gallon of Coke, bag of popcorn, and we'd have our own little picnics down there. I even helped the guy put the numbers on the board, read the ticker tapes and things like that. You could see through some open holes and get a real nice view of the game. I loved it out there. When you get used to seeing the game from out in the bullpen it's really a whole different game than the one that you see from the bench. One night Gene Mauch, he was with the Phillies then, and his team was hitting. He called time and had the umpire come throw us out of the scoreboard because he said that we were stealing signs, and his team was hitting. I couldn't believe that, stealing signs? Hell, his team was at bat.

If you're talking about hitting, how about 1956? Dale Long hit the consecutive home runs, eight in eight days, and that was really something. The whole ball team really enjoyed it. When we were on the road we'd have a half hour batting practice and if Dale wanted to take the whole half hour we'd just stand around and watch him, he looked so good swinging. I remember after, I think he'd hit his seventh home run in Philadelphia, and we were leaving to go back to Pittsburgh. For some reason Dale was late getting back on the bus and Nellie King realized that he wasn't there. So he ran out and lay down in front of the bus and said, "This bus doesn't leave 'til Long gets here."

I had a nine-straight game appearance record that year. I guess the thing that I remember about that is a game that Ronnie Kline was pitching in Brooklyn. I had pitched six or seven straight games then and he'd gotten in trouble in the eighth inning. Bragan went out and asked him, "If you were managing what would you do?" And Kline said, "I'd put in Elroy!" That was my seventh or eighth game. That was a good year for me, one of my first real good ones.

There are always going to be hitters that you'll have some success against. Hank Aaron only hit one home run off of me and that was my last year. But Richie Ashburn gave me trouble when I first came up. And Walt Moryn of the Cubs, he gave me a fit. When he came to Pittsburgh later, it was a good trade for me. I never went through a period where I thought that I was losing control of the pitch but there was a period when I was getting hit pretty good. I remember one game in particular in Atlanta. Walt told me that I was doing something to give my pitches away, and then I was able to correct it. What I was doing was this. When I was setting my forkball I was dropping my hand down below the glove and then they could see more of my hand than they did on the fastball or curveball, so they knew the forkball was coming. And naturally the word was out. Those hitters are going to tell everybody else in the league.

I don't remember much about those last five games that I won in 1958. I know that they led into the consecutive wins of the 1959 season [18–1].

I guess what I recall best about that run of games was this. When they realized that we had a streak going, we had a fellow where we used to park our cars. It was an Esso station right across from Frank Gustine's restaurant. I think that he charged two dollars and gave it to the players for a dollar. And I think I was 5–0 early in 1959, and he said, "Elroy, you don't pay until you lose!" I parked for free until September.

Another thing that I remember about the string of wins is that I could have lost about seven or eight of those games. There were so many of them that it's hard to remember any particular one. Dick Stuart probably hit three or four home runs to win ball games for me. He may have made errors to put us behind—he wasn't known as a real good fielder—he'd boot one but then he'd do something like hit the home run in the ninth to win it. I remember that I used to come in from the bullpen and I'd have to walk by first base. And he'd kick the dirt and work his way around so that I'd have to walk right close to him. And if the tying run was on first base he'd say, "Hey, don't throw over here to me. I don't want to foul up and lose the game." So I'd be afraid if I tried to pick the runner off that I might pick Dick off. Of course, there were a lot of line drives that were caught and some miss-hit balls that fell in during that string. I remember the game that I lost that year in Dodger Stadium in the 18–1 season. I got beat on a Charlie Neal hit, a broken bat single that just dribbled between third and short.

I don't remember how many saves I had in 1960, probably twenty-some [twenty-four] but I think that record-wise—not wins and losses but record-wise—that I had a better year than I had in 1959. I saved a lot more ball games. We won the pennant and then won the World Series and there are plenty of memories there. In Game One I came in for Vernon Law. What I remember the most about that one is that I struck Mantle out. He said it was a curveball, but it wasn't. It was a forkball. And it broke pretty good, and I think that I struck out Maris with, I think, one or two guys on base. In Game Four I came in in the seventh [the score was 3–2 Pirates] and got, I think, eight straight. But I also believe that that was the game that Virdon made the great catch in right center on Skowron. I wasn't sure he was going to catch it. Skowron really hit it good and he ran it down out there in right center by the scoreboard. Bob Prince was announcing and I understand that he kept saying Face—forkball, forkball, forkball. And I threw very few forkballs in that game. Most of them were sliders. I was breaking it in on the left-handed hitters' fists—Dale Long, Blanchard. I probably threw no more than five or six forkballs, the rest were almost all sliders. That ball that Skowron hit, that was a slider out over the plate. He hit it to right center field, way out there in Yankee Stadium. I turned in time to see Virdon jump and take it over his shoulder and fall against the wall. And you know, I think the next inning that Mantle made a catch just like it, running away in right center to rob Virdon.

In Game Five I came in for Haddix and had success [two and two-thirds innings of hitless relief]. I guess that I remember the shadows in Yankee Stadium on that one. They're real tough on the hitters because you're coming from the sun to the shadows and so you throw more hard stuff, mostly sliders.

I think that I got the saves in Games One, Four and Five. The thing that I remember about Game Seven was coming in for Vern Law and giving up the home run to Berra. It was a slider down and in on him. It wasn't a good pitch. But to be honest, my arm was tired. That was the seventy-second ball game that I was in that year and my arm was a little bit tired. But that was no excuse. I threw a bad pitch, got it over the plate, down and in to him and he hit it off the right field screen. That put the Yankees ahead and that was the top of the eighth inning. In the bottom of the eighth Cimoli pinch-hit for me and got a base hit. Then Hal Smith hit the home run that put us two runs ahead again. Then we brought Friend in to pitch the ninth inning and

160

then Haddix. They tied it up off of him. I was in the clubhouse, so I missed the ground ball that hit Kubek in the neck and all the fireworks in the eighth. And I missed the home run by Maz to win it. I was in there listening to the radio. Law was in there with me, and probably a couple of bullpen guys, I can't recall who. We were sorry we'd missed seeing it but we were so excited that it was over. . . .

[Pirates play-by-play man] Bob Prince missed it too and there's a good story about that. He was on his way down after we got our lead. Somebody told him to get back up to the booth. The Yankees had tied it. As he was coming into the booth, Maz hit the home run and he heard the roar and so he headed back down to the clubhouse. When he came into the locker room he still didn't know what had happened. When Maz came into the room Bob was interviewing the players and said something about, "Well Maz, how does it feel to be world champs?" and just brushed Maz off. He had no idea how we'd won it, didn't know that Maz was the hero.

Pittsburgh that night was something. I didn't get downtown. We had a victory party at the Webster Hall Hotel. And I was over there and then Burgess, Maz and I had to leave the next morning. We rented a station wagon because we had to go up to New Jersey and play an exhibition game. So we didn't stay out that late. But in 1971, I worked for a restaurant and we had fried chicken. Jack Wheeler had a night talk show. After I closed the restaurant, I'd take some chicken up, and I walked in one night. He was talking on the phone to a woman and when I walked in he says, "Here's Elroy Face, do you remember him?" She says, "Yeah, I remember Elroy. My son and I went down into Pittsburgh the night they won the Series and we asked him for an autograph and he refused to sign for my son." And through the window I said, "Jack, can I talk to her?" He motioned me to come in and so I got on the phone and I said, "Lady, you said I wouldn't sign an autograph for your son? The night you're talking about I wasn't even downtown. I was over at Webster Hall at a team party." She said, "Well, I *thought* it was you!" Ten years she'd been saying that I wouldn't sign an autograph for her son. I very seldom ever refused an autograph for anybody.

I remember one ball game, this was late in my career with Pittsburgh we were playing in San Francisco, Pirates vs. Giants in Candlestick. I came in to relieve and we had a two-run lead I believe. Tom Haller was the hitter and Harry Walker was the Pirate manager at the time. I think this was about 1966. Haller hits a two-run homer and so we go one run down. I get them out. We come back to score a run in the top of the ninth and tie it up. Now I get the first guy out in the bottom of the ninth, so the Giants send up this little old left-handed hitter, an outfielder. I can't remember his name. Jesse Gonder is catching me and Jesse didn't know it, but Harry had left the bench and was halfway to the third base line to take me out of the ball game. Neither of us see Harry coming to hook me. Gonder gives me the sign and I make the pitch and this little left-handed hitter hits a fly ball which we catch for an out. Two away. Now Marichal, the pitcher, is the next hitter. So Harry sees me get the fly ball out and stops dead in his tracks. He figures Marichal is the next hitter and we're out of the inning. Walker turns around and heads back to the dugout. But just as Harry's taking his seat in the dugout he hears the crowd roar, looks up and sees one of my fastballs leaving Candlestick. Marichal hit one out to beat us. Harry never said anything about coming to get me. But Pagliaroni saw it and told Gonder and me about it later. "Hell, Harry was coming to get you, then he saw Marichal and turned around and took a seat!"

Pittsburgh was a great place to play. I played with some great ballplayers there. The nicknames were put on most of those guys by Bob Prince—the Tiger was Hoak, the Quail was Virdon, Donkey Stuart, the Dog was Skinner in left field. Dick Groat was one of the first players to come right out of college and never play minor league ball. I think the guy that was the biggest inspiration on the team was Hoak. He's the one that fired the guys up and kept them on their toes. Don probably had seventy-five or eighty percent ability, but he gave a hundred and ten percent effort. He was a good ballplayer but the effort made him even better. He had a reputation for fighting, and I don't know that he won too many, but he'd fight if he had to. I remember Don was playing tag at a swimming pool at a friend's house, started up the ladder, slipped on the rung and the doctor put seven stitches in him. Don never missed a ball game. He never limped on the field. Between innings he'd come in and go down the runway and hold his leg because it was killing him. He tore stitches out of it and had to restitch it. He'd come in after the game with a shoe full of blood and Murtaugh never even knew he'd been hurt. He was just a great competitor.

Mazeroski was like a vacuum cleaner out there. If you were in trouble you hoped that they'd hit it to Maz. Groat wasn't a player that had a lot of range, but he knew the batters and he was always in position for the hitters. The same type as Aaron. You wouldn't see the outstanding catches like Mays or Clemente because he was always in position. Virdon just had the instinct. He'd turn and run and just turn around and that's where the ball was. I'd just as soon have Virdon in center field behind me as anybody, Mays or anybody. He could run. And offensively Groat, he could handle the bat. In fact Virdon became the manager at Pittsburgh and he made this statement one time. In the seven years that he and Groat batted one-two, he said he could probably count on one hand the number of times with less than two outs that Groat didn't advance him. And Groat was one heck of a basketball player, played for Duke. An All-America, I think.

We had a Pirate basketball team that played high school and college alumni teams for charity. It was me, Frank Thomas, Groat, Ronnie Kline, Bobby Del Greco, guys around Pittsburgh. We went up to play a team in Erie one time. We got beat 72–70, two or four points. But out of our seventy points, I think Groat had about sixty of them. We'd just get the ball and give it to Groat. You know he didn't have too much hair on his head and he used to tell us about playing at Duke. He was under the basket one night, they were warming up for the game. And Groat was feeding the balls out to the guys practicing their shots, and these two little kids walked by and one kid said, "I wonder which one's Groat?" And the other one said, "Let's ask this old bald-headed guy here!"

When you play on a team with Bill Virdon and Roberto Clemente, you're going to see a lot of great catches over the years. And with Clemente there were always stories about his throws. Somebody recently told me about a catch that Clemente supposedly made out by the iron gate in right field. Mays was on third base and Clemente threw him out after he tagged up at third. Now if Mays was running there's no way that you could throw him out at home. There's no way that I can get a ball and throw it 400 feet before a guy runs ninety feet, especially a guy like Mays. I saw a number of great Clemente throws, I've seen him throw a guy out rounding first base, a ball hit to right field through the hole, and he throws him out at first base. Clemente had a great arm but I don't believe that it was that accurate. Maybe it was accurate, but a lot of times he'd overthrow third base. Very seldom did a guy hit a ball to right field with a man on first that the guy who hit the ball didn't end up on second base. Because Clemente would try to throw him out at third all the way in the air and wouldn't give Groat at shortstop a chance to cut the ball off and hold the hitter at first base. So, if he misses him at third, now you've got a guy on second and third, two guys in scoring position. And he had a strong enough arm to, at times, throw guys out like that. But you've got to give the other guys a chance to cut the ball off if you know that you're not going to get him.

One memory that sticks in my mind was my last outing for the

Pirates. I was going to tie Walter Johnson's record of 802 appearances for a single club. And that is my favorite statistic. I feel like I'm in pretty good company being in with Walter Johnson. Eight hundred two ball games with the same club. I don't think anybody is going to touch that for a while. The twenty-two consecutive in-relief [appearances] and the 18–1 won-loss is pretty safe, I think, percentage-wise. If they lose two ball games, they've got to win thirty-six. But the 802, here's what happened the day I set that record. I remember Larry Shepard calling me in before the game and handing me the ball. He said, "You're going to start!" and I said, "No, I'm not." He wondered why and I told him that I had five hundred and some games without a start and that was a record at the time. And he said, "Well I didn't realize that." So I said that I wasn't starting. And he said, "Okay, we'll start Blass then." So that's what he did. He started Blass, and put Carl Taylor in left field. Then he called me in to pitch to one batter, put Blass in left field and then he brought Blass back in to pitch to the next hitter. Then he put the regular fielder in left. I got the hitter, I think it was Felix Millan. And when he came out to take me out he said, "Joe Brown wants to see you in the clubhouse!" Well, I knew then that I was sold. That was the first that I'd heard from the manager or GM. But prior to the game one of the ushers came up to me and said that he'd heard at the Pittsburgh Athletic Association, a men's club there in town, that I'd been sold to Detroit. When Shepard called me in and said, "You're starting!" I knew something was up. But he didn't tell me then either. When he came out on the mound and told me to go to the clubhouse to see Joe Brown, I knew that usher was right. I wasn't really that disappointed. I stayed around a couple innings after they told me. I stayed around in the stands behind home plate and gave autographs to the kids back there.

I went over to the Tigers in 1968 and when I got there they got thirteen straight complete games. I pitched one inning in two ball games, a third of an inning in one and two-thirds in another. I didn't do hardly anything. I wasn't eligible for the World Series. I went on the first of September and you had to be there before the first. But I do have a great memory from Detroit. I was in the bullpen and I recall Denny McLain. I think it was his thirty-first victory. We were playing the Yankees. And that was Mantle's last year and I believe it was one of his last at-bats. Detroit had like a three-run lead and had already won the pennant. The stands were full, maybe fifty thousand people there. McLain asked Mantle where he wanted it. So Mantle gave him a gesture, about letter high out over the middle of the plate. And he threw it and it was up and in a little bit. So Mickey gestured to make it out and down a little more. Denny laid it in there and Mantle hit it in the right field seats. When he rounded the bases he got a standing ovation from fifty thousand people and as he touched third base, he tipped his hat to McLain and McLain tipped it back to him. And McLain got the next guy out and walked off the field. They gave him a standing ovation for throwing the pitch. But that shows you what kind of a hitter Mantle was. I mean batting practice when they're just laying them in there, how many guys can hit them out? And Mantle did it. Everybody knew that he was grooving it because you could see them. McLain was saying, "Where do you want it?" And Mantle gestured. A great moment!

I finished up in Montreal, had a decent year being forty-two years old. When I was released I had a choice of going on a voluntary retirement list or they would release me. Mauch called me in and he said, "It's up to you. I can't say you're done pitching because maybe you're not, but we have to make room for some younger players that we want to look at." It was their first year of baseball. So I said, "Well, if you release me you have to pay me a month's salary, so go ahead and release me." After that I did sign with Hawaii. But the next year I didn't show up for spring training. I stayed in Pittsburgh and threw batting practice for the Pirates. Eventually I wrote to the club out there and they said, even though it was late in the year, to come on out. They were going into the play-offs. I went in July and finished the season. I was only there from the end of July until September but I struck out Leon Wagner with a couple of men on base and that game won the championship of the division. Then we lost four straight in the play-offs.

But here's something we let out later, during the play-offs Ronnie Kline and I always had fresh orange juice in the bullpen in a cooler. And all through those play-offs we were lacing it with vodka. The umpires were coming down between the innings and getting a drink. I don't know whether the umpires knew, but they sure kept coming down for drinks. A lot of repeat business! We lost four straight, so it didn't help our team.

One last memory, one of my favorites. Murtaugh was great to play for. As long as you did your job, he left you alone. I remember one game at St. Louis. I threw a forkball down and away and Musial hit it on the right field roof. And I think I'd been twenty-one innings without giving up a run and we lost the ball game on that, a good pitch. After the game I'm sitting at my locker and Murtaugh—he had this dry sense of humor—he comes in and slaps me on the back and says, "Relief pitcher my ass!"

RYNE DUREN
Right-Handed Pitcher

BALTIMORE ORIOLES, 1954
KANSAS CITY ATHLETICS, 1957
NEW YORK YANKEES, 1958–1961
LOS ANGELES ANGELS, 1961–1962
PHILADELPHIA PHILLIES, 1963–1964
CINCINNATI REDS, 1964
PHILADELPHIA PHILLIES, 1965
WASHINGTON SENATORS, 1965

- **Known For 95-MPH Fastball, Wildness, And Coke-Bottle Glasses**
- **Saved League-Leading Twenty Games In 1958**
- **Averaged More Than One Strikeout Per Inning**
- **Hit An On-Deck Hitter With Wild Pitch**

Ryne Duren has just returned to his Wisconsin home from a 1961 Yankee reunion at Trump Castle in Atlantic City. Mantle, Ford, Kubek, Berra, Skowron—all the great ones were there. So my timing was right. I caught the big right-hander soaking in memories . . . literally soaking. My call goes through. One ring, another, "Hello, this is Ryne Duren." The quality of the phone reception is poor. I ask if he's talking on a speaker phone.

"No, I'm on a portable," Duren says, "got to be, I'm in the bathtub." We both laugh. The conversation takes off—reunion, minor league towns, Stengel stories. Ryne Duren—ex-fireballer, major league wild man, and reformed alcoholic. It's not just the sixty-minute tub bath he took during our conversation—the man has truly cleaned up his act.

The first thing I played when I was a kid wasn't baseball. It was the drum. I played bass drum in the marching band in high school—until the first parade. I dropped my drumstick, bent over to pick it up, lost my balance and started rolling along like crazy. After that I played the trombone. And baseball. I grew up in Cazenovia, Wisconsin, and played my high school ball there. I really wasn't much of a baseball player. I didn't have any talent as a hitter. The only talent that I had was throwing, I could throw hard. One of the first times I pitched I hit a kid and broke two ribs. The coaches identified this as a detriment and moved me to the infield where I played out a rather undistinguished scholastic career.

When I was fifteen I had rheumatic fever and spent a lot of time in bed. While I was cooped up I listened to the Cubs games on the radio. Bert Wilson was the announcer and I wrote him a letter telling him that I was sick and that I enjoyed listening to the broadcasts. Then one day, I was lying there in bed listening and Wilson says, "I'd like to wish a speedy recovery to a young fella up in Cazenovia, Junior Duren." Junior was my nickname. I almost fell out of bed. And that, listening to the Cubs games those months when I was sick, was when I really started to develop a real interest in baseball.

Unfortunately it was about that time, when I was a teenager in Cazenovia, that I also developed a real interest in alcohol. It was a community thing, what the men in town did. Drinking caused me and my family a lot of trouble when I was a kid. In fact it didn't stop. It haunted me my entire major league career and eventually almost killed me. I'll get to more on that later.

In the spring of 1949 the St. Louis Browns offered me $300, a bonus, to sign. Well, half of it was the bonus, I think I got like $150 up front and the rest as salary. I accepted and reported to Wausau of the Wisconsin State League. That was D-ball. There I learned to chew tobacco and polished up my drinking skills. The drinking I could do, but the manager, a guy named Joe Skurski, taught me to chew. Nobody could chew like that guy. He could work two wads at once, one in each cheek. As a pitcher I didn't set the world on fire. I was still very wild. I struck out a lot of hitters, about 115, but walked more than that. From there I went to Wichita Falls, Texas. That was wild. The Sputters—named because of the oil fields. As I said in my book, *The Comeback*, this sent me off on a minor league career that I have looked back on with wonder. I wonder how I ever survived.

There was Pine Bluffs, Arkansas, the St. Louis Browns minor league complex. My clearest memory of Pine Bluff is that we won the pennant that year in spite of some unbelievable carousing and drinking. I won fifteen games. In one game I hit a lead-off batter in the head on the first pitch, no plastic helmets in those days, knocked him out cold. I beaned another guy in Greenville, Mississippi, and the Greenville manager charged the mound. Our manager, Harry Chozen, cut him off. And all of us, the whole team, stood and watched. It was one hell of a fight. I pitched in Dayton, Ohio, the next year, Class-A, won seventeen and then went to San Antonio, Texas. At San Antonio I pitched for a guy named Jo-Jo White, a funny guy. I pitched well but was usually wild. I always went 3–1, 3–2 in the count, long counts, and Jo-Jo, a pretty impatient guy it seems, decided to ship me out. He just called me in one day and said, "Kid, you can throw but I can't stand them long counts, too many 3-and-2s. You got to go." And so off I went. From there I went to Anderson, South Carolina, Scranton, Pennsylvania, and then back to San Antonio, Texas, again. San Antonio, the second time around was 1954, and at the end of the season I got hit on the hand by a pitch and broke my knuckle. I couldn't hold the ball or bat for that matter without pain. As luck would have it, [that] was the time that the Orioles decided to give me a call to the majors.

I pitched two innings that year in the big leagues, against Chicago, and did it with that broken knuckle. But the one thing that I remember—it was a short stay because the next year Paul Richards shipped me out to Seattle—the fans loved to watch me throw. The word was out on my arm, how hard I threw, so when I warmed up on the sidelines, it was like when Ted Williams took batting practice. People watched. That was 1954, just a cup of coffee, before I really made it to the majors. There were more demotions. As I said, Richards sent me to Seattle. Then I went back to San Antonio and finally to Vancouver in the Pacific Coast League, all still part of the Orioles chain. When I joined Seattle that first time I flew in and met the team on the road, they were playing in Hollywood. The team was on the field playing, something like the eighth inning when I suited up. Fred Hutchinson was the manager. He introduced himself and sent me off to the bullpen and told me to heat up. It wasn't too long until I got the call. I came in with the winning run at the plate and blew it, gave up two runs and we lost. After the game the guys were walking around in the clubhouse whispering, "Who the hell was that guy?"

From there it was back to San Antonio again, and that's where I ran into arm trouble, a nerve in my arm. I was pitching with a lot of pain. So much that I really was afraid to throw hard and my record began to show it. I got shipped to Vancouver, a team that the Orioles had a working agreement with in the Pacific Coast League, where I pitched for Lefty O'Doul. But there was a game there that I think saved my career. Like I said, I had been afraid to throw hard with the arm pain. And then in this game against San Francisco, the Seals, we were ahead seven to nothing. I'd been pitching well and all of a sudden my fielders dropped everything that was hit at them, errors everywhere you looked.

The score gets to be 7–6 and O'Doul comes out to the mound and laughingly says that it looks like the fix is in or something. He knows that I'm not a part of it, he says, but he's got to take me out.

I say, "Well I don't have anything to do with it and I'm not coming out, I'm throwing alright. I'm going to stay out here and pitch my way out of this." And Lefty reminds me that I've gotta come out of the game because this is his second trip to the mound. And I said, "No you don't! You take yourself out because I'm not going anywhere." So that's what he did. Lefty was a drinking guy and I'm sure he was ready for a cold one. So he says, "Hell, I've seen enough of this anyway. Besides, I could use a beer!" I stayed in the game, pitched mad and I think that I struck my way out of it. We won the game seven to six. But I was pitching a good ball game. What I proved to myself that day was that I could pitch with the pain. I think I was something like 1–6 at the time and ended up 11–11 and that was with a last place club. So I was throwing hard again, still wild at times but much more effective. I'd pitched my way through the pain.

In the fall of 1956 I got traded to Kansas City. I wasn't pleased. In fact I began to wonder if I'd ever have a chance at making it in the majors. But I reported to West Palm Beach, the A's training camp that spring. Lou Boudreau was the manager. And I had a good enough spring to go north with the club. And that year, in early May, Boudreau gave me my big break, my first start in the majors. And it was a real break because that was the day that I impressed the New York Yankees, the team that I'd eventually play some of my best baseball for. I think my speed would have impressed anybody at that time because I was really throwing hard. But one thing that sticks in my mind about that game is that the only run we got I knocked in with a two-out drag bunt. At the reunion in Atlantic City, Mickey and Whitey and I got to talking about that game. We were talking about Billy, of course. Billy was hitting further down in the lineup and the first time he came up Mickey said that the guys told him to watch me because I could really throw. What I remembered was going over the hitters before that game. When I came to Billy they told me to be careful with him because he handled the fastball pretty good. So when he came up the first time I thought, well I'll try to run the fastball in at him, that pitch would either run in or sink for me. And of course, I didn't have that kind of control but that's what I was trying to do to him. So I threw him a fastball. Now Billy's coming out to get it and the ball is running in and all of a sudden he was falling and swinging trying to stop the bat. And it's right on his fists, breaks the bat off, saws it off in his hands. The ball bounces right back to me at the mound and I get it

169

and just toss it to first. Well, you know Billy, he was hot. He comes back and makes a little circle around me in front of the plate, cusses me out and calls me Four-eyes and a number of other things. When I got the ball back I could hear him over in the dugout. I looked over and they [Mantle, Bauer, and Berra] are just all holding their sides laughing. Everybody but Billy. He was up on the dugout steps, still hollering at me calling me Four-eyes.

And I think that game did make an impact on the Yankees. At least Hank Bauer always said it did. I threw so hard and Bauer always said that he went to Casey Stengel after that game and told him to get me. That they [the Yankees] were married men and that Stengel would be doing the team a tremendous service to get Duren. "Pitch him or send him out! Anything to keep us from having to face him." That's what Bauer told me later.

I played for Casey in 1958, 1959, and 1960. Ralph Houk took over the Yankees in 1961. Ralph had been a Yankee coach before that but I had also played for Ralph in Denver, their Triple-A team. I reported there when I was traded to New York from Kansas City. In fact I threw a no-hitter in my first start with Denver. A nice beginning but things weren't always that rosy. Ralph and I were laughing about one of my escapades in Denver at the reunion last week. Believe me, it's a lot easier to laugh at these things now because I'm sober. But, anyway, I'd gotten into a pretty nasty fight. We were playing in Louisville, Kentucky. I had a snoot full after the game, and evidently—I rarely remembered anything when I was drinking—had insulted a guy's wife in a bar. Some words were exchanged but we—me, Jim Pisoni and Norm Siebern—got out. Pisoni left but Siebern and I went into a coffee shop. And here's the guy whose wife I'd insulted, sitting in there in a booth. He starts giving me a hard time. And I finally grab him. Suddenly a guy appears with a blackjack and starts working me over, really cut me badly. I'd been set up. Boy, they really worked me over. So after about twenty-two stitches I find myself in jail—creating a disturbance, disorderly conduct, and resisting arrest if you're keeping score at home—and again I don't remember. For some reason they also picked up Siebern. So he's in jail too. When Ralph Houk comes to bail us out he starts back to the cell to see us and the desk sergeant stops him, tells him he can't go back. Now what Ralph doesn't know is that it isn't just me and Norm, they've got another one of his players locked up. When Ralph hears the other player's voice he tells the desk sergeant that if that guy can go back to visit, then he sure as hell can, because he's the manager and there to bail us out. Of course the player he heard wasn't a visitor. The Louisville police had arrested him on other charges, booked him for patronizing a prostitute. So he wasn't there to visit us. And he sure as hell wasn't pleased to run into Ralph Houk on his way out.

I still get questions about how hard I threw. I wasn't the greatest baseball player in the world but I could throw. In fact I think I probably had the edge at that time, and the reason I think so is because I led everybody in strikeouts per relief inning. I think that there was one guy that may have beaten me but he never started any games. I wasn't strictly a reliever then. I started four or five games for the Yankees. And then I started quite a few games for the Angels and for Philadelphia. My strikeouts at the end of my career were still over one per inning. And I wasn't always doing it in short bursts as a reliever. For relief appearances I would imagine that they [strikeouts] averaged about one and a half per inning. I think that's a good indication of how hard I was throwing. And I believe that in those days batters didn't strike out nearly as much as they do today.

I think the glasses, the wildness, and the speed all worked together to help keep hitters off-balance. They wrote about my eyes a lot when I was playing. They were really that bad. They have never been corrected to 20/20. They're not quite 20/30. Along with that I had very bad depth perception. There were times when I'd be waving at line drives that were already over second base. Hell, I'd never see 'em. I did have several tints of lenses. Rose-colored ones for night games, and shooters' glasses, sort of an amber color for twilight time. And others too. I don't know, I guess they were a help. My night vision was really poor. One night in Baltimore, Casey Stengel came up with an idea that was good in concept but didn't work. The lights were notoriously bad in Memorial Stadium and I couldn't see Ellie Howard's fingers to get the signs. Dark hands, bad light and bad eyes. So Casey goes to the team doctor and gets a bottle of methiolate and pours it all over Howard's hand. Did it help? No, I'm afraid not.

Of course, the Yankees did have great players and great drinkers. I think that I said that once, or somebody did. But anyhow, joining the Yankees in 1958, I was in awe of these guys. And if people like Mickey and Whitey asked you to run with them, that was really something you know. On one side I had Jim Turner, our pitching coach, telling me to stay away from them. But on the other side they were having all the fun and the laughs and hell, for me that's what it was all about. So it was like telling the fox to stay out of the hen house.

There are so many stories. Here's one that Whitey and I were talking about at dinner the other evening at the reunion. One winter, I think it was 1958 or 1959, Mickey was opening one of his bowling alleys in

Dallas, Texas. We were invited down for the opening. It was supposed to be a weekend, just Saturday and Sunday, something like that. We started phoning around and I don't know, a bunch of us decided that we'd come in early so we arrived about Wednesday. Now we're playing golf, drinking, having a lot of laughs and the alley is supposed to open on Saturday. Somebody Mickey knew was opening condos so we're staying in these condos. We're all there together having a hell of a time, Whitey, Billy, the whole crowd. Golf all day, partying at night. And without getting into much detail there were a lot of Dallas millionaires, the swingers, a lot of gals around. Pretty soon it's Sunday and we're still there and the wives are calling trying to get us to come home. Mantle had to be getting pretty tired of us by this time too. Well, finally I flew down to San Antonio. I was living there at the time. When I got there, it was wintertime and the airport was all fogged in. We circled around for a while and then they turned it around and took us right back to Dallas. So that night I'm back knocking on Mantle's door. You should have seen his face. All he said was, "Oh no!" He got me on the first available flight. I was out of there early the next morning.

One of my all-time favorites is a story about me and Casey and this happened in Chicago. We told this one at the reunion the other day. Billy Stafford [Yankees pitcher from 1960 to 1965] is just getting over a heart attack and heart surgery and that was the only time I saw him get tickled. We [the Yankees] were in the old Del Prado Hotel in Chicago. Casey was just coming out of the bar where he'd been holding court with the writers half the night. It's past curfew. I'm in my usual condition and I run into Casey at the elevator. Stengel looks at me and says, "Drunk again!" and I said, "Yeah, me too, Casey!"

Before Casey died I ran into him at an Old Timers game and he was congratulating me for my alcohol rehabilitation. We started talking about my alcoholism and I asked him, "Casey, when we were playing did you know how much we were drinking?" And he said, "Well, you know, if I'd ask a man he'd never lie about that. The man would say 'I had a few.' What he wouldn't say was this—that they was as big as piss pots!"

Casey Stengel was a very witty man, and a bullshitter with it. He threw a lot of bullshit my way but I enjoyed it and I liked him. He'd pat me on the back and tell me how great I was. That was Casey's way and I got a tremendous kick out of him. Some of the guys, the ones who didn't like him, thought he was a buffoon. But I thought he was very sharp and had a lot of smarts, and the writers thought so. And he did a tremendous job of PR with the New York writers. In that town they were always on somebody's ass. And if it hadn't been for Casey they'd have had to handle it themselves. But he was the master at that, taking the heat off the players, working the writers, deflecting the attention by saying something funny or quotable. He did that great, a buffer.

Talking about the control thing, I was wild and that's well-documented. But I would cut one loose every once in a while, during warm-ups, just for the hell of it, sort of a message pitch. Casey liked that. Everyone talks about me throwing one up on the screen while I was warming up to come in to the game. But I used to like to throw one into the other team's dugout all the way from the bullpen. This was Jim Hegan's idea. He was our bullpen coach at the time and after he'd get me warmed up, I'd fire one all the way from the pen, which was in deep right center in Yankee Stadium, on one hop into the third base dugout. This would put them on notice. Back where I was throwing there in the pen it was about 500 feet from the dugout so it took a pretty good pitch. The business about me firing them up on the screen is true but that really started in Yankee Stadium. Bob Turley had the mound flattened and when I came in the very first time after the ground crew had changed it, I threw the first pitch and I thought my knee was going to hit me in the jaw. It threw my stride off and the ball ended up on the net behind home plate. That was the first time, an accident. But after that the coaches were after me to do it, to shake up the hitters. Frank Crosetti was always trying to get me to put one on the screen. Let's just say that I did it from time to time.

And my warm-ups did get quite a bit of attention. People would watch me heating up. Casey said that when I came in the fans would put down their beer and popcorn. Casey was a master at building confidence. And with me confidence or lack of it was an ongoing thing and Casey was good for me in that respect.

I remember one time we were playing the Senators in Griffith Stadium and it was a doubleheader. The second game was getting ready to start and Casey said, "Duren, some of these folks were late getting to the park today. They may not know what a real star looks like, except in your pictures. So I want you to take your jacket off and stroll on down to the bullpen. I'm not going to use you today. I just want these fans to have an opportunity to take a look." That was Casey just bullshitting around. But I went right out there. If he said go, I went.

I guess one of the biggest games that I pitched for Casey was the pennant clincher in 1958. It was a doubleheader in Kansas City and after the second game we all started drinking. There was a victory dinner and then after that a long train trip to Detroit. I was drunk, and the deal with Houk which Leonard Shecter reported made national news. It wasn't really a fight, but it made nice headlines. It was like guys are when they're drunk and raising hell. I'd had an especially good year. We'd just won the pennant, which was special, so I got specially drunk. Drunks don't need excuses anyway. I was drunk and it's very vague in my mind and always was. I really don't remember the incident clearly, but I came into the car and they were sitting at a card table there on the train, Ralph and a bunch of them. Houk had a cigar and I pushed it into his mouth. He got mad and came up swinging. No, he didn't really come up swinging—what he did was hit me with the back of his hand and cut my head with a big ring he was wearing. One of those five championship rings. So what I did, according to reports, was get angry. Then Larsen jumped in, grabbed me and took me off, back to my Pullman car. So that was it. Most of the writers who covered the teams had filed their stories and were in on the celebration. Shecter, the *Post* reporter, didn't drink and saw fit to print the story. It made headlines, and as I said in my book, might have done me a service by bringing home my addiction, in bold black headlines. But I chose to ignore it.

In the 1958 Series, that was really exciting, so exciting that I actually didn't drink the night before the game. And in the first game when I got the call to come in I was so nervous that I almost couldn't get the bullpen gate open in County Stadium.

I guess Game Six of that Series would be one of the most memorable games, considering what was on the line. I came in with one out in the sixth and the score tied, pitched four and two-thirds innings and struck out nine, I believe. Anyway we won. That was the game I got fined in. I gave the home plate umpire, Charlie Berry, the choke sign. He didn't see it but Ford Frick, the president of the league, did and fined me $250.

After the game, Jack Lescoulie of "The Today Show" was in the clubhouse and we had this nice long interview. I really turned it on and he told me afterward what a fine job I'd done. The next day I got up, watched and it had been cut to something like fifteen seconds. Before the seventh game, Jack's in the locker room again and I asked him what happened to the great interview. He apologized and said, "When we got the film back to New York, they ran it. Yogi Berra was behind you wandering around naked, going back and forth to and from the shower, scratching his rear end." So much for my big interview. But I did have a pretty good Series. I think I pitched nine innings and struck out fourteen batters.

A lot has been written about the Yankees' letdown in 1959 and I would have to say that it's true that the players weren't as hungry as they had been. But the thing that happened that year, more critical than anything else, was this. Skowron got his arm broken. Skowron always drove the big ones in. You know we lose a one-run game and we lost quite a few of them that year. When you lose a one-run game it kills you. Mantle never helped you in the one-run games. He'd make the score five to two or ten to three. But in that one-nothing, two-to-one game that's when Skowron could take a good pitcher to right field or go back through the middle. Once in awhile he'd bomb a pitch to the opposite field. Unpredictable. Yogi was kind of the same way. But Mantle you could just about set the clock by who he could hit and who he couldn't hit. He'd break games open. But real tough pitchers, a Frank Lary or Billy Pierce, those guys were tough. I don't single Mickey out, everybody knows how great he was. But Skowron, and once in a while McDougald and Hector Lopez—damn those guys!— that was the type of guy who later made the 1961 Yankees great be- cause they all had great years. But in 1959 Moose wasn't around. Coot Veal ran into him on a play at first base and broke his arm. We lost him. Hell, we got off to a rough start anyway.

A game that was probably as memorable for me as any in my big league career was the one that I got the hit off of Turley. This was a regular season game after the Yankees had traded me to the Angels in 1961 and a real kick. They [the Yankees] were up one to nothing and with two out in the sixth inning and the bases loaded, Rigney let me bat. He wouldn't have let me bat if there'd have been one out and he wouldn't have let me bat if it was the seventh inning. Bob [Turley] got two quick strikes on me and then the next ball was down and away on me. So the next pitch, I figured he was trying to set me up. It was up in my eyes and I just hit it right, got just enough to bounce it past Kubek and Richardson. That drove in two runs. Then Albie Pearson followed me with a home run. We ended up winning the ball game five to four, I think. I struck out something like twelve Yankees in seven innings. It was a big game because it was the Yankees. They were beating everybody. Mantle and Maris were hitting all the home runs. Mantle hit a home run off of me that day, over the light tower. He hit it left-handed. That was old Wrigley Field where the Angels played. Quite a game. I'd just been traded by them and well, you'd a thought we'd just won the World Series. Then you've got to remember, the fans out there then were so hungry for big league baseball. And it was the Yankees and that park was just jam-packed with people and they just wouldn't sit down. When the game was over and we were in the locker room you could hear them up there. It sounded like a tornado. You'd have thought there was still a big rally going on. I think that was June. You can look it up. Casey always said that, used to tell the reporters, "You can look it up!" Inevitably he was right.

Gene Autry [owner of the Los Angeles Angels] was such a kind man and I know that that win was one that he treasured. He loved baseball. He had made an offer once to buy the Yankees, you know. So any of us that came from there were special. Whitey and Mickey told me this later. After that game he came into their locker room and apologized for us beating them. It's true.

Memories from the bullpen? There's a favorite bullpen story on the Yankee team and I'm going to be careful how I tell this. But the first time I went down to the bullpen in Yankee stadium—tunnels and catacombs down underneath the stands behind the pitching area—there was a guy down there, one of our ballplayers and he had a gal out there and they were . . . well, let's just say it was a sexual encounter. Of course, when the ballplayers get together, that's one that always comes up. One of the famous Yankee stories.

Great moments, catches, are hard to remember, there were so many, unless there's something to trigger the memory. The World Series moments are often the ones most remembered, of course, and like [Admiral] Halsey said, "There's no such thing as heroes, only opportunities."

The 1960 World Series against the Pirates was one of those opportunities that I guess we'll be talking about forever. When the 1960 Series came up at the reunion we had to be a little bit careful because Coates and Terry were there. [Jim Coates and Ralph Terry were called in relief late in the final game and Duren never saw action.] Hal Smith hit a three-run home run in the eighth off of Coates to tie the score and Bill Mazeroski hit the game-winning home run in the bottom of the ninth inning off of Terry to win the Series for the Pirates.] You know I didn't pitch bad in that Series up to that point. I must have been on the trading block or they were trying to make a deal for me to get me out of there. I don't know why I was so much in the shit house but I should have been in Game Seven before Coates. Hal Smith hit the home run off of Coates. Casey told me later, out in Los Angeles, the time he told me about the drinks as big as piss pots, he said he only made one mistake managing all those years. That was when he didn't put me in that ball game in Pittsburgh, the time when he put the other guy in, the one who gave up the big home run.

I direct an alcoholic rehabilitation program at a hospital here in Wisconsin and I've been speaking openly about my own alcoholism for years. I'm not a preacher. I'm not some jockstrap Carrie Nation. And

I'm not against drinking but I am against ignorant drinking. I'm a firm believer in getting the word out about the disease. I think that we all have to be better informed about substance abuse. It's certainly not new to baseball. And I guess I was the perfect example. There were warnings, messages that I got and didn't accept about my drinking when I was playing. When I was with the Yankees, Whitey and Mickey came to me and told me that I shouldn't drink. This was after a night in Washington when I'd been out with them. I had flipped out and done something really crazy, something that I couldn't remember. They came to me the next day very seriously and told me flat out how they felt. And my response to that was to challenge Mantle without ever telling him. I decided that I'd stick with him drink for drink after that. And when it was time to go home I was still, well, relatively sober, and he was dead meat. So that was part of my denial, "There, how's that for a guy who can't drink?" That's how I thought. But you see I had to challenge him, had to out-drink him. It's a funny thing the way that we go about trying to justify denial. It's a weird, weird sickness.

At the end of my career I was with the Senators and had a sore arm. I was getting shots for it all the time. There's a story which I tell about a bad game with the Yankees. I got so drunk after that game that the [Washington] D.C. police found me on a bridge threatening to commit suicide. Gil Hodges came and got me, talked me down in the middle of the night. It was another one of those blackout things. What I know about that story I learned at the ball park the next day. I was just sick and crazy at that time. I got my release shortly after that and the word was out on me in baseball. "Stay away from Duren, he's poison!" Later, among all the other tragedy, I passed out in my home drunk in San Antonio and burned down my house. My wife took my son Steve and left me. Later I tried to commit suicide in San Antonio—parked my car on the railroad tracks and thought about headlines like "Ex-Baseball Star Killed By Train." A policeman spotted me and hauled me off the tracks and into jail.

Looking back at the baseball and the drinking and where I am, I think this career that I have in alcohol counseling is a lot more meaningful than the baseball. This is the real career. As to the talent that I had, I'll never deny that. I think that I had the greatest right arm that God ever gave a man. Maybe my hands were small for a pitcher. But my body was so strong, I should have been playing right into my forties. The alcohol prevented all that. In fact I proved later that I could still play. When I was first running the rehabilitation program I got myself into good shape. And my pitching abilities were amazing.

177

I played in a game against some pretty good local players here in Wisconsin, pitched eleven innings and struck out twenty-five guys. My central nervous system was in order, I was in control for the first time in my life. I had great presence on the mound. I could move the ball and still throw hard enough to go up and in to a left-hander, and I was forty-three. And that experience, it wasn't something that made me look back and regret the fact that I'd let all that slip away. I'll tell you what it did. It wasn't a regret.

You see they interviewed me afterwards for a big write-up in the papers. And it started me thinking, "Hell, with this kind of ability I could go right down to Milwaukee and be a good relief pitcher." But here's what happened. I woke up the next morning with an arm so sore that I couldn't lift it. That was for the best. And I knew then that the Lord had answered my prayer. I'd always thought that what I needed was insight into what pitching would have been like without the [alcohol] problem. I really needed that, so I could share it with young people when I talked with them. And now I had it. And I do now, I bring that up every time I give a talk that's athletic in nature. I always work that into my message. Now I know what it might have been like without the booze. Listen, I don't care who it is, adversity is the greatest thing that there is—once we've lived through it and have gotten on top of it. I know now when I talk to people about this that what I'm saying is right. I've lived through it. And that's why I feel so comfortable about being open about my alcoholism. I've got nothing to sell, nothing to sell but the truth.

ROGER CRAIG
Right-Handed Pitcher

**BROOKLYN DODGERS, 1955–1957
LOS ANGELES DODGERS, 1958–1961
NEW YORK METS, 1962–1963
ST. LOUIS CARDINALS, 1964
CINCINNATI REDS, 1965
PHILADELPHIA PHILLIES, 1966**

- **Combined With Ron Taylor In Relief To Hold Yankees To Only One Hit In Eight Innings In Game Four Of 1964 World Series**
- **Lost Record Number Of Games (Twenty-Four And Twenty-Two Respectively) With New York Mets In 1962 And 1963**
- **Split-Finger Guru**
- **Started The Last Game The Brooklyn Dodgers Played**

Roger Craig is a Lyndon Johnson look-alike. Perhaps it's a case of clothes making the man today, but the LBJ look is definitely there. Craig, dressed in boots and a string tie, is leaning back under a big gray Stetson watching airport traffic pass by. The manager of the 1989 National League champion San Francisco Giants has come East to his home town of Durham, North Carolina, for a round of post-season rubber chicken affairs. And as he awaits his return flight to San Francisco, the man who made "split-finger" a (club) household word takes a few minutes to talk about his days in the pen. "A book on bullpen guys? Here's a trivia question. What was the last ball park where the bullpens were right on the field? The Polo Grounds! It was made like a football stadium and the pens sat right out on the field in front of the fence. They had this little awning over the bench to keep the fans from spilling beer on you. It was that way when the Giants played there and in the early years of the Mets."

Roger Craig, you're the guy who lost forty-six games with the Mets! I still hear that. But as I look back, it's magnified now. I know that I pitched well, and I also know that I learned by the way we lost games. And frankly, that experience has helped me as a manager. Now when my teams go into a slump and they lose three or four games in a row, I can bring up some things and relate to them because I went through all that. One thing about the Mets that people don't realize, if you look at the Mets records, I only pitched two years there, 1962 and 1963. I had twenty-seven complete games and nowadays nobody completes a game. I wasn't even what you'd consider a good hitter.

Yes, we lost a lot with the Mets but baseball has always been a lot of fun to me. I also took it as a job. I just said to myself, I know we're not going to win much and we're going to lose a lot of games but I'm going to start. I'm going to go out every time thinking that I'm going to win and I'm going to do the best job that I can. I took it more as a job because we weren't going to win anything. It was the best possible thing I could do. And of course Casey was fun to play for.

He used to always let his starting pitcher go over the lineups before each game and we'd talk about how you were going to pitch and where the fielders should play. I was pitching this game against San Francisco. Casey had a great wit and sense of humor even in defeat, which added a lot to the ball club. I remember this one game. I was going over the hitters with him and I got to Willie McCovey and I said, "Well, McCovey's a good low-fastball hitter, I want to play him deep in the outfield and play him to pull." And Casey said, "Mr. Craig"—he always called me Mr. Craig—"wait just a minute, Mr. Craig, where do you want to play McCovey, in the upper deck or lower deck?" And of course the players just cracked up.

One thing about the Mets, we had pretty good offense and we could catch the ball and play some defense, but we just didn't have very good pitching. Craig, Jackson, Hook, Miller, Anderson, Moorhead, MacKenzie—good guys but not exactly your Hall of Fame names. I know a lot of times after I'd pitched a nine-inning ball game on the days when I was supposed to throw in between starts, Casey would say, "Wait until late in the game before you throw." Then when we'd have a one- or two-run lead in a game, and if our pitcher looked like he was getting in trouble he wouldn't even have to say anything to me. He'd just look at me and I'd get up and go down to the pen and start to throw. A lot of times he'd bring me into the game. And I was a starter then.

New York was great to play in during those days. When the New York Giants and Brooklyn Dodgers left New York, they lost their National League teams. The Mets come into town and so you've got the Giants fans and the Dodgers fans all becoming Mets fans. We really did pretty well at the gate for a club that was as bad as we were. We played a lot of doubleheaders because we drew well. We had like twenty-one scheduled doubleheaders and everyone of them drew like 50,000 fans. It was something. New York is probably the greatest town in the world for a major league ballplayer as far as being recognized—the kids, the cab drivers, everybody knew who you were. Many times I'd go to a downtown restaurant to eat and I'd go to pay my check and they'd say that some fan had paid it. They'd already be gone before you could thank them. And I've ridden in cabs and the cabbie wouldn't charge you because you were a ballplayer. They idolized their players. The fans could be tough, but to me they were very knowledgeable and they expected a lot. With the Mets they really didn't expect us to win a whole lot of games. The one thing that I'll always remember was that every time we won a game, which was very seldom in the Polo Grounds, the clubhouse was way back in center field and behind the clubhouse there was like a little balcony where you could look out on the street. The fans would get out there on the street and whoever was the star of the game, in their opinion, they would call out, "We want Craig, we want Kranepool, or Ashburn," and you had to go out there on the balcony and just wave to them. That's all they wanted. It was great.

Great memories from New York, first the Dodgers and then the Mets. But some of my earliest baseball memories, and some nice ones, took place right here in my home town of Durham [North Carolina]. As kids we used to stand outside old Durham Athletic Park, peek through the fence and watch the Durham Bulls play. We'd wait for foul balls to come out and chase them down. If you'd turn them in, they'd let us into the ball park. If the ball was scuffed we'd do that, but if it was a good one we'd keep it to play with on weekends.

Later when I signed with the Dodgers—and believe me, they weren't paying the kind of money they're paying today—anyway I was delighted, couldn't believe it. Because as a kid my dream had always been to be a Durham Bull. That was the big leagues to me. I'll never forget that first trip to spring training, I rode with Branch Rickey Jr. in a big Cadillac. He kept falling asleep so I made him let me drive the rest of the way down. I got in camp and I think we had like six guys in a room. I said to myself, how in the world am I ever going to make the major leagues with all these great ballplayers? But I guess I was born with it, the desire and determination to make it. Then I just looked around and I said, heck, these guys are no better than I am, I can be as good as they are. I went on and pitched pretty well the first couple of years that I played in professional baseball. Then I went in the Army for a couple of years. I was in Fort Jackson and fortunate enough not to have to go to Korea. I played both basketball and baseball there.

In 1954 I got out of the service and I was playing basketball. It was the night before spring training, and on the last play of the game I intercepted a pass and someone tripped me and I went down and broke my left arm or elbow. And my mother and brother were there and they took me to the doctor and I talked him into not putting a cast on the thing. I said, "I'm going to spring training tomorrow, and they'll take care of it down there." So he put an Ace bandage on it and let me go. I went to spring training and for two weeks I didn't tell anybody about it, just wore the Ace bandage around it during the day when we were practicing. When we were playing catch, a lot of the times I'd just let the ball go by like I didn't see the catcher throw it or catch it with my bare right hand. I couldn't do push-ups with two hands let alone one hand. But I wanted to be a professional baseball player. Finally it got to hurting so bad that I had to go to the doctor and tell him the truth. And he said, "Kid, what have you done?" He looked at the X-ray. The X-ray at the time that I broke it was a little fracture, about an eighth of an inch, and now it was about a half an inch long. And he said, "You aren't going to play any baseball this year." They sent me back home to Durham and I worked out with the Durham Bulls. Finally I got myself back in shape and then ended up going with about three ball clubs that year. I ended up with Newport News where I had a pretty good year.

This is a true story, this was 1954. I hadn't pitched much and I always had a problem with getting a blister on the end of my finger until my finger got in good shape. I used to take Benzone and put that on it and rub the finger to get a callus on it, smooth it with a flat rock so it wouldn't hurt. They had sent me from Pueblo, Colorado, which was Class-A ball, to Newport News. My wife and I drove all the way there from Colorado, and I'll never forget it, I pitched the night I got there. Norm Sherry, who's my pitching coach now, caught me. About the third or fourth inning I noticed my finger started to bother me. About the fifth inning the umpire walked out there and he said, "Son, let me see your hand." So he grabbed it and the end of my fingernail was about to come off, and he said, "You can't pitch like that." I said, "I drove 2,000 miles, I'm going to pitch this ball game." Then my manager came out and he said, "I can't let you do this, Roger. You're one of our prospects and if you get hurt, I'll get fired." And I said, "Well, you might get fired but I'm not leaving this ball game." So I pitched the whole nine innings and won the ball game, had a real good year—was 10–2 or whatever—but I was what you might call an overachiever. I just wanted it very badly. These are some of the things that I tell my players. If you want something bad enough, you can get it if it's within reality.

My rookie year in Brooklyn was 1955 and that season ended with us winning it all. My first year in the major leagues, to win a World Series game and to be able to start. That was something. I remember we had lost the first two games and then we won the next two and I hadn't appeared in any of the games. I was in the bullpen warming up. About the middle of the fourth game Walter Alston called down to the pen and told the pitching coach to sit me down. I was upset, thinking, why are they sitting me down, I want to get into this thing. And then when it was over, we'd won the game, he came to me and said, "Kid, you're starting the game tomorrow." And that was really a thrill, because it was a rubber game. We'd won two and lost two. I started and I pitched pretty good for six innings and Labine came in and saved it. I'll never forget that night. My mother and I went downtown to Jack Dempsey's restaurant and he said, "Anything you want!" He cooked us country ham and grits.

That was a great Series. Robinson stole home in the first game. I saw that from the bullpen. I can't say that I was surprised by the play because from Jackie Robinson you could expect anything. He was such a great competitor. That's why I've always said that he'd have made a great manager. He would beat you in so many ways, with his sliding, base-running, throwing, hitting, he could intimidate you. When Amoros made the catch in Game Seven on Berra I was in the bullpen again, so I got a great view of it. He had to run a long way and you could see the ball drifting and drifting. At first I thought it was going to go in the stands, but he kept running and running and never gave up on it and made a great play on the ball.

And here's something else I remember from 1955. I can just picture Clem Labine walking out to the pen. He did it so many times. And he was like a lot of them, your so-called stoppers, he wouldn't even go down to the bullpen until the sixth or seventh inning. If you had a lead, there was this thing where about the seventh or eighth inning where he'd get up, sort of a ritual, and walk down to the bullpen. It was always when the crowd would notice him. Clem Labine was good at that, because Clem was kind of a cocky, arrogant type, which was good, I liked it. He'd fold his glove up and put it in his pocket. I can see him now strutting down to the bullpen and the fans cheering. Nowadays you don't see that.

I hurt my arm in 1957, that was in the last game the Brooklyn

Dodgers ever played. It was in Philadelphia, and it was a cold, rainy, sleeting night and I felt something snap in my shoulder in about the fourth inning. I said to myself, well, it's the last game of the season, no need to tell anybody about this. The score was tied 1–1 and we got beat something like 2–1. I pitched seven innings. I never thought much about it. I rested my arm most of the winter. Then when I started playing a little catch I noticed the twinge in my shoulder. I guess it was what they call a rotator cuff today. They would have probably operated now. But I went to spring training about a month early and I started throwing against the wall, took my kids out of school early. I worked out every day before anybody got there and this thing kept stinging in my shoulder. And even today when I try to throw batting practice it still hurts. I still salvaged the career. I went back to the minors and became a stuff pitcher. At one time I could throw the ball pretty hard. I could throw in the nineties and had a pretty good curveball. When I had to go to the minors I had to learn how to throw a good sinker and a good slider. I couldn't throw hard anymore but I still pitched seven more years in the major leagues. I had great control because I just worked on it so long.

In 1959 I had a good year, pitched mostly as a starter. I was, I think, 11–5 and I had some big wins down the stretch. But the game I remember from 1959 was certainly one of the best experiences that I ever had as a reliever. This was in July in Milwaukee. I threw eleven innings of shutout relief, threw something like eighty-eight pitches. I came in like what, the second inning. I don't think I had three balls on one hitter, I had such great control that day. I could throw the ball anywhere I wanted to. It was just one of those days. You think about the great games you pitch in baseball, and this was probably the best game I ever pitched and I pitched it in relief. I think that Norm Larker hit a grand slam to win that game. I remember kidding the guys the next day saying that, if I can pitch eleven innings in relief, then why can't I start?

In the 1959 Series, I remember that we had just come through that pennant race. I'd had a great close. I'd won something like five in September and I had like three straight complete games at the end of the season. I started a World Series game and we got beat. I didn't pitch good but we played bad and when the game was over, we got beat 11–0. It was almost like, okay, we're still going to win. And we won the next four out of five. That was the Series that Larry Sherry had all the wins and saves.

I guess Game Four of the 1964 World Series had to be one of my greatest thrills. I was with St. Louis then and we were playing the

Yankees. Frankly, I was disappointed that I didn't start that game. I thought that I had a chance to start it. Our manager, Johnny Keane, told me before the game, "I don't want you to run or throw," he said, "as soon as this game starts, as soon as Ray Sadecki throws the first pitch, I want you to go down to the pen and start warming up." And so I thought, well, why don't you start me then? So Ray gets in trouble and I come in. I remember I had real good control that day, and I think that the shadows in Yankee Stadium helped me, but I struck out eight men in four and two-thirds innings. I picked Mickey Mantle off of second base. Then Ron Taylor relieved me, and he pitched the last four. I got the win and, of course, Ken Boyer hit the grand slam and that was a good one. I was pretty dominating and it was just one of those days when everything I did was right. Bob Uecker, who was my roommate at the time, tells a story about that day. They had a bullpen fence in Yankee Stadium that was about as high as that lunch counter over there and Uecker says that I never even opened the gate when Keane gave me the call, that I just came flying over the fence. Well, I was pretty anxious to get into that game, I know that.

As I look back, I've been managing in the major leagues what, six or seven years, and all I ever really wanted to be was a pitching coach. I love working with pitchers. And when you talk about the split-finger fastball, yes, I've taught it to some people who have experienced some success. I think that you'd have to say that it has had a major effect on relief pitching. A lot of your good relief pitchers are coming up with the split-finger. Bruce Sutter was the first guy to start throwing it, and I didn't have anything to do with teaching him. He had probably the best one, but there are a lot of good relievers who are throwing it and effectively. And the one thing it does is when you're managing, you look for a good pair of right-handed/left-handed relief pitchers, lefty to face left-handers, right-hander to face right-handers, but if you have a guy that has a good split-finger, it doesn't make any difference. If he's got a good split-finger, then you don't have to make those [left/right] changes all the time. But it has definitely made a change in the bullpen and how you use it. For instance, I use a guy once in a while, a guy that I have confidence in as a get-out-of-an-inning man, a guy who can keep the ball down and possibly get me a double play. We taught Jeff Brantley, who did such a great job for us last year, the split-finger and he's got a great one, he came in last year into a lot of jams and got some big double plays on some great hitters with that pitch.

Of all the pitchers that I've worked with, one of the most amazing stories that I've witnessed in baseball happened last year with Dave Dravecky. Dave had a cancerous tumor in his left arm, and he had it operated on and came back. What a miraculous thing this was to witness, to watch, and as his manager I could not believe what he did. I watched him throw every day in simulated ball games and he'd say, "Roger, I'm going to make it, I'm going to make it, I'm going to pitch again in the big leagues." And I'd say, "Well, if anybody can, it's you, Dave. One reason is because you have the Guy Upstairs on your side. You have a direct line to Him, you can call Him anytime you want to." The first game he went out and pitched in A-ball. We sent him out on a rehab program, and he went out and pitched a seven-inning shutout, complete game. The next game he pitched Double-A, a nine-inning three-hitter, unbelievable. We just couldn't believe this at the major league level. When you have something like this happen to you and to even be able to throw a baseball. . . . The third game he pitched another complete game victory. We brought him back to the big leagues. The day that he pitched that comeback game, a day that I'll never forget as long as I live. As many games as I've seen—and I was there when Don Larsen pitched that perfect game in the 1956 Series—this was even more incredible. He got a standing ovation when he came out of the bullpen after warming up. When he threw the first pitch it was incredible, everybody up. And believe me, this guy is a very, very strong person. He threw a one-hit shutout into the seventh inning. We were on the bench and just couldn't believe what we were seeing. In the eight inning he got a little tired and gave up a three-run homer and we got him out of there with a one-run lead and the win. And of course the next game was when he broke his arm again. You talk about a feeling as a manager when a pitcher with that much courage and that much guts on one pitch goes out there and breaks his arm, it was incredible to witness. And the last thing he said on the stretcher on his way to the hospital was, "Win this game, we need this game to win the pennant." And of course we did win it and we won the pennant.

MOE DRABOWSKY
Right-Handed Pitcher

CHICAGO CUBS, 1956–1960
MILWAUKEE BRAVES, 1961
CINCINNATI REDS, 1962
KANSAS CITY ATHLETICS,
1962–1965
BALTIMORE ORIOLES, 1966–1968
KANSAS CITY ROYALS, 1969–1970
BALTIMORE ORIOLES, 1970
ST. LOUIS CARDINALS, 1971–1972
CHICAGO WHITE SOX, 1972

- **All-Time Bullpen Prankster**
- **Hero Of Game One Of 1966 World Series, Striking Out Six Consecutive Dodgers**
- **Once Gave Bowie Kuhn A Hotfoot**

What God is to Heaven, Moe Drabowsky is to the bullpen.

"Have you talked to Moe yet?" "You've gotta talk to Drabowsky!" "You can't write a book about the bullpen without Moe Drabowsky." I heard it everywhere I went. So it was a big day when my mail-back postcard arrived with the following message: "Heading for Sarasota shortly, don't know where I'll stay but drop by and we'll talk. Thanks, Moe."

Several weeks later I arrived at the White Sox training headquarters prepared to talk high jinks. But there was one substantive question that begged for an answer.

Why hasn't there been a contract out on Moe Drabowsky? How does a guy like this survive seventeen years in the majors, out there on the front lines daily, slipping snakes into lockers and pockets, firing M-80s under stalls of occupied toilets? Hell, the guy once gave a hotfoot to Bowie Kuhn, the commissioner of baseball.

I found my answer inside the Sox complex. "That's Drabowsky over there in the bullpen area," A PR guy said.

Moe Drabowsky is one big dude. Six-three, maybe taller. A good 210 pounds, and looking fit for his fifty-five years. The guru of bullpen high jinks and minor league pitching coach for the Chicago White Sox was a bit of a surprise. I didn't know that practical joking could be discussed as an art form. And I found Drabowsky intelligent, well-spoken, a man who accepts his "pen's bad boy" reputation with a great deal of modesty.

"Hey, I lit up a few shoes, kept a couple of snakes. I don't know, I've just always looked at the game in my own special way," he said.

Was I a prankster as a kid? Oh, I don't know if I was a prankster, I was always getting in trouble. Just an average kid, breaking windows and police showing up at the house and stuff like that. If that's average I guess you could say I was an average kid.

I was from Connecticut and I went to a small liberal arts school there called Trinity College. This was the fifties, and at that time they only had sixteen major league clubs. They didn't have a draft system in effect, so anybody who was interested in anybody could sign anybody. It was a free market, and I was pursued by a number of clubs. Having grown up in Connecticut I was a Red Sox fan and a Yankee-hater. Both the Red Sox and the Yankees were interested and I thought that I would probably sign with one of those organizations. But then the Cubs showed up and said that if I signed with them that they would have me in the starting rotation in the big leagues in ten days. So I thought, "Well, if they're nuts enough to offer it, well, I'm nuts enough to take it." So I went from college right into the big leagues.

I signed with the Cubs in 1956. Stan Hack was my first big league manager and I was twenty-one years old and single in Chicago. I happened to be in a supper club one night and they had a hypnotist performing on stage. They asked for volunteers from the audience. They'd go up on stage and be put to sleep. It looked like a big phony act and later in the evening when they asked for more volunteers, I went up there in a flash because I was sure it was rigged. So he's telling me all these things that I was feeling, and I was feeling them, and pretty soon my eyelids were getting heavy. Anyway, I guess I did go under, I had tingling sensations. And while I was under he'd given me a post-hypnotic suggestion. I didn't realize it at the time but Stan Hack, our manager [for the Chicago Cubs], was in the audience. He suggested that when I got back to my table that when I heard the word "psychology" that I'd go to Stan Hack's table and yell "Hurrah for the Chicago White Sox!" Well it worked. I did it. And the crowd, well, they loved it.

But when I got to the park the next day there was a message in my locker to report to the general manager. I went up to see him, a fellow by the name of John Holland, and he said, "Moe, I understand that you were out entertaining last night." I said, "I don't know whether that was entertainment but . . . I thought it was educational and enlightening and I wanted to find out what it was all about." And he said, "Your performances should be in that little box in the middle of the green grass, right there between the white lines. Not in a supper club in Chicago." So I don't know, maybe I ended up taking my act to the bullpen. I stayed offstage in Chicago after that.

I spent about five years with the Cubs and hurt my arm and I went to Milwaukee for a year, that was 1961. Bob Uecker was in Milwaukee in 1961 but I didn't survive the whole season there. And when I went back to Louisville, their Triple-A club, that's when I met Uecker. We were in that bullpen together on that club. You never knew about Bob. He was always interviewing people at airports and pretending he was with "Candid Camera" and trying to get people to do crazy things. There were some escapades that Bob and I were involved in but I'm not sure that we should share that with people. I know he told Johnny Carson about one of our stories and Johnny said, "There's no way we can tell that on the air!"

I think the view from the pen is fantastic. The further you are away from the action the better off you are. If you really like to isolate yourself, you don't like pens that are down the foul lines and in full view of everybody. And I guess I have a reputation of being one of the guys that was pretty loose down there. The greatest bullpen feat, I guess, was the Lew Krausse story, being able to manipulate another team's bullpen by using the stadium telephones. We were in Kansas City and I had played for them the previous year. Having been their player representative there were a number of times when I'd have to call Charlie Finley, the owner, or call somebody up in the press box. They had a direct dial system throughout the ball park. If you knew what the numbers were to the various locations, all you had to do was pick up the phone, dial three digits and you were connected. So I knew what the opposing bullpen was. We were in the Oriole pen and it was about the sixth inning of the game. Jim Nash was pitching a two-hit shutout against us, just breezing. It wasn't really a premeditated thing on my part but I called over to their pen to find out what players were in the doghouse, whose wives were expecting babies, just get caught up on all the local news. When their coach, a fellow named Bobby Hofman, picked up the phone, I don't know why but I hollered, "Get Krausse hot in a hurry!" and hung up the phone. All of a sudden two bodies came charging out of the bullpen and they proceeded to heat up. Nash is still cruising along on this two-hitter and he looks down there and wonders what in the hell is going on. So I let them throw for a while and then called back and said, "That's enough, sit 'em down."

We always had a lot of fun with the phones. There were plenty of times when the starting pitcher was getting his brains knocked out and the manager would be trying to get through but the phone would be tied up. Beep, beep, beep . . . redials and it's still busy. I was a stockbroker and I used to get on there and call New York to check on a certain stock. I'd be in California and the New York market would be closed. You'd want some closing prices or be in Milwaukee in an afternoon game and in a lot of those places all you need to do is pick up the phone, dial 9 and *Boom!* There you go! An outside line. I know that after we won the pennant at Baltimore in 1966 and then finished in the second division in 1967, one of the first meetings that Hank Bauer had in spring training in 1968 he said there will be no more long-distance calls from the bullpen and there will be no more charcoaling in the bullpen. He came down pretty heavily on us, me largely responsible for it, I guess.

Another story from Kansas City—Joe Gordon was the manager, a big drinker, and when we got back from spring training the first year that I played for him, we had a clubhouse meeting and we were talking about setting curfews for the season. He asked for my advice. So I told Joe, I've been on a lot of clubs and some say two hours after the bus gets back to the hotel or two and a half hours after the game is over. And I never did like those because some guys didn't take the bus back. You've got a tough game that you've lost, then you don't want to look at the clock right away. So why don't we set one time every night. Joe said, "Yeah, I kinda like that idea, let's make it two A.M. every night." And then he said, "No, I'll tell you what. It's going to take us twenty minutes to get from the bar to the hotel. Why don't we make it two-thirty, and then if the game runs late, we'll adjust." I said, "Ah, this is wonderful." What a guy to play for.

Another Kansas City bullpen story, Joe Gordon managing, and as I said, Joe was loose. One day I looked in our bullpen and the game was going, we've got nine guys on the field. In the dugout there's Gordon, and a couple of coaches and I don't see another soul up there. Then I say, "How many fucking guys do we have in this bullpen?" I count and there's twenty-three guys in the bullpen. Well, we were having a party and the word got out. It was a Sunday game in the fall and we're in Chicago, we had a TV out there and the Bears were on. So we had twenty-three guys. How creative can you be with twenty-three? One of our guys, Wally Bunker, had had a tough night the night before and he's curled up in the corner sleeping. So I decide to have a little mock burial ceremony for him. And we scratch out a five-by-eight foot area for the grave there in the dirt. I put three pallbearers on each side of him, and I'm at the head giving him the last rites. All of a sudden I look up at the center field camera and the red light is on and they're pointing it right at me. So we bowed our heads and completed the ceremony. I found out later that the switchboard started to light up. Mr. Short, our GM at the time, called Joe Gordon and said that we were making a mockery of the game and good old Joe just laughed at him and said, "Hey, nah, let my boys alone, they're having fun down there."

So after the funeral I had to come up with something to occupy the twenty-three. Chicago has a wire fence with a covering in front of it so you can duck behind the covering and nobody can see you. So I had all twenty-three ducking down and gave them each a number. When I called their number they'd come popping up. I had the odds come up, then the evens, then one and two, six and seven. Well it made a pretty entertaining thing for the fans and the TV people were interested, of course. A nice change of pace from a bullpen funeral.

The Detroit bullpen was a favorite of mine. It offered a wonderful opportunity but you had to suffer a little bit. The pen was down in the ground and they had a big tarp underneath this long bench. What I liked to do was get down there early and hide under the tarp. Then when my buddies arrived I'd be down there under the tarp with all the ants and maggots. So I'm under there and they play the national anthem. Everybody stands up—anthems are great for hotfoots—so out I come and slip the matches and cigarette fuses to about four or five unsuspecting shoes, get things lit and wait for the howl to go up. I was always willing to endure a little discomfort for a good hotfoot.

I guess the practical joking and my reputation for it all got started at Baltimore. When you're with a losing team, management kind of frowns at antics. It's kind of funny. If you're on a losing club it's bad, you're not showing team spirit and all that sort of stuff, but if you're on a good club then the reputation is of the guy who keeps everybody else loose. We need that. So you need it on winning clubs and you don't need it on losing clubs.

The bullpen wars were another thing. This time, I'd gone from the Orioles to the Kansas City Royals in a trade. It was our first trip into Baltimore and I decided to have a commando attack at 2100 hours. It was dark and we took our jackets down into the bullpen. We had all sorts of rocks and dirtballs in our jackets and we got some blackened cork and blacked our faces. We had a bunch of young kids in the KC pen, guys who had hardly ever been in the big leagues before. It was the first year for Kansas City and I was one of the old guys on a youthful team. So anyway at 2100 hours we snuck over behind the Oriole pen. The game was going on and they're all sitting in the pen watching and we cut loose with the rocks and dirt on the roof of the pen and really blew them out . . . Watt, Richert, Turkey Hall, the same old crew. Scared the hell out of them.

That was done under the cover of darkness. And the next afternoon, Watt and Richert retaliated but those dummies—it's broad daylight and here's Harry Dalton, the Orioles GM, with the binoculars watching his bullpen pitchers crawling along behind the fence in center field, and he's wondering what in the hell is going on. So they got caught. They did get our plates in the bullpen, painted them orange. They got out early and painted our plates and the pitcher's rubber bright orange.

I used to like to put goldfish in the big clear drinking jugs of the opposing teams' pens. And on occasion I'd whistle some sneezing powder into the other team's clubhouse through the air conditioning system, just to keep them on their toes. I didn't carry a kit with cherry bombs and sneezing powder but I usually had something available.

The stories about the snakes are all true. I used to have them from time to time, hang them in lockers, put them into play at unsuspecting times out in the pen. My favorite target with the snakes was Paulie Blair. In fact I got him again just a couple of weeks ago at one of the Orioles Fantasy Camps. Here's how the snake business started. Frank Robinson always carried an attaché case and back in those days, in the sixties and seventies, not too many players had occasion to carry them. So we were always on him, wondering what he kept in there, kidding him about carrying all his money. On the bus or plane he'd be catching a lot of grief from all of us. So one day he finally opened it up and pulled out this rubber snake. There were a lot of guys who were petrified of those things—Paul Blair—and that went on for a number of days or weeks, I guess, with Frank throwing the snake and then other guys getting into the act. So I thought that it would be nice if I could substitute a live one for that rubber one. I didn't have the opportunity to put one into Frank's attaché case. But we did get out to California for one series and I'd visited a pet shop and got myself a king snake and a boa constrictor and threw them in a bag. I was at the ball park early and I had one of my snakes draped around my neck. As Blair entered the clubhouse he saw that thing, took a few steps near me admiring the new rubber snake—just as he got to about within five feet the snake's head popped up and the tongue flicked out. Paul was in reverse at about 100 miles-per-hour and didn't stop until he got to the dugout. And he wouldn't come back in. The clubhouse guy had to take his uniform out there and he suited up for the game out there in the dugout.

Charlie Lau was another one on that club who wasn't fond of snakes. You know how boas like to wrap around things. I just wrapped the boa around his uniform in his locker, draped it around the hanger, buttoned the uniform shirt over the snake. The snake was very docile and comfortable. Charlie would come in and unbutton the shirt and just go berserk.

Another time with Charlie, he was sitting in the Angel bullpen in a golf cart. I'd found this huge pipe about twenty feet long. He had his feet up relaxing. I'd put the pipe on his shoulder and he'd knock it off. I'd put it back and he'd knock it off. Finally I put it back and he said, "Oh shit, I'll just let him be." So I had the pipe about six inches past his ear, resting on his shoulder. Down the other end I started cramming a snake. Charlie's sitting there watching the ball game and about five minutes later out comes the head, right next to Charlie's ear. Yowl! Believe me, when he knocked it away this time, that was the last.

Usually I'd borrow the snakes from a pet shop or someone that I knew. I liked them and took good care of them. But I know that I didn't endear myself with the maids in some of the hotels because I'd often leave them in the room curled up on the bed, under a couple of sheets. So I'm sure that it wasn't just ballplayers but a number of maids that I drove crazy with my snakes.

Hotel high jinks? Of course, Bouton enlightened the American populace with the stories of the beaver-shooting at the Shoreham Hotel in Washington [D.C.]. That was a favorite pastime for a lot of the guys. Easy access to the roof and also guys up there on the roof in the middle of the night, you could have had a party up there. But, of course, there have been a lot of things from hotels over the years. I recall one time in San Diego they had a Shriners convention and the hotel was in various stages of being remodeled. They were putting new numbers on the doors. On a couple of the floors the numbers were being written in in pencil. So when I saw that, it didn't take me long to get a big eraser and a pencil and go to work. I do recall in the wee hours of the morning hearing the guys in the funny hats coming in feeling good. . . . It took them hours and hours to get into their rooms. A lot of havoc in the halls.

There were accusations about tearing up the premises, there were some fairly substantial bills. Often I'd have a delayed reaction to a tough loss or poor outing. Not every outing, but some hurt more than others. Some guys would come in right after the game and kick a water cooler or whatever. I was usually pretty calm at that point, maybe it was more for show for my teammates, but about four or five hours later the fuse might go off. So we had some unfortunate experiences, not always my total blame. But with my reputation, the finger usually pointed at Drabowsky.

For example, at Kansas City we had a team party late in September. It was a Saturday night in Chicago, my hometown, so I asked a couple of guys to come out to the house for steaks. I figured that nobody would want to come. Chicago's a place where there's so much to do, but they said sure, they'd love to come. So pretty soon, well, I'll tell you how big the crowd was. After the game I asked the manager if he wouldn't mind catching a cab back to the hotel because the team bus was going to my house. The bus driver joined us. We had quite a night at the house. Then we had this suite at the hotel, the Executive House, and we all went back in there and continued to party. We had a day game the next day so I spent the night in the hotel and things got a little bit out of hand. When we got back to Kansas City the general manager, Cedric Tallis, called and said, "I've got a telegram here from the general manager of the Executive House in Chicago. It states something to the effect that there was quite a brawl in Suite 2218, which was yours, and estimated damages are $5,600." And I said, "Cedric, I'll tell you what, we did have a party but I'll guarantee you there's no $5,600 worth of damage. Maybe $2,500 or $3,000, but I don't think I can justify the $5,600."

I always enjoyed the fans. You do get to know some of them out there. There are some who like the bullpen area and they're there in every city. It's nice to see a familiar face. In New York there was this guy who used to carry political science books under his arm and he knew everything about the Dodgers and Yankees and all of the ball clubs for that matter. I do remember one fan story in Philadelphia in the old Phillies ball park, Shibe Park, I guess it was. They didn't draw too well back in those days and they had one guy sitting in the left field stands during batting practice. The upper deck was right there and we had a game where we'd try to throw the ball off the facing of the upper deck. This one day I threw a ball that hit right on the edge of that facade. It came straight down and there's only one guy sitting there and all of a sudden he's like grabbing his face and down he goes. The ball got him right above his left eye. I felt very badly for him, so I went down to the first aid room where they took him and gave him a baseball. But before I did, I changed my uniform and visited the sick in someone else's uni. I figured if he decided to press charges that he'd do it to another number. They like to sue people in Philadelphia.

Another thing I had fun with the fans with were these fake ten dollar bills. It looked like a ten dollar bill, not folded in half but folded in quarters. A friend of mine had to get permission from the Treasury Department to get these things printed. One side looked extremely real and the other side had his ad on it, a broker, "Buy Through Us." So I had a whole box and I was with Kansas City at the time. I'd use these things in the hotel lobbies. Let's say that the carpet was green. I'd go out and get green thread. I'd walk up to the cashier and when I'd get change I'd drop that fake ten out and kind of reel the thread out and find myself an easy chair, sit there with my magazine or paper where I could get a good view and wait for someone to come along. One night a guy saw it, dove for it. I jerked it, he dove, pretty soon I had him chasing it all over the lobby. I used to pass them around. One of our guys had a wad of them and a rubber band around it. He ran across a hooker one day and said, "Hey, this is all yours." Boy, she popped that in her purse and off they went. Another case of a disappointed hooker, I guess.

The practical jokes were rarely premeditated. I'd just look around and say, "Gee, I could probably do something there." And I always tried to have M-80s around. I always delighted in petrifying guys, so if someone would go into a bathroom stall, I'd like to sneak in there and light up an M-80, walk out and blow them off their toilets. And the hotfoot stories are numerous. The guys that you like to get will try to be creative in stopping the hotfoot. As an example, when I was with Baltimore we had a writer named Jim Elliot who was really easy pickings. He'd be interviewing somebody and we'd light him up, and you'd hear this yowl. He was really so easy. To increase the challenge I'd use all twenty matches in the book, ten on one side and ten on the other. And when we'd get one of those double deals lit up it and flaming it would look like a battleship going down in the Pacific in World War II.

So then as he interviewed guys he would always be looking down at his feet, talking to Jim Palmer, "Okay, Jim, what did you throw him? . . ." Always looking down here. So while he was staring at his feet I'd set fire to his notes. And one guy, I think it was a guy named Chan Keith, I got him on what I called my skin-to-skin. I wedged one of those wooden matches under his sandal, right under his big toe. About ten seconds later, he was recording the interview with one of the players and you just heard this ungodly screech. It was just mind-

195

boggling. On WBAL or one of the radio stations they used to play that on the air during the day. "Sounds of the Oriole Clubhouse," they called it.

I guess my all-time hotfoot would have to be the one on Bowie Kuhn. I lit up the commissioner one day. Bowie was in the clubhouse after one of the World Series games. I stuck a book of matches under his foot and then got a can of lighter fluid. [I] ran a trail all the way back through the room about forty feet away, all the way into the training room. So I lit it up from back there and all of a sudden you see the flame snake out to where the book [of matches] was and it exploded and it lit Bowie up real good.

But it wasn't all jacking around, I had some pretty good years. In 1966 I had a good year in Baltimore and then there was the World Series game which is mentioned a lot. But I had a more satisfying game that season. Our staff was really decimated that year with injuries. We only had twenty-three complete games from our starters. At that point there had been the fewest number of complete games ever from a pennant-winning club. We had some problems in the starting rotation. Hank Bauer needed a starter one day and asked me if I'd pitch against Washington. I did and I went out and he wanted to get just five good innings out of me, just to give the bullpen a little rest. I went eight and two-thirds and beat Peter Richert, 2–1. Frank Robinson hit a two-run homer and that was it. So that was a very satisfying win. They wanted five and I gave them eight-plus. This gave everybody in the pen a chance to rest, which is really important in a stretch. But who the hell would remember beating the Senators 2–1 in August!

So now the Series game. It was the first game of the 1966 Series against the Dodgers and I came in in the third inning. Brooks and Frank had homered in the first to put us ahead but then McNally got into trouble. I think I struck out eleven batters [six of them in a row] but I really had no idea of the impact of that at the time, or the impact that a World Series game would have. It was such a blur that to tell you the truth, I don't even remember striking hitters out. I really don't. I know that when the game was over and they started asking me about the row of strikeouts, I was surprised. I would have thought that there would have been a pop up in there somewhere. But all that was was tremendous focus, fastball down and away, fastball up and in, slider down and away. And intense concentration on every pitch. And there were other moments. I was in the bullpen the night that Frank Robinson hit the ball out of Memorial Stadium, the first and only fair ball ever hit out. We were sitting in the pen and all of a sudden we saw this ball that was crushed. We were wondering where it was going to hit and I remember watching its trajectory and thinking this thing is really ripped. It just kept carrying and carrying and then it was gone, out of Memorial Stadium. It came right over our heads. A pretty sight! Others not so nice, but memorable nevertheless. I lost to Early Wynn, when he won 300. And I gave up Stan Musial's 3,000th base hit so that's certainly a moment you don't forget. A very treasured moment for Musial but not for me particularly. I do get remembered by all the trivia buffs. It was a curveball on the outside part of the plate by the way, the count was two and two and he had fouled off a number of pitches and they had a couple of blown up pictures of it in the paper the next day and when you looked at it you could tell that he was actually fooled by the pitch. Because he was way out in front like this and you really don't want to hit like this because all your back side's gone and all of your weight is on your front side. But the bat was back and all of a sudden he just shot that ball down the left field line for a double.

Here's how I knew it was time to hang it up, end the career. I was with the Cardinals, this was 1972, my last year in the major leagues. We were playing in Atlanta, so again, I've got some M-80s with me. Atlanta is not drawing too well, it's the end of the season, and I'm sitting out there in the pen looking down the right field line. And so of course you've got Knock-A-Homa out there in his tepee in right, the Indian mascot who dances for all the Braves home runs. He probably hasn't had an opportunity to dance in weeks the way the Braves are going so . . . I decide to whip an M-80 in his tepee, stir him up a little. So I put the M-80 on a cigarette and with a cigarette as a fuse, you've got about twelve minutes with a cigarette. So now I wind up and fire it at the tepee, and that's the moment that I knew my career was in trouble. I didn't even come close, it barely cleared the outfield fence and landed in fair territory. So now I'm checking the scoreboard clock and know that it's twelve minutes and counting, do I go out and retrieve it or let it tick? I'm thinking here's Lou Brock, a Hall-of-Famer, bending over to pick up a ground ball double or something and this thing going off in his face and blowing his eyes out. Fortunately, nobody hit the ball in that area, and about twelve minutes later there's this huge explosion. Brock jumps and I come flying out of my bullpen seat and start screaming, "There he is! There he is!" at some poor unsuspecting guy in the upper deck.

Now that I have the prankster reputation I try to carry on the tradition, at Old Timers games and in the Orioles Fantasy Camps. Shaving cream on umpires' caps, a hotfoot now and then. And then of course I've still got Paulie Blair and my collection of snakes. This year at the

Orioles Fantasy Camp, we had an awards ceremony at the end of camp and Paul was receiving an award. Blair watches me like a hawk, never takes his eye off of me, but he got engrossed in the award, and just for old times' sake I slipped a boa on his shoulder. I'd alerted the TV people so I'm sure the fans in Baltimore will see this one on the Diamondvision. I dropped that thing on his shoulder and he screamed and did a fantastic lateral move about fifty feet. And after I did it I found out that he'd just had arthroscopic surgery on his knee. So I'll tell you I was really impressed by that doctor's work. That was unbelievable the way he moved.

LARRY SHERRY
Right-Handed Pitcher

LOS ANGELES DODGERS, 1958–1963
DETROIT TIGERS, 1964–1967
HOUSTON ASTROS, 1967
CALIFORNIA ANGELS, 1968

- Only Relief Pitcher In Major League History To Win Or Save Four Games In A World Series
- Part Of The Last Brother Battery To Work In Major League Baseball
- Led National League In Relief Wins In 1960
- Once Cost Walter Alston A World Series Ring

The best time to ask a favor of an ex-major league ballplayer is after he's played a round of golf where all the putts went down. When my phone call went through to Sherry's residence in Mission Viejo, California, he had just pulled the cork on a bottle of wine and was settling back to celebrate. "Just came in off the course. Two over, thank you. No, not too shabby," he laughed. We agreed to meet during the summer in southern California.

The rendezvous took place several months later in Solvang, California, a little Danish village known for its quaint European shops and old country look. It was a clear, cool, smogless California afternoon—a great day to cut the wives loose with the credit cards and a great day to talk baseball. So that's just what Larry Sherry and I did. Sherry is a big man, young for his fifty-five years. Maybe it's the golf, I thought. I asked about the previous day's round. "Four over. Missed some putts," he said. We said good-bye to our wives and retired to a sidewalk cafe. I floated a joke about the expense of this interview, considering the beating my Mastercard would take. "Hey, join the club!" Sherry laughed. We ordered iced tea and slid into some baseball talk.

Let me tell you about my first trip to Vero Beach. The Dodgers had eight, nine hundred players in that camp. And there must have been a hundred of us free agents that had *FA* [Free Agent] on our uniform. And my uniform number was *156 Brown*. The number on my back was brown, not even Dodger blue. So that was my introduction to the Dodgers. Larry Sherry, *156 Brown*. Until you got into a Double-A or above—Montreal, Ft. Worth, or one of the higher clubs—you got the off-colored numbers—oatmeal, salmon. So I just got the *156 Brown*, that was it. I came out of Los Angeles, me and another guy, Don Kenwick.

I was a very gangly, awkward kid. I graduated from high school at 6'1" and 135 pounds. I didn't throw very hard. I happened to hurt my ankle my senior year before the season. I was running down some stairs coming out of school. When the season started I was going to play first base, I played first and second base. I couldn't move around. The coach suggested that I pitch. He was short of pitchers. And so I proceeded to go out and pitch two no-hitters in my high school senior year. And by the end of the season I was his number-one pitcher. Not much of a fastball but I had a good curveball. And I had pretty good control. When I signed, Lefty Phillips signed me with the Dodgers in 1953. He signed Drysdale the following year.

I started out by playing ball with my brothers. Norm, of course, [was] a catcher in the major leagues. In fact we were the last brother battery in major league baseball [from 1960 to 1962 with the Los Angeles Dodgers]. My other brother George played one year with Pittsburgh. He hurt his arm, he was a pitcher. My older brother Stan was a fairly good athlete but he went into the Second World War in 1941. He didn't get to play, he played some semi-pro ball in the outfield. But the three of us played quite a bit of baseball as youths. I was going to Fairfax High School in Los Angeles. When I came into school the coach knew that one more of the Sherry brothers was coming along. At the time I didn't realize it, but it's just like breeding lines of horses. You see a lot of that in the major leagues today—fathers and sons. And so the coach at the school says, "Well, I got another Sherry coming along."

Back to that first spring training, there were thirty-three pitchers on that team. And we're thinking about who we have to beat out. I've never seen so many pitchers' toe plates in my life! Everybody we'd look at, it seemed like they had a pitcher's toe plate on. So finally at the end of the camp we're trying to figure out where we're going. And of all of us—all those toe plates—I think only one of us made the club. It would be about five years before I made that Dodgers club—Great Falls, Bakersfield, Pueblo [Colorado], and Los Angeles. The Angels were in the Pacific Coast League. This was before the Dodgers came west in 1958.

And looking back, from 1954 to 1958 I used to sit in spring training and look at Snider, Furillo, Robinson. I'm a kid, dressing in the same clubhouse with these guys. I had Sal Maglie's uniform that first year, number 35. And Rip Repulski dressed on one side of me. And across the aisle is Pee Wee. Really hard to believe. And what happened, 1958 was the year that Roger Craig, Don Newcombe, Carl Erskine, and Ed Roebuck all had sore arms. Drysdale and Koufax were in their six-months military service. Seven of their ten pitchers coming to L.A. from Brooklyn couldn't do anything. I felt like I had a chance to make this club, coming out of that good season in Double-A. And Dressen was coaching with the Dodgers then. Alston is managing the club and it seems like there's always some young fresh face that stands the camp on ear. My year!

I pitched twenty-six innings and gave up one earned run. What they try to do to the young ones is let them pitch themselves off the ball club. And I didn't. I ended up going west. L.A. boy makes good. Here I am out in California and I'm in the Opening Day parade. Drysdale and I were the only two local boys on that club. The club was bad. I got a few chances to pitch early and didn't do well and they sent me back out. They sent me to Spokane and that was the only year that my brother and I played together in the minor leagues. Norm had a good year. But that was a letdown for me. Making the big club and then being sent down. My daughter was born that year but that was about the only good thing that happened. I was 6–14 and never got it going.

The next year I go to spring training, 1959, and I get sent out to St. Paul. But I start out pretty good. I win the first two or three games and they're putting it in the paper that I'm going to be going to the big leagues. Meantime, about July 4, there's two doubleheaders in Chicago and Podres comes up with a bad back. I was six and seven but I was leading the league in strikeouts. One of the scouts had seen me pitch and of the six wins I had, three or four [were] shutouts so I got the call.

I go into Chicago and pitch the first game of the doubleheader and I get beat 2–1 against Banks and those guys. They got two earned runs off of me. Moon let a ball drop in and we lose the ball game. Next game I come into the ninth inning 1–1 against Cincinnati. Roger [Craig] comes in to relieve, gives up a base hit and I'm 0–2. Now I pitch a little bit and get a win in relief, my first, against the Phillies, a last place club, pitched five scoreless innings. But the game I think that turned it for me was in St. Louis. I relieved Podres. That was the turning point because I relieved him in the first inning and pitched eight and two-thirds innings and I was three-for-four, hit a home run and drove in three runs, I struck out the side in the ninth. I struck out Musial, White and Boyer to end the game. Durocher was doing the Sunday "Game of the Week" or whatever and I got a watch for Player of the Week. Walt Alston's headline quote was "Best One Man Performance In The History Of The Game."

That game is a vivid memory. I remember the strikeouts but even more so I remember the balls I hit. I got out of the first inning for Podres. We're down 3–0 and come up in the next inning or something and I hit one off the wall. Ernie Broglio was pitching. I hit a high curveball. I drove in Zimmer, that was the first run. And later Zimmer, I think he was hitting eighth . . . and I got another high curveball and hit it up in the bleachers. So now it's 3–3. I had one tough inning, a couple guys on base and the game could have gone the other way. And it's hot—St. Louis in the middle of the summer—and Snider hits one right over the clock in right field to put us ahead. Alston let me go into the ninth. I was afraid that he'd take me out but he let me in there. I'd never faced Stan Musial until that day and when he came up I struck him out on three pitches. He went down on a curveball in the dirt. I remember that. And then I got Boyer, a right-hander, I got him on a back-up slider inside. Roseboro comes out and says, "Hey, you know if he turns on that he hits it out of the ball park." But that happens. You get away with stuff like that when you're going good. Then I got White on a curveball too. I think that's when I felt like I'd joined the Dodgers. I was finally there, you know. Everybody has something like that in their career when they know. And it was right in the middle of the pennant race. I remember Hodges coming in during that game from first base, rubbing the ball with pine tar, calming me down. And Pee Wee was coaching then. There I am with those guys. Four or five years before [I] was sitting in the stands in my Dodger hat, watching these guys play.

As we got into the end of the season my only shutout game in the big leagues came when I blanked Pittsburgh in the second game of a doubleheader. That was August 31 or September 1. From then on I didn't start, they put me in the bullpen. Labine wasn't doing the job and they had Art Fowler the first part of the year. They tried Don [Drysdale] a little bit, but that didn't work. Don didn't win too many games in September, although I think he won seventeen that year. So when we got into September, I remember winning the last three or four games of the season. I pitched the first game of the last series in Chicago, against the Cubs, and won. And then we went right into Milwaukee and I won a play-off game there. And I know my ERA was something like 0.74 in relief. So I really got it going in September. In the play-off game we're in Milwaukee. It's drizzly and you're on the road and you've played all these games and the guys [the Dodgers] had been there before. They knew pretty much what they wanted to do. By the way, Danny [McDevitt] was a character, the only guy I ever knew who pitched with his wedding ring on, then took it off as soon as the game was over. I don't think he'd mind me saying that, he's been married four or five times since then. That's what he did. He'd stick that ring in his wallet as soon as the game was over. Anyway, Danny's pitching and gets into trouble in the second inning and I get into the ball game. I can remember Spahn and Burdette screaming at me from the Milwaukee dugout, "You're gonna choke, kid!" "Rookie, choke!" And I remember getting away with some pitches. I threw a hard slider, a pitch I'd just come up with before that season in winter ball. Well, we beat the Braves in that best-of-three play-off series. I won the first one and then Stan Williams took Game Two. And the success I had was for the most part due to that back-up slider. I struck Aaron out with it twice and he was tough to get out. Roseboro hits a home run in that game and I get through seven and two-thirds innings for the win, my seventh after losing two in a row, so now I'm seven in a row.

Then we win the second play-off game at home, back in California, after being behind 5–2 in the ninth inning. And I'll never forget Vince Scully's comment, we heard it later. "Bad throw gets by Torre! We go to Chicago!" So now we're going to play the go-go White Sox. It all has to happen so fast that we don't have a pennant party or anything. We went right to the plane that night.

Now the World Series—my first year and I'm playing in the big one. First game! We get beat in Chicago 11–0. We come back in the clubhouse and I'm really wired but Hodges and them guys are just going about their business. They've been there. So, and this is the irony of the Series, there wasn't one complete game pitched, the first time in Series history that a relief pitcher pitched every ball game. I got the record, finishing with a win or save—all four of the Dodger wins. It's funny, the next year Elroy Face came very close to tying this. I tied about a half a dozen guys with two wins but no one to that point had finished all four with either a win or a save. And with a staff like Drysdale and Koufax you'd never expect something like that to happen.

But the situation came up from our side [the Dodgers] to bring me in relief. Between Alston and Dressen they just said, "Sherry's got the hot hand, we go with him." So Game Two, we're down and then Chuck Essegian pinch-hits a home run, Gilliam walks and then Charlie Neal hits a two-run shot. I hung in there and we won that one 4–3. That was a big one because we couldn't have let them go 2–0 in the Series. In Game Three with Drysdale pitching I came in in the eighth inning and relieved him with a 2–0 lead. Furillo had a pinch-hit single in the seventh with the bases loaded to break a scoreless tie. We go up 2–0 and eventually win 3–1.

Now we go to the fourth game. Roger Craig has like a 3–0 lead and I think Sherm Lollar hits one out with two on. That makes it 3–3. I come in in the eighth again and then Hodges hits one out to win it. Now I've got two saves and a win. I'm like on cloud nine. I'm on a real roll. But here's what I'm really proud of. In the fifth game I didn't appear as a pitcher. I pinch-hit in the top of the ninth inning. How many pitchers are called on to pinch-hit in a World Series? I grounded out to third but I got two hits in the last game and hit .500 for the Series.

We lost Game Five 1–0. We go back to Chicago leading three games to two and play Game Six. Here Podres has an 8–3 lead and we bang out seven runs or whatever it is. I think somebody knocked somebody down. So they told John to knock somebody down and John doesn't throw at guys. In my career, when I was younger I threw at guys, Drysdale threw at guys, so our players got protected pretty good. But that wasn't John's style. Landis comes up to hit and I think he was going to fake a bunt. He moved in and John hit him in the head. I know John felt bad. I've got it on that film. I don't think it would have hit him if he weren't going to bunt, moving in. This shook John up a little bit. He walked the next guy. I think Kluszewski hit a three-run homer and then he walked the next guy. They figure we've got an 8–3 lead and they never get me up that early in the ball game.

And they get me up and ask if I'm all right. If I wasn't, I'm not going to say so. So then I go in and I give up a base hit. And I got booed. I remember getting booed. I used to have this gait when I came in from the bullpen. I mean just strut. And center field from the bull-pen in Comiskey—they didn't have a cart and so I got booed a long way. Anyway that's in Chicago and I go something like five and two-thirds in the game and we win it 9–3.

Afterwards, we have this victory party and I'm getting interviewed by everybody. I get called to go on the Ed Sullivan show the following Sunday and some guy calls me up and wants to be my agent. This was 1959, right? I mean, there weren't that many ballplayers with agents in those days. For the Ed Sullivan show I had to go out and buy a suit. I didn't own one. I didn't even make the minimum salary that year.

Hell, my World Series check was double my salary. We got the big World Series check, something like $13,800, because we were playing in the Coliseum.

After that Series, my whole world changed. I wasn't home. I'd call my wife from all over the country. I'd have trophies sent home. Everywhere you spoke, they had to give you something. I was working out of New York and I just couldn't leave because all the engagements. I'd never been treated so well. But I also had to learn to . . . I don't know, be a little stand-offish because people were coming at me from a dozen directions. "I've got an investment for you!" "I've got a proposition that can't miss!" But what I did was, I got the Dodger attorney to help and a friend of mine, an ex-third baseman who I'd played with who was an attorney. I consulted him a little bit. I was at least that smart. But it was quite a winter. I did at least twenty banquets in January. I met a lot of people. And I'll tell you one thing, I sat in Chicago at a banquet between Stan Musial and Joe DiMaggio and that was pretty darned good company. And both of them were great gentlemen. I'll never forget at the banquet, DiMaggio drank a little Scotch and he had them bring it to him in a coffee cup with a tea bag on the side of the saucer. A lot of class. Everybody else is drinking theirs right out front. Not Joe. That's how classy Joe DiMaggio is. I never forgot that. And at the Boston dinner I met Ty Cobb, I had my picture taken with him. Big guy, about six-feet-something, a pain in the ass. He sat next to me at the dinner, poked me in the ribs all night. "Hey, kid!" this and "Hey, kid!" that, a big guy. I look at it now and I wish I could get hold of the actual picture. Someone sent me a copy of the newspaper it was in. But I'd love to frame the original. I have all four balls from the last outs of the 1959 Series. I've got them in a case [with] my glove and my shoes from that Series, which I'll send to Cooperstown if they ever want them.

But it wasn't just 1959 and that Series. I have some great memories from L.A. I saw the Davis boys [Willie and Tommy] come up, saw two of Koufax's no-hitters. In 1962 he no-hit the Mets 5–0 and then the following year it was, I think 8–0 and he blanked the Giants. Speaking of Koufax, here's a story. . . .

My brother, who caught for the Dodgers in the early sixties, was quite instrumental in Koufax's breakthrough. And it's true. This was back when Sandy was still trying to find himself and get his control problem licked. We had a spring training game, and we used to have split-squad games. And the Dodgers had their own Convair 440 plane. One team took the bus. Then they sent a second squad by plane that Hodges was going to manage to play somewhere else. Koufax was going to pitch the B-game because he was having such control problems. In fact, most of the time he really wouldn't pitch until May or June because he was so wild.

The rest of the pitchers stayed in Vero, the guys who weren't involved in the two away games. And we had it pretty easy then, only one coach to supervise us. We'd work out for about an hour or so, run a little bit, throw on the sidelines and then head off to the golf course or race track. We're coming out of the clubhouse to work out and here's this pitcher, George Anderson. I think he made the club that year. He looks up and sees the Dodger plane going over and says, "Oh man, there goes the Dodger plane. I'm supposed to be on it!" He was supposed to be the second or third pitcher for the B-game that day. So that leaves Koufax with just one other guy. Koufax was just supposed to pitch three or four innings in that game. Now they've got only two pitchers. And Hodges knows that he's got to pitch Sandy at least six or seven, you know. And here's what happened. Norm, my brother, was going to catch that game. So he tells Sandy, "Look, why don't you just try to get the ball over. Don't overthrow." And Sandy had been trying a new delivery. So Norm says, "Forget all that extra movement in the delivery. Just ease the ball up there, nice and smooth like, because you've gotta go at least six today."

That evening, they come back from this game. And now Alston's waiting to find out how the B-game went. This is how Norm tells it. Walt asks Hodges, "How did you do?" "We won," Hodges says. "We shut them out!" "Well, how did Koufax do?" "Well, Koufax went nine! Struck out fourteen and walked two," Hodges says. "You mean he walked fourteen and struck out two," Alston said. I don't know the numbers exactly but it was really something, a real mind-boggler and here's what happened. That was the game that Koufax realized that he didn't really have to rare back and throw the ball. With his stuff, all he had to do was get into the rhythm. And that was the beginning of the Sandy Koufax that wound up in Cooperstown in the Hall of Fame. My brother caught him a lot. Sandy had those big hands and Norm said that his fastball spun so good and so fast that when guys were trying to hit off of him it looked like when the ball got to within seven or eight feet of home plate, it looked like somebody threw it again! It just jumped and guys couldn't get around. Now that was the spring of 1961. Sandy won eighteen ball games that year. And if you'll look at that fabulous career of his, 1961 was the year and of the 165 games he won, almost all of them came in the next five or six years.

Sandy was a perfectionist, a that-tie-doesn't-go-with-that-shirt kinda guy. A perfectionist in everything he did. I think that it was really tough on him earlier in his career when he didn't do as well as he knew he could, really frustrating. But boy, when he got it together, he got it together. And he had good killer instinct, he'd get two strikes and boy, look out! The only time we'd worry when we sat in the bullpen was in the early innings. Because when Koufax and Drysdale were pitching, it was almost an automatic night off for us. But in the early innings Sandy could be a little wild and it had to do with his big, heavy muscles getting loose. He was always concerned about this. He was the only person I ever met who used a whole tube of Capsulin to rub on his back before he pitched. Capsulin is the heat stuff, the stuff that guys used to sneak into the rim of your jockstrap as a joke. I'll tell you, it is so hot that you can't stand it. Sandy would rub it on his shoulders and back. He had real thick skin, said it helped him get loose. And it would be eighty, ninety degrees out there and you'd go by him and you could smell that sweatshirt. It would make your eyes water. He'd bring his arm up and ohhh! But it was a great thrill to play with a guy of that caliber and Don was overshadowed while Sandy was still pitching. Those two guys were something. And Drysdale was a great one, he'd knock you down. Stan Williams was another one. Stan would make notes, keep a little book of guys he had to hit.

Here's one about my brother and me. We were in winter ball together down in Venezuela. Pete Reiser was managing the ball club and had to go home for some reason and so Norm managed the ball club. You've gotta understand the sibling rivalry, it went back to when we were small. Some guy slides into our second baseman and cut him up in the leg pretty good. I get mad and the bases are loaded. Norm's catching and managing and he comes out and says, "Come on, bear down, settle down." So all of a sudden I just lost it and started screaming, "I'm sick and tired of listening to you. I've listened to you all my life. If you're so damned smart, you guess what's coming!" And now I'm pitching with the bases loaded and he missed all three pitches. All three runs come in, right? So the next day in the paper it has, "Hermanos Guerran [Brothers Fight]. One brother going back to the United States." I didn't go but if the truth be known, Norm was very instrumental in my career. Norm was older and a really good player and you couldn't ask for a better teacher. He knew me so well.

Walt Alston, a very good manager. A quiet presence. He didn't talk much to the players. I think the first couple of years I thought that maybe there should have been a little more communication. But then I learned that that was what he was like. And if he had any applause for you you read about it in the paper. There's a famous story about Alston losing the diamonds from his World Series ring that I'm right in the middle of. Koufax and I were—this was in spring training, 1960, maybe 1961. But we were ready and it's like a week from the end of spring training and you're bored and you want to get on with the season. Sandy and I decided to go down to Port St. Lucie to get a pizza. We don't make curfew and when we get back it's late, but not that late. Now Williams is Sandy's roommate and I'm in with Podres. We're in the barracks at Dodgertown on the other side. And just as we're coming in a poker game breaks up in Williams's room, which is right across the hall from where Alston's room is. Walt has probably been asleep for hours and he wakes up and is mad and looks in the room and sees that Koufax isn't there and says, "Where's Koufax?" Now here we come walking into all this semi-innocent. Unfortunately, we have to come up the stairs and go right by Alston's room. Now Sandy starts to go in his room and I head on down the hall. Walt comes firing out and starts, "Hey, where in the hell have you two been?" Then he yells at me, "Sherry!!!" So I went on in my room. There was this little night latch on the door and I turned it. Alston's right behind me, trying the door. It won't open and he's out there shouting for me to open the door. I just didn't do it. So he starts banging on the door and when he did, he knocked the diamond out of his 1959 World Series ring. Never found it. A real sore point because he never found it. So I got fined. But they needed something like that to get the team going. After that Koufax was always yelling, "Sherry, check your door for diamonds!" And Buzzy Bavasi [Dodgers general manager] liked that. He thought things like that helped get the club fired up. They fined me about $300. But later Buzzy gave the money back.

There was a lot of fun in the bullpen when you're out there with guys like Stan Williams. Here's a Williams story. Frank Howard, the gentle giant, about 6'7", probably one of the strongest guys to ever play in the majors. He wasn't playing a lot and he wanted to come down and watch the games with us from the bullpen. In Philadelphia they've got this maintenance room right next to the pen and they've got dirt piles and tractors and stuff in there. They had this rope down there. Stan makes this noose and gets on top of this dirt pile. He decides we'll invite Frank down there and get him to go into the maintenance room. Then we'll tie him up, keep him in there during the game. So, Stan's 6'4" and he goes about 225. We lure Frank in there, Williams comes pouncing down off the dirt pile with the noose. And Frank just picks him up and tosses him back over the dirt pile. The rest of us ran for the bullpen. Frank comes out and just looks at us and says, "You oughtin' to be doing that. You oughtin' to be doing that!" Didn't even lose his temper.

But I'll tell you what—I saw Frank mad one time and that was enough. That was in St. Louis when Turk Farrell was in the Dodgers pen. It was St. Louis, because it was Sportsman's Park. They had the metal bar and then they had rocks in front of the dugout. I guess it was so the fielders would know they were getting close. And Alston was doing an interview in the dugout. Howard was playing pepper in front of the dugout but down aways. Farrell lines himself up at an angle behind the pepper game. He's hiding behind the corner of the dugout and he starts bouncing balls into the dugout right next to Alston's head. Walt's trying to concentrate on the interview and these balls keep caroming off the rocks and hitting the dugout wall right next to his head. After about the second one Walt loses it and screams at Howard, "Frank, if you can't play pepper, take that damned game out in the outfield!" This embarrasses Frank. This was 1960 or 1961 and the pitchers on the road will do their running and then go back in and put on a dry shirt. Frank, instead of taking his outfield throws and staying to take his fly balls like they do in the outfield before every game, he came right into the clubhouse because he knew all the pitchers were in there. Now Turk's a pretty big guy, he's like 6'4", 225. And so Frank says, "Farrell, you're the one throwin' them balls at Alston and you got him mad at me!" And Turk says, "You're a liar!" Boy, I'll tell you. Frank says, "You called me *what*?" Now the veins are standing out on Howard's neck. It took about five of us. We got in front of Frank. And we told Farrell to get the hell out. Farrell says, "Oh, he ain't gonna do nothin'!" Then Frank says, "Nobody calls me a liar!" Farrell's starting to get the message because the veins are just throbbing. And Frank is the kind of guy we could do anything with him in fun—slap him . . . hell, I've seen them throw at him in a ball game and he'd come in and say, "Oh, he wasn't throwing at me." But not that time. They got Farrell out of there and nothing happened. But that was big league history there because nobody had ever seen Frank Howard mad. None of us ever wanted to see it again, I'll tell you that.

Farrell was something. A major character. There are so many of the old Dalton Gang stories. That was the bullpen crew's name in Philadelphia—Farrell, Morehead, Owens, and Meyer. Jim Owens was on the Houston club in 1967 and then worked as a coach and he told me these stories. It got so bad in Philadelphia that they put them all in the same room. So at least the rest of the guys would be all right. They carried guns, started bar fights. Hurt a reporter real bad up in Buffalo—beat him up, dropped something on him, I don't know what it was. But they, the Dalton Gang, were renowned and Farrell was the ringleader. And yes, I've heard the story about *Sports Illustrated* writing the article about them, calling them the Dalton Gang and that Farrell was going to sue. But he couldn't because everything in the article was true.

Characters? I was in Detroit from 1964 through 1967, split a year between Houston and Detroit in 1967 and ended my career with California in 1968. But now in Detroit—Denny McLain, I've got some McLain stories. The year he won twenty, 1966, I must have saved, oh, six or eight ball games for him. We had a chance to win at the end of the season, to finish second instead of third. It was his chance to pitch but he'd already won his twentieth game and he didn't want to pitch. Man, I got out in the outfield before that game and I chewed his ass out. He was great between the lines when he took the ball, but boy, I didn't like that. And the other thing was, his favorite line was, "If I'm lying, may God strike me dead!" And when there were thunderstorms in Detroit, the first bit of lightning, everybody would scatter from McLain. Yeah, he was a character.

Here's another one. A bullpen guy—Tracy Stallard, the guy who gave up the home run to Maris. I played with Tracy. We were in spring training and Bill Faul was a bullpen guy with the Detroit club for years. Faul was the guy who used to bite the heads off dead frogs and hypnotize himself. Faul was married and he had his car down there in spring training. And you've gotta know Tracy Stallard. He's from up in the hills of Bristol, Virginia. We're having a few drinks and we want to go down to Daytona. So Tracy asks Faul to borrow his car. And Bill says, "I'm not giving you my car, you've been drinking. You might crack it up." And Tracy says, "Yeah, but you wouldn't know about it until I brought it back!" That was Tracy, that Southern drawl—the way he said, it didn't really sound so bad, kinda made sense. He was a character. He missed a starting assignment in New York when he got traded over there to the Mets from Boston. This was when the Mets were going bad and they played a twelve o'clock game. Tracy is supposed to start. Well, he shows up thinking it's a one o'clock game. The game's on when Tracy arrives and Stengel says, "Stallard, where the hell were you? You were supposed to start!" And Stallard says, "Case, you schedule a game at twelve o'clock. I don't get through throwing up until about eleven."

I'm jumping ahead here but the Stallard story reminds me of another one. Pitchers are hard to keep happy. There's only one out there at a time and so there's a lot of unhappy guys waiting in line. In 1977, 1978, I'm the pitching coach with Pittsburgh. Chuck Tanner is the manager and we've got Will McEnaney, the guy who was so good with

Cincinnati when the Big Red Machine was rolling. Tanner uses Will early in the season in Chicago, brings him in to pitch to two left-handers and he can't get either of them out. After that, Will hasn't pitched in about two weeks and so he comes to me and says how he'd like to get in the ball game. And I understood. I kept a running chart and so I tell Chuck that Will's upset and wants to have a meeting. Well Chuck gives him the old rah-rah—it's a twenty-five-man team and you're part of the . . . the whole build-up thing. So that day we're down about 7–1 in the seventh inning. Our pitcher's due to hit, so I come up to Chuck because this is the pitching coach's job. I say, "Who do you want to get up? Do you want to use McEnaney?" And Chuck says, looking at his chart, "Let's see, if Stennett, Moreno, and Taveras get on and Stargell hits one out, then we're only two down. . . . No, get Tekulve up." He just wasn't going to use him. McEnaney was pretty discontent.

At the end of that season we're playing at home, in Pittsburgh, and now Will's got a twin brother. They're identical and both have these full beards. It's time for the National Anthem and I'm standing there next to Will. As the anthem starts, I hear Will say to the guy on the other side of him, "Which bullpen are we in?" And I look back and it's his twin brother. He's in Will's uniform ready to head out to the pen. Will had dressed and left the park. Now I'm thinking what happens if Tanner calls for McEnaney. It would have been bombs away! He didn't get the call. But the twin was out there all day. Showered after the game, the whole deal. But I'll never forget that double take I took during the anthem. 'Which bullpen are we in?' I'm thinking, I've got a guy pitching for me who doesn't even know which bullpen we're in!

TIM McCARVER
Catcher

ST. LOUIS CARDINALS, 1959–1961, 1963–1969
PHILADELPHIA PHILLIES, 1970–1972
MONTREAL EXPOS, 1972
ST. LOUIS CARDINALS, 1973–1974
BOSTON RED SOX, 1974–1975
PHILADELPHIA PHILLIES, 1975–1980

- **Won Game Five Of 1964 World Series With Extra Inning Home Run**
- **Runner-Up To Orlando Cepeda As National League's MVP In 1967**
- **Steve Carlton's Personal Receiver**

Tim McCarver, baseball's four-decade player and energizer, just won't quit. He's still going. McCarver, one of the game's great analysts for CBS-TV and WWOR-TV in New York City, is the best in every booth he's ever been in. We met in Port St. Lucie, Florida, at the Mets winter home during the strike of 1990. As we sat perched on little blue stools in the Mets empty locker room, it occurred to me that this must be what it's like in the pen. Two catchers, one a great talker, one a great listener, engaged in topical conversation—a little hitting, a little pitching, a couple of laughs every now and then. "Now Bob Gibson—Gibby was something. This is a good bullpen story," McCarver laughs.

This was spring training, 1973, when I was with the Cardinals. We were all asked to go over and talk to the minor leaguers at their camp to relate our experiences, give them a feel for what it's like in the big leagues. So every week one guy from the big league camp would go over. This one time Gibby's over there talking to them and this little guy, about nineteen years old, a reliever, raises his hand and says, "Mr. Gibson, I seem to have good stuff in the bullpen, but when I cross the white lines I don't have as good a stuff." And Bob very seriously said, "Well son, there's a nerve that goes from the shoulder to the asshole. When you cross that white line your asshole has a tendency to shrivel up." And the kid is shaking his head, going, "Uh huh, I know what you mean."

We all about fell over laughing. But you know, it is true. A lot of guys throw well in the pen and then once they're in the game and they put that hitter up there, it's different. That's something that you learn when you come out of the pen.

I know that the opinion that most people have is that it's a zany feeling in the bullpen and that relief pitchers have to have a couple of wires loose. Maybe that's true. We used to say, you have to have brass balls to be a short reliever, and you really do. That's one of the reasons that so many of them are viewed as zany, wacko and crazy, because they're doing something to relieve the pressure. Because every time they come in they're in a pressure cooker. The zaniest by far was Tug McGraw. I didn't know this, but in 1975 when I went back to the Phillies, he told me this story. When he was out of high school [playing for a junior college] I was a catcher with the Cardinals and we were playing in that 1964 Series. He said he used to listen [to the radio] and he'd imagine just throwing to me. Because my name was McCarver and his was McGraw. Tug McGraw and Tim McCarver. In 1975 we were together in Philadelphia and you would think that the story has a great ending. Wrong! Every sign I put down for Tug there was a line drive on the other end of it. I mean Tug and I were so bad together. It seemed like every pitch I called would backfire on Tug. It's funny now but wasn't then.

I had an opportunity to catch some good ones. Lindy McDaniel, in St. Louis, was one of the first great pen guys or relief pitchers that I had the pleasure of catching. He's a preacher, and has a church out in Kansas City, I think, now. Lindy was very stoic in the bullpen, concentrated on everything and rarely, if ever, messed around with anything.

Joe Hoerner was an excellent relief pitcher. Joe pitched for about a dozen years in the majors and did it with basically one pitch, a fastball. And he really didn't throw all that hard but he had a lot of guts, and that's what a reliever really has to have. One of the best fielders I've ever seen was Bobby Shantz, and he pitched quite a bit of relief. It made it that much more difficult because he was a reliever. Relievers have to get good and loose not only to throw the ball but to field their position. And another guy who was very serious was Gene Garber. Gene always wanted you to hold your mitt in a certain spot and you did what they wanted you to do. Hal Woodeshick was a good relief pitcher, he had that great year with Houston, I think twenty-three saves in 1964. I was with him later in St. Louis for a while. Nobody in the pen wanted to get up to catch him. You'd almost have to draw straws to get someone to catch. He was nasty, had that sinker, and he was real wild. And a lot of the time he'd throw the ball in the dirt and you'd have to "olé" them, but he was a member of the 1967 Cardinal team.

Mike Marshall was a great relief pitcher. I caught him for a while in Montreal in 1972. Mike and I didn't really get along, but Mike was blatant about blaming somebody else when a guy got a hit off of him. That happened to me once in Montreal. I didn't catch him that much, usually John Boccabella was his catcher. He preferred to throw to Boccabella. But Mike Marshall was the best reliever that I have ever caught. He was the Cy Young Award winner in 1974 but he was not a real likeable guy.

Another relief pitcher was Al Hrabosky, the Mad Hungarian. I was with the Cardinals before Al really came into his own as a short reliever, which was like 1975, 1976, 1977. There's a great Danny Ozark story about the Mad Hungarian. I was with the Phillies then and we were sitting on the bench one day. We couldn't get a hit off of Al to save our tails and Danny was fuming. Finally he just stood up and shouted, "Come on guys, let's send this guy back to Hungaria!"

And yes, I think some of them like to perpetuate the fearsome image. Gossage, for instance, with the Fu Manchu mustache, and Hrabosky, they're both out of the same kennel. Again, of the pen guys that I caught, Gossage certainly ranks up there. He was fastball/slider, and definitely one of the top—McGraw in the 1980 Series. Of course the game is changing, the Sutters, the split-finger, I guess they'll be coming up with another pitch. Ted Williams said that the slider made it tougher to hit because it was just one more pitch to look for. And any pitch that can serve as the illusion of a strike and have a hitter swing.

My name is linked to Steve Carlton because I was his catcher in Philadelphia. Lefty wasn't a relief pitcher but the bullpen is also involved when a guy starts. Carlton used to go into a trance-like state in the pen before he would warm up and I used to think that he was just taking a nap. But what he was doing was visualizing the outside lane and the inside lane of the plate under the theory that thought precedes action and you keep the ball away from the fat part of the plate. And it worked for him.

Bill Faul was one of those guys who practiced self-hypnosis in the bullpen. He was a reliever and starter for the Cubs and he was goofy as hell. They had stories about him biting the heads off of live frogs. But Faul proved that even with hypnosis, if you don't have a good fastball you can hang it up. He may have been a good hypnotist but. . . .

One of the guys that I was with at St. Louis certainly qualifies as the quintessential pen man . . . Bob Uecker. I was with him in St. Louis for several years. And I guess one of my favorite memories of Uke was during batting practice in the 1964 Series, he was shagging fly balls with a tuba.

One more bullpen story. One of my all-time favorites was a guy named Ron Willis. Ron died back in the 1970s. He was a good relief pitcher with the Cardinals in the mid-sixties and a very funny guy. Always with the self-deprecating humor. Well Ron had no chin and one of his favorite lines was that he liked to help his wife around the house but, "You know the chin hurts me with this one chore," he'd say. "I'm really weak . . . putting pillow cases on pillows."

But it's not necessarily always zany or screwy out in the bullpen. The guys actually try to watch the game. And when pitchers and catchers get together, for the most part, they talk about hitting and pitching. We all tried to watch the game and everything. As a youngster you tried to pick up as much information as you could. I remember once, and this still sticks out in my mind. Eddie Mathews was a notorious off-speed hitter and one day he hit a changeup for a home run. Gene Oliver was behind the plate. Our pitching coach out in the pen was Howard Pollet. And he just berated Ollie—this is a typical pitcher talking—he berated Ollie for calling the pitch as opposed to Larry Jackson for throwing it.

Here's another for instance, the kind of story that you'd hear in the pen. Hank Aaron was the best hitter that I ever played against. When I played with Musial, he was in his late thirties and early forties so I never got a chance to see him in his prime. I saw Aaron in his prime. I never saw Aaron break a bat, I never saw him get jammed. He hit balls on the good part of the bat probably more than any hitter I ever saw. Lew Burdette and Warren Spahn told me that they picked up Aaron's bat in June one year. He'd used the bat all spring and there was this little ball and a half area right on the sweet spot of the bat where there were ball marks. There were no marks anywhere else. Nowhere else, just in the sweet spot.

We used to talk about pitchers getting away with bad pitches and hitters hitting good pitches. Hitters will do that too. There are danger areas in the strike zone and you have to know them. There are pitchers that have had so much preached to them about keeping the ball down that they think that if a ball is down and in, that it's a good pitch. Well I used to tell them that if down and in wasn't a good pitch to hit, they'd make golf tees a hell of a lot higher. So you don't jam guys and get outs on pitches down and in. Down and away is a different deal because now you've made him reach. But if you raise that ball inside to the hands, that's where you can jam them and that's a great pitch.

The beauty of the game is this. It changes, each situation differs depending on the hitter, pitcher and game situation. But generally you want to stay ahead and expand the strike zone. The more you're ahead, the more you can afford to tease the hitter and throw the ball out of the strike zone. But if you're not ahead, you squeeze the strike zone. And you are more inclined to throw the ball on the fat part of the plate. So it's not necessarily a walk that gets pitchers in trouble. It's what happens before they have a chance to walk the guy, what they do to prevent a walk, it's the 2–1 or 2–0 pitch right down the heart of the plate, and the guy gets the good part of the bat on the ball. A lot of people think that if a guy is wild then he walks a lot of guys. But it's the guys that are what Don Drysdale calls "wild in the strike zone" that get into big trouble because their pitches are too good. I mean you can throw strikes but if the catcher never catches it? All of this is the beauty of the duel.

As far as throwing at hitters or coming inside, I don't think relievers have the luxury of doing that as often because, if they walk or hit a guy, then the cat's out of the bag. So they are often in a position where they have to throw strikes and there's more of a sense of immediacy with the short man than with any other player. He's in there to close the game. For a short reliever, you really have to get ahead of the hitters. I think a short reliever should be used to start innings.

Sometimes you can't help it, sometimes you feel like a guy's got good stuff and for some inexplicable reason he goes out there and guys get hits and he can't get anybody out. So then you have to bring in your short man in the middle of an inning, but I think that most good managers bring in the short man at the beginning of the inning to keep out of trouble as opposed to getting somebody else out of trouble. You've got a little more leeway if you do get somebody on. Then you can get the double-play ball. But if you come in with the bases loaded, then it's imperative that you stay ahead because if you walk somebody, it can be the tying or winning run.

Some managers use bullpens better than others. Often the reason for that is because they have better bullpens to use. I don't think that anybody gets any more mileage out of their relief pitchers than Whitey

216

Herzog. He's always thinking ahead and always has the right guy up regardless of whether the guy's in trouble or not. If you can get beat by the home run then he's going to bring in the best pitcher that he has to deter a guy like Strawberry or McReynolds. Nobody does it any better than Whitey. Whitey, number one, knows the value of left-handed relievers. You know left-handed relievers can neutralize both left-handed and right-handed hitters better than a right-hander. The reason is complex. It's various things with various pitchers, it's different with each pitcher.

Bruce Sutter came in and was so phenomenally successful with the split-finger over a period of time. That pitch helped neutralize the left-handed/right-handed relief pitcher decision, because when it's effective it's as tough on the left-handed hitters as it is on the righties.

And of course the prominence of the relief pitcher is here today, much more so than ever before. Has it made the game better? I don't think that there's any question about it. I think that the hitters, Williams is one who has said that it's tougher to hit today, and the reason is because you have a lot of left-right advantages. Back in the early sixties there were few teams that had pitchers who were all quality starters. When you went into a town you knew that you were going to see at least two starters that you'd pay your way into the park to have the opportunity to hit against, guys that you knew didn't really have great stuff. But with the advent of the bullpen and the age of speciality, I think it's made it very difficult to hit. Even if you are a switch hitter you're going back and forth across the plate and taking a different look. Usually if you face a starting pitcher the chances of getting your bat on the ball goes dramatically up the more times you see him. So if you face him the second time the chances of you getting a hit are greater than the first time, the third time even more so. You've seen the guy, he's weakening and you're getting more familiar with his stuff. But of course the bullpen has grown in stature, really changed the game. Those starters are rarely around when the game winds down.

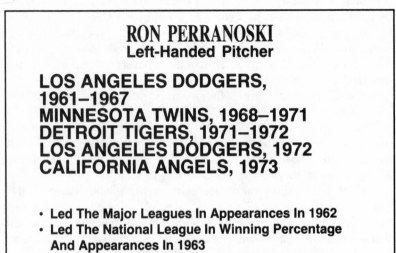

RON PERRANOSKI
Left-Handed Pitcher

LOS ANGELES DODGERS, 1961–1967
MINNESOTA TWINS, 1968–1971
DETROIT TIGERS, 1971–1972
LOS ANGELES DODGERS, 1972
CALIFORNIA ANGELS, 1973

- **Led The Major Leagues In Appearances In 1962**
- **Led The National League In Winning Percentage And Appearances In 1963**
- **Named *The Sporting News* American League Fireman Of The Year In 1969 And 1970**

Ron Perranoski is dressed Florida-casual today—white knit golf shirt, fawn slacks, white loafers. It's spring training, 1990, and I've caught the Dodgers pitching coach relaxing behind the screen in Dodgertown's Holman Field. He's watching a big right-hander from Los Angeles's Albuquerque Triple-A Club work a few innings of relief.

Perry is smiling and tanned from a winter of golf. Seeing him up close confirms my opinion. Ron Perranoski does look a bit like Bill Dana, the comedian who played Jose Jimenez on the old "Steve Allen Show." A fan stops by and asks for an autograph. He obliges, but the eyes never stray from the mound. I glance down at my notes, have second thoughts, then go ahead and test his sense of humor. "They called you bad body in high school?"

Yes, it's true they called me "Bad Body." And rightfully so. I only weighed about 130 pounds my freshman year in college. I'm from Fair Lawn, New Jersey, and I got started as a pitcher there in high school. I was really thin but I got scholarship offers to Michigan State and Notre Dame. And Dutch Dotterer, a Chicago White Sox scout from Glen Rock, made arrangements for me since I didn't want to sign right away. He made the connections with Michigan State so I received a scholarship there. I always had a pretty good breaking ball. My ball moved but I didn't throw the ball all that hard. We won a state high school championship at Fair Lawn High. Then I went on to Michigan State, pitched four years there and then signed with the Chicago Cubs organization. Then there was a trade where I went to the Dodgers for Don Zimmer. That turned out to be the biggest break of my life for me career-wise, even after my playing days were over, because I've been with the Dodgers organization now for twenty-five years.

I had always had a curveball but there was a time when I had a problem with it. It was my senior year in college. I hurt a muscle in my forearm and I really lost my curveball then. So I came up with more of a slider-type breaking pitch, so I kind of limited myself and couldn't really break off the curveball. I started getting the confidence back in throwing the curve in Montreal [Dodgers Triple-A club]. And a lot of that was due to the help of Ralph Mauriello, a Montreal pitcher. Mauriello, Al Campanis and Tommy Lasorda all helped me. So I started coming more over the top, finally got the rotation again, and the break came back. I went to winter ball, came to spring training with the Dodgers and made the ball club.

Danny Ozark was the manager at Montreal and he was the guy who sent me to the bullpen originally. And to tell you the truth, when that happened there in the minor leagues and being that young, I didn't understand the thinking behind it. But in 1961 when I came to spring training, that was the next year, I knew where the opening was on the Los Angeles Dodger pitching staff. It was in the bullpen. And then once I got a taste of it [relief pitching] that spring, they used me in relief that whole spring, and I just loved the challenge. I took to it right away. I'd developed the sinker in winter ball, and as a matter of fact, my fastball always did sink, but I really started concentrating on it in winter ball. It came about during a game I pitched in San Juan in the play-offs. I won the ball game and after the game, a fellow by the name of Ron Samford, a second baseman who played for Roches-ter, came up to me and said, "Ron, you know your ball sinks so much that when you make a mistake, you still get away with it." And that kind of stuck with me and I thought, you know, all these years that was just kind of a natural sink. If I kept the ball down the bottom would fall out. Then I started concentrating on keeping the ball right around the hitter's knees, and ended up developing the consistent sinker. They ended up swinging at balls down out of the strike zone. They had to, because if I got ahead they had to swing at my pitch. And I always had the confidence in the breaking pitch, so one pitch complemented the other.

Nineteen sixty-one was my rookie year. And when I think of that, I have to go back to the spring before because again, I knew the opening was for a lefty in the bullpen. I remember that Don Newcombe was making kind of a comeback at that time and with all his experience as a big league pitcher and the great star that he was, I didn't know what they had in mind for their staff. But they kept putting me out there and kept putting me out there and, fortunately, I kept getting people out. I remember that we were going down to West Palm Beach to play Kansas City, who trained there at the time, and Larry Sherry who was, of course, the star of the 1959 World Series. They started him that particular game and he pitched seven innings, a 2–0 shutout. Newcombe was warming up and then all of a sudden they got me up. To see if I could hold the lead, I guess. And I knew that that was the most important game of my spring training. They were really going to test me. When I came in there were men on first and third with nobody out. And who's up there but Hank Bauer. My God! I grew up watching Hank Bauer with the Yankees. He, of course, was with Kansas City then, and I ended up throwing him a 3–2 curveball and he hit the ball back to me. That was one out and then I got a double play to get out of the inning and I shut them out the rest of the way. I remember thinking at that time that was it, the biggest game for me. Even after the season started, people would ask if I was nervous during big games in my rookie year. I wasn't really nervous because the biggest pitches that I had to make were in that spring training game in West Palm. I had to make those pitches to make the club. I had no contract and after that I signed a Dodger contract. It's kind of like league play-offs and the Series. The Series is the biggest thing in the world but you have to win the play-offs to get there and that's where the pressure is.

In 1962 I had seventy appearances. I was used against both left-handed hitters and right-handed hitters and I have to give a lot of the credit for my success to Larry Sherry for helping me in the mental part of the game. He taught me how to warm up. Being the only left-hander in the bullpen in 1961, hell, if they were in trouble I'd get up in the first inning, again in the sixth if they were in trouble, in the eighth, the twelfth, keep getting up and down the whole game. And after about four or five days I was worn out. And I hadn't even been in a ball game yet. Sherry really talked to me and helped me as far as my warm-up procedure was concerned.

I guess one game that sticks out that year was the play-off game in 1962. We had come down to the end of the season having an opportunity to win the pennant outright and for whatever reasons couldn't seem to do it. The result was a best two-out-of-three play-off with the Giants. It was the last game of the play-offs. Ed Roebuck had a two-run lead but he loaded the bases and Stan Williams and I were both warming up. They brought Stan in to pitch to Cepeda. The next hitter was Ed Bailey, the left-handed hitting catcher. I think that there was an out and now we were down to a one-run lead. I had told Stan, I said, you get Cepeda and I'll get Bailey. Well he walked Cepeda and ended up pitching to Bailey and walking in the lead run too. I'm still in the bullpen. In fact, Drysdale and Koufax are both down there too. Then I came in and got the final out, struck out Bob Nieman, but it was too late. But that was a tremendous learning experience for me. Because fellows like Duke Snider were still on the ball club. It was kind of the end of his career but you know darn well that one more World Series would have been great for people like that. And I really got the feel of the atmosphere in that clubhouse after it was over, what it was like to lose a pennant like that. It was devastating.

And I think that it had something to do with the way we bounced back the next year and won the pennant and World Series. [Perranoski was 16–3, with twenty-one saves in 1963.] There was a period during that year where I think I pitched thirteen games without giving up a run. What I recall about that particular string is that you just get into a groove. There was one game against the Cardinals that I think I pitched six innings. You just get into a roll where you go out there and feel so comfortable. You make a pitch knowing that you are capable of making it when and where you want to. It's a lot of fun being out there. The plate gets bigger and you're moving the ball around. You're making the pitches according to the situation and you just have full command.

I guess because of the circumstances the big game that year was the one in September against the Cardinals, considering how things had turned out with the Giants the year before. We had lost the first game in the series and then Koufax came back and beat them in the second game. But if the Cards won the third game, they'd have been something like three games back with only a couple of weeks in the season. When I came in, in the eighth inning, it was 5–4, the Cards up by one. I got them and then in the ninth Dick Nen hits a home run to tie it up for us. I think this was his first big league hit. Now it's tied 5–5. I pitch the bottom of the ninth and get them in the bottom of the tenth. Then in the eleventh it's still tied of course. Dick Groat led off the bottom of the twelfth with a triple and Walt [Alston] came out to talk to me. He wanted to know if I wanted to walk the bases loaded. And I looked at the next hitter coming up and it was Gary Kolb, a left-handed hitter. I believe that Ken Boyer and Bill White were behind him. So I said, "You know, Walt, if they let Gary Kolb hit, I'd kind of like to pitch to him and see if I can strike him out. Go for a strikeout and if that happens then I wouldn't mind walking Boyer and White to load the bases." They were experienced hitters who could certainly handle left-handed pitching. And he said, "Well, whatever you feel like doing is alright with me." So that's exactly what happened. I struck out Kolb, we walked Boyer and White and then got two ground balls, a ground ball force at home and a ground ball to third to get Mike Shannon. Then I went on to pitch through the thirteenth and get the win. And that one turned around what would have been a two-game lead to a four-game lead in September in a pennant drive. I would have to say that one is probably as big a game as I ever pitched in and won. There were so many but that one stands out. The year before, after losing the pennant like we did, I think that every writer and media person in baseball covering that St. Louis series was wondering if the Dodgers would fold. Again, it ended that year with us beating the Yankees four in a row.

Somewhere before that Series I was quoted as saying that the left-handed Yankees didn't worry me. But I'll tell you I would have never said that. My God, I think that some writer must have said that. I always had more respect for those guys than you can imagine—Mantle, Maris, Berra, Blanchard—I just tried to go out there and do the job that I had to do, and hoped that I could get away with it. In that particular series I think that Ron Fairly and I were the only two, other than the starters, that got into the Series. I came into Game Two and got the save for Johnny Podres. Koufax struck out fifteen in the first game and then Drysdale three-hit them in Game Three. My memories of that series? Growing up in New Jersey and going to all those Yankee games as a kid I had watched number 11, Joe Page, jump over that bullpen fence to come into the games. As a kid, I'd say, "Someday I'm going to do that." And I did. I jumped it just like Joe did when I came into Game Two.

Billy Martin? Martin gave me the opportunity to pitch when I was traded over there to Minnesota in 1968. He was the third base coach. Cal Ermer was the manager, and being new in the organization, Al Worthington was their stopper and a great one. So they'd bring me in to pitch to a left-hander and then take me out and then bring in Al. I only had like six saves that year and eight wins. Then during the course of the year they sent Billy to Denver to get some managerial experience. But before he left I had asked him to do me a favor and talk to Cal Ermer. And Billy did. He told Cal that I really enjoyed getting right-handers out and that he'd taken the guts right out of me by taking me in and out of the games like that. I did understand that

Worthington was the stopper, but if there was an opportunity I'd like to have the chance. The next year Billy Martin became the manager of the Minnesota Twins, and he gave me the opportunity to really pitch. The toughest thing with Billy, everybody knows what a competitor this guy was, I mean he wanted to win about as much as anyone I've ever seen. And so we went to the first game of the season. Tommy Hall was the starter. This is the first game that Billy Martin ever managed in the big leagues. And I came in and pitched two and a third innings or whatever, and they pinch-hit for me. I didn't give up any runs but we lost the ball game in extra innings to Kansas City. We get to the second game, the same thing happens. I pitch like three and a third innings, he finally pinch-hits for me. I ended up pitching in like four straight games and not giving up a run. Billy still hasn't won as a big league manager, and in that fourth game, I pitched like an inning and a third and I was going to be like the second hitter the next inning. Billy comes out to the mound and I can see that his veins are jumping out of his neck. Game Four and he still hasn't won. And he says, "How do you feel?" And I say, "Billy, I feel fine," which I did. But I said, "If you don't hit for me I might have to pitch at least another two innings and, if that happens I won't be able to pitch for you tomorrow." So he hits for me the next inning and we ended up losing again. So we're 0–4. I hadn't given up a run, Billy's really upset but he came up to me after that game and he thanked me. He said, "Ron, God Almighty, I know that you don't want to come out of a game but I wanted to win that first game so bad that I'd lost sight of what was going on here. And I appreciate you reminding me how much you'd been used. Thanks for reminding me." We finally ended up winning the fifth game. That was the year that I went on to have thirty-one saves for him, we won the division, quite a year.

Now Billy Martin—oh Billy—there are some stories there, some that I can't tell, of course. But there are some great memories of Billy. I do have one Martin—again, he was such a great competitor and a great friend of mine. I flew back to New York for the funeral. But, I remember one time when I was with Minnesota, 1969. We'd already clinched the division and we were playing a day game in Metropolitan Stadium in Minneapolis. There was hardly anybody in the stands and I had given up a single to a left-handed hitter. The ball skipped between first and second and a run scored. We'd already clinched and I probably already had twenty-nine or thirty saves at that time. Now keep in mind that the stadium is empty and all of a sudden I hear that water cooler being kicked in our dugout. It's Billy. I can hear him over there kicking the hell out of the cooler, swearing like crazy, and I know that he's second-guessing the damned pitch.

So I snatched the rosin bag from behind the mound and I threw it as hard as I could at the dugout. I was trying to hit him. And luckily it didn't get that far. It landed on the warning track and rolled a little bit. I was mad as hell and I didn't think, I just threw the damned thing at him. Billy never did see it. About a week and a half later, I'm coming out of the clubhouse going down to the bullpen in this runway in Metropolitan Stadium that ran down the right field line. And here comes Calvin Griffith, the owner, he's strolling along heading to his seat. He says, "Ron, I'd like to see you for a minute." I said, "Yes sir," of course. And he proceeds to say, "You know, Ron, I received a letter from a fan a couple of days ago and I'm a little perturbed about this. The fan said that you gave up a base hit in a meaningless game, and then lost your temper, and showed some unsportsman-like conduct to all the kids in the stands by throwing a rosin bag into the dugout." So I just apologized and said, "Yes sir, Mr. Griffith, I got a little mad at myself." Fortunately neither Mr. Griffith nor Billy Martin ever knew who I was aiming that rosin bag at.

When you've been in the game as long as I have, you're going to witness some really great moments—some from the pen, some from the bench and a number of them come when you're out there on the mound. I saw Willie Stargell hit three home runs in Dodger Stadium. The fourth one was hit right down the right field line and it was caught right in front of our bullpen. That was unbelievable, something to watch. Another incident that has gone down in baseball history is the Marichal-Roseboro fight. I had a rather unique perspective of that. At that particular time I had pulled a hamstring covering first base in a game the day before. So I was in the training room, and they were working on me trying to get that fixed up. So I heard the fight on the radio. I'll never forget, all of a sudden they bring Roseboro into the clubhouse. He was bloody all over, his head, his uniform. I'd just listened to what had happened and here he is all bloody. And then Willie Mays came in and talked to John. So I kinda got in there and listened to what Willie was saying. Willie was a peacemaker. What he was doing was apologizing for the use of the bats in the fight. There were apparently some other ballplayers who were going to use bats too, and he was just really upset with that. Not the fight but the fact that anybody would use a bat.

Some nice moments, there were so many. I had the privilege of seeing Koufax no-hitters. The one in 1962 against the Mets is the one that I'll never forget. I used to sit up against the fence in the bullpen in Dodger Stadium and when you sit up against the fence in a chair, you look from there out onto the field. The way the field's sloped you're a little bit lower. And you can see the first deck, the second deck, the third deck and then that fourth piece up there, everything is above you.

It usually took Sandy an inning or two to get going, but in that first inning he threw some curveballs that, from that angle, looked like they were coming out of the third deck. And I said, "This team is in a lot of trouble today." That ball was breaking so big, you knew damned well that he was always going to have a great fastball. And he ended up striking out the first three men on nine pitches and going on to throw a no-hitter. Now that's a memory that you don't forget.

Memories of hitters? Cepeda, and this is one that can be looked up in the record book, but I would say that he probably hit more home runs off of me than any other player. I was mainly a curveball, sinker-ball pitcher and it seemed that he just stepped into those pitches. His groove was right were my ball was sinking and he'd hit me to right center, left field, wherever. And Henry Aaron, I think, hit two home runs off of me, but he never beat me in a ball game. He hit one to tie a game. In fact Sandy Koufax still brings it up to this day. Sandy had a 1–0 lead and I come in in the top of the ninth. The first pitch was to Henry and he hit it over the center field wall out there in Dodger Stadium between those flagpoles. That tied the game. I ended up pitching two or three innings and getting the win. Here Sandy had pitched eight innings and shut them out and then I come in and . . . I really felt terrible about that because it's not my job to come in and let them tie it. Then we come back and I hang on and get the win. But speaking of Aaron, I do remember this. At one time he was eight for eight off of me. And that might have been over the course of a year, but I knew that he was eight for eight. I threw him a sinker and he finally dribbled one, a little roller to first base and I had him. On the way to first base to cover, I'm thinking it's over, I finally got the son of a gun, and I pulled a hamstring muscle. And he beat it out. Nine for nine!

When it comes to bullpen guys, Moe Drabowsky was a real beauty. Moe was a veteran over at Kansas City when I was with the Twins. I still have a souvenir presented to me by Moe and the Kansas City bullpen. What had happened was this. Moe used to have these parties for his bullpen buddies up in his hotel room. In fact Moe would invite guys from the other club over from time to time and one night he invited me and this other guy on our staff, Joe Grzenda, up to have a couple of drinks with them after a game. One night I walked in and Moe's at the hotel in his room in his full dress uniform. That was Moe. On this other particular night, it was in Minnesota and he'd invited Joe and me over to their suite to have a party. I said, "Moe, thanks a lot, Joe and I are going to go out to dinner and then afterwards we might stop by and have a drink." There was a day game the next day. I didn't know whether we would because I knew what Moe's parties were like. I knew damned well that I'd probably be in the next day's game. So, we went out and had dinner and I asked Joe if he wanted to stop by and have a drink. So he said, "Yeah," and we agreed that it would be proper if we brought some refreshments with us. And so I bought three or four bottles of VO and three or four bottles of gin and Scotch. And we brought it up to the room. I walked into that party and they had just a half hour before run out of liquor and the bars were closed. I walk in with that stuff and Joe and I are sudden heroes.

The next day in the bullpen here comes this gift from the Kansas City bullpen. It's an autographed baseball signed by the whole staff. I've got it to this day. It's got the time—12:07 A.M. "To Ron Perranoski from the Kansas City bullpen, thanks for the greatest save of the year."

Moe never forgot his friends. One time they tore up a hotel in Chicago to the tune of about $5,000. He sent me a copy of the bill and a note to Minnesota saying, "Ron, sorry you couldn't be at the party but if you'd like to share in the tab. . . ."

In 1965, John Kennedy was traded over to the Dodgers for Claude Osteen. I ended up rooming with him. John was a great utility infielder, great hands. Along about the end of May, we're playing in Cincinnati and after the game I come back to the room. We had like a couch in this room and here's John sittin' there with his head down. And he had a letter in his hand. I was afraid that someone had died. I walked in and I said. "God Almighty, John. What's the matter, are you okay?" He says, "I just got this letter, it's from the scout that signed me with Washington." He said, "Read the letter." And I read it. It stated how he hoped that everything was going fine with John now that he was with the Dodgers and so on and so on. Then he said, "But I'm a little bit disappointed in you in the fact that when you come into the games, you're not taking charge. You're not going in and talking to that pitcher in tight situations."

This really got to John. He says to me, "Jesus Christ, Perry. Maury Wills is the captain of the team and I come in late in a utility situation. I can't do that!" So I said, "Oh John, you're doing a super job, forget it. This game is tough enough. A guy who comes in to play defense, all he can do is make a mistake. You're expected to make every play so it's almost a no-win situation. The guys love you and you're doing a hell of a job, so just forget about it."

226

It gets to be September, months later, and we're in a big game. I've got the bases loaded, one out, top of the ninth inning. John's playing third and I'm rubbing the ball up, getting ready to make a big pitch. I'm trying my damnedest to concentrate and here he comes from third base, shouting encouragements and carrying on. He gets twenty feet from me and I turn and say, "John, I read that goddamned letter in May. You get back there and play third base and let me do the pitching." Later we laughed, of course, and he said, "No, the scout who wrote the letter wasn't there today, but how the hell did you remember a thing like that in that situation?"

When I was in the pen, I'd really start to pay attention about from the seventh inning on. But before that I'd do crossword puzzles, sit around and relax. I remember in Minnesota, it had to be 1970 because Stan Williams was with us. And we had a day game. It was late in the season and we'd clinched the pennant. It was one of those September afternoon games and hardly anybody came to the games, it was so cold. We had started playing this bullpen game called "coverup." You'd throw the dice and you'd draw twelve numbers in the dirt. The object was to cover all the numbers up. So there was a shed out in right center field where we used to go. You couldn't really see the game from there. We were playing this game and Tommy Hall was in our pen. He was a black guy, a left-hander. Tommy was a real great guy and he always wanted to play the game. And they, as a joke, just wouldn't let him play. So I made up these signs and had him parading up and down in front of the game, waving these signs about discrimination. On that particular day we got involved in the game. We had these little trophies and it was like our championship coverup game—Stan Williams, Tom Tischinski, the pen catcher—we're playing this game and it's coming right down to the nitty-gritty. When it finally ended and we walked out, the stands were empty and they were dragging the field. The damned baseball game had been over for twenty minutes and we didn't even know it. There are so many fun memories of the bullpen but looking out there at that empty stadium, here's the tractor dragging the infield. That's one I'll never forget.

BOB UECKER
Catcher

MILWAUKEE BRAVES, 1962–1963
ST. LOUIS CARDINALS, 1964–1965
PHILADELPHIA PHILLIES, 1966–1967
ATLANTA BRAVES, 1967

- The Most Famous Man In Baseball History To Hit A Career .200
- Operated Baseball's First One-Man Exploding Scoreboard
- Wowed World Series Fans In 1964 With Spectacular Catches In A Tuba
- Grew Up To Be Mr. Baseball

I've got a couple of names for the all-time bullpen battery. Trust me, these guys are solid, you can go ahead and ink them in. "Pitching . . . Moe Drabowsky! Behind the plate, Bob Uecker. Mr. Baseball is your catcher!"

I caught up with Uke in the dugout at Baltimore's Memorial Stadium just moments before he took the mound to pitch batting practice to the Milwaukee Brewers. A busy, busy man—BP pitcher, play-by-play man, author, star of radio, television and cinema.

He is tanned and looking surprisingly good for a man who spends his life being chased through airports, hotels and ball parks by fans screaming, "Bingo! Front row seat!"

I tell Uke that his friend Moe Drabowsky suggested I ask him about the (Drabowsky) story that Johnny Carson wouldn't let him tell on "The Tonight Show." Uke laughs, and in a voice that sounds suspiciously like Mr. Baseball, politely declines. "It was nice of Moe to mention that, but no, I'm not going to tell you that one. The reason is that I don't want to see it in your book!"

I guess you could say it was a forerunner to the exploding score-boards. I used to put on fireworks displays out of the pen in Louisville, Kentucky. That was the Milwaukee Braves Triple-A club. I got the idea at the Kentucky State Fair. I'd seen a pretty impressive display there so I got one of the guys who worked there to leave us about twenty big jobs, those humongous cannons that they shoot off during the fireworks displays. I dug a hole in the bullpen and mounted my launcher in there. And the first time it happened—a very impressive explosion—it shocked everybody. Nobody knew where it came from and I think it was Neil Chrisley who had hit a home run when I fired the first salvo. He was between first and second when I lit it and then it took another two or three seconds before it got to its maximum height and then it blew. Very nice, a lot of color. It was huge, unbelievable really. And well-received by the crowd. It got to be a habit until some of the neighbors started complaining about the noise late at night. But if there was a home run hit I lit one. I didn't care, didn't wait for a signal from management or anything. I started firing them on my own and if things weren't going well and we got a base hit, I'd light one. A walk, anything to get the team going—a single, a walk—I'd fire one of those babies up.

I did some early announcing out in the bullpen. But no particular game comes to mind. We did play-by-play out there every day. And I'm sure that there are similarities in the bullpens today as to what goes on out there. Games that they play, guessing games, name games, word games and everything else. It's boring out there. I mean a lot of times you got a good ball game going and you're into the game. But the blowouts and stuff, what do you do out there? Hell, you sit out there every night. So you do a little play-by-play, light a few of those cannons up.

When I played, I don't know what it's like today, but we never wanted starters out in the bullpen. They used to come out there and try to hide or something. But that was our place. It was for the bullpenners—the pitchers, the relief pitchers and the catchers. You know bullpenners, mostly catchers, you're not good enough to play every day but you're still important to the club because of what you do out there. I've often thought, wouldn't it be great to just send in a pitcher without warming him up. You know they make fun of the bullpenners [catchers]. We'll send him in there cold. They'd probably rip him and kill him and his arm would fall off. This would be great because it would illustrate just how important bullpen catchers are.

When the starters came out to the pen we'd aggravate them, aggravate them to the point where they didn't want to come out there anymore. I don't think that they belong out there. They could go out there before the game to do their throwing or whatever, that's fine. Once the game is underway, unless the manager sends somebody down there to throw in between starts, that's different. But to hang around down there every day between starts like you're a bullpenner, that was a no-no. That was no good at all.

There's a serious time and there's that time, as I said before, where if you're getting blown out of a game then you find other things to do. When you're a catcher, if you're getting blown out you're usually warming everybody up you know. There's always a time to get serious. In Philadelphia the pen was in left field and we had access to the street out there. All you had to do was open the back door where they used to bring in the equipment and everything, all the dirt and tractors out there. And we had that out-of-the-way pen for a long time until Gene Mauch changed it. He put the Philadelphia Phillies bullpen in right field where he could see them because he couldn't see out of the dugout into the pen in left. But we used to go out on the street in our uniforms in Philadelphia.

We had a little bullpenners club in Milwaukee, a nice place until one day Bobby Bragan—he was coaching at the time—he came out there and tore it up. We'd hung a snow fence up underneath the stands and we'd sit there and play cards and you know the usual stuff, light people on fire. We had a little table out there and chairs where we used to sit. When it got cold during the spring and the fall, we'd bring wood out there and burn it. We'd bring stuff out of the clubhouse and light it up—chairs, anything that would burn, we'd break and bring out there. And we had no concern as to who the chairs belonged to, we were just looking for warmth.

Later, this was when I was with Philadelphia, and this had nothing to do with the Milwaukee pen, but we lit Bragan on fire. He was the Houston bullpen coach at that time. Turk Farrell asked me to get some lighter fluid. That was during the bullpen's hotfoot era, everybody was getting them and giving them. And I had gotten tired of the hotfoot business. So instead of waiting to hotfoot somebody, I'd just throw some lighter fluid on their shoe and throw a match on it. Farrell and I did that to Bragan. Farrell just sprayed Bobby's leg and threw a match on it. It was kind of a sick bit of humor, but a very nice flame. Striking colors—and he was moving around pretty good. It didn't last very long but it was pretty impressive.

If you start naming guys who would make good bullpenners—Roger Craig, Tim McCarver, Bill Lee, Warren Spahn, Bo Belinsky, Moe Drabowsky—all good friends and we all had our own little things and laughs. John Boozer, a Phillies pitcher, every time I think of John I think of him eating bugs. That's what he used to do, eat bugs. Anything that you'd put up, he'd eat it. He used to make a lot of people sick doing it but if you enjoy that sort of thing, then I think that you ought to do it. Everybody has their own little thing. He'd pick stuff up and eat it. He liked to do it in front of people. It made them sick but it was a big kick for John.

The tuba incident happened during batting practice at the 1964 World Series. That was something that might be described as bullpen behavior. It was unfortunate, cost me about $250. I don't remember if they took the money out of my World Series check but the club got the money from me. I don't know if the tuba guy ever got reimbursed. It was just one of those things, the Cardinals had a couple of bands playing during the World Series batting practice. One was in right field and one was in left and they took turns playing. And when the band in left field put their instruments down to take a break, they just laid them in the grass over in the corner. I went over and picked the tuba up and started shagging fly balls. I caught a few. A couple went down the hole but more than a couple hit the rim and dented it pretty badly. I made a few running catches with the thing, nothing spectacular. I put the tuba back down when the band was ready to go again. But it was bad, it was damaged. The guy couldn't play anymore. Some of the balls that I caught were jammed down there in the stem of the tuba.

In St. Louis I ran the batting practice league. We chose teams and played out a season during batting practice. One of the teams was called the Avengers. These teams were made up of pitchers, a lot of bullpenners in that BP league. I was the judge because it was my job to throw to the pitchers every day during batting practice. Ray Sadecki managed one pitchers' team and Ron Taylor managed the other pitchers' team. And they had to post a lineup card every day, just like you would in a regular game. My job was to judge each hit and give out points for line drives, singles, doubles, gappers, major league fly balls, balls that rolled to the warning track, that kind of thing. They took the season seriously. Toward the end of the year it was getting pretty close and there was a lot of money riding on the thing. One of the last games that year—it was really getting close to a tie season, I mean it looked like a possible play-off situation—and one of Ron Taylor's guys hit out of turn. Sadecki came to me and filed a protest. When I went to get the lineup card to check it, Ron Taylor ate it. So I had to follow him around for a couple of days, sort of waiting and watching, hoping he'd pass the thing so I could make some kind of a ruling. But the protest went for naught. I never was fortunate enough to be at the right place at the right time. He must have passed it but I wasn't there to make the call.

Great moments? *My* great moments coming out of the pen? I remember coming to the plate and striking out on a Sandy Koufax curveball. This was the strikeout that tied Koufax for the record, most strikeouts in a single season. I'm particularly proud of that. Then Mike Shannon came up behind me and broke the record. It pissed Shannon off. I guess he looked at it differently than I did. But when you start talking about the really big moments, for me it would have to be the spring training game. It was the first intra-squad game in 1964, and in the ninth inning with the bases loaded, I took the pitcher deep in the count, 3–2, and then fastball outside. I walked. I forced in the winning run. You don't forget moments like that.

JIM BOUTON
Right-Handed Pitcher

NEW YORK YANKEES, 1962–1968
SEATTLE PILOTS, 1969
HOUSTON ASTROS, 1969–1970
ATLANTA BRAVES, 1978

- **American League All-Star In 1963**
- **Won Games Three And Six Of 1964 World Series**
- **Wrote Parts Of *Ball Four* On Popcorn Boxes While Hiding Behind Toilet Doors In Major League Bullpens**

Jim Bouton is talking on the phone from the Teaneck, New Jersey, offices of Jim Bouton's Big League Cards. Speaking of Cards, it's been twenty-six years since Bouton beat St. Louis twice in the 1964 Series. But in a sense he's been in the big leagues ever since, vagabonding around the majors and minors trying to sell managers and manuscripts, creating big league products like Big League Chew—a tobacco-pouched shredded bubble gum; Big League Cards—the personnel, products and services card of corporate America; and Big League Ice Cream—a bat-shaped stick complete with autographs from twenty-six of the greats of the game. The guy just won't stop pitching. And summer nights circa 1990, Bouton, the senior (by decades) member of the Little Ferry staff in the northern New Jersey league, was back at it again, baffling hitters in the state's semi-pro Metropolitan League with his "storied" knuckleball.

"Hello, nice to hear from you, yes, I recall your letter. But you'll have to refresh my memory, exactly what is the book again?" I give him the rundown—boy who wanted to spend his life as a bullpen catcher decides thirty years later to check the pulse of the game's great pensters. "The book's name is *Pen Men*? Bob, that title could be a bit misleading in today's climate. Profiles of the game's great pen men—let's see, Denny McLain, Joe Pepitone, Ron Leflore, Pete Rose. Heck, if you wait you may be able to add Steinbrenner to the list. George could do time," he laughs. I sputter. "No, I get the idea, sounds like a fun project. Let's talk," he says.

Giants fan when I was a kid. My dad's favorite team was
my favorite team, so I started rooting for the Giants. And
ieir progress or lack of progress through the late forties and
es. The team didn't have to win in order to love them.
... as a matter of fact, in my neighborhood in Rochelle Park, New
Jersey, you weren't a real baseball fan if you rooted for the Yankees.
It just took more courage, more character to be a Giants fan or particularly a Dodgers fan. These were the Giants of the late forties and early
fifties—Eddie Stanky, Whitey Lockman, Alvin Dark, Walker Cooper
and Sal Yvars, Dave Koslo, Jim Hearn.

When my brother and I weren't talking baseball and listening to the
Giants on the radio we were down the street from our house under the
viaduct. We always played under the viaduct when it rained. That was
the forerunner of the domed stadium. We played stickball. One guy
would take the sidewalk on one side of the street and pitch to the guy
standing on the sidewalk on the other side of the street. There weren't
too many cars back then so we didn't get interrupted too often. The
pitcher would throw into a box drawn on the wall and if you threw it
into the box it was a strike. We used a rubber Spaldeen. And the viaduct was constructed in a way in which they had horizontal lines. If
you hit it in the lower section it was a single, the next section a double,
and if you hit it up where the pigeons roosted it was a home run.

The thing about our games was that we took turns being the Giants.
Sometimes you were the Dodgers but whatever team you were, you
had to come to bat as the actual big league player. Whitey Lockman.
You came to the plate left-handed and it didn't matter if the game was
on the line or whether you were a good left-handed hitter or not.
When Whitey was up that's the way you hit. You also had to adopt
his batting stance. We had them all down pat. I still today can do
Monte Irvin's batting stance and Bobby Thomson. And we were the
voice of Russ Hodges and when we won a really close game we'd
shout, "The Giants win the pennant! The Giants win the pennant!
Bobby Thomson hits it in the lower deck!" We had that memorized of
course.

In fact that moment, the Thomson home run, was the greatest moment of my life as a child. I had just gotten home from school. I had
run home and in those days, the World Series and play-off games were
in the afternoons. So you could listen to them on the radio while you
were in school. Somebody always had a radio. And you could walk
into the halls and people were all asking, "Who's winning? What's the
inning?" And sometimes right during class someone would poke their
head in the door and say, "The Giants went ahead, it's the bottom of
the seventh." Everybody knew what was going on.

So on that famous day in October, 1951, I ran home and got there in time to hear Thomson hit that home run. The first thing I did was start running, out the front door and off to Robert Iriana's house. Robert was one of my best friends and a Dodgers fan. We were in a constant Dodgers-Giants argument. Well, when Thomson hit that home run I ran non-stop from my house. My mother was ironing, "Where are you going?" "Thomson just won the pennant, I'm going to Iriana's house!" He lived way across town and it was the longest run. I think it was about three miles. But I didn't stop, I could hardly wait for some serious rubbing it in. I got to his house and the shades were drawn and the door was locked. And his mother said, "He's not coming out." I stayed out there screaming, "The Giants Win the Pennant! The Giants Win the Pennant!" He didn't come out and not only that, he didn't come to school the next day. He didn't come to school for the rest of that week. His mother wrote him a note saying that he was sick. And she wasn't lying. I'm sure he was sick. He had a broken heart.

That was the greatest moment of my life to that point. And my brother and I would go to the Polo Grounds by bus and subway. We had to learn the routes and figure out how to get around in the city. Eventually we knew our way around, got to be pretty sophisticated little kids. We were going to visit our shrine and it didn't take us to long to figure out the best route to get there. Always got there early and we were always looking for doubleheaders. When we'd hear people say that baseball games took too long, we didn't know what they were talking about. For us they couldn't take too long, they could not take too long. We used to go to the Polo Grounds four hours before a ball game. Then you could get the players coming out of their taxicabs. In those days they took cabs into the park and you'd catch them pulling up and get their autographs. We'd wait out there for the gates to open and we'd have our lunch in a brown paper bag. Our mom would make sandwiches for us, liverwurst or peanut butter and jelly. After about two hours in the hot sun you could tell what everybody was having for lunch because you could see it seeping through the sack. The purple bags were the grape jelly sandwiches. Or you could smell the liverwurst. Sometimes you'd be sitting there in the bleachers and say, "Oh tuna fish!" And then, of course, we'd go up into the bleachers and try to catch the guys hitting home runs during batting practice. We'd run around the Polo Grounds and try to get the balls that the guys hit. A player would swing and we'd be like, "Oh, here it comes!" Your perspective as a kid was, "Oh, that one's going to go out!" And it would fall in somebody's glove way short of the fence. But to us it looked like everything was hit nine miles. And we wanted to catch the balls so badly that we finally got scientific and developed this net, a fish net that we lashed to a bamboo pole. And we practiced in the street in front of our house. We'd throw long fly balls and try to catch them in the net. We did pretty good at home, probably about eighty percent, but lousy at the Polo Grounds. We never caught one in the net. It was so hard to run through the stands because you were banging people in the head with this net. And invariably you'd misjudge the damned thing, but when you're twelve years old . . . Well, it seemed like a good idea. We never got one in the net. We annoyed a few people and got a few fans in the back of the head but we never actually caught a major league baseball in that net. A good idea, in theory.

And we'd shout at the players, pick a number out like, "Hey 48, 48!" Then we'd scramble around and look up the number in our score-card and 48 would be some kid up for a tryout. A high number guy. But the nice thing about the high number guys was that they would turn and wave to you. And one of our things was we'd shout, "Hey, wave to me, wave to me!" It was like we had arrived when they waved.

It was always so fantastic to walk into the stadium and see that green field. And you know what was exciting? To watch the grounds crew, lining the foul lines, manicuring the infield and grooming the grass. So much anticipation. It was like something very important was about to take place. And it was! And we were going to get to watch it.

Then we'd sit there and watch the game and finally look up and say, "Damn, it's already the fourth inning. The game just started and already the fourth inning." But we knew that it was a doubleheader so we always had the next game to look forward to. We always stayed to the last out. We never left early, watched the players take that long stroll to the big clubhouse in deep center field. And to us it was like a whole play or something. You stayed for the stroll. You didn't leave before the last act.

That was the Polo Grounds but later when we were in Illinois—my grandmother had died so my family spent some time out there—and while we were there my brother and I would go to Wrigley Field. One day the Giants came to town to play the Cubs. My brother and I were the only Giants fans in the place and before the game we went down to the Giants dugout. And I was leaning over the top of the dugout shouting at Alvin Dark. My brother had me by the feet so I wouldn't fall in and I'm shouting, "Alvin, Alvin!" I thought it was important and necessary at the time that I explain to Alvin that I was not a Cubs fan, that I was a Giants fan, that I was one of his. I said, "Alvin, wait a second, I'm not a Cubs fan, I'm a Giants fan. I'm from New Jersey, we go to the Polo Grounds all the time, we're just out here visiting relatives!" I gave him my life history and I was sure that it would have some meaning to him. "We're visiting in town, my brother and I have been for you guys since the mid-forties. . . ." I really thought he'd turn around and say, "Oh Jimmy, okay, glad you could come out here, great to see you in Chicago!" Instead he turns around and says, "Take a hike, son!" *Take a hike!* Now my brother still has me by the ankles and so he pulls me back and he says, "Well, did you see anybody?" and I say, "Yeah, Alvin Dark." "Did he say anything? What did he say?" "Take a hike, son!" "Alvin Dark talked to you?" He was so excited and so was I, just the fact that he'd talked to me. My brother was so proud of that, "Hey, Alvin Dark told Jim to take a hike!" And that became a Bouton family put-down line. *Take a hike, son!*

I wrote about that in *Ball Four* and some reporter asked Dark whether he'd said it, and Dark said, "I didn't even know Jim Bouton when he was a kid!" Is that a hoot? Alvin Dark topped himself.

A lot of the book was written in the bullpen and the pen was certainly a great place to have fun. The locker room could be very intense before a game. And the dugout is where the guys are serious, coming on and off the field. The managers and coaches are trying to make decisions there. But in the bullpen it's "Hey, we're not in the game, no pressure on us, pass the sunflower seeds, check the girl in section sixteen!" You are near the battle but you definitely aren't in the front lines. Occasionally the phone rings and that's a mortar round hitting nearby. But for us, no big deal, life was fun and games and the question was, "Do you eat your popcorn now or maybe a hot dog because you're the long man and you could have to go in on a full stomach so. . . ." Decisions, decisions, you know. So you tried to plan your lunch menu as to when you thought you might get into the game. The games and things were usually run by the senior members of the pen. They'd establish the etiquette. I remember Johnny Blanchard being out there when I was a rookie with the Yankees, telling me that he thought I ought to try a little tobacco, that it would help me concentrate. And he was right, it concentrated my lunch. Fortunately I didn't get called into the game because there's a rule in the American League. You can't pitch when you're green. I don't know, maybe that was the inspiration for Big League Chew, the shredded bubble gum that Rob Nelson and I invented.

Some guys had their favorite seating arrangement and it was a lot like pulling up your easy chair at home and watching a ball game. Very relaxed, talking, telling jokes. And of course the first bullpen joke pulled on me, and it's one that all rookies get, usually it happens before you get to the majors. They got me on this one in Greensboro, North

Carolina, I believe. Anyway it goes like this. The crowd will be coming into the ball park and somebody will say, "Good crowd tonight, looks like there's between two and three thousand!" "Two and three thousand, shit there's not that many people here!" And of course the guy swears that he thinks there is and eventually they get you to bet them a dinner and a beer or whatever. And you know you've got them because there's no way there's more than 2,000 people in the park. And they call down to the press box and say, "Well, 955 fans. Pay up!" "Pay up hell! That's not between two and three thousand!" "Sure it is! Five hundred is between two and three thousand." Hell, four is between two and three thousand. And so they've got you. Then you pass it along, a bullpen tradition, another guy in another bullpen.

There were so many good lines that I heard in the bullpen, and many I wrote down and used in *Ball Four*. In the sixties and early seventies there were a lot of players using uppers—dexadrine—we called them "greenies." We'd be sitting in the pen and an outfielder would dive to make a catch and just miss. "Looks like he came up about a greenie short." One day Wilson, one of our pitchers, was warming up and didn't seem to have it. His arm hurt and then he went into the clubhouse, came out and started throwing BBs. "What the hell got into Don?" I said. "About four greenies," somebody answered.

The bullpen in Yankee Stadium is in right field, right center, and in order to get to the pen you could either walk across the outfield or walk around under the stands and go through a little door. And right under the stands, there where all the grounds-keeping stuff was kept—lime, bags of dirt and stuff—you could go back in there and sit and be completely out of view from the park. And I remember walking back there one day and there's Whitey Ford. He's sitting in there at a little table having a pizza for Christ's sake. And he's got a little red-and-white-checkered tablecloth and a wine bottle there. It looked like a little Italian restaurant. And that's right in the Yankee bullpen. This wasn't a game day for Whitey. He'd pitched the day before and was just celebrating I guess.

And then another time Pedro Ramos had a BB gun out there and during the game, there we are under the stands, we've got Coke bottles and cans lined up and we're having target practice. And then sometimes the phone would ring and rudely interrupt. "Whattya mean I've gotta start throwin'? It's my shot! Come ahn, I'm up next!"

And it wasn't always just BB guns. Sometimes the guys had girls down there. The girls would come out of the stands and they'd take them in the back. So I've seen everything in the bullpen.

I remember playing in California. I think it might have been under the Coliseum or perhaps it was Dodger Stadium. Anyway they had these poles under the stands out there and there was this huge area under these poles. And they had these two golf carts to take the pitchers out on the field. And one day we got into those two carts and started slaloming around the poles, using them as an obstacle course. I mean we were flying, "*Rrrrrrooooommmmmm!*" It sounded like a LeMans. Great fun.

There were some great characters. Joe Schultz, the manager of the Seattle Pilots, was one. He stayed away from the bullpen but he would have made a nice addition out there. One day we're losing the first game of a doubleheader—down a couple of runs and Schultz calls John Gelnar over. Gelnar's keeping the pitching chart. "C'mere a second." Now Gelnar figures he's going to get some wisdom from Schultz about pitching and he sits down and Joe says, "Up there near the Section 23 sign. Check the rack on that broad." In the eighth inning of the same game he comes through with the lunch menu. "Well, boys, between games today we have a choice of roast beef, baked ham and tuna salad."

One of my favorites from Schultz was the day he got tossed from a game. He'd been up at home plate giving the umpire the business, kicking dirt and carrying on. He gets the thumb and just as he's about to step down in the dugout he looks up in the stands, sees a good-looking woman and says, "Hiya Blondie, how's your old tomato?" Now we're in hysterics on the bench laughing. Who knows what the hell he meant by that? Nobody to this day knows what he meant by that. But it was funny as hell!

In many ways, the off-the-wall comments reminded you of Casey Stengel. One of his favorites was, "Boys, let's go out there and kick the shit out of them and then we'll come in and pound the Budweiser!"

You can see why the city of Seattle had a hard time taking the Pilots seriously.

Back to the bullpen and *Ball Four*. I made a lot of notes out there. I'd hear a line or a conversation and I'd be like writing it on a popcorn box, and I couldn't write fast enough because some of it was so fantastic. The guys saw me writing but they just didn't know what I was writing about. They thought that I was just making notes on the game. Stuff like "It was a hot day today" and "This has really been a tough series," and "The pitching has been weak and I hope that we'll do better when we get home from this road trip." They had no idea that I was recording the real thing. People have asked, "Did you make some of that stuff up?" But that's something that you can't say. There's a

239

ring of truth there that makes you know it's the way it was. I couldn't have made that stuff up. They knew that I was writing a book but they just didn't know what. Like Fred Talbot said, "Hey, Bouton, writing notes is worse than whispering!" And Ray Oyler said in the back of the bus one day, "If you're writing a book, Bouton, leave me out of it!" No, they knew I was writing a book alright, they just didn't know that it would have that kind of a slant to it.

I remember Jim Owens asking me if I was going to use names in the book. I said that I might once in a while and he reminded me of the story *Sports Illustrated* did on the Dalton Gang—Owens, Turk Farrell and a couple of other wild men in the Phillies bullpen. According to Owens, the Dalton Gang sued and would have gotten a hell of a lot more money in the settlement if one of the guys hadn't attacked a hotel maid a week before the trial. Another Owens line on the Astrodome—"It isn't much but we call it home."

The censorship, I didn't really have a problem with. I decided that I wasn't going to put anybody in bed with anybody. In spite of the criticism from the players I didn't put anybody in bed with the wrong people. All the sexy stories are anonymous. And when it's about somebody's roommate, well they may have had twelve roommates and it could have been about anybody. Like the story about the ballplayer who has the baseball Annie in bed and she says, "Please just tell me you like me!" "Like you?" he says, "Hell, I love you!" So the sexy stories were anonymous and I never quoted anybody making any anti-Semitic remarks or racial slurs and I heard those all the time. So I did use judgment and I didn't just write down everything. Well, I did write down everything because I decided that I wasn't going to try to edit this thing in my head. I was going to be like a recorder. I would record it all and then I'd decide what I was going to put in later.

Lines like Greg Goossen's were tough to lay off of. We're riding in the team bus by some government buildings in Washington and somebody reads a sign that says, "Erected in 1929." Goossen—"That's quite an erection."

Some of the book didn't come during the season. The closing line has been quoted a lot ["You see, you spend a good piece of your life gripping a baseball and in the end it turns out that it was the other way around all the time."] I don't really know when that came. The opening of the book came as a result of a question-and-answer thing between my editor Leonard Shecter and me. He simply asked me why I play baseball and I said, "Well, I'm thirty years old and I have these dreams."

The idea? I did use to take notes because I liked to do talks and things and I've always enjoyed telling stories. I used to do this at my church. I liked telling the stories and they liked hearing them. In 1968 Leonard Shecter did a story about our adoption of David, the Korean baby, and we got to talking. He suggested that I write some stuff down and maybe it would make a book. I don't even remember if we got an advance. I know that the idea didn't turn on the world, about me and the Seattle Pilots. We may not have even gotten an advance, just a "we'll take a look at it." So what happened is the first day of spring training I started taking notes. At the end of the day I'd spread my notes out on the bed and then read them into a tape recorder. I'd write down crucial quotes and fill in the story that night. I did that nightly. Sometimes the quotes I heard at the park were so terrific that I'd have to run to the bathroom, close the stall door, and write it in longhand. The bullpen john and the locker room johns were my writing rooms. Of course, while I was in there I was probably missing a lot of good stuff. I'm writing and finally I get about two weeks' worth and I sent it in. I got this call from Shecter. I had no idea what he'd think. I said, "Is it any good?" and he said, "Bouton, we've got a fuckin' book here!" He says, "This is great shit, if you can keep this up we're in business. Give me a little more physical description, I want to know what these guys look like." He said, "The quotes are great, keep it up." So I just tried to sharpen it up. And still must have missed fifty percent of what happened.

One day I'm standing in the outfield and I'd given up a couple of doubles the day before. One of our pitchers, Skip Lockwood, a really funny guy, comes over to me, all serious. So I figure he wants a tip of some kind. He's got a ball in his hand and he says, "Say, Jim, could you show me how you hold your doubles?"

It was Jim Pagliaroni, a day when we're all getting off the plane, coming off the road, the wives are out there waiting for us, and Pagliaroni says, "Okay everybody, act horny!"

Fred Talbot was one of the wittiest guys in baseball. He was a tough guy, from a tough area. There's a story that Talbot told about shop class. The day they taught them to weld. The first thing they did was weld the classroom door shut. The teacher was welded out of the room. Then they welded all his tools to a tractor.

Here's the thing, I always thought of Fred Talbot as being, you know, a guy I could never be friends with, but I never appreciated Fred Talbot. He didn't like me, what I stood for. I'd look over and in the locker room he'd leer at me. Just the fact that I read the front part of the newspaper offended Talbot. What was interesting when I started to keep notes, I found myself writing down all these things that Fred

241

Talbot would say. I realized that this was a very, very funny guy. I actually came to like Fred Talbot because now I was no longer looking at him as a ballplayer with opposite politics from mine, but as a guy who was a great source of material. When I think of some of Talbot's lines they're hysterical. Just the other day I opened up the book and there was the story about Marty Pattin. Pattin had lost about five games in a row. Well, after his last loss he'd come into the locker room and torn it up. Broke light bulbs in the runway, just tore the place up. So we're in the locker room the night before Pattin's next start and everything's real quiet. Talbot says, "Marty, if you shouldn't win, what are your plans for after the game tonight?" There were so many good Talbot lines, the night he's getting blasted and Schultz finally comes out to hook him, he says, "Joe, what kept you?"

As I said, Talbot and I were at opposite poles politically. One time I was taking the guys to one of my favorite restaurants in Washington, D.C. Talbot looks up and says, "Well, if Bouton recommends it, you can be sure to get some good Communist dishes!"

The greatest put-down line I ever heard in my life was a Fred Talbot original. We're running in the outfield before a game in Minnesota, doing our wind sprints and we're tired. It's hot out there. And every time we come close to the stands there's this one big fat guy sitting up there. He's got like one tooth and and he's giving us all grades of shit. "Hey, you guys sure got your ass kicked in Baltimore!" "Hey, I just figured out your team earned run average. It's 9.3." "You guys got a nice streak going, nine straight losses." And every time we come over to his side of the field, this guy's got more lines, and every time he hits us with one of these put-down lines everybody in the stands is laughing. They think this guy is a real comedian. Every time he says something goofy they all turn around and laugh their asses off. The players aren't saying anything, not even acknowledging him. But we're hearing it, you know. Finally we come back to his side of the field and we're all bending over tired, sweating with our hands on our knees and this guy comes on with another line. And Fred Talbot just looks up, doesn't even take his hands off his knees, and says, "Hey pal, nice teeth you got there!" Everybody in the stands turns around and here's this guy with a goofy look on his face and these two teeth hanging out. And the crowd got hysterical and it was like letting air out of a fat balloon. This guy just collapsed, totally deflated. That's all Fred said, "Nice teeth you got there." No "You're full of shit," "Go fly a kite," or even "Take a hike, son!"

Players are used to hearing that kind of stuff but to me, a writer now, I'm thinking how great that will be for my book. So suddenly

I'm hearing all these lines and I'm thinking of Fred as a terrific guy because I realize he will be a wonderful source for great lines.

He had another funny comment after the telegram incident. The story goes like this. The Pilots had this "Home Run for the Money" promotion, where if a listener gets his name drawn and the guy up hits a home run then the guy gets a jackpot. So Fred Talbot hits a home run with the bases loaded and there's a bonus if the bases are loaded. So a guy in Oregon named Donald Dubois won $27,500. Now I send Talbot a telegram from Dubois thanking him for the home run and saying that there's a check in the mail to Fred for $5,000, an expression of gratitude. I even misspelled Fred's name which I thought was a nice touch. Talbot gets the telegram and falls for it hook, line and sinker. Needless to say, when the word got out that I'd sent the telegram, Talbot was gunning for me. But here's the funny thing. Pagliaroni hit a jackpot for a guy and the fan actually sent him a check. This is like rubbing salt in Talbot's wound. One day we're all sitting in the locker room and somebody, within earshot of Fred, is tallying up what percentage Pagliaroni got from his fan and what that would have amounted to if Donald Dubois had come through for Fred. Talbot says, "Here's what I hope Dubois did with the money. I hope he bought a new car, I hope he got drunk and I hope he got in the car and went out and killed himself!"

There were things that you'd hear in the bullpen or locker room that you didn't actually experience, just good stories or funny lines. And like I said, when the stories started there were times when I couldn't write fast enough. This actually happened out there, during a period when the Pilot pitching staff is really getting hammered. We've got Gelnar starting the game, and somebody asks Bob Locker who's pitching. And he says, "Gelnar . . . and a cast of thousands."

I remember hearing the story about Al Lopez and Bob Shaw. Shaw was one of those guys who had a great hairdo. He was single and he'd come out of the locker room early and strut around in front of the dugout, checking the babes, what the hell, living it up as a ballplayer. So Al Lopez lays this line on him, "Hey, Shaw, I see you with a different broad every night. You really must be a lousy lay!"

Whitey Ford and Mickey Mantle used to love to tell Bill Miller stories. He was up with the Yankees for a short period of time, and certainly wasn't a name player but he made the best of his celebrity. Whitey Ford used to love to tell this one. Miller would go into bars and say things like "Bartender, if there are any phone calls for Bill Miller of the New York Yankees, I'll be in the back!" Mantle had a Bill Miller story that he liked to tell. The first time Casey Stengel put

Bill Miller in a game the Yankees were down by two runs. So Miller gives up like four more runs and now they're down by six. But the Yankees manage to come back and win it. So Miller's the winning pitcher. The next day Casey puts him in in relief again and this time the Yankees are ahead by a couple of runs. Miller gives up four runs again and they lose. So now after the game the writers are all grouped around Miller's locker and he says, "That's baseball, gentlemen. Hero one day, goat the next!"

The beaver shooting that I talked about on the roof of the Shoreham Hotel, in the book, you know nobody ever denies that. It was universal, everybody went up there. Pagliaroni was the guy who had the telescope, Norm Miller had the hole in the dugout.

We had a lot of all-star teams that we made up in the bullpen—All-Ugly. One that was fun was the All-Celebrity team—celebs, if they were ballplayers what position would they play. Smooth-fielding center fielder? Duke Ellington. Alcoholic pitcher? Rip Torn. That kind of thing.

I guess if I were going to make out a lineup card for Jim Bouton's All-Bullpen team, Drabowsky would have to be the captain. And I'd have to have George Brunet out there, quite a character. George is the guy who never wore any underwear shorts. He was the guy that I wrote about. I came into the locker room one day and George was pulling on his pants with no underwear. I asked him why he didn't wear underwear. He said he was afraid that he might leave them somewhere, too risky, why take a chance? I remember when George joined the team Joe Schultz went through this big clubhouse meeting for George explaining the rules of the Seattle Pilots. When he got to the curfew the whole room just cracked up. The idea of George Brunet obeying a curfew was just hysterical. And of course, I'd have to have Talbot out there. Another great Talbot line. We had lost like twelve of our last ten games. We're sitting out there listening to the National Anthem and Talbot says, "Boys, if we get a lead today let's call time out." And you know the funny thing is that in that game we did get a lead and Fred's out in front of the bullpen making the T-sign.

Catchers, let's see . . . I think one of the funniest discussions I ever heard in a bullpen was between Fred Talbot and Merritt Ranew. So let's make Ranew my catcher. They were arguing over which part of the South was the dumbest. And it went something like this. Talbot is telling Ranew that the farther south you get, the dumber they get, so his part of the south isn't as dumb.

Great moments? The first time I ever got called into a big league ball game for one inning of relief, I was with the Yankees in Cleveland.

This was early in 1962 and I remember walking across the grass and somehow the days in the stands in the Polo Grounds came back to me. It was a feeling that here I was, I had arrived.

Another one and this is a trivia question—I was the first pitcher in Yankee Stadium to ever ride in from the bullpen in a cart. We used to walk in at the stadium and that was a walk where time stood still. Usually when you came in you had your mind on the game. Most often it was mechanical stuff, your motion, that kind of thing, the thoughts had to do with your craft and the game situation. But every once in a while you'd look around and you'd say, this is really something important here, walking across that outfield grass. You'd especially feel that way at an All-Star game or during a World Series. Sometimes the size of the event would overwhelm you. I remember standing on the mound before facing Don Drysdale in the 1963 World Series and thinking, "Oh shit, I'm in a World Series." And I recall saying something to Ralph Houk before that game that it was going to be fun, just pitching in a World Series. For every major league ballplayer there are moments. We all need to remember, we all need to stop from time to time and enjoy them. You know what it is, it goes back to when my brother and I were kids in the Polo Grounds watching them prepare the field. That was something. Our fantasy was, jeeze, if we could just get down on that field, run out there and slide into second base. Just kick the base, wouldn't that be great? Just to see that beautiful brown-colored dirt and see if the grass was really that green. Dick Baney, a Seattle pitcher, said to me one time, you know walking across the outfield grass like this with organ playing, it's really special, and you know he was right. I think that sometimes you forget to tingle out there.

DICK RADATZ
Right-Handed Pitcher

BOSTON RED SOX, 1962–1966
CLEVELAND INDIANS, 1966–1967
CHICAGO CUBS, 1967
DETROIT TIGERS, 1969
MONTREAL EXPOS, 1969

- **Named Fireman Of The Year In 1962, His Rookie Season**
- **Led The American League In Saves And Again Named Fireman Of The Year In 1964**
- **American League Relief Point Leader, 1962–1964**
- **Called "The Monster"**

Detroit kid. Six-foot-six, 230 pounds! Led American League in relief points three years in a row, struck out more men per game (9.67) than any pitcher in baseball. Three of the greatest years in relief in history—what happened?

I'm shuffling through a stack of 3 × 5 note cards, listening to the phone ring in the Boston home of Dick Radatz. Radatz and I have been playing phone tag for almost a month now trying to get together for our bullpen conversation.

It sounds like another strikeout. The ringing continues. I attempt to read a semi-legible pencil scribble. *Who named you* "The Monster"? *Did the name have anything to do with the fence in Fenway?*

Click!

"Dick?"

"Yes!"

"I'm calling about the bullpen book?"

"Great, I'm glad we could finally get together!"

I turn the first note card over. "I'm not sure if this is a good way to start but . . . how did you get named 'The Monster?' Were you named after the wall in Fenway or what?"

No, it wasn't the wall [laughs]. I had a lot of succ\
Mantle. I think the stats read that I faced him sixty-one tin,\
struck him out forty-two. It was just one of those things. I co\
get Kubek out to save my tail. But I owned Mantle. I'd just\
him out with fastballs around the waist and go up the ladder. ɹr\
some reason he just couldn't move on it. It got so that he was\
bunting with two strikes. In fact it was Mickey who gave me the\
name "The Monster." But I'll tell you what, there were about\
fourteen four-letter adjectives in front of it before he finally got to\
"Monster." I struck him out in Yankee Stadium with the bases\
loaded and boom, ba-boom, ba-boom, he started cussing and "Mon-\
ster" came about the tenth word. He was cussing so loud that the\
press heard it. Hence the nickname. It stuck with me.

And I don't know whether I'm a monster or not, but I was a\
pretty good-sized guy out there on the mound [Radatz is 6'6" tall].\
And to be honest, basketball was always my number one love. I\
played baseball because my friends played it. I got three letters in\
high school in basketball, three letters in football and two letters in\
baseball. I never was really that serious about baseball, not until I\
got into my sophomore year in college. I went to Michigan State\
on a combined basketball and baseball scholarship. I really thought\
I was John Havlicek. As it turned out, I played more like Mrs.\
Havlicek. But I wasn't quite as good as I thought I was. A fellow\
came into Michigan State at my position, a guy named Johnny\
Green, Jumping Johnny Green, and he sort of put me on the\
pines. And I wasn't a candidate for MIT by any stretch of the\
imagination. About that time my grades started to slip a little bit,\
and two sports was just too much. So I made a decision to go strictly\
to baseball and it was obviously the right one. I was a starter and we\
had a great staff on the Michigan State baseball team. We had Ron\
Perranoski, whom I roomed with, a fellow named Eddie Hobaugh who\
pitched for three years with the Washington Senators, and a guy who\
quite honestly threw harder than any of us named Larry Foster, who\
signed with the Tigers. I think that he got as high as Triple-A but never\
did make it. So we had some talent. We didn't even win the Big Ten,\
but practically everybody on that pitching staff went to the big leagues\
and a number of the other guys signed.

I got serious about baseball about my sophomore year. We had\
a great old coach by the name of John Cobs. He was crazy really\
but I had a lot of respect for him. He told me that it was time\
to get serious about the game because I had an opportunity to do\
something. And as it turned out I did. When I went to Michigan

State I was 6'6" and had a 29" waist. I'm still pretty tall but that waist is long gone now, I can tell you that. I was growing quite a bit, I put on thirty pounds my sophomore year, went from about 209 to 240. I really filled out, to where I should have been, I guess. I just really quite honestly wasn't mentally into the game. I played my heart out in basketball and gave maybe seventy-five percent to baseball until the light went on. It just dawned on me that football wasn't going to happen and basketball wasn't going to happen and this is what you've got left, pal, so let's get on with it. I ended up making All-Big Ten as a junior and All-America as a senior. I took a lot of pride in that and I still do. I remember there was an incident in South Dakota when Ron [Perranoski] and I were together. I had quite a temper and if an umpire missed a close pitch I had a tendency to get a little wild about it. I think that hurt me. In fact, I know it did. I got into a conflab with an ump in Mitchell, South Dakota. I was pitching against Don Schwall. We both had double no-hitters going out there. Don became one of my close friends and teammates later on. We both had no-hitters going in the sixth inning and the umpire missed five or six pitches in a row that I thought were strikes. And I charged him and he threw me out of the game. I ended up pushing him against the screen, and there just so happened to be a Boston Red Sox scout in the stands and he wrote a bad report on me. "Great talent, bad attitude." That stayed with me and when I signed with the Red Sox, right after I got out of college in 1959, they mentioned that. It probably cost me a little money. But as it turned out everything was fine. It's the old story. You never know who's watching!

How did I become a relief pitcher? Well I started out with the Red Sox in Raleigh, North Carolina, that was A-ball, and I had a so-so year. Then I came back the next year and did quite well and they called me up to Minneapolis, their Triple-A club, at the end of the season. So it was the following spring, a spring training game against Rochester. It may have been Harry Dorish, the pitching coach, who made the suggestion, I don't know, but someone convinced Johnny Pesky, the Minnesota manager, that I'd be effective in relief. I always gave the credit to Pesky. But the fact was that that was the turning point in my career. I went down to spring training with a sore arm that year, I'd been playing a little touch football and I hurt myself. It wasn't anything severe, but I told Johnny Pesky who was the manager. I said, "Johnny, I'd like to have about a week down here in this warm

248

weather to get my arm in shape." I said, "I've got a little pull in there or something that I need to work out." I didn't tell him what had happened.

So about two or three weeks passed and I still hadn't thrown yet. And when he started to cut the roster he said, "Look, I'm going to have to have you pitch." So he did and I went over to Daytona Beach against Rochester and struck out eleven out of twelve. I don't know how I did it because my arm was killing me. The Lord was on my side, I guess. The next day I went to the ball park and Johnny called me into his office and said, "Dick, we're going to take you to Seattle with us." [The Red Sox Triple-A team had moved from Minnesota to Seattle.] And he said, "But we're going to make a relief pitcher out of you." In those days that was a demotion. I said, "I don't agree with that, you can send me back to Allentown. I want to pitch every four days." And he said, "No, I'm going to take you with me and I'm going to teach you how to pitch every day." And I said, "Well I can't do that!" And he said, "Well, I'm going to teach you," and as they say, the rest is history!

Well that [Pacific Coast league] was a hitter's league too, there's no doubt about it. I got so I sort of liked it a little bit, you know. But that year and even the following year when I went to Boston and was Relief Pitcher of the Year, I still didn't feel like I was a part of the ball club. I felt like an add-on and still felt like I had been demoted. That was 1961 when I pitched in Seattle and 1962 was my rookie year in the big leagues. I had the good year. I was 9–6 and won the Relief Pitcher of the Year award. Again, I still didn't feel like I was a part of the club. I felt like I was an extra type guy. And it wasn't until 1963 when I had the real good year—I was 15–6—that I felt like I was there. I lost the Relief Pitcher of the Year award to Stu Miller on the last day. Twenty-five saves, that was a real good year. I did have quite a run, in 1962, 1963, 1964, 1965 [24, 25, 29, 22 saves respectively]. Somebody computed that. If the save rule had been the same then as it is now, I would have had, in I think in 1964, something like forty-nine or fifty saves. I don't know how rich I'd have been [in today's market], but there'd have been a lot of zeros in the figure. I told Ted Williams that. He asked me last year at a card show, he said, "What do you think you'd be making today, Bush?" And I said, "Well, Ted, I'd have to be looking at two, two and a half million." And he said, "Well, I'd have to agree." And then I said, "Well, how about you?" And he said, "Well, I'd be writing your check because I'd own the ball club." And that's probably true.

In the first year I played for Pinky Higgins and then later Johnny

Pesky and Billy Herman. I replaced Mike Fornieles in the short role. Mike and I became very good friends. In fact we roomed together for a while. He was a big help to me mentally, how to approach the game. I got off to such a good start in 1962 and Mike said, "Now don't let this thing get a hold of you, kid. There's some awfully good teams in this league!" And I think the first fourteen games that I pitched in I only allowed eleven runs. I said, "Mike, let me live it, brother." I said, "It's feeling awfully good." And he said, "Well, things are going to happen to you that aren't going to be pleasant. When they happen in Fenway Park they're going to hurt you. So just stay within yourself!" And I tried to do that. I was always, I thought, amiable with the press. When anybody wanted to talk to me, I'd talk to them. I never made a big deal out of it. People know how good or how bad you've been and you don't have to tell them. Let the record speak for itself and keep it all in perspective. I've always said there are millions of people out there who do what they do better than anybody else and nobody knows about it because they don't get their names in the paper.

Looking back gives you perspective, of course. I always pitched with the attitude that, well it's contradictory. I went out there with the attitude of, if I screw up what are they going to do, put me in jail? So I developed sort of a flip type attitude. But now on the other hand I loved the challenge. When you get right down to it, I loved embarrassing the hitter. I think it's pride in every sense of the word and you don't dwell on it, especially the relief pitcher. The toughest thing for me to do—and of course there were a lot more doubleheaders in those days—the toughest thing was to screw up the first game and then a few hours later go out there again. Boy, that was tough. You can have a bad day and go out and have a couple of libations and come back the next day. But boy, when you screw up the first game and have to go back out there, that made it awfully tough.

I developed a pretty good slider but the fastball was my pitch. The relief men, especially the guys who come in there late, are usually one- or two-pitch pitchers. The way I looked at it was, "Here comes the fastball, see if you can hit it!" It's not because it was my pitch but I believe that they can play this game for another five hundred years and that they'll never come up with a better pitch than the fastball. And only for one reason. It tests the hitter's reactions better than anything else. If you can throw it for strikes, I think that you have ninety percent of the battle licked. If you make mistakes with fastballs you have them swinging and missing and often they'll foul them off. And if you hang a forkball, curve or whatever you want to talk about, they have a tendency to get banged pretty good. I was blessed with a pretty good fastball and I had good control. I think that there were guys who threw harder than I did, but it was the movement of the pitch. And I had a slow windup. Al Kaline put it in perspective, he said, "He puts you to sleep watching that windup and then all of a sudden the catcher's throwing the ball back." So I sort of put them in a trance with it. It wasn't a deliberate herky-jerky Tiant-type thing. I've heard and read where people said that I threw a really heavy pitch. But Bob Tillman, my catcher, used to say just the opposite. Tillman said that he could have caught me with a Kleenex.

I did get off to a good start my rookie year and had a very good per-inning strikeout ratio. But there's a story behind that. I was what they call a stand-up pitcher, all through the minor leagues, and I had a good strikeout ratio in the minors. Sal Maglie was our pitching coach in 1962. I always had a lot of respect for Sal. He taught me how to use the rubber. He said, "Big fellow, you're 6'6" and weigh 250 pounds and you're doing it all with your arm." And he taught me to get my quote-unquote butt into it a little bit. And jeeze, it turned out that I was averaging better than a strikeout per inning. At least for those three or so years. And it turned out that Sal helped me a lot. I played against Frank Howard in college and he said, "You're throwing a lot harder now than you did in college." And I credit that to Sal.

I guess if there was a game that rookie year it was the one in late August in Yankee Stadium. [Radatz came into the game late and held the Yankees scoreless for nine innings, finally getting the win in the sixteenth inning.] That was quite a thrill. There was something about playing in Yankee Stadium. I don't think I ever failed to walk out to the monuments and read them. I did that every time I played there. The aura of the place and of course, they had that great lineup. They had guys like Clete Boyer hitting eighth. They were loaded. And that was just an extra challenge for me. I hooked up with Marshall Bridges. Marshall Bridges was an outstanding pitcher, and the thing finally went into the sixteenth. By the way, it was one of the few games that I ever had saved for me. Chet Nichols came in and got the save. I think I pitched eight or nine innings or whatever it was, and Bob Tillman tripled in the top of the sixteenth. I was the next hitter and they pinch-hit Billy Gardner for me and Billy squeezed in Tillman. Then Chet came in and saved me. That was a tremendous ball game.

I remember that Ralph Houk made a statement when he took me to the All-Star game in 1963, something about he wanted the National League hitters to see what he had to face. But you know I had varying degrees of success in the All-Star games. I think I pitched four and two-thirds innings, struck out nine in those two games and have nothing to show for it but a loss and a high ERA. The first one, that was 1963, I pitched the last two innings of that one and struck out McCovey, Groat, Javier and Snider. [The American League lost 5–3.] And then it was the next year that Callison got me with the home run to win it. [Callison's three-run homer gave the National League a come-from-behind victory in the ninth inning.] But I struck out five people that day too, including Aaron and a few other people. It's funny, I don't know whether it was the great Ellie Howard who was catching me or whether I was just pumped up, but I don't ever remember having a fastball like that. I think it was just the pump of the game itself but I don't think that I ever threw fastballs like I did in those two games.

It was almost like the atmosphere put a couple of extra miles on my fastball. I had great stuff. I struck out ten of those guys in less than five innings, that was 1963 and 1964. I really felt bad about the 1964 game because we had them beat 4–3 in the bottom of the ninth inning and I threw Mays a 2–2 slider. An exciting ball game, I got caught up in it. There were 63,000 in Shea and Willie's town—he'd come home. I threw him that slider, a real good slider and Mays thought it was strike three, he started walking toward the dugout. The umpire called it a ball. And then I walked him on the next pitch. Oh, it hurt! I'd had great success against Willie Mays. I'd only pitched against him a few times, spring training in Arizona and the All-Star games. Willie told me one time and I've never forgotten it. He said, "Let me tell you something, big boy. I don't think that I'm ever going to put a ball in play against you. But I'm going to tell you something, I'm going to wear out a whole lot of people in the times in between." And needless to say, he did.

But for me to walk him that way, the crowd just absolutely erupted. I stepped back off the mound and just listened and thought, boy, this really is something. And then I got it back together. But Mays stole second. Then Cepeda blooped a ball over first base and Bobby Richardson threw it home. The throw went wild, over Ellie's head, and I backed up the play. That tied it. Then I walked John Edwards intentionally. Callison came up with two on and two out—it was tied at the time—and he was the only guy that I faced twice in that ball game. He had hit the first ball pretty good. Hit it to Mickey in center field at the warning track. He got my attention there. But when he hit the home run, I tried too hard. I tried to slip a fastball deep in on him, the first pitch. I was just trying to back him off the plate, I wanted to get a little bit more of the plate. I didn't throw it for a strike, I didn't mean to. But it turned out that it caught the inside part of the plate and he cow-tailed it. There wasn't really any doubt. I was just hoping that it didn't have time to get up. I looked up and there was my good friend Rocky Colavito out in right field and I knew he wasn't going to get to it. I knew that was the end of it.

That one took me a while to get over. . . . How long? I don't know, but I'll tell you what. I went into that game and if memory serves me right, I was 8–1 at the All-Star break. In about three weeks I was 12–1, so as the regular season goes it didn't bother me. But I did have a few sleepless nights over that one. And my mother, God rest her soul, put it in proper perspective after that game. My whole family was there and saw it. I walked out of Shea and she said, "Son, it's an honor that you were even here, chosen to pitch in this game!" And I said, "Yes, I hear what you're saying, but I really can't see it in that light right now." Now my vision and perspective has cleared somewhat. I've got relatives in Detroit who love to kid me about that. Every time I talk to them they say, "Hey, have you talked to Callison lately?"

And the funny thing is that I did see Johnny, saw him for the first time this summer at an Old Timers Game. First time since that day and he had had two or three bypass operations but he looked great. And I said, "Johnny, you don't mind if I slip one up under your ribs at the game tomorrow, do you?" And he said, "Don't do that, I'll need another bypass!" I said, "Well, if I hit you it wouldn't hurt you." But that was a good reunion. This was one of the Equitable Old Timers Games.

A lot of people ask what happened to Dick Radatz. Yes, I did have a run in the mid-sixties. There was a good stretch, something like thirty-three innings without allowing a run. I remember that, of course, and as far as I know, the record still stands with the Red Sox. Somebody made a run at it—it may have been Clemens just recently—I'm not sure but I think that's one of the few [records] I've got left over there [in Boston]. It wasn't a highlight for me although it's something that I take pride in. I think the run [in 1964] when I won ten in a row and went to 12–1. Then I started getting tired during the dog days and I ended up 16–9. I did go long in the count, a lot of 3–1, 3–2 counts, and that probably is the thing that led to my quote-unquote downfall.

After the 1964 season, this was one of those deals where if the wheel's not broken, don't fix it. And it certainly wasn't. Ted Williams got me in spring training in 1965. He never asks a question that he doesn't know the answer to. And he said, "Who gives you the most trouble, Bush?" And I said, "Well, the left-handed contact hitters, the guys that are just trying to move the ball around. They see the ball pretty good!" And he said, "You're exactly right. With your motion you should be able to come up with a halfway decent sinker and you wouldn't have to throw so damned many pitches. Wouldn't you rather throw one or two pitches instead of five or six every at bat?" And I said, "Yeah, I really would." He said, "Why don't you work on something!" And I'll be doggoned if I didn't come up with something. But in doing so, I changed my motion. I dropped my arm a little bit and I didn't realize that I'd done it. We didn't have the luxury of videotape. And I wish we had. People kept telling me, "Dick, your arm's not as high as it used to be," and I always thought it was. When it came time to throw my good fastball I was throwing a sinkerball. I lost some velocity and it had a tail on it and then it became a mental thing. I never did hurt my arm, it never got tired or sore. But it became a mental thing and my control went and by the time I got it back . . .

I even went and got hypnotized on the suggestion of Randy Hundley. When I was with the Cubs [1967] I'd pitched a ball game against Tucson in the spring. I walked the first six guys on twenty-four pitches and none of them were even close. And after the game Durocher called me in and he said, "Jesus, Dick, you're not a minor league pitcher! But hell, you can't pitch in the big leagues throwing like that!" And I said, "Well, I understand." And he said, "I'm going to have to release you. Good luck to you. Do the best you can. You've still got the talent!" So I went back to the clubhouse and Randy Hundley, the Cubs catcher was there, Randy and I had become pretty good friends. He said, "Dick, why don't you do what I did? I got hypnotized." So I thought, "What the hell is there left? I feel good," so I went back to my home town—Detroit, Michigan—saw a hypnotist and it worked! So then, right after that Jim Campbell [the Tigers general manager] called and offered me a pretty decent contract with Toledo. He wanted to start me so I could get as many innings in as possible. I went down there and it was strike, strike, strike. So it worked.

I pitched well in Toledo that summer but I never really made it back. I made the Detroit club in the spring of 1969. And I started out very, very well and I thought, "Jeeze, this is great. I'm in my home town and if I can get two or three years here, this would be a nice way to end it." I was pitching short relief, and it was funny. The last day of spring training there were four relievers—myself, Don McMahon, John Wyatt and Elroy Face—four pretty good country relief pitchers, and they were only going to keep two. They kept McMahon and me and released Wyatt and Face. I was 2–2 and had a couple of saves and had a decent ERA and I was the number one man out of the hole. For some unknown reason Mayo Smith sold me to Montreal. And Johnny Sain, our pitching coach, ended up quitting. It upset him and he had sort of taken me under his wing as his private project. He took a lot of pride in getting me back to the big leagues and I was pitching pretty good ball for him.

I was in Montreal in the bullpen there with Elroy Face, but Gene Mauch was into a youth movement. Gene made a funny comment before they released me. I said, "Gene, I've always had a lot of respect for you. You're the only guy I ever played for twice." I'd played for him in 1960 in spring training with Minneapolis before he went to the Phillies. I said, "Can I still pitch in the big leagues?" And he said, "No doubt about it. But not with us!" And we both laughed. And that was it, 1969, the end of the line. I went home that winter with all intentions of going back and hooking on somewhere else. But my son, he was ten and he said, "Dad, how about doing a little fishing next summer?" and I said, "I think that's a good idea." And right then and there I hung it up.

It was tough the first couple of years. You don't miss the game so much, you miss the people in it. Some great friends, guys like Gary Bell, some great stories, unfortunately most unprintable. Dick Stuart—the guy they called Stone Glove. There was a character. A big handsome guy and he took great pride in the way he looked, how he dressed. Some people just flat out didn't like him but I thought he was great. I really enjoyed being around him. One story in particular, this was 1965 or 1966 and I guess I was the highest-paid player on the ball club, making about $42,500. Carl [Yastrzemski] was making about $40,000 and Dick was making around $41,000. And Stuart would go around the clubhouse on payday to the rookies, guys like Conigliaro, with his check and say, "Excuse me, could you cash this for me? Oh, I'm sorry, too big?" Well, I'd let him go around for a while and then I'd say, "Stuart, do you want to bring that over here? I think I can take care of it." And he'd say, "I'm not talking to you, Radatz."

I roomed with him, nobody else would. Oh, he was a funny, funny man. I remember 1963, Johnny Pesky's first year. Stuart lived in Connecticut and we got rained out in Boston the first two days of the season. On the third day Johnny said, "We're going to play this game no matter what." The rain hadn't let up and we had a team meeting at twelve o'clock noon in the clubhouse—how to pitch to Maris, Mantle, whatever. And we were going to cold-jock it, no hitting, no infield, just take the tarp off and play. Stuart doesn't show up for the meeting. And lo and behold, he walks in about 12:30 and the game starts at 1:00. Pesky was irate. And now Stuart dressed immaculately, he's wearing a burgundy suede sport coat. He had on $100 shoes and this was when $100 shoes were something. A big handsome devil. And he walks in and puts his arm around Pesky and says, "Well boys, here I am, eat your hearts out. I know you all want to be me but you can't. . . ." Well Pesky cuts loose, a lot of four-letter words, with some "get your uniform on" mixed in. "And Stuart, I'll see you later." We continued to go over the hitters and we got down to the end and Pesky said, "Now some of you guys who haven't played for me, I want to explain the curfew situation. Day games I want you in bed by twelve o'clock when we're on the road. Night games, two and a half hours after the bus hits the hotel I expect you to be in bed." And he said, "If you're not, it's going to cost you five hundred dollars. The second offense will be a thousand and if there's a third, there are no guarantees, but you probably won't be with the ball club." Stuart raises his hand and says, "Johnny, I'd like to get back to the first two offenses, the $500 and the $1,000?" Pesky says, "Yeah, Stuart, what is it?" Stuart says, "Johnny, is that tax-deductible?" Now everybody is falling off their stools laughing. End of Pesky's first meeting.

But Stuart was something. About his fielding I'll tell you what, he wasn't bad, he was lazy. He would say, "If they hit it to me I will pick it up. Don't ask me to go two or three feet one way or another. You're taking a big chance there." He'd say, "I get paid to do one thing and I do that very well and that's to hit the ball out of this bandbox [Fenway]." His poor fielding was so renowned that he once picked up a hot dog wrapper in Fenway and got a standing ovation. And that's a true story. I saw it! He was something. Stuart made a comment which was one of the great comments of all time. Dick and Harmon Killebrew were tied with forty home runs apiece and it came down to one of the last series of the season. Now they [Minnesota] were playing us. Harmon hit four in that series and Dick hit two. After the last game a reporter in the clubhouse asked Stuart how he felt about losing the home run title, with Killebrew hitting four and him hitting two. Stuart said, "If I could have hit against our pitching staff I'd a hit six!" Well, Bill Monbouquette, Earl Wilson, myself, every pitcher in the clubhouse fell off their stools laughing on that one. That was Dick Stuart.

There were a million characters. Sam McDowell, who was never sober. We thought he was just stupid and it turned out that he was never sober. And, of course, he now is one of the foremost authorities on drug and alcohol rehab in the country. I was always in awe of the arm that McDowell had, despite the drinking problem. Sam McDowell may have had one of the best arms of all time, a command of all the pitches, but he always wanted to trick people with his changeup or something else. According to him there were times when he played hammered, hung over, sometimes he could disguise it, sometimes he couldn't.

Luis Tiant and I were in the pen together and this isn't just indigenous to Luis. A lot of your great starters did not like that bullpen. It was funny, Luis was out in the pen with me that year I was in Cleveland. And the phone would ring and Tiant would say, "Tell them Luis no here. Him in the whirlpool, got bad arm!" He didn't like that bullpen work at all.

For some reason no-hitters are a popular subject in the pen, games you've seen. And the guy who originally told this story was Joey Amalfitano. You know when Koufax threw the perfect game against the Cubs he struck out the last six hitters. Joey went up with one out in the ninth inning and, of course, struck out, and Harvey Kuenn was the on-deck hitter. Now Joey's walking back to the dugout. Harvey didn't strike out much, even when he was old. Harvey passes Joey on his way to the plate and says, "Joey, what do you think?" And Joey says, "Harvey, don't go up there!"

That reminds me of another one. I almost got killed out there one night in Boston. You always have some problems and in Boston you're right in the stands, it's out there in right center. It's right up against the bleachers and people could lean out and touch you if they really wanted to. I remember one day and I'll refer to something that I said before. I'd pitched the first end of a doubleheader and I'd screwed it up. It was a twi-night doubleheader and I came out in the second game to warm up. In those days, probably much like today, there were a lot of college kids out there and not too many of them sober. I got a smattering of "your mother this," and jeeze, somebody threw a full vodka bottle at me. It screamed by my head and hit me in the ear and crashed against the bullpen fence. I think that if it had hit me in the back of the head it might have killed me. And that's the only game—well I shouldn't say only—but that was one game that I went into without throwing a warm-up pitch. I took my warm-up pitches on the mound.

That was one of the hazards. But as I said before, there are so many good people and memories. Hoyt Wilhelm paid me the ultimate compliment. He came in here to Boston when he was being honored. Hoyt and I weren't real close, we'd hooked up a couple of times in big games but I didn't know him that well—a golf tournament or two after we'd retired. He came into Boston after he'd been inducted into the Hall of Fame and the Boston sportswriters were going to give him an award. Hoyt said, "Doesn't Dick Radatz live up here in the Boston area?" and they said that I did. Hoyt said, "I'd like to have him up here with me when I receive it, I think that Radatz was as good as there was." And boy, I'll tell you I took a lot of pride in that!

But I'm a big believer in longevity. One of the things that saddens me about my career is that I really would have liked to have gone a few more years. If I'd have had another pitch, who knows, maybe I could have, but when you talk about the great relievers. . . . Was I a great reliever? I always say yes, for a minute. When I look at guys like Rollie [Fingers], Elroy [Face], Hoyt [Wilhelm], and my good friend Perranoski well . . . you look at their numbers sometime, brother, they put up the big ones.

THE GOLDEN YEARS OF RELIEF

At the close of the 1970 season some rather telling figures were in evidence in baseball's record books. For the first time ever, the individual marks in the save column were greater than those denoting games completed by a starter. This was due in part to the story in Cincinnati about Captain Hook. Never before in baseball history had managers yanked starters as quickly as Sparky Anderson. His moves on his regulars resulted in sixty saves. Cincinnati starters completed only thirty-two games. Both of these numbers were major league records. Anderson, however, was counting trips to the mound.

> Everybody says that I was Captain Hook, but the bullpen wasn't built that way. Our situation was that we didn't have good starting pitching. We felt strongly that we had to defense our starting pitching, so we did it with our bullpen.

The teams that won had good men in the pen. Cincinnati had Granger, Carroll, and Gullett. Pittsburgh had Giusti; Minnesota, Perranoski; New York, McDaniel; and Baltimore, Watt and Richert. And the following season, in 1971, when Dick Williams arrived in Oakland, he took the A's to a Western Division title by developing a left-right combination in Knowles and Locker. They worked the middle innings until the game wound down to the eighth and ninth. Then Williams presented the ball to Rollie Fingers. This flip-flopping by Williams and Anderson helped win pennants. Before long, anybody who knew anything about baseball began to talk about the "bullpen by committee."

Dick Hall, one of the pen's keener observers, served on a committee for Earl Weaver during this period of new awareness.

> I had my role with Weaver. Those days the long man would finish the game. But my role was in the seventh inning in close games or in extra-inning games. That was the only time I pitched. If it was out of reach, he didn't use me for mop up. In the seventh inning of a close game when the Baltimore Orioles needed a pitcher, I was number one.

In 1973, the designated hitter rule raised its ugly head in the American League. Second only to the outrage it brought from the game's purists—the idea of a pitcher not swinging his own bat was heretical—was the effect it had on complete game totals. Surprisingly, this figure jumped more than fifteen percent. As baseball historian John Thorn points out, "Strangely, though relievers were being used less, the percentage of games in which a save occurred increased. Seemingly the major effect of the DH was to permit more starters to absorb route-going defeats where previously they might have been pulled for pinch hitters."

The DH wasn't the only news around baseball. Several bullpenners made headlines that season. In Montreal, Gene Mauch called on Mike Marshall a record ninety-two times. Tug McGraw convinced the baseball world that "You gotta believe" by his last-minute heroics during the Mets' successful drive to the pennant. And perhaps the most believing penner of all was John Hiller, a Detroit right-hander who staged a miraculous comeback from a heart attack and set a major league relief point record with a total of forty-eight.

That was 1973. The following season Mike Marshall moved from Montreal to Los Angeles and took relief pitching into its golden age. His league-leading fifteen relief wins, twenty-one saves, eighty-three games finished, and thirteen consecutive appearances in 1974 brought trophies and acclaim to the pen, most notably the Cy Young Award. A relief man had never been so honored.

Players like Marshall, McGraw and Hiller turned in great individual performances—teams in Oakland, Cincinnati and Baltimore won with well-formed committees. There was, however, no star system in the bullpen. The year 1976 would change all that.

A modification of the reserve clause in the players' contracts enabled twenty-four players to play out their contracts, become free agents and go for the long-term contracts and the big bucks. Over a dozen players landed contracts worth more than a million dollars that season. Rollie Fingers, one of the great relief pitchers of all time, found himself in the middle of a monumental court case over this free agency.

Another plus came in 1976 when Warner-Lambert, a New Jersey-based pharmaceutical company, wrote up a prescription that would ultimately help loosen some baseball coffers.

The Rolaids Relief Man Award, appropriately named for a pill which soothes nervous stomachs, was just what the bullpen doctor ordered. Before the R-E-L-I-E-F Awards, you could count the number of "big names" in major league bullpens on an umpire's indicator. What Rolaids did was devise a scoring system to evaluate relief pitching. Initially, to gain credit for a save a reliever had to come into a game with the tying or winning run on base or at the plate and finish the game with the lead. Rolaids relief men were chosen by calculators. This was not another one of the game's popularity contests. Bruce Sutter places his R-E-L-I-E-F Award on the very top shelf.

I'm still not so sure that the Cy Young Award should be given to a relief pitcher. We have our Rolaids Award. I don't get all hepped up about awards where you get voted on. Somebody doesn't like you and you're screwed. Of course, the Cy Young has a nice place in my home. But so do the Rolaids trophies because that's something that they don't vote on.

Bill Campbell of the Minnesota Twins and Rawley Eastwick of the Cincinnati Reds were Rolaids' first honorees. And the winners who followed? The list reads like a bullpen "who's who"—Gossage, Fingers, Sutter, Kern, Quisenberry, Holland, Reardon, Righetti, Worrell, Bedrosian, Eckersley, Russell, Franco, Davis and Thigpen. The once-maligned profession now had the save as an official statistic and yet another measuring stick. Like hitters and starting pitchers, it was something to bargain with at contract time.

Even the best of medications takes time, of course. Mike Marshall had been the first relief man to earn $100,000 back in 1975. Fingers jumped to the Padres in the winter of 1976 and signed a five-year pact for $1.6 million. The following season, Goose Gossage played out his option in Pittsburgh and made a six-year deal with the New York Yankees for a then-mind-boggling sum of $2.7 million.

Free agency had opened some wallets. But most of the big money was still earned by starters and hitters. Whitey Herzog constructed one of the first good economical pens in Kansas City in 1977 and did it without the aid of power tools.

I never really had what I'd call a glorified closer. I always had to go with left-right, left-right, to keep two left-handers and two right-handers out there in the bullpen. If I had three left-handed starters I wanted my number five man to be a right-hander. I wanted my long reliever to always be the opposite of what my starting pitcher was. So basically I started shaping the pens that way in Kansas City.

Later in St. Louis Herzog got that heavy-duty equipment he'd been looking for, and with a dash of running, a bit of hitting and a lot of relief, he won his first World Series in 1982.

When I came to St. Louis in 1980 they had a terrible team, but the major weakness that the Cardinals had was they had no bullpen. So I went to the trading wars and I traded fourteen ballplayers and got eleven. The first thing I had in mind was that I wanted to get me a closer. I wanted Sutter and I ended up getting Sutter and Fingers. I didn't want both of them in the same bullpen because I knew that would be trouble, so I traded Fingers away. In the meantime while I was getting Sutter, I was also getting Bob Shirley to get me a left-hander in the pen. And I started getting the balance that I wanted out there. We picked up Doug Bair from Cincinnati and then the next year in spring training we got Jeff Lahti. I think that people fail to realize that, especially in the National League, the setup men—before the closer—are the most important people.

While Whitey matched up righties and lefties and built pens in America's heartland, on the shores of the Chesapeake Bay, Earl Weaver crunched numbers, marked them down on 3×5 index cards and then at the appropriate time turned the cards over and made pitching decisions.

Computer managing, no! The only thing a computer can do is spit out what you put in it. So no, we didn't run the bullpen by computer. We had all our information on index cards that you could go to. If you talk about how we handled pitchers in Baltimore, we had definite research on what one pitcher could do to a certain hitter and we made our call to the bullpen accordingly.

While Herzog pen-shaped and Weaver number-crunched, Dick Howser, George Steinbrenner's latest manager, stacked New York Yankees relievers in a way that would change the meaning of the term setup man. In 1980, Howser matched up two of the game's best arms, Ron Davis and Goose Goosage, and won the American League East. Davis took the ball in the seventh and eighth innings, exclusively. When the ninth rolled around, if the Yanks had a lead, R.D. would politely pass the ball to Gossage. The stopper with the Fu Manchu mustache would then stalk in and blow the ball by the final three or four hitters. Howser rarely let Gossage work more than six outs. If he got him up he pitched him. Orioles/ESPN broadcaster Jon Miller recalls Gossage calling Howser's system, "the best way that I've ever been used."

This was in 1980. Martin and Lemon may have done some of this but Howser is the guy who had Davis setting up Gossage. And as a result Gossage had an incredible year, something like ninety-nine innings and only seventy-four hits, over 100 strikeouts and a microscopic ERA. He was untouchable and never got overworked, never had to go around the batting order. He usually pitched just the one inning. That was the first time I saw the setup so regulated, and I think a lot of teams saw that and followed suit.

But what about the starters, all those guys who wanted to go the whole nine? How are you going to wrestle the ball from them? Earl Weaver says free agency and the multi-year, million-dollar contracts made this new committee work more palatably, for starters and relief men alike.

The biggest difference though is this. Today you have the big three-and five-year contracts for starters and relief guys. If the starters still had to complete games when they talked contract each year, well, then you'd see a lot less specialists in the game. And these long-term contracts have affected the attitudes of the relief pitchers as well. When they were on a year-to-year basis, you'd bring in a left-hander to face a left-handed hitter. You took your right-handed relief guy out, there was a little animosity and a show of temper at times because they wanted the save to talk about at contract time. But just as soon as they [the save] didn't mean as much and people were satisfied with their contracts, then the relief guys became more specialized and very happy to pitch to the two or three guys that they knew that they could get out. I'm not saying it's any better or any worse, but it's changed, just different.

The bullpen was evolving in a steady progression. Things were getting, in Weaver's words, "different." But relief work was still no exact science. And regardless of how rich the contracts or how evenly management distributed the work load, even star relievers like Fingers and Sutter were going to blow saves and lose ball games. But as Jack Buck, the St. Louis Cardinals play-by-play announcer points out, the mistake market will never be cornered by the guys who groove fastballs and hang curves. There are times when managers under- and over-manipulate, even the great ones like Red Schoendienst and Whitey Herzog.

The way relief is going today the starters like it because it prolongs their careers. But you take a fellow like Bob Gibson, his prime thought was to go nine innings. The last thing he wanted was to have somebody come in and screw up one of his games. In fact we lost the pennant in St. Louis in 1974. Hrabosky was in the Cardinals bullpen getting everybody out at the time and Gibson was pitching.

Schoendienst was managing, Montreal has a runner on first. We're ahead by a run, two out in the ninth inning and Red didn't change pitchers. I said to Shannon [Buck's broadcast partner], "Here goes the pennant." *Bong!* Mike Jorgensen hit a home run, beat us, knocked us out and the Pirates won the pennant that year. So that's one of the things about using the bullpen. You have to have confidence in them. Gibson was pitching and I think Red was afraid to take the ball away from him.

Whitey Herzog, he didn't care what anybody else thought. He just made his moves. And he's certainly had his share of success. But every once in a while, every once in a while these people get caught up in it [the bullpen switches] and I'm talking about the left-right, left-right. At Kansas City, in Game Six of the 1985 World Series, the one where the umpire [Don Denkinger] missed the call at first base, Dayley was pitching, just throwing the hell out of the ball. Nobody was going to hit him. And he [Herzog] brought in Worrell [a right-handed pitcher] because he was afraid of McRae [a right-handed Kansas City hitter] who was on the bench. McRae has told me since that he was hurt and that he couldn't even swing. It didn't work. There was a passed ball and an intentional walk, to set up a double play, and eventually Dane Iorg, a left-handed hitter, ends up getting the two-run single and Kansas City wins it 2–1. Nobody's ever one hundred percent right, you know!

Relief pitching was not perfect as yet, but its craftsmen were trying. Let's visit with the men from the pen's golden age—Gossage, McGraw, Fingers, and Sutter among others—the men who brought the bullpen to a point where the art gets dangerously close to science.

VOICES FROM THE PEN

SPARKY ANDERSON
Manager

**CINCINNATI REDS, 1970–1978
DETROIT TIGERS, 1979–present**

- **Managed His Bullpens To Three World
  Championships**
- **Named Manager Of The Year Three Times**
- **Won More Than 800 Games In Each League**
- **His Penchant For Pulling Starters Earned Him The
  Nickname "Captain Hook"**

Decor in the manager's office in the visitors' locker room in Baltimore's Memorial Stadium is early attic—metal desk, retread chairs, sagging sofa—the perfect environment for one of baseball's great old shoes. George Lee "Sparky" Anderson is dressed in his pre-game uniform, Tiger gray pants, a blue-sleeved baseball underjersey, sanitaries, a pair of shower clogs. Behind a puff of pipe tobacco is the Anderson trademark—a big smile and a shock of white hair.

I explain my mission by reminding Anderson of his rookie year managing the Reds. Nineteen seventy was the first time the number of saves in the major leagues surpassed the number of games completed by starting pitchers. Anderson tamps fresh tobacco into his pipe and nods knowingly. I remind him that 1970 was also the season that his starters completed a niggling thirty-two games and that he called on his pen for help more than occasionally. "Sixty saves. That was a record I believe," I said.

"Yes, I went out there and got them," he said and struck a match. I pushed my recorder past the ashtray and into the appropriate flight path. You get a lot of smoke and wisdom in a Sparky Anderson chat.

Our situation at Cincinnati in the 1970s was that we didn't have good starting pitching. Everybody says that I was Captain Hook, but the pen wasn't built that way. We felt very strongly that we had to defense our starting pitching, so we defensed them with our bullpen. We had Granger, Clay Carroll, Don Gullett, Tommy Hall. So what we had was two right-handers and two left-handers and we just criss-crossed with them. If it got into the eighth or ninth inning and we had a lead, well, we had you. You were in trouble with those guys. We would match up with who you sent up there. But I don't remember many times using all four of them in the last inning just to get three outs.

There wasn't one game or one stretch. I think we did it with the bullpen all the time during those years. Clay Carroll, he was our number one guy. The sinkerball and he had a great curveball. He was like Eckersley. His stuff was starting pitching stuff. And everybody accused him of throwing a spitter. He never threw a spitter in his life. The pitch just fell out of the sky. I can say it now that he's done and through. The Hawk never threw a spitter. He wouldn't know how to throw a spitter. He just had a natural sinking fastball. It exploded on you, and a great breaking ball and a great changeup too. He wouldn't change up a whole lot, unless he was going to pitch more than one inning. If he was just going one inning, he'd come after you with his sinker and the breaking ball. But I don't think I ever had a better relief pitcher over a six-year period than Clay Carroll. Later on we had Eastwick and we had McEnaney. We always made up our bullpen with two and two, two left and two right. But that was our staff. In 1970 we started out with a great staff, Simpson and McGlothlin and Nolan. They were pitching extremely well, but we always, when we got into the eighth and ninth, we got into our bullpen. The hitters hadn't seen them and they'd already seen the starter. I always felt this way, I felt that my starters should not lose after seven good innings. They should not become the losing pitcher. If we were going to lose it, it would be out of our bullpen. We had the talent in the pen and so we did it that way.

I don't think that I had too many happy starters. Yes, they were unhappy. At that time though, I was truthfully a very brash, young, thirty-five-year-old manager that never had any thought or care about that. I don't think that I'd do it the same way now. Twenty years later I think that I would probably go longer with my starters. I hate to say that, but I would. In those days I knew that I could get it done out of our bullpen. I just went ahead and got it done, and I didn't care how they felt about it. I didn't talk to them at all about it! My pitching coach was the only one who talked to them and he was having holy hell all the time. Larry Shepard, a very rough, tough guy who didn't take any crap from nobody, he used to tell me. He'd get mad at me many times, you know. In fact, me and him had had a few go-arounds about it. I know he was right now, when I look back on it. But I had no fear of anything. I did exactly what I wanted to do and I could care less what anybody else thought.

I didn't get the idea of using the pen that way by seeing it done anywhere else. I truthfully have never done anything in baseball that I've consciously copied. I've never been one for reading about baseball. I never read a book. I never read anything. I go just by how I feel and that's how I felt about the bullpen. That's the way I felt at that time. And like I say, when you're thirty-five, you're a totally different person. You think that you can lick the whole world and nothing ever bothers you then. I know that they [starters] were a very unhappy group, they were. I can say that very honestly. You can ask any one of them and they will tell you that they were never happy.

Some of those great relievers that I had—there were two guys in that bullpen that I would let face right or left, Gullett and Carroll. I never took them out according to right or left. The other two just came in and did a special job. They were in and out. But Carroll and Gullett, if they were in there, they usually finished it, Carroll always. If he was in there he was going to stay. You had to beat him. I always had a theory. If I'm going to take the starter out once he gets a man on, then why should I ever let him go out there? I like to bring my relievers in at the beginning of an inning. And I stuck to that. I always started an inning off with my bullpen. If I was going to finish you off, it would be from a position of strength at the beginning of an inning, because now I could really play with you. They'd get me in a criss-cross if I brought them in in the middle of an inning. You could hit and I couldn't do nothing about it. But if I started off with my guy, then you had to make a move and I could counter. And I'd have you. And I kept all four of them ready.

Granger came from underneath and everything sunk for him. He didn't last too long for the simple reason that the hitters stopped swinging at the ball. Very similar to what happened to Quisenberry. The hitters just stopped swinging. It was almost always a ball and the hitters got to the point where they took on him, made him throw a strike. And that's what hurt him. They made him bring the ball up and after about two years he was just not nearly as effective.

Gullett just overpowered you. He never threw a break in those days. If he did, it was a little nickel slider, but it was hard. He just blasted away at 92 [MPH] to 94. And he'd just come in and literally overpower you.

Pedro [Borbon] had to hate me most. I think Larry Shepard, the pitching coach, had more trouble keeping him in line than anybody else. Pedro never got a chance to finish, very seldom. He was the middle man, the guy who always had to do the dirty work. He did a tremendous job, but we never ever let him finish. He might have had eleven saves, maybe one year fourteen, eighteen or so later, but he never got up into the thirties. He was always the guy doing the dirty work and he just never ever got the credit for it. Pedro is the one guy who, I would say very honestly, had every right to be unhappy. Pedro was a piece of work. I remember in the World Series against Oakland in 1972, we've got 'em beat by a run and a man on first. I go out to the mound and I tell Pedro, "Now look, I don't want you to go to first," because when he did, he had a tendency to throw hard and wild. And I turned around and walked back to the dugout. Before I could sit down, there was the ball going over to first and past the first baseman. And I said, "Now how can this be. I just went out and told that man not to throw and here he goes. . . ."

That's another thing about great pitchers. When the game is on the line, guys like Eckersley, Rollie Fingers, Gossage, they know exactly what the problem is. Nobody has to tell them that a base hit beats them, a home run has got 'em. Nobody has to tell them the situation. They know it and they don't want you to tell them the situation. Because now you're putting something in their minds. They know if there're two men on and they've got a three-run lead, that this man at the plate isn't gonna hit a home run. He ain't gonna get no ball that he can drive. And they also know which guy between the guy hitting and the guy at the bat rack they can get out. If it's the guy in the on-deck circle, then if this guy at the plate hits one, he's gonna have to hit one hell of a pitch, because he's not gonna see anything. That's one of the differences between the great ones and the rest. The great ones know.

The great ones are all competitors, they can hardly wait to get into the game. They fight you like hell when you try to take them off. Now I got one guy, a starter, Jack Morris. Jack has actually broken blood vessels in my fingers slamming the ball in my hand. He broke them on Opening Day this year. It was cold and he slams the ball so hard in my hand that he breaks the blood vessels. But that's all right with me. Jack's almost a madman. He gets wild, he'll watch me. I'll be on the bench and I won't look. But I know he's staring at me, daring me to come out there. He just stares. Where other guys I honestly know that they want me to come out. But him, he's very ornery. Every game he pitches, I know that day, if I have to take him out, that my hand is gonna have to take the punishment. I do know that, I'll say one thing, he's never ever said anything. A couple times he's thrown out

270

a couple of words, not at me. They're *at* me, but they're not said towards me. He gets really nasty. Which is good, it's great. It's so nice to see people that really care. I've had too many guys in my career, that I'd say, "Man, that cat wanted out of there bad," he laid that ball in my hand so soft. He's a happy cat. Or lookin' at you to come and get them. I've had that too. I call them genuflectors. They go behind the mound and start looking up and down, man, they want you to come out there and get them. Give me a Morris!

I think in every bullpen that there is one reliever that will always be unhappy. I don't care, every great bullpen. Honeycutt over at Oakland. Honeycutt's just going to get them to a point and then Eckersley is going to come on. Left-handed hitter or not, Eckersley's coming anyhow. It's all over now. Eckersley's coming. And so each staff that has a great bullpen is going to have one guy that's going to pay! Murphy at Boston, it looks like that's the way they're setting up. Murphy is going to do all the dirty work and Reardon is going to get the payday. That's the way it works, the setup, I mean. Somebody has to do it. Usually the guy that's doing that is doing the most important job for you.

Communication. I believe in it now. Your pitching coach has to really do it. It's tough enough handling a bullpen situation, but Larry Shepard [at Cincinnati], was about as tough as I've ever seen. He was tough both ways. He was tough with the men and he was tough with me. I think that was the thing that was so good. The fact that he was able to be so tough with them and also very tough with me. He would come in and fight for them. They didn't know it but he would fight like hell for them. And he wouldn't go back and say, "I fought for you but couldn't win." But he would fight me tooth and nail. Many times on the bench he would try to stop me. He'd know that I was going. But he'd try to talk me out of it, and I wouldn't listen. He'd raise hell after the game. So that's why I've always loved him. He had the fortitude inside to fight for what he thought was right. And he was right! He only wanted fairness for his pitchers and he wasn't getting it. And he has a right. It wouldn't make no sense to have a pitching coach if he wasn't going to fight for his pitchers.

Bob Hertzel [a writer] named me "Captain Hook." Hertsie gave me that name. He's in Pittsburgh now. My reaction to the name? Well, the reaction was that he was right. Because at that time we had a bad staff. That was around 1973 or 1974. We were really short on starting pitching. We had Tommy Carroll, Dick Baney, Pat Darcy, we were really short. If we could get them to five innings, that's all I hoped for. And that year, I don't know how many games that we went without a complete game, I know we hold a record for it. But there was just no way.

And I think that I was maybe the first one to take two relief pitchers. I took Carroll and McGraw, maybe I took three or four relief pitchers to that All-Star game. Tug McGraw was unbelievable. He was pitching for the Mets then and Yogi was managing. Tug was so good, and me and Yogi used to have a thing going all the time. When we got to the ninth I knew that Tug was coming in and Yogi would give me the old nose-thumb from his dugout. I'd give him the bird back. But Yogi and I were such good friends that we could do that. Oh, he knew that I didn't want McGraw in there. And Tug was great. He had the good fastball and he had that great screwball. I want to tell you something, his screwball was a legitimate screwball. He could pop you with that fastball and set it up. And Tug had no fear. Tug's a loony bird. He had no fear of anything. And that's the type of guy that it takes to be a great reliever. The greatest to me of all relievers is Rollie Fingers. I don't believe that we'll ever see, in our time, a relief pitcher that could go the distance for seventeen years the way Rollie did. And I know his theory because I asked him. His theory was, "Shithouse or castle!" He never worried about it. He came in and was going to throw strikes. If you get him, fine. If you don't, fine. He never worried either way. I thought he was the greatest relief pitcher of my time.

Eckersley is the big man today. He reminds me so much of Fingers. Their stuff is similar. They throw strikes at all times. They know which guy can hurt them and which guy can't. They go after the guy who can't hurt them and the guy who can, they make hit their pitch. They're that good with their control. I just feel like Eckersley right now is the guy who is the man. He has no fear. He believes so much in himself that he believes he's going to do it. I just don't believe that you can be any better than Eckersley, he's so consistent.

About handling relievers, I think the greatest manager in recent years has been Whitey Herzog. You see, Whitey has shaped his club but his main thing has been shaping his bullpen. Whitey's whole thing has been based around the bullpen. He's had speed, of course, very little power, and he plays in a big ball park. He tries to beat you with his speed and his bullpen. I would say the last five years that Whitey Herzog has been the number one bullpen manager, along with Tony La Russa at Oakland. Tony over there took Honeycutt from a starter to a reliever, Eckersley from starter to a reliever, took Burns from a starter to a reliever. And the one I almost forgot—the right-hander who used to be with Chicago—Nelson. Now you see Nelson and Burns do their dirty work. Then on comes Honeycutt and then on comes the big guy. You can almost go right on down his staff, he's shaped his bullpen.

I remember Tony asking me the year before last—they'd beat us a ball game the night before and Honeycutt was pitching real well. They had a lead and he brought on Eckersley to start the ninth. And he asked me, "Was I wrong?" And I said, "Tony, let me tell you something, you'd a been wrong if you don't bring your ace. Any time you can bring your ace on to finish a job, I don't care if Superman is hitting, if you can and you don't, you're going to be wrong. And that's what Tony does now. He doesn't care who's pitching or what—Eckersley's coming on.

From now on, in our game it will be a game of bullpens. Why didn't it start sooner, come to the game any quicker? It used to be that if you were in the bullpen you were a bad pitcher. You were down there because you couldn't pitch. Now today the guy in the bullpen can make more money than the starter. Mark Davis makes more money than any starter, Eckersley is going to make more money than any starter, Smith and Reardon are making a tremendous amount of money. You're going to see that the bullpen guy is the guy. They've won the MVP, Hernandez. I know one thing, that today there will always be a bullpen guy up in the top five on the MVP ballot. Always in the last six, seven years. The bullpen is the game. It's all settled now.

TUG McGRAW
Left-Handed Pitcher

NEW YORK METS, 1965–1967, 1969–1974
PHILADELPHIA PHILLIES, 1975–1984

- **Made The Phrase "You Gotta Believe" Famous During Mets' Amazing Finish In 1973**
- **Winning Pitcher In 1972 All-Star Game**
- **Final Game Hero Of 1980 World Series**
- **Named Tug As An Infant For His Aggressive Feeding Habits**
- **Wrote "Scroogie," A Nationally Syndicated Cartoon**

Here's the scene, the way I thought I'd always remember Tug McGraw. When the Mets had that miracle finish in 1973, I remember Tug pogo-sticking off the mound, screaming, "You gotta believe!" Scene two took the place of that image. It was played out in the restaurant of an Embassy Suites Hotel in Philadelphia. Tug, napkin tucked under his belt, is on his feet, imaginary bat held high, showing me—and a bewildered waitress—how he designed an out against Hank Aaron in the 1969 National League championship series. "You have to realize this was more than Hank Aaron, more than an out!" McGraw explained. "It was about confidence and a young pitcher coming of age."

It was against Atlanta in the 1969 play-offs. I learned something that confirmed everything. I relied heavily on my catchers for the signs, because I really didn't have the confidence to know what to throw. When I developed the screwball, with that came my whole cube theory, the strike zone was no longer a plane to me. And Aaron, it was Aaron in the play-offs. This whole series was supposed to be a pitchers' duel. It turned out to be a sluggers' duel. In a key situation I had to face Aaron. I struck him out on four pitches, he fouled one off. And Grote was the catcher, a very, very ornery catcher, a very much in-charge guy. If you didn't do what he said—like if you finally did talk him into changing his sign, if you shook, shook, shook. He'd keep putting the same sign down, thinking, "McGraw doesn't know what's going on out there, I do." I'd been a yes-man out there but this time I kept saying no, no. If you shook, and you didn't throw a strike, the next pitch came back from Grote harder than you threw it in there. He had a cannon. And just before those play-offs, I was pitching real well—this was the end of 1969—and we were still having these problems with the signs. He wanted to call everything, and that was fine because I was learning at the time. But the more I wanted to call them, the more I started thinking about what was going on. In order to step over that bridge and get real stubborn about it, I had to really be sure about what I was doing. And there were times when he'd fire that ball back and just about rip my head off. And finally I called him out to the mound one time. I said, "Hey, Jerry, I understand where you're coming from with the signals. I know that you know the hitters better than I do, but you're not doing anything to help the situation when you fire the ball back like that. And," I said, "it pisses me off. The next time you do it the fucker is going out into center field. Because I'm not going to catch it. If I want to shake off a sign, I'm sorry, that's the way it's going to be." There was a major growl, but I really think that's what he wanted me to do. What he really wanted was somebody out there with balls. And as long as he could get away with calling the shots, you were a wimp in his eyes. You [had to] challenge him and [say], "Goddamn it, it's my fucking ball game. I'm the one that's going to get the win or the loss. It's my ass on the line and not yours." He wanted me to say that. He was going to keep busting my chops until I finally told him, "Okay. *Enough!*"

We got into the play-offs and Aaron was up and Grote called for a screwball right off the top. I wanted a curveball. I didn't think that Aaron was going to be looking for a curveball. So I threw a curveball and he took it for a strike. And then Grote called for another screwball and I never like to throw my screwball behind a curve. It's two off-speed pitches in a row and that's not much of a change. You're going like this and going like that [demonstrates with a wrist flip]. The curveball comes out of a high plane and goes down. And so a lot of times after a curveball I liked to throw a high fastball. It's that same plane and a fraction of a second longer for the hitter to decide that it's not going to go down. So I came with the fastball up and in and strike two. He took it. And now Grote throws down the screwball [sign] again. And I thought, "No, man, now it's 0–2, Aaron is just going to be protecting the plate. He's looking for a screwball and if I throw something off-speed he's just going to be . . . he's got those quick hands, you know." All this stuff is going through my head. I'm going to make him think that it's a screwball and I'm going to throw him a fastball hard off the plate low. In the same area that the screwball would be. And I swear to God, it's a good thing that it was off the plate. Because Aaron was looking screwball and he was, fortunately, about that far outside. He just went *whoosh!* and hit that mother straight back foul on the screen. He was right on it. And if I'd a thrown a screwball he'd a been out in front of it that much more and that baby would have been a souvenir. And I said, perfect, that's exactly what I thought he might do. Either that or take it. It was almost like I saw all this before the sequence started and that everything was going right in order. And now it was time to throw the screwball, in my mind. But not out there [outside]. Grote called for a screwball again, and he always gave you location. He puts down screwball and he goes like this, he wants it outside. I go yes, and then no. Yes to the pitch, no to location. He didn't need to put down another location. He knew it wasn't going to be outside and that I was going to drop one inside. Usually hitters are always looking for tips, when you say yes and then no. They think fastball because not too many guys shake off location on their breaking ball. This gave me an advantage throughout my career because I used to shake off location on my breaking ball a lot and a lot of hitters thought, "Oh, that's fastball!" I mean, how many guys spot their breaking ball? I threw the screwball right at Arron's hip. And Aaron locked because he thought it was going to be an inside fastball, and it dropped right over the inside corner for strike three. And now I'm out on the mound having one! I punched out Hank Aaron just the way I saw it. It was like designing an out.

I started my professional career as a suspect, not a prospect. They didn't want to sign me—my brother made them. I wouldn't even have gotten signed into pro ball. Hank got me signed. He was in the Mets organization and he threatened to quit if they didn't sign me. Later, when I received my first major league contract telling me to report to spring training with the Mets, we both thought it was for him, a mix-up because he's Hank and I'm Frank. We figured somebody screwed up, some secretarial typo in New York. So I called them and said, "Hey, you got my contract wrong. You got my brother's name on my contract!" They said, no and explained the protection rule. They were real short on left-handed pitchers and they had plenty of catchers so they didn't have to protect Hank. They reassured me that it didn't mean that I was going to make the team, that it just meant that I was going to be on the forty-man roster. Hank was going to be invited to spring training too. We'd probably be playing together somewhere down in the minor leagues.

I didn't have a real powerful fastball and I was only like 5'10" and 165 pounds. What I did have was pretty good control, particularly for a left-hander. Left-handers usually don't have good control, especially when they're young. When we were in high school I had an awesome curveball. I had a really good tight rotation on it. When the Mets started looking at me in a more serious way, that and the good control probably caught their eye.

I guess Clyde McCullough was probably the first legitimate Mets coach in the minor leagues who said, "This guy can play at the major league level." I think that Clyde thought I had something and he passed the word along. I didn't stay in the minor leagues long—rookie leagues in Florida, near Cocoa Beach, Auburn, New York, and back to St. Pete in Florida—three teams in one summer which might be a record. And all this time I'm starting. A little relief, but mostly a starter. The fact that I got rushed to the big leagues eventually is probably what made me a reliever because everything happened so fast. I hadn't developed any system for myself, how to budget time, budget energy—when to focus, when not to focus. When to relax. Here I am in Shea Stadium and the World's Fair is right across the street. This was 1965 and suddenly I'm with the Mets. I don't want to make this sound like I do drugs because I'm not a druggie, but that whole rookie year was like an LSD trip. It was one big high all the time. I'd come in and mop up a game. I was the last pitcher on the team and I'd come in and clean them up. We'd be losing terribly and Casey would say, "Get McGraw ready!" And I'd go out there with the idea that we were going to win, I believed that we were going to have this miraculous comeback and that we'd win it. Nine-to-nothing in the third inning and I'd go out there all pumped up saying, "Hey, we got a chance!"

The Mets were so bad. They'd gone with all the old guys when they established the club, and little did we know but the marketing plan for the Mets was—Number one—see if New York is ready to accept a National League franchise. Because New York was pissed. They were pissed that the Dodgers and Giants had left. So Mrs. Payson and her gang got the Mets together—old guys—it looked like a gum card show, ex-marquee names—Hodges and Ashburn, Duke Snider, just to see if there was interest. The press knew that if they could sell National League baseball to New York again that they would all have jobs. So the media guys, rather than bury the Mets, they made them into folk heroes. Hot Rod Kanehl, Marvelous Marv Throneberry, Choo Choo Coleman. These guys were not really good ballplayers. They were leftover Yankees and from other organizations, guys who had experience but were teetering, couldn't quite cut it in the big leagues. Yet with expansion those guys get a chance, so the press just made good comical fun, made characters out of those guys. They could rally all that around Stengel. Casey was the perfect guy, the marquee name to pull it off. Once they started drawing fans and they saw it was going to be a viable franchise, they went ahead and built Shea Stadium. It was all tied into the World's Fair, I mean it was a marketing phenomenon. Once that happened and the turnstiles started clicking, then in 1964 and 1965 they started rushing up all these young guys. Cleon Jones and [Bud] Harrelson and [Ed] Kranepool—Kranepool they brought up earlier because he was a local boy. They started gradually filtering the younger guys in. I remember in 1965 Casey saying, "It's time to start developing the youths of America!" So the marketing strategy changed from drawing people to trying to develop a club that could win. They figured that they could finish last without these old guys. They brought up everybody that they thought had major league potential and I got caught in that wave in 1965.

That first Mets team that I played for was something. Casey brought Jesse Owens to spring training to teach us how to run. Jesse showed up at spring training and the first day he was there he got a hip pointer and couldn't run. He's out there giving us exercises and everything and he hurt himself—that was vintage Mets—they're going to be a base running threat because we've got Jesse Owens as a running coach. We had a big time with him. We'd say, "Hey, Jesse, you've got us doing all this running, when was the last time you threw a baseball to get in shape for track?" We used to always bust his chops. Then he gets hurt right away, "Thanks, Jesse, now we know what not to do!" But Jesse Owens was a great guy. He was in kind of a strange environment there. But Jesse was great. Number one, he was really honored to be invited down by the Mets and number two, he was proud of his experiences in the Olympics. He was great at sharing that with people. Number three, he was just a kind guy. I really liked him.

Warren Spahn was the pitching coach. And Spahnie and I were a lot alike. I had Spahn tendencies. Spahn was all business on the mound but in the dugout, in the clubhouse and outside the arena he was a lively character. A good time guy, always pulling jokes, a ballbuster. He and Lew Burdette. I wasn't around then, but they were notorious for some of the things that they used to do. And of course, there was Casey. Even though I was there, I didn't have any way of evaluating Casey's performance. He was way over my head. I was a rookie and I just sort of watched him, but stayed my distance. The only thing that I remember him saying directly to me, really personal, directly, was in regards to Warren Spahn. One day in the locker room Casey nodded toward Spahn and says to me, "While you're at the ball park don't leave that man's shadow! But when the game is over, I don't want you to go near him!" Casey didn't even know my name yet but he must have thought of me as some sort of a Spahn protégé. He wanted me to learn as much as I could from him, but I guess he thought we'd be trouble away from the park. One day Casey walked up and wanted to know if I was related to John McGraw. I said "No," and that was that, end of conversation.

But that whole evolution of me coming to the big leagues at a very young age was something. Being with the Mets made it even more so. It took me until 1969 to come out of the fantasy, the dream part. I was in awe of bonus babies. I was in awe of the other players. Even in the minor leagues I was in awe of guys who came out of good colleges. I was just really naive and awestruck. Major league heroes were all over the place, Whitey Ford, Warren Spahn. When I was a kid playing in California, Mickey Mantle was my hero. And then one day, here I am pitching to him. Here's a ridiculous crazy story.

That first spring that I went to the Mets camp on the forty-man roster, after I was there for a while, the Grapefruit League had started and we were going over to Ft. Lauderdale to play the Yankees. I called my dad and said, "Hey, Dad, we're playing the Yankees tomorrow." And to him, just the fact that I was there was like I'd been in the big leagues all my life. This was spring training and I hadn't pitched an inning yet. But my dad is telling everybody that his son is a major leaguer, telling the world. I told him we were playing the Yankees tomorrow and guess what, I'm pitching. And to him, it was like you're starting in a World Series. Of course, to me it was too. So he says, "Those guys are tough, son!" They've just played in the 1964 World Series. They still had Maris, they still had Mantle, Howard, Boyer, Pepitone, Kubek, Richardson, and he's telling me they're tough. So Dad says, "Really tough, they were just in the World Series." I said, "Okay, I'll let you know how things go!" And then just before he hangs up he says, "I don't care what you do, I'll be proud of you. But do me a favor, son. Strike out that Mickey Mantle for me!" So I say "Oh sure, Dad!"

I gave up, I think, seven runs in the first inning. Got one guy out before Casey hooked me. I struck out Mantle. So I call my dad after the game. He's all over the place. "How did it go, how did it go?"

And I said, "Well, I got your deal done. Struck out Mantle." That's something I won't forget. I got him on a fastball. I'd thrown him some curves and I was ahead in the count. And I think he must have been looking for a breaking pitch. That whole experience was something.

My first game memory from Shea? Well, that was when my dad threw up. That was the first major league hitter I ever faced. I think that was in the first game of a doubleheader on Easter Sunday, 1965. Orlando Cepeda. I struck him out on a 2–2 curveball. It was his first time up in 1965. He'd had knee surgery in the off-season. But I remember when he first stepped to the plate. I clearly remember wondering how I was going to miss his bat. How could I miss that? The bat looked like a big, huge telephone pole. I just didn't know how I'd miss it. The first thought that I had, how am I going to miss that sucker? I grew up near San Francisco so my dad was as usual "watching" the game on the radio. "I watched you on the radio. I could see everything you were doing!" He used to say that all the time. That's the way dads are. So I struck out Cepeda. He had some friends over at the house with him. They said as soon as, I guess it was Russ Hodges, the radio guy, said, "And Cepeda goes down swinging to the young left-hander," my dad jumped up off the sofa, ran into the bathroom and threw up. That was it, my career was underway. Hello john, hello Shea!

I wasn't much better in the nerve department. In April, when it's cold they have those tanks of hot bouillon in the dugout to keep warm. A consommé. I was like this, shaking like crazy. I only pitched that inning and they took me out for a pinch hitter. The next guy after Cepeda, Hal Lanier, grounded out to second. Then they hit for me and I was out of there. So I'm vibrating. And I go into the locker room to take an aspirin and the trainer—this is how baseball has changed—the trainer walked in and I still had my shaking cup of soup. He says, "What the hell's the matter with you?" I said, "Boy, this is fun, isn't it? I can't wait until I call my dad." He said, "Are you all right?" And I said, "Yeah, I just get this way. This is the way I get." And he says, "We got another game. You can't pitch if you're like that. You've gotta calm down. Here take these." And he gave me Valium. They didn't know in those days. I remember later on I earned a start and I was pitching the second game of a doubleheader against the Cubs in Chicago, Wrigley Field. The trainer says, "Look I know how you get, here take this," and he gave me a Valium. And I went out and I warmed up. I got on the mound. The first guy got on, second guy got on, third guy got on. Fourth guy, Billy Williams, grand slam, four to nothing, nobody out. Bottom of the first. Casey came to the mound and said, "Kid, I don't think you got it today!" And I said,

"I'm alright now, Casey, I was just a little nervous." "Too late, hit the showers!" he said. Took me out of the game and I walked out of the dugout. In Chicago you've gotta go down those stairs to get out of the dugout. I see the trainer and I say, "Don't you ever give me another one of those things." I said, "I just gave up a grand slam and I don't even care. I'm not pissed! There's something wrong!" I never took another one.

One of the things you have to learn to deal with is failure, of course. I remember what Spahnie said when I gave up my first major league home run. It was to Hank Aaron. And I gave some up—there's a lot of guys who wouldn't be in the Hall of Fame without me. I mean Aaron creamed it. It disappeared into the night. It was majestic. It banged off one of the light towers in Shea Stadium, above the fence, way up. And you know I firmly believed that I'd never give up a home run. All rookies believe that. They should anyway. I firmly believed that I wasn't going to give up a hit. When that happened I wasn't going to give up a run and I was never going to give up a *home run*. The process of elimination and I was all pissed off about the Aaron deal. So I did my young rookie thing, threw my glove in the dugout, and plopped myself down next to Spahn. And he says, "You gotta throw a ball real hard for it to go that far, kid!"

I've always been a great rememberer of firsts—first time I give up a dinger to Aaron, the first time I beat Koufax. That was a big breakthrough. Sandy was the pride of New York. Howard Cosell interviewed me on his program the next day, it was like instant credibility. I think the Mets lost a lot of money that night because since then, at least 300,000 people have come up to me and told me that they were at that game. And then there was the first time I got myself ejected from a ball game. That came in September of 1965, my last start before I was to report to the Marine Corps for basic training. There'd never been a no-hitter thrown in Forbes Field. So I'd made up my mind that I was going to throw a perfect game. I was going to finish strong. And the first three guys up *boom, boom, boom*. I get them all. Second inning all three down, *boom, boom, boom*. Third inning, *boom, boom, boom*. I was perfect through three. And then in the bottom of the fourth, error, maybe a walk and then Clemente hit a chopper in front of home plate. I saw it go up and it was going to come down to me and it hung up there like a hot air balloon. It just wouldn't come down. Finally I got it and I turned and looked at first and he was already past the bag. I just had to eat that son of a gun. There went my no-hitter. And then Clendenon came up, big son-of-a-bitch. Curveball—I thought it hit the ground before he hit it. It was a great curveball, a super curve, ankle high and he just golfed that sucker. I had to go up on my toes to keep it from hitting me in the *cojones*. It went right between my legs. Hickman, the center fielder, had to come charging in to catch it in the air. That sucker went between my legs and then went up. *Wooo!* Hickman is coming in to try to catch the line drive in the air. That baby was nailed. He missed it. He tried to shorthop it and it rolled out by the batting cage in center field. A friggin' grand slam single. By the time Hickman retrieved the ball Clendenon was coming into third. They overthrew third. I went over and got the ball and now Clendenon is going home. I think I got him in some kind of a rundown so now all of a sudden I'm backing up the catcher. And the ball got over his head and I ended up coming to the plate. I don't recall how I got the ball but there I was at the plate with the ball and putting the tag on him. The umpires says, "Safe!" I remember cussing my brains out. My eyes were closed and I was just cutting loose. When I opened them up, there was the umpire and he thought I was talking to him. He had nothing to do with it. But he took all this conversation personally. I guess it was while I had my eyes closed cussing, he'd given me the boot. But I still don't know this so I head on back to the mound. Wes Westrum came out to the mound, this was after Casey had broken his hip I believe. Wes came out to the mound and he said, "Hey, you're outta here. It's over." And I say, "One little chopper and a horseshit grand slam single, and you're taking me out?" He said, "I'm not taking you out. See that guy down there behind home plate? He's the one that asked you to leave." Then I snapped. I'm screaming, threw my glove, I'm kicking it all over the infield. Quite a display. Awesome. Finally I get it all together and I'm walking through the Pirates dugout heading to the tunnel for our clubhouse. I really was pissed, but it was almost tongue in cheek at that point. And I'm walking through there and Clendenon is standing there not too far from where I've gotta go down the tunnel. And the Pirates, they're all just having a good time with this, "Look at that kid out there, he lost it!" And so Clendenon says in this real deep voice, "Hey, kid, what'd you say to the umpire to make him send you home like that?" And I said, "I wasn't talking to him, I didn't say nothin' to him." And so Clendenon says, "Well, who were you talkin' to?" And I said, "You!" "Well, what'd you say to me?" And I said, "Fuck you, you motherfucker!" And I took off running, down the runway into the clubhouse and slammed the door behind me. There's this board that you can pull down so nobody can break in. I pulled the board down, locked it up, I thought the whole Pirate bench was coming after me. Ironically Clendenon got traded to the Mets in 1969 and we started reliving that story. I told him, "I swear I thought every one of you guys were coming after me." Clendenon said, "We couldn't." I said, "Why?" "Because our legs wouldn't work, we were too busy laughing. You had us rolling on the dugout floor!"

One of the things that I remember most about the early years when I was basically starting, other than getting Mantle in that spring game, was how wired I always was. It took me two minutes to warm up. As soon as they handed me the ball I wanted the game to start. And you know, it was always that way, that's the way it was when I was starting. When I was starting I'd wake up early. Usually on a game day you'd wake up at nine or ten o'clock or something. But the day I was starting I'd wake up at like five o'clock. I couldn't sleep and then it would be time to eat breakfast at ten o'clock. I'd be there at eight o'clock and I'm like eating lunch at noon instead of two o'clock. You're supposed to be at the ball park at five and I'd be there at three. The whole waiting process, I couldn't deal with it. Between starts I just never learned how to handle it. Didn't know what to do with my energy. "Aaaaah!" [He screams and pulls at his hair.] I was always playing catch between starts. I just wasn't cut out for that pace that a starter has. What happened with me was that when the start finally did get there and I was going to have a good night, I'd breeze through everybody the first time. I might give up a few hits, walk a few guys, but I'd get through it. And then the second time around I'd say, "Oh man, they know what I'm going to throw them." And then if I'd get through that I was dead. I just didn't know what to do now. "God, they've seen me twice. They know my mother's middle name." So I'd just psyche myself out and make something bad happen. Coming out of the bull-pen I could face anybody, go through the lineup one time and nobody had a chance. Tomorrow night do the same thing, the next night do it again. And it's weird, very strange. Top guns, your relievers, they need that speed fix. And I wasn't one of those guys who could block the other factions out. One of the reasons I think that I was able to enjoy my career so much was because I learned early that I couldn't do that. By the time I blocked everything out I was, "Aaaaah-hhh!"—wired. No function. I listened to the guys in the dugout, they like to get on your case. I listened to people in the stands. I heard everything. I never went back and forth with them. If you do that they think they've accomplished something. If somebody yells something, you can glance over and they know you heard them. They're going to have a bat in their hand one of these days. So you play that game, but nothing like, "What?" My role was kind of fun and I wasn't easily intimidated.

The screwball developed like this. I needed a third pitch and I was down in winter ball. Ralph Terry, the Yankee great, wound up his career with the Mets in 1967. This was the winter of 1966 and Terry was trying to decide whether he was going to try to continue in baseball or try professional golf. I spent a lot of time on the golf course with Ralph. We were always talking about golf balls and slicing the ball and drawing the ball. And backspin, when the ball would bite and pull up on the green. We'd just switch the conversation back and forth from baseball to golf, talking about rotation and all this stuff. It was all a learning experience and he said, "You know, with your changeup you might try what I do when I want to take something off of my sinker." And he didn't even refer to it as a screwball. He said, "You just place it back in your hand a little bit more. Adjust your grip a little bit more." And he'd show me. And he said, "When you finish off the pitch, instead of having your wrist flop straight down like you normally would on your fastball, flop it a little bit inside the ball. Just have your wrist follow through. Flop inside the ball and it will be back in your fingers a little bit further. You won't be able to get the velocity on it like your fastball does and it will tail a little. And that will be a good moving changeup. Try it and see how it feels." So everyday I'd play catch with him and he'd say, "Nah, nah, that's not it, you're exaggerating your this or your that." One day I finally got that little flop. I got that little rotation that he was looking for. And he said, "How does that feel?" And all of a sudden it was there. And my thought was, "I understand!" But the palm ball, the window shade curve, all of those pitches, I never understood. The concept I could appreciate but I just didn't have them. It wasn't there. But with Ralph, that little wrist flop and that little rotation. Oh, yes I could see it. And I threw it all the time, pepper games, batting practice, pitch and catch. In games, making the normal mistakes with it and the next thing you know it evolved into the full opposite of the curve. The screwball. I could change speeds with it. It opened up a whole new world for me. I was like a carpenter with a whole new set of tools. It's like you have all these power tools with no electricity. Well, the screwball provided me the electricity. It turned all the other pitches on.

Gil Hodges was the Mets manager then. He and a lot of the Mets people were skeptical of the pitch. They were afraid that it was going to hurt my elbow. So what I had to do was call it a changeup. When I started throwing it, I'd watched Brewer with the Dodgers throw it. And I did hurt my elbow. I hurt my shoulder throwing the pitch. But as it turned out those were growing pains. So pitching in Jacksonville, Florida, in 1967 and 1968 I got a chance to develop the pitch. If I'd a stayed in the big leagues those two years they wouldn't have let me throw it and I may have never developed it. By going to Triple-A I was able to develop it and to learn how to use it. And that's when pitching became a whole new world for me. When I came back in 1969 with the Mets, that's when [as a pitcher] I really had a clue. That's when all of a sudden with that screwball, the whole strike zone became more than just a plane. The strike zone became like a big cube and you could use the front of it, the back of it, the top, the bottom, the inside, the outside. There was so much more to work with.

I had some great catchers who worked with me—Duffy Dyer in the minors and then Jerry Grote later with the Mets. I think because I was small when I came up that I was one guy whose fastball improved and that helped set up the other pitches. Most guys spend four or five years in the minors and when they get to the big leagues, what you see is what you get. But when I first came up in 1965 I didn't have much yet. But now when I came back in 1969 I had been through the Marine Corps. I'd spent a couple of years in Jacksonville in Triple-A. I'd filled out and I'd worked hard and I'd ironed out a lot of mechanical things in my delivery. I'd developed what I considered a high-performance functioning delivery, which all the Mets pitchers evolved into. Seaver, Koosman and myself, we had great mechanics.

Now 1969 was the year of the Miracle Mets. I had a great season out of the pen, good play-offs, but I didn't pitch in the Series. I remember distinctly in the early part of 1969 Hodges came in at the beginning of spring training and he said, "I'm going to take you north with me as a relief pitcher. I can't take you as a starter. If you want to start, you'll have to go to Tidewater [the Mets Triple-A Farm team]. If we get an opening I'll call you up. I really need help in the bullpen, but I know you want to be a starter." So I said, "Look, I'd rather be a reliever in a major league bullpen than a starter in the minors. I'll be your first baseman, your center fielder, whatever . . . just take me north." So I came up north as a reliever. I had the best spring that I'd ever had in my life. Just unbelievable. They had expansion after the 1968 season where Montreal and San Diego were added to the league. Nobody took me in the first three rounds. Then the Mets protected me. When I got to spring training they had a lot of young pitchers. Even though they'd finished last in 1968, the Mets were really starting to rumble. And Hodges was emphatic on winning. He had a lot of pitchers in camp and had I not had a good spring, I may have been off to one of the expansion teams. So when I got to spring training I went to Rube [Walker] and I said, "Am I going to be allowed to throw my screwball this spring?" The previous two springs they wouldn't let me. Rube says, "Kid, you can throw whatever you want because you're going to have to really do something to make this team this year. It's up to you!" I said, "What, you're not worrying about me hurting my arm?" He said, "You're not going to be here. So we don't care. It's your life. When you were younger we tried to help you develop but now you're at the point where you gotta do it!" And that was probably the best advice that Rube ever gave me. "Do what you gotta do!" So I ended up not walking anybody all spring. I think I had close to two strikeouts an inning and only gave up one or two hits. None of the hitters had ever seen me throw the screwball. I didn't throw the pitch even thirty percent of the time. But my fastball and my curveball were still hot. I probably threw it a couple of times to each hitter and I had a lot of long counts because I always dicked around with the strike zone. I always had long counts. Maybe thirty-five percent screwballs.

I made the team and Hodges used me in early trouble. Not even as a setup man—as soon as a starter got in trouble. I was the first guy. And in six weeks I was 4–0 and I'll never forget he called me in to talk. I'd been coming in and slamming the door and we were winning. Some of our aging hitters were starting to hit—Agee, Jones. And suddenly we had comeback capabilities and I was holding teams. So if we had trouble, Hodges boomed, "McGraw!" The next thing you know Hodges called me into the office, I think it was like the middle of May and he said, "Tug, I'm going to give you my opinion about your role on this team. This club is on the verge of going somewhere and I see you playing a role on this team that's very valuable. If it doesn't fit into what you want for your career, we'll make some changes. Because you really are a good young pitcher. Here's the way I see you on this ball club. I need a stopper." I didn't even know what a stopper was. Something for the bathtub? He said, "I need a guy who can come in in the late innings and slam the door." And I said, "You mean I'll only get to pitch a couple of innings?" Because I'd been pitching three, four and five innings and loving it. He said, "That's right, just a few but you might have to do it every night!" And I said, "Oh, that's almost like being a regular. You go to the ball park, you know you've got a chance to play." And he said, "You're a good pitcher. In my view you probably will be around for a long time. As a starter I think that you'd be a pretty good pitcher, maybe better than average. But as a relief pitcher, if you learn how to come in and learn how to slam that door for me, I think that you can probably be one of the best in baseball. I don't think that you can be one of the best as a starter. So what I'm going to tell you is—if you haven't already figured it out, you dumb

286

little shit—that you can make more money as a real good relief pitcher than you will as an average pitcher. Also, this team with a great stopper has a chance of going somewhere and you can be a part of that. As a relief pitcher you can have a much longer career. That's the way I see your future with the Mets. Do you have a problem with that?" I said, "Where's the bullpen?"

In the 1969 Series, I spent most of that one on the bench. I wanted to be close to the action but I went down in the bullpen. As soon as I'd see something stir up I'd run down there. I knew that I wasn't going to be the stopper for that one. Ron Taylor was pretty much going to be the guy. There were so many thrills in that Series, they're not crystal clear. But I do remember sitting in the bullpen and when the phone would ring—sometimes you had them or you didn't, so sometimes it was signs from the dugout—tall guy, little guy, left-hander, physical signs to let us know who to get up. You'd see the pitching coach get up on the steps and my heart would be like "*Wump, wump, wump.* It's going to be me." For me they'd always turn the left hand over, the screwball sign. When you see the guy step up, almost hyperventilating time, and then when you'd see it was somebody else, it was, "Aw, shit. Hey, go get 'em, let's go now! Like, shit! Yeah!"

I had a starter's repertoire. And I got to enjoy this with the Phillies more than I did with the Mets because I was experienced and I'd learned things—you could really go to the mound like you're Picasso or Christian Dior and design something. And that's why I used to pitch deep into the count almost every time. Because I was always trying to design an out. Work the hitter to the point that when I make this pitch, this is the one that I'm trying to get the ground ball with. This is the pitch that I'm trying to get the strikeout with. This is the pitch that I don't care about, this is just setup stuff. When you're doing that sometimes you miss. I mean you really gotta be careful. Sometimes you fall behind in the count because of that. You can't miss somewhere where he can hit his fly ball or ground ball. I got most of my ground ball double plays with the slider, which I learned to throw after I joined the Phillies in 1975. This really made it fun when I learned how to throw that. They'd be looking for the screwball and you could sneak that slider in on the hands. They couldn't wait long enough. Then they get out in front a little bit and they hit a ground ball to shortstop. Your infielders, your shortstop, second baseman, third baseman, they know that you're trying to design this ground ball double play. They've seen you do it and you've talked with them about it over drinks, at breakfast or on the bus, and they believe in you. And baby, when it works and you set them up and then pull the string, it's great, really great.

The "You Gotta Believe" was something like that, one of those moods. That was with the Mets in 1973. The team was struggling. We had a team meeting and I was screaming, "You gotta believe!" because that was the mood I was in that day. That's how that all started. Joe Badamo, a friend of Hodges, had said it at lunch that day, "Hey, you gotta believe." So I came to the park saying it, to the fans in the parking lot, and later at a team meeting. M. Donald Grant [the Mets Chairman of the Board] happened to pick that day to give a pep talk to the team and here I was all wired running around saying, "You gotta believe." Well, I hollered it when he was making a point. He thought I was mocking him, but I wasn't. I was just being me. I had to go and explain it all later. That's how the "You Gotta Believe" got started. And that was 1973. I hadn't been able to get anybody out the whole first half of the year but I felt great. I'd just lost confidence in myself. I didn't have a clue as to what I was doing wrong. Hitters would be coming up to me around the batting cage, saying, "Tug, what's wrong? You used to get me out with that shit and now I'm wearing you out!" And I'd say, "I don't know, you tell me." And they all just said that they didn't know. What it was, I think, I got into the habit of not really focusing on the hitter. I was just pitching mechanically and I was trying to throw a strike. I didn't really have that special feeling of purpose. You know there's a big difference between reason and purpose. And the first half I had no purpose. Somehow just running around saying, "You gotta believe" made me focus. And the shortstop and second baseman out there knowing that you're doing this or that, they're ready. The outfielders are on their toes. It's contagious. That's what happens when you start pitching with a purpose and that's what happened to me in the second half of 1973. I got hotter than hell, an entire year's success into about eight or ten weeks. I really got on a roll. And the same thing happened in 1980. It's very hard to explain. It's like a golfer who's struggling. And then all of a sudden some little thing that's been throwing everything off clicks. You make that one adjustment and it pulls everything back together.

Yogi was managing then. This was 1973, and he started me a couple of games, just to try to get me back in the groove. That's the opposite of how they handle a starter. They'll send a guy in the regular rotation to the pen when he's struggling to try to work it out. Hell, here I am a relief pitcher having problems and they give me a couple of starts. I can't say what it was but something did click and I got hot. At the end of the year I think the division race came down to about five teams. Up until the final week, five teams could have mathematically still won the division. In the final game, Seaver pitched and I came in and

288

we wrapped it up. I don't remember too much about that game at all. I know that it was very draining. The play-offs, of course, [were] a hard-fought series. And then the seven-game Series with Oakland. What I remember most about that was how I felt when we lost the last game. I was warming up to go into the game because I think we were losing like 5–2 and something started happening. Oakland made a couple of mistakes. I'd have been in if we'd tied it and then it was over. I remember sitting in front of my locker and it was the only time in my life that I was glad that a baseball season was over. That whole last month of the season and then the play-offs when Pete and Harrelson got into a fight. It was such an intense period of baseball from the middle of July through October. It was very intense. I mean 1969 was a cakewalk. Nobody expected us to win it that year. But this was grueling. I mean every time you went to the ball park you could feel it, feel the pressure. The New York crowds, the New York press. But I think for the young player to have an opportunity to break in in New York is a great challenge. There are so many things on the field and away from the arena that you have to deal with. We did the cartoon "Scroogie" in New York. At that time baseball was going through all these labor negotiations and there was a lot of bad publicity about baseball. I thought we needed something with a fresh, fun approach to balance out all these negative headlines. We had an artist and a couple of guys wrote it. I got the idea with Danny Frisella. Danny threw the forkball. And when he went into the game from the pen they'd say, "Fork 'em, Danny!" and when I went in they'd say, "Screw 'em, Tug!"

I took that New York experience to Philly with me. Everybody used to talk about how tough the Philly fans were—[they'd] boo Santa Claus, boo the Easter Bunny, boo Kite Man—and I came down here and I led the Phillies in grand slams. I wasn't a hitter and yet the press and the fans were all in it together. I never fought them and they never fought me. We just always got along. And I had some bad years, 1979 like I said, I led the league in grand slams. We finished fourth after winning our division three years in a row and the bullpen had a lot to do with that. And so that could have gotten real ugly. But when the going got tough down in Philly, I was schooled. I understood, these people just wanted it, that's all.

I was traded to the Phillies in 1975 and played there for the rest of my career, which ended in 1984. Nineteen-eighty was a great year in Philadelphia, play-offs, World Series, I could go through each year but it's like driving through an art museum on a motorcycle. You see all the paintings but it's somewhat of a blur, "Let me go back and check that again!" I just know that 1980 was a lot like 1973. Some time in the middle of the season, you think, "Uh-oh, I can smell it. I think we're going to be there again." And then all of a sudden you go to another level. That's what happened. [McGraw saved Games One and Four in the National League play-offs, then won Game Five and saved Games One and Six in the World Series.] When you get into the flow, you have a feel and a touch. When the ball leaves your fingers you know it's going to do exactly what it's told. I can remember feeling as though my pitches had vapor trails behind them, that I could see the flight of the ball. Before I threw it, I could see exactly where it was going to go. I could sense pulling the hitter out to me. I knew when he'd be out in front and sense when to take just a little bit more off my fastball. The last game of the 1980 Series, I had bases-loaded situations a couple of times in the last game and got out of it. In Game Five, I got Jose Cardenal with the bases loaded, struck him out in the bottom of the ninth. I had that feeling then.

I mentioned my first appearance in Shea Stadium and how nervous I was after facing Cepeda. The ironic thing is that the last game I pitched in Philadelphia, the same damned thing. The nerves, the shaking, I felt like I had palsy out there. The last game and I felt just the way I did when I faced Cepeda. I guess that's good but it sure made it hard for me to shut it down. Since I've retired, people ask me what I miss most about the game. It's that daily pump that a short reliever gets. I remember when I first retired driving around with a jar of jelly beans in my car, just for the sugar, eating sweets because I didn't have my daily adrenaline pump at the ball park. It was unbelievable. And then I put on weight. You come to realize that going to the ball park and putting on that uniform and walking out that tunnel into that arena is a very, very special place to be. And then later on in the night when you're walking in from that bullpen, what a rush! And you don't take it personally. My view of it was that it was an experience that we were all sharing. We all had a role to play. Everybody in the stadium. My role was being focused upon until I let go of the ball. And then it was like whoever the ball went to after that. Then it was the role of the fans to respond to that. Because without their response it's all changed. It wouldn't be any fun to do. Everyone of us, whether we were getting paid, or whether we were paying to be there, everyone in that stadium was just as important as the other. And the only difference was that when you had the ball in your hand as the pitcher, you initiated the action. That was my job.

ROLLIE FINGERS
Right-Handed Pitcher

OAKLAND ATHLETICS, 1968–1976
SAN DIEGO PADRES, 1977–1980
MILWAUKEE BREWERS, 1981–1982, 1984–1985

- **Elected To The Baseball Hall Of Fame In January, 1992**
- **Most Valuable Player And Cy Young Award Winner In American League in 1981**
- **Appeared in Five League Championships And Three World Series During His Seventeen-Year Career**
- **Entered A Game Following A Bullpen Snooze With His Waxed Handlebar Mustache Drooping Thanks To A Melt Job By Penmate Darold Knowles**

It's Mayberry Night at Greensboro's War Memorial Stadium. In an hour or so the Class-A Greensboro Hornets will play their Sally League rival from Spartanburg, South Carolina. Out in front by the main gates is the police car they used in "The Andy Griffith Show." And yep, smiling and schmoozing with the in-coming crowd are two guys in ill-fitting cop uniforms. Satellite trucks—TV-types laying cable—all this for a look-alike Andy and Barney? There's more. And this one's no fake. Rollie Fingers, one of the game's all-time save leaders (341), Cy Young and MVP award winner, is going to throw out the first pitch.

Local TV guys line up for pre-game interviews. "What brings you to Greensboro, Rollie?"

"Well, I'm here for the big gum card show tomorrow and here tonight to see if I can throw one more strike!"

After Fingers had thrown that strike, reportedly a slider, he took a seat in the stands behind home plate, sipped on a beer, pulled on a cigarette and talked about his days in the pens of Oakland, San Diego, and Milwaukee.

"This is kinda nice. It's been a long time since I've been in a ball park that has words on the fence," he said.

The mustache? That came in 1972. We did it, the guys on the Oakland ball club did it [grew beards and mustaches] just to get Reggie Jackson to shave his mustache off. He came into spring training in 1972 with a mustache and wouldn't shave it off. So Catfish Hunter, Darold Knowles, Kenny Holtzman, myself, we started growing mustaches. We figured if we started growing mustaches that Dick Williams would tell us to shave them off and when he did, then he'd have to make Reggie shave his off. But Charlie Finley, Mr. Promotion, got wind of it and thought the mustache idea was great. So he said he'd give everybody on the club who had a mustache on Mustache Day three hundred dollars. Those guys would have grown mustaches on their ass to get three hundred dollars out of Charlie! Everybody got their three hundred dollars and that's when mustaches got into baseball again.

That was how the mustache thing started. I got started a lot earlier than that, no mustache [laughs]. About 1956, 1957, I was playing Little League, playing shortstop and pitching. Then I went to Colt League, and it was basically the same thing there. Then in high school, this was in Cucamonga, California, for Upland High, I was a starting pitcher and did real well. I did okay in Little League and Colt but nothing outstanding. I guess the first game that sticks out in my memory is a no-hitter that I threw in American Legion ball. I think it was against Chino in southern California. But a lot of the games that I remember were in the American Legion World Series. We played in Little Rock, Arkansas. I pitched two games in Little Rock. I beat Charlotte, North Carolina, which was one of the better ball clubs and then I ended up pitching the final ball game and beat them again 3–1 for the championship. I threw a two-hitter against them. I led the country in American Legion that year as a hitter with a .450 average. So I got some attention from the major league scouts. They were looking at me as both a pitcher and an outfielder.

Now as far as my signing a professional contract—the Dodgers were going to give me I think $18,000 or $20,000 as a signing bonus and they were my team. I grew up idolizing guys like Perranoski but I looked at that Dodger staff and saw Koufax and Drysdale and Stan Williams. They were just really deep. I thought if I go there I'm going to spend at least six or seven years in the minor leagues. So Charlie Finley offered $13,000 and I knew that the Kansas City organization was kind of a minor league to the Yankees and they really hadn't done that well. But they had just signed a bunch of young prospects, I think from the Olympic team and prospects out of college. I thought, well I've got a better shot with Kansas City, a quicker route to the majors.

I signed as an outfielder out of American Legion ball in 1964. They tried me out at both positions, outfield and pitching. I hit like .320 in spring training that year, but they figured that I'd be a better pitcher than I would a hitter, so somebody knew what they were doing. I'm just kind of glad the way it worked out.

In 1965 I was with Leesburgh. That was Class-A ball, Florida State League. I really didn't have that bad a year. I think I was 8–15 and had a real good ERA. We just had a terrible ball club. And the next year I went to Modesto and had a real good year in Modesto. That was 1966. I was 11–6 there, played with Dave Duncan, Joe Rudi and Reggie Jackson there.

Here's a trivia question from Modesto. Name the pitcher who saved Reggie Jackson's career. I think that someday I might be credited with putting a guy in the Hall of Fame because Reggie might not be around today if it wasn't for my forgetfulness. I used to pick Reggie up every day at the hotel in Modesto and take him to the ball park. And this one particular day I just forgot him. I don't know why because I picked him up every day. I just went right by and never thought anything about picking him up. It was really weird. Two blocks later a car ran a red light and hit my car and rolled it over on top of a bridge. And had Reggie been along, sitting in the seat where he always sat, he might not be here today. It was just one of those things, you know. I forgot to pick him up.

The next year I went to Birmingham and Opening Night I was starting. Fred Kovner hit a line drive back and it hit me in the right side of the face, broke my jaw, shattered my cheekbone. It's funny what you remember: "Bear" Bryant was at the game that night. I was in the hospital for about nine days and I had my face wired together, lost about eight or nine teeth. I ended up being allergic to the medication they were giving me. I threw up with my teeth wired together for the whole time I was in the hospital. They finally figured out that I was allergic to the medication. But I went from about 205 pounds to 165. I really didn't think about my career and whether I'd be able to play baseball again. I was more concerned about seeing. The first two days after I got hit I couldn't see out of my right eye. I was blind or blurred, so I was thinking more about whether I'd even ever be able to see again out of my right eye. But it slowly came back. I was on the DL for about two and a half months. And my first game when I came back I had to face Kovner again, the same guy that hit me. So that was probably the best thing that could have happened. I know I won that ball game but I couldn't tell you how I did against Fred Kovner. I know he didn't hit me with another line drive. I'd remember that. After that I never even thought about it. I did make sure that my glove was up there from then on.

I was a starter in Oakland in 1969, did a little bit of relief in 1969, and did most of my starting in 1970 and the first part of 1971. Dick Williams sent me out to the bullpen, oh, mid-season in 1971, and that's when I became a short man. We just ran out of pitchers one day, we were playing the Yankees and ran out of pitchers. And we were getting beat like 9–1 in the third or fourth inning. He'd gone through about three or four pitchers and he got to the eighth inning. We were ahead 10–9 and I was the only guy left out there. We were in Yankee Stadium and I pitched a shutout inning and we won. The next night I came back again and got the save, and so I got those two saves in a row in Yankee Stadium. From then on, Dick, just every game, went to me in short relief. That's how it started. I sort of backed into it.

It wasn't something that I wanted. I think everybody coming up from the minor leagues, you want to be a starter. You know back then that's where the money was at. I was sort of disappointed at the time but . . . being a short man I really didn't mind it, because my arm adapted pretty quick. I didn't mind throwing every day. I could throw two or three innings. And an inning—just about any day I wanted to, I could go out and throw an inning. I had the type of arm where I could do that. So it just worked out great.

First big moment in relief? The American League Championship series. This was in Oakland and we're playing Detroit, Game One, a big one in 1972. They brought me in with the score tied, nobody out, 1–1 in the ninth, I know it was the ninth and men on first and third. Gates Brown and Jim Northrup coming up. I was trying to strike out Gates Brown, because you know, first and third. I usually didn't pitch guys inside. I can't remember who was catching, Tenace or Duncan, but they called for a pitch outside. I made a mistake and the ball ran in on Gates and he swung and hit it on his hands, just happened to pop it up to Sal Bando at third base. So I had one out and Northrup up. When Northrup got up, there were still men on first and third and all I wanted him to do was hit something on the ground. I think he hit the first pitch, a ground ball to Dick Green at second base and he turned the double play. And that's probably the biggest inning to that point that I'd ever pitched.

The 1972 World Series where we struck Johnny Bench out with a fake pitchout, that was a big one. It was the eighth inning in Game Three and I had a 2–1 count on Bench with runners on first and third.

I threw a pitch that was kind of away and it kind of got away from Gene Tenace, our catcher, a little bit so the runner on first, Tolan, went to second. And I ended up with a 3–2 count with Bench up and first base open. Sal [Bando] came over and then [Oakland manager] Dick Williams came out and called time. I asked Sal, "What the hell's he gonna tell me with Bench at the plate in this situation?" Dick gets there and he starts gesturing all over the place. He's pointing at the on-deck circle and then to first base. All the time he's telling us that Tenace is supposed to stand up when he gets behind the plate. I'm supposed to go into my stretch like we're gonna intentionally walk Bench. And he wanted me to throw a slider for a strike. He wanted to make sure that in case we didn't fool Bench, he wanted it to be a breaking pitch that he'd be swinging at. And so as I went into my stretch, just as I went into my motion, Joe Morgan was on third base and he kind of yelled and said, "Be ready!" So I didn't know if they had picked it up or not. But I just happened to throw a perfect pitch. I mean, it was a slider right there on the outside corner. It was strike three. Bench told me later that that was the most embarrassing thing that ever happened to him in baseball. We ended up losing the ball game but yes, that's one that will probably be remembered for a long time.

I guess the most memorable moment would have to be the first World Series in 1972. I got the last out in the 1974 World Series, but I think the first one, you remember a little bit more. It was Game Seven of the World Series against the Reds, 1972, and I came in with two guys on base in the eighth inning. The score was 3–2, and I came in in the eighth inning and I got out of the inning. I think I came in with runners on first and third. They scored one run and it went to 3–2 and then I got out of the inning. The next inning a ground ball to Dick Green and I think the next guy popped to Campy and then I hit a guy. That really pissed me off. Because Dick Williams had Vida Blue warming up and Rose was up. He was going to come out to the mound and take me out. But Dave Duncan, our catcher, met Dick at the third base line and told Dick that I was throwin' the ball good and not to take me out. So he got to the mound and we talked and he let me pitch to Rose. All he said was, "Just keep the ball away from him!" So the first pitch I threw was a fastball—in fact it was a ball—up and out over the plate. He went after it and hit a fly ball to left field and that was the World Series. That was it!

There's another game that people talk about. When I was with Oakland there were four of us who pitched and combined to win a no-hitter. The thing that I remember best about that game is that I won a dinner off of that. Vida started that game and went five innings. Then Abbott and Lindblad came in and pitched, I think, an inning and then I got the call for the final two. This was right at the end of the 1975 season, like the last day of September. I came out of the pen in the eighth inning and Kenny Holtzman said, "Fingers, I know you're gonna blow it!" And I said, "I'll bet you a dinner on it." So I got out of the eighth inning and Holtzman's in the dugout now. I said, "Do you want to make it any more, up the bet?" and he said, "No, let's just stick with this!" So I ended up getting through the ninth with the no-hitter intact. I don't recall whether it was a steak dinner or what, but I collected on that one, I do remember that.

Winning that bet was fun but there's more to it than that. The one thing a relief pitcher hates to do is to screw up a win for a starting pitcher. That's one thing that I never wanted to do for the obvious reasons and also because you take a lot of heat from the guys on the ball club. Especially in that no-hitter deal. Any time I came into a ball game I didn't want to screw up a win. I think the biggest role for a relief pitcher is to come into a game after a starter has gone eight innings and busted his ass and has a one-run lead. To lose it for him is, well. . . . They get paid for their wins and I get paid for my saves. I've got something like 114 wins and I'd just as soon trade them all for saves. That's what I got paid for.

And if you want to know my philosophy on relief pitching, it's very simple. "Shithouse or castle!" When you're a relief pitcher that's it—"Shithouse or castle!" You know it when you walk out there, you're either going to end up in one place or the other. You're either going to do it or you won't. It's like a field goal kicker in football. You either miss it or you hit it. You'd rather be in the castle than the shithouse but you're going to have those days when you're in the outhouse. You just try to minimize them. Coming out of the bullpen you really have to have good control, and pitching like I did in situations where there was usually a one-run lead, I thought you could get in more trouble inside. They could take you long in there, so I pitched outside. I tried to stay away. I'd just as soon give up three singles to right field rather than one swing of the bat for a homer. When I did come in, I usually didn't try to throw a strike. I came inside and off the plate. Starting pitcher, it's a little bit different. And that's one thing that you can't do being a relief pitcher. You can't let bad games affect you. If you give up the home run to lose it in the ninth, the sun comes up tomorrow. If you continue to think about it then you're just not going to do well.

Finley stories? Working for Charlie Finley one of the *highlights* of my career? One of the lowlights! He was a beauty to work for. Yes, he was as bad as the press made him out to be! [laughs]. You know we had our run-ins, me and him. I hung up the phone, slammed it down on him several times. And he hung up on me a number of times too. Charlie liked the phone. He was constantly calling the dugout all the time. When Alvin Dark was there and Dick Williams was there, Charlie was always ringing them up. One time I came down from the bullpen in about the fourth or fifth inning to get a drink of water and the phone rang. I was standing right by the drinking fountain and when it rang I picked it up and said, "Hello Charlie!" It was Finley and he said, "Who is this?" I said, "This is Fingers!" and he said, "Well, this is Charlie!" He said, "Is Alvin there?" and I said, "Yeah!" and then he said, "Fingers!" "Yeah?" "Don't ever answer the phone that way again!" But we had a good time with him. I didn't mind him that much. The mule and the white shoes and all the Finley stuff. I remember one time, me and Kenny Holtzman were in the outfield and Charlie used to come down to the dugout and sit there during batting practice. So Holtzman and I were in right field shagging fly balls. Every fly ball that we caught we'd stick in our pocket because we knew Charlie was in there. We had about seven or eight of them and finally when he turned his head, me and Kenny fired all the balls right in the dugout and ran. He didn't know where they came from. We hit him with a couple of them too.

Well the trade to Boston. That was kind of crazy. Charlie knew that I was going to become a free agent—me, Rudi and Vida Blue would be free in 1977—so he was just trying to unload all of us. He sold me and Rudi to Boston for a million dollars each. And he sold Vida Blue to the Yankees for one-point-five million. The Red Sox just happened to be in town so Chuck Tanner, the A's manager said, "Hey, you've just been traded to Boston." So I packed up all my stuff. It didn't make any difference to me because Boston was a contender at the time. I was going to be leaving Oakland after the season anyway, because Charlie wasn't going to sign me. I went over to the Boston clubhouse and got into the Boston uniform. I was over there for the whole series, a couple of days, warmed up in their bullpen and stayed with them until the last game. And when Boston was getting ready to leave town to go on the rest of their road trip, Bowie Kuhn calls Charlie and nixes the deal, says that Rudi and I can't go to Boston and that we're staying in Oakland. Okay, I packed up my stuff and went right back to the Oakland clubhouse. Boston left town without us. Me and Joe

Rudi sat there for almost two weeks and didn't do nothing. Charlie wouldn't play us. It came to the point where the other guys on the ball club said, "Look, we're going to boycott." Minnesota was coming to town and our guys were going to boycott. They told Charlie, "If Joe Rudi's not in the lineup against Minnesota we're boycotting, we're not going out on the field." And about fifteen minutes before the game Chuck Tanner came into the clubhouse and read the lineup. Joe Rudi's name was in there. And in fact I got a save that day. And Joe played. But of course, what really hurt was that we lost the Western Division by a couple of games that year. I think we lost six or seven games where Joe and I were out. So it could have made a difference.

I finally got out of there, ended up being one of the first free agents. I had other offers but San Diego was a young ball club and they had the Cy Young winner in Randy Jones. I enjoyed San Diego. Then I went to Milwaukee in 1981—Harvey's Wallbangers—and we had some real good ball clubs there. In 1981 we had a great ball club, finished first in our division. I had something like twenty-eight saves. We lost to the Yankees in the division play-off series three games to two. Then in 1982 we beat California in the Championship Series and lost to St. Louis in the World Series. In 1983 we played pretty good until about the first part of September and then we kinda went into the tank. But I enjoyed my years with Milwaukee, it was a good organization.

I'm starting to get questions about the Hall of Fame. Until this year I really hadn't given it much thought. But to get in there, that's the icing on the cake for a ballplayer. That's the ultimate. You win Cy Young Awards and MVP Awards, and Fireman of the Year Awards, those are awards that you win over a period of one year. But to get into the Hall, that's a career honor, and really something special. So if I get in there that's the ultimate, that would be great.

When did I know it was over? Well I didn't. I thought I could still pitch. In 1985 I had seventeen saves at Milwaukee. My earned run average was up but me and George Bamberger didn't see eye to eye on a lot of things. He was a starting pitcher's manager. He left the starters in longer than I thought he should. And I had a clause in my contract, a performance clause where I got so much money for every appearance. It came to September and we were fifteen games out. There was no way that they were going to run me out there just to get some work in, because they would have to pay me. So at the end of the season I told them that if Bamberger was coming back to Milwaukee in 1986 that I just couldn't play for them. I needed to work. I didn't pitch the whole month of September in 1985. So I asked them to trade me and they ended up giving me my release. I was expecting to hook on with some ball club and to go to spring training in 1986 but no one called. I think I was a part of the collusion deal where the ball clubs just didn't have anything to do with me. So I'm involved in the lawsuit—"Collusion III" I think it is right now. I still thought I could pitch. In fact Pete Rose wanted me in camp in 1986. Cincinnati called me up and they wanted me to come to camp but they said that I'd have to shave my mustache. Marge Schott wanted me to shave my mustache. And I said, "What difference does it make whether I have a mustache?" They said, "Well, that's Marge's policy." So I told them, "You tell Marge to shave her St. Bernard and I'll shave my mustache!" That was the last I heard from that.

In January of 1992, Rollie Fingers was voted into the Hall of Fame.

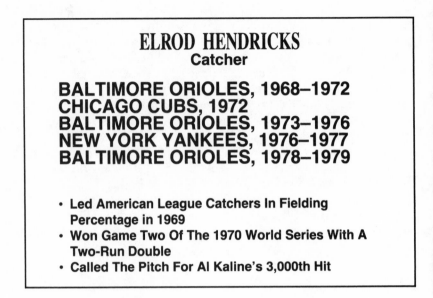

ELROD HENDRICKS
Catcher

**BALTIMORE ORIOLES, 1968–1972
CHICAGO CUBS, 1972
BALTIMORE ORIOLES, 1973–1976
NEW YORK YANKEES, 1976–1977
BALTIMORE ORIOLES, 1978–1979**

- **Led American League Catchers In Fielding Percentage in 1969**
- **Won Game Two Of The 1970 World Series With A Two-Run Double**
- **Called The Pitch For Al Kaline's 3,000th Hit**

As a wet February snow falls on the tarped field of Memorial Stadium, Elrod Hendricks leads a parade of pitchers through the hallways and tunnels of the old ball park. Mike Flanagan, Kevin Hickey, Pete Harnisch and Gregg Olson traipse along—barbs, jive, there's talk of a basketball game the Orioles played the night before. The parade comes to a halt at a green doorway. Hendricks fumbles for, then produces the key. Two tarps are removed revealing dirt mounds and rubbers. Sixty feet, six inches away rent-a-catchers—college kids who catch the morning workouts—squat and thump their gloves. Hendricks directs Hickey to one mound and Flanagan to the other. "Twelve minutes, easy. That's all, twelve. And no breaking stuff, Kevin!" He pulls a stopwatch from his uniform pocket, looks at me and says, "You wanted to talk about the bullpen? Shoot!"

I started my baseball playing in St. Thomas in the Virgin Islands. I was born and raised there and I really didn't start playing baseball until I was thirteen years old, mainly because of an injury. My dad's car rolled over my feet and crushed my insteps. It took a while to rebuild, so I didn't play any sports at all until I was thirteen. At the age of seventeen I signed with the then-Milwaukee Braves. I stayed in that organization for two years. That was 1958, my first year of minor league ball was 1959. And after the 1960 season I got released. I had broken my ankle during that winter playing in Puerto Rico and so when the Braves released me I signed with the St. Louis Cardinals. That was the winter of 1961. I stayed with them for two years, in the Cards organization. And there were guys ahead of me like McCarver, Joe Torre—he was in Triple-A in the Cards chain and Uecker was there with him. Then Joe got called up. I got released again, so I went to Mexico in 1964 and that's where I developed. I got to play, which is really what I needed, more playing time. I really didn't do a lot of baseball playing before I signed, only played a total of twenty-six games before I signed. So I needed the experience. I got that experiénce playing in Mexico and playing winter ball in Puerto Rico with the San Souci ball club.

I guess when you talk about highlights, great moments, the 1969 World Series was big for me. As a youngster you always dream about it, all boys dream about getting into a World Series. Even though I was twenty-eight years old at the time, my second year in the big leagues, I was like a baby. My first at-bat in the Series I got a base hit. In fact my first at-bat in the big leagues I got a base hit, right here in this ball park [Baltimore's Memorial Stadium]. I got the first major league hit off of Jim McGlothlin. Then in the World Series in 1969 I got a base hit in my first at-bat off of Tom Seaver, here in Baltimore again. Hit it in a pretty good spot, to right field. And little did I know that that would be my last one in the Series. I was one-for-ten. I hit the ball fairly well but that was the only one that fell in in that Series.

One of mine that didn't fall is one that will be talked about, I don't know, maybe forever. You know Agee made two great catches in that Series, both in Game Three. They saved maybe five runs. The two catches—one was in right center and of course, the one I'll never forget was in left center. I don't even know where Tommie Agee came from, or why he was playing me there. Because if the Mets scouts had done their homework, they would have known that I never hit the ball to the left side of second base. I was a dead pull hitter but I hit that ball to left center field. I hit the ball good and when I hit it, I said to myself, "That's a sure triple!" I had triple in mind and the longer I ran, the crowd's reaction, well, the less the triple seemed a reality. Tommie caught it right in the webbing of the glove out there in left center, and there was some ball showing when he caught it. I saw the catch, I was rounding first base at the time, so I had a good view of it, and it was most disheartening. Because it seemed like everything we did in that Series was wrong. We hit the ball hard, they caught it. That was not our year. That was the year of the Miracle Mets.

And then in 1970 we got into the Series again, this time with Cincinnati. I guess they felt the same way about us because that was the year that Brooksie made all those great plays, two great plays in Game Three and well . . . that's baseball I guess. That Series was very rewarding for me, because I thought that we had the best team in 1969 when we lost to the Mets. The next year it was Cincinnati, and they were supposed to be the big bad Red Machine. We weren't even supposed to be able to play in the same ball park with them. I had a fairly decent Series. In the first game I tied the game with a home run and in the second game I hit a two-run double to put us ahead, scoring Brooksie [Robinson] from first. The first time in my life I ever hit an opposite field base hit. I hit it inside the third base line. That's the only reason Brooksie could have ever scored from first. That wound up being the winning run, so those were highlights in my career.

And yes, there were times when I sensed that I was, I guess you'd describe it as sitting in on baseball history. I was catching when Al Kaline got his three thousandth base hit, a double. I'm not sure who was pitching—I think it was McNally pitching. But it was a double right here in Memorial Stadium. I remember thinking, here's a man who grew up in Baltimore, went to high school practically across the street from this place, and he comes home and gets his three thousandth hit here. That was great. It was a breaking ball. He hit it down the left field line and when he got to second base I felt like going out there and shaking his hand. But we were still battling, in contention in a pennant race, and you just don't do those things but I wanted to.

There were others. I caught Palmer's no-hitter. I caught the twenty-game winners in 1971. I think the toughest one for me was Palmer's twentieth win because he was the one I expected to get it first and he got his last. And he had to get it that day. He had one more chance but I sure didn't want to see it go down to the very last day, because of the pressure. I didn't want it to be a situation where in his last start he had to get his twentieth. It was a big thing for me, the fans and the ball club, and of course that pitching staff, to have an opportunity to catch four twenty-game winners [McNally 21–5; Palmer 20–9; Cuellar 20–9; Dobson 20–8]. Yes, that was something, some happy moments.

I remember catching two "almost" no-hitters in one week. McNally's and Mike Cuellar's. They both lost the no-hitters late in the ball game. I had already caught Palmer's at that time. As the catcher I never really felt any pressure when a no-hitter was in progress. You are fully aware of what's going on, you just keep calling the pitches, go with whatever is working best for them. You hope that the guys behind them make the play. I never looked at catching as pressure. I always felt like the pressure was on the guy out there [the pitcher]. My job was to help as much as I could, help the guy on the mound do his job, try to think along with them, two heads, one mind. Help them do their job without having to think, "What do I do next?" I would say my piece, especially when Weaver came out there. I would say things for them. I knew exactly the way he felt about a lot of things. I knew when he came out just about exactly what he was going to say and there were times when I'd just be ready and cut him off. Other times when he came out and had differences with the pitcher I'd say, "Look, that was my call, I called the pitch! I was the one that insisted that he throw it!"

Now as the bullpen coach, it's changed slightly from my catching days in that I'm always honest with management now. I can't lie to these guys because it could be a ball game. It could mean two ball games. I'm up-front with them. And all I ask of my players is to be up-front with me. Let me know. If there's an arm problem, whatever, don't try to hide it because sooner or later I'm going to find out. I've seen them all throw long enough. I know when they're throwing right and when they're not. I don't worry about what they think when I have to say, "Hey, you don't have it today." I used to be concerned about that but I'm not anymore. That's the job and I know all these guys very well. They know I'm doing it for their good and the good of the club. So I'm very honest with the manager and the pitching coach because their jobs, mine, everybody else's, depend on the arms out there on the mound.

I have so many good memories from the bullpen. I guess I always go back to Moe Drabowsky. You'd have guys who maybe had a tough Saturday night and he'd come out there to the pen with books of matches, and he'd be giving them a hotfoot—both feet actually—and when he'd see somebody drifting off, going to sleep, he'd just light them up.

And then you had Stanhouse who was again a character. Basically he stayed in the game, mischievous but always asking questions about the hitters. He always wanted to talk about how he'd pitch a guy and then wanted our feelings. He would say things like, "How did we say we're going to pitch this guy?" And he was good for the younger guys. Once I started to coach he was good for me because he made my job a lot easier, keeping the guys in the game by asking where was the last pitch. He would ask them, "What was that pitch? Where was it?" The man who named him "Stan the Man Unusual" is right here [points to Mike Flanagan who grins and continues to work easily, pushing off the mound]. Of course it stuck, because he was, well . . . *unusual.*

Sparky Lyle, on the other hand, when I was with the Yankees, he was a mile a minute. He'd sit there in the pen and he'd be talking about some ball game in the past, "Do you remember this, and when they threw this guy the breaking ball how he reacted? Do you remember when the ball got by Thurman or Fran Healy?" Things like that. He was more the character before the game, usually during batting practice. Sparky was also a good example. When it came to doing his running he was very good and led by example. In fact, he took Guidry under his wing, even though there was a possibility that Guidry could have taken his place in the pen. When Guidry came up he was a reliever. And he didn't mind teaching Guidry. He taught him the slider, and it wasn't exactly like Sparky's but it got the same reaction.

You're talking about guys here who were unselfish. All of them characters maybe, but they were secure in their positions. They liked to fool around but from the seventh or eighth inning on, they were a bundle of nerves.

There were so many great relief jobs that I've seen over the years both as a player and bullpen coach. But I guess the one that stands out is one back in Detroit, with Dick Hall. He came into a game with the bases loaded and the count three balls and no strikes. I was catchin', nobody out. I don't know if it was 1970 or 1971 but we were in a pennant race and we were playing in Detroit. I think it was Horton, Freehan and Cash. I don't remember what order they hit, but he came in there and it was strike one, strike two, pop up to the infield, strike one. . . . He made it look so easy the way he did it. I'm sitting back there—strike one, strike two—and that was a pennant drive. I'm getting excited and he's just so calm and cool out there. The next thing you know we've got a ground ball to first and the ball game is over. I remember running up first base to back up and I'm looking at him to see his reaction. He doesn't show any emotions one way or another, just another day at the park. That's the mark of a great bullpen guy. And for some reason that made a fantastic impression and was very special to me.

Dick Hall was very calm. But now as a bullpen coach I've learned that you have to handle the pitchers differently for the simple reason that different people have different personalities. I learned that from Earl Weaver. Earl taught me that as a coach. He tried to know each ballplayer as an individual. He wanted to know what motivated them, what made them tick. Sitting beside him when I played I picked up little things that he did as a manager. And I listened a lot, and I learned a lot. When I was out in the bullpen as a catcher, I was with Charlie Lau and I learned from listening to him. He'd tell pitchers, this works or that works, and I took it all in. He knew the little things, little quirks that would get them going. There are days when they don't feel as ready as others, but they're professionals. It's my job as a bullpen coach to get them mentally ready, to watch the way they're throwing and to correct any flaw that they might have in their delivery before they go into a game. I know what the motion is supposed to look like. I know when the leg comes up where it's supposed to land, I know when he releases the ball what it's supposed to do. It's simply preparation to go out there and if I don't see that, well. . . .

In the case of a short man, I might have to hurry him more than I would a long reliever. Now with the present crop, with Gregg Olson, I know how long it takes him to get ready. I know them all, but there are days during the season when they're different, when they're a little stiff or tired, the night before—I'll know that. So it's my job to tell Frank [Robinson] and Al Jackson [the pitching coach] this guy needs more time, or if you get him up, put him in the game. Because he just can't take two warm-ups. If you get him up, don't let him sit back down because if you do he'll be stiffer and it'll take you longer to get him ready. Mentally these guys bounce back a lot quicker after pitching. Sam Stewart, he was a different breed. He'd say, "I'm tired but I can give you an inning." And you'd say, "Hey," and he knew what it would take to warm up and knew what it would take to get ready. There is a point in time during the year when these guys get loose a lot quicker. When they hit that nice groove it'll take them only maybe ten or twelve pitches, in some cases only a minute or two to get ready. That's when they're in tip-top shape.

I don't have many rules, but the rules that I have, when somebody comes into the Orioles bullpen, if anybody forgets, the other guys will remind them. One of my rules is to have a baseball ready at all times. When you get the call, you're going to have to look for your glove and a baseball. Have that ball ready. I don't want anybody saying, "Where's my glove?" I want that glove there with them with a baseball in it. When that phone rings I want them ready to go. The manager and I want you ready now. The other rule that I have is, "Let me know where you're going to be at all times." They'll come to me and want to go to the bathroom and I say, "When we're hitting! Go then!"

This is nice, working in the Baltimore bullpen. After all the releases early in my career to have spent so many years here as a player and then to be able to stay here and coach. . . . Well, I'm still working for a living and hopefully when I end my career it will be right here in Baltimore.

TOM HOUSE
Left-Handed Pitcher

ATLANTA BRAVES, 1971–1975
BOSTON RED SOX, 1976–1977
SEATTLE MARINERS, 1977–1978

- **Bullpen's First Psychologist**
- **Uses Footballs To Teach Rangers Pitchers Proper Throwing Mechanics**
- **Caught Hank Aaron's Record-Breaking Home Run Number 715 In Atlanta Bullpen**

Tom House, the pitching coach for the Texas Rangers, has a Ph.D. in psychology. He looks a bit like John Denver in double knits, and writes books on pitching mechanics and why some professional ballplayers can't cope with the everyday world. Just a tad too intellectual for the pen, don't you think? Not exactly the kind of guy you'd expect to find out there with the guys who enjoy setting fire to each other's feet.

Tom and I talked at the Rangers winter home in Clearwater, Florida. As expected, he is intelligent and articulate. But House was quick to set the record straight. "I have some of the bullpen in me. Remember I am a left-handed pitcher!" House admits spending a great deal of his major league career marching double time to a different drummer. "I drove some managers and coaches nuts," he laughed. "But I'm hardly typical of what you'll find out there. Let's see, how can I describe them, the Goose Gossages, Mitch Williamses and Sparky Lyles? How about the game's jet jockeys, Mach III with their hair on fire!"

Yes, managers do tend to take the hyperactive and send them to the bullpen, in some cases just so they don't bug everybody. In fact when Mitch Williams was with Texas, [manager] Bobby Valentine used to say, "Mitch, go! Just get off the bench. I don't want you here, just go to the bullpen where you belong." And these people [pen men] seek each other out because they understand each other. The only chemistry that doesn't quite work is the frustrated long man who wants to be a starter. And they're a cross between the starter and the relief pitcher. But the committed bullpen guy, it's like their own little subset of a family system.

Are pen men different? Yes, you're like an island unto yourself out there. You know it used to be that you got banished to the bullpen and while that mentality is different now because of the special role involving the middlemen and stoppers, you know there's some credibility out there now. And usually the free spirits are out there. No matter what their personality appears to be, these are guys who seek out that adrenaline situation and thrive on it. They like to be on the dance floor. And as a starter many of their temperaments can't handle it. Mitch Williams couldn't. One of the things that I did with Mitch was, I said if this kid has three or four days between starts he's going to figure out a way to screw it up. If he's out there [pitching] four out of five days he doesn't have time to think about it. And that's why he should go to the bullpen. And there are physiological reasons why people should be in the pen too. Some guys' arms are just not capable of handling the intense workloads of 125 to 145 pitches every fifth day. But they can take three days at thirty-five or forty pitches each, bounce back and be real effective. So there are psychological and physiological reasons. But more likely than not, your bullpen pitchers are going to be the jet jockeys. They like being in the arena. They get the instant feedback of success and failure as often as they can out there.

I don't know whether there is a hierarchy—short men the highest and the bullpen catcher the lowest. I don't think so. I played for Clint Courtney. Clint was quite a character and his definition of a short reliever and a long reliever differed from everybody else's. "My short relievers are the guys who can't get anybody out, so they ain't out there too long. My long relievers are the guys who are gettin' everybody out so they're gonna be out there a long, long time."

But in my era, when the bullpen was starting to present itself as a specialty, [in the] mid-seventies, the way the managers worked it was . . . they would ride the horse until the horse failed. When you failed you'd go to the bottom of the heap and have to work your way back up. Now the roles are more sophisticated, more defined. There are setup men and stoppers. There's more consistency and a little bit more predictability. Athletes can prepare themselves a little bit better than they used to.

I had the advantage of coming from an athletic family, being brought up by a dad who knew something about conditioning. My father was a football player at the University of Washington and athletics were a part of our existence from Day One. I never remember not having a football or baseball game on TV, even back when [we had] those little TVs with all the snow in the fifties . . . when Dizzy Dean had the guys "sluddin'" into third base. As it turned out I liked all sports but I never really got big enough to play a big man's sport. Being left-handed and being able to throw strikes, I kind of fell into being a left-handed pitcher. If I were six-foot-three and weighed 210 pounds I might have been a football player or a Stan Smith-type tennis player, I don't know. But baseball presented itself as something that was fun and something that I was good at.

I had a real good high school career. I was what you would call a big fish in a little pond. I put up the impressive numbers. I was a real low draft choice with the Cubs in 1965, the first year of the draft. When I saw what I was offered and where I was drafted I decided to go on to college. I had a number of scholarship opportunities and I ended up going to the University of Southern California on a baseball scholarship. I played there two years on a real good ball club under Rod Dedeaux who was the god of college baseball at that time. I signed after my sophomore year with the Braves and then spent five and a half years in the minor leagues finding out that I wasn't the athlete that I thought I was.

The bullpen came about after my third year as a starter. It became apparent that I didn't have the durability or the fastball to be a day-in and day-out starter. I think Eddie Robinson and Clyde King were the brains behind moving me into the bullpen. I could throw a curveball for a strike. They just started bringing me in against some left-handed hitters. I had some success with that and I yo-yo'ed back and forth between the major leagues and Triple-A. And then in one instructional league someone said, "Why don't you try to throw the screwball?"

The screwball came real easy to me. I don't think that any one person taught it to me. I talked to Jim Brewer, talked to Arroyo, talked to Clyde King and found out what worked best for me with the pitch. Like I said, it did come fairly easy to me. With the screwball, I was able to make my fastball look better than it was. So I was now able to go in and pitch against left-handers and right-handers. And finally I got called up to Atlanta in 1971. I was finally a major leaguer.

My best year in the majors was 1974 [House won six, lost two, with an ERA of 1.92 and had eleven saves]. The thing that got that year started so specially was catching Henry Aaron's 715th home run. I figured that there was nothing going to take the place of that, ever. It was a very special thing to me. I happened to be standing at the right place at the right time, in the bullpen. We [the bullpenners] had separated ourselves into geographic territories as a function of our time in the big leagues. We knew that the next one would be the big one and we didn't want a big fight over the ball. So what the bullpen members did was divide the pen into about ten-yard areas. If it came into our area it was ours. And we weren't going to violate anybody's area or territory. The only pitcher with less time on the staff than me was Buzz Capra. He was to my left, which was the closest area to center field. And then me and the other five or six bullpenners who were out there. You see, Henry hit most of his home runs right down the line, so the senior pen man had the territory closest to the foul pole. Guys like me, the low men on the totem pole, got the power alley in left center where he was least likely to hit it. As it was, the ball was hit right to me. If I had stood still and let it come through, it would have hit me right in the forehead. I ran in and presented it to him. In fact I think that was *Life* magazine's picture of the year. It had my hand in it and Hank with tears in his eyes hugging his mother. And that's the picture that's in the Hall of Fame too. I caught the ball on the fly, and ran it all the way in. That catch got me in the Hall of Fame. I had no prayer of making it as a player but what that did for me was even more than that. Just having that moment somehow made pitching a baseball a lot easier. Now I had been associated with a great moment in baseball history and as a result of that I felt really good about myself. It was one of those years where you matched up physically and men- tally. I got off to a good start and had a great year.

I've been in the game for twenty-five years now and I've seen and had some special moments. I guess the one that's second in my mind was sitting there and watching Nolan Ryan get his five thousandth strikeout. That was a special pleasure for me. This time, as the pitching coach for Nolan, I wasn't in the pen. I watched it from the bench. Of course, it was exciting to watch him lead up to it. And this year [1990] is a special year because he will be making his run at three hundred wins. With a guy like Nolan Ryan I wouldn't say that I'm a coach as much as I am a reinforcer. I know what to look for in his delivery and motion. It's very easy dealing with someone like Nolan because he, like Charlie Hough, is a long-time professional. They both know their bodies, know what they need to do to be successful. Coaching isn't really the key with these guys. I think that it's more of a business rela- tionship, as opposed to the younger kids who haven't really gotten a feel yet for what they're supposed to be doing to be successful in the major leagues.

I happen to have a Ph.D. in psychology and yes, I guess that I do try to intellectualize the game to a certain extent. One of the criticisms that baseball has of a person like me is that I over-intellectualize. I've always been considered a bit of a flake. And because I was a marginal athlete I had to ask "why" a lot of times when I should have just shut up. And when an instructor would tell me to do something and I couldn't see the reason, I would say, "Well, why?" A lot of times in baseball you don't have an answer, it's just what's been done for 115 years. When they couldn't provide the answer and I couldn't see why we were doing it, there was some friction. So I know that during my tenure in the game that I pissed a lot of people off. But I love the game as much as anybody. My problem was when I couldn't see the logic I'd ask why. That's one of the reasons I continued my education in biomechanics, exercise physiology and psychology, because I felt that there were pieces of the puzzle in this game that were missing. Kids that weren't being instructed, informed or taught properly, it's been a continuing effort on my part to bring as much to the party as I could.

Now as a coach, whether the education has helped, it's really hard to quantify. When you get into professional athletics these guys are elite athletes and they will often times succeed regardless. One of the kids that I've been associated with I mentioned earlier, I've known Mitch Williams since he was sixteen years old. I know that his abilities would have probably gotten him into the big leagues no matter what. But I think that our friendship and the information that I was able to learn off the field about him helped him get to the big leagues sooner. Maybe it will also allow him to hang around longer. He signed as a real young kid with the Padres and then went right to the rookie league up in Walla Walla, Washington. As a minor league pitching coach I got to know him then. Because he was a bit of a left-handed flake we were naturally aligned with each other. So Mitch would be one that I helped on the mental side of things.

And I'm actually pretty proud of some of the biomechanical adjustments that we made with Nolan Ryan. This isn't Tom House's information. We got it from the computers, a motion analysis system, a company called Biokinetics in California. It's objective information. To a guy like Nolan Ryan, you say, "Nolan, the computer says if you did this, you might get more results this way." And he's a good enough man and a good enough athlete to say, "Okay, I'll see what happens." In a game of course, you always go with your money pitch. He always had the great fastball and curve, but he has a great change as well. When it gets down to what am I going to get beat with, you don't want to get beat with your second or third pitch. Since he's gotten older he realizes that if he gets his breaking ball and changeup even close, then his fastball is that much better. He has become a pitcher with maturity, rather than a thrower. Nolan Ryan has always been able to throw the ball. But probably toward the end of his Angel years and during his Astro years he learned what being a pitcher was all about.

We've gotten a good bit of publicity because we have our pitchers throw a football as a means to perfect the throwing motion. But it's just a piece of the conditioning continuum, a piece of the puzzle. I wish that the football were my idea. It's not. The original idea came from a Dr. Atwater at the University of Arizona. Many of her students went on to become athletic trainers and physical therapists. Dick Dent, who's a trainer with the San Diego Padres, is one of her students. The point with the football is that you can't throw it wrong mechanically and make it spiral, so there's positive feedback and reinforcement for your mechanics. Thirteen ounces means that there's some weight training and conditioning involved. Motivationally, it's called cross-training. It's very acceptable now that people are doing it throughout sports, but cross-training is a way to keep an athlete's motivation muscle up. It's fun. They'll throw a football for five or ten minutes way more consistently and with more effort than they would a baseball. It's a three-tiered device. It's only a piece of the puzzle and not the only answer.

The only frustrating thing was that when we first broke it out with the Rangers, we had a pitching staff that had an ERA of five and change and were on our way to losing something like 112 ball games I think. I pat Bobby Valentine on the back for allowing our pitchers to use something like this to get better. When Nolan Ryan came to the Rangers last year and picked up the football in spring training for me, that was the final word that it is a valid training tool. In fact, there's a bubble gum card with Nolan Ryan throwing the football that I understand is worth about sixteen bucks. So Nolan has helped me solidify this training. Just about anywhere in the country around baseball, you'll see somebody throwing the football, professional, collegiate or at the high school ranks. Because it's been accepted.

My book has been somewhat of a topic of conversation. [House is the author of *The Jock's Itch: The Fast-Track Private World of the Professional Ballplayer.*] It's been quite well received, surprisingly so by the players' wives. I went into the writing of that book with a lot of trepidation. I didn't want it to be a name-the-name book. What I wanted to do was elevate the awareness of what mind-set is, what this closed system is all about and why the athletes appear to the general public the way they do. And while they are responsible for their actions, they have been programmed by society to be that way. I don't think, unless they are made aware of it from Day One that eventually they are going to have to act like real people, that they should be criticized as much as they are. I use the analogy, now that I've gotten a little bit better at explaining it, that athletes are a Nintendo, the rest of the world is like a Macintosh personal computer. The capacity of both systems is the same but the software that makes them run is entirely different. One is programmed for games, one is programmed for Spell-Check. You can't take Spell-Check and put it in Nintendo, and you can't take Super Mario Brothers and put it in the Macintosh. If there's some cross-compatibility, the software will work in both systems. But until society in general and the people in sports get better at synthesizing the two worlds, then there is going to be a pretty frustrating existence for the athletic community. Athletes are pampered while they're playing and very abused when they've finished their careers.

It's getting better but is still very bad. At this point I'm convinced that if a guy has played professional baseball for four or five years, then he's probably never going to be happy doing anything else. There are exceptions of course, but across the board, he may be successful and he may be good at what he does, but he won't get the same satisfaction or fulfillment. The syndrome is called the terminal adolescent syndrome. These guys were allowed to be kids up until they were thirty-four or five years old. Because of that they don't have real life understanding and real life skills.

It's more than just never attaining the great highs again, without getting too far out over our skis. It's accountability versus responsibility. Athletes are always responsible, but they're never held accountable. So the athletics gets in the way of their role as people. As long as your numbers are good you can do anything, socially. The system protects them. It's a very conditional acceptance. I don't like to name names, but they're out there, a Pete Rose.

If I were to try to discuss this subject in the bullpen? If I were talking about all this to a bullpen guy, [laughs] he would give me the glazed doughnut look and then about two-thirds of the way into it he'd probably fire up a hotfoot, or give me his attention while someone was doing something lewd and lascivious behind my back. What would be a real good, real-world analogy for the pen? If you gave five twelve-year-olds $500,000 a year and told them that they could do whatever they wanted to do out there . . . well, what you'd have would be your typical major league bullpen!

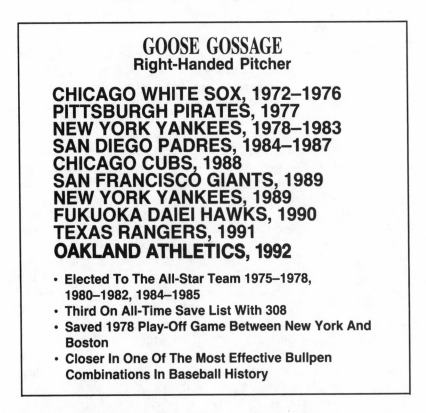

GOOSE GOSSAGE
Right-Handed Pitcher

**CHICAGO WHITE SOX, 1972–1976
PITTSBURGH PIRATES, 1977
NEW YORK YANKEES, 1978–1983
SAN DIEGO PADRES, 1984–1987
CHICAGO CUBS, 1988
SAN FRANCISCO GIANTS, 1989
NEW YORK YANKEES, 1989
FUKUOKA DAIEI HAWKS, 1990
TEXAS RANGERS, 1991
OAKLAND ATHLETICS, 1992**

- **Elected To The All-Star Team 1975–1978, 1980–1982, 1984–1985**
- **Third On All-Time Save List With 308**
- **Saved 1978 Play-Off Game Between New York And Boston**
- **Closer In One Of The Most Effective Bullpen Combinations In Baseball History**

Richard Michael Gossage isn't the goose I expected. I tracked him down by phone in Japan, where he was working as the bullpen ace of the Fukuoka Daiei Hawks. And as the phone rang for our prearranged talk all I could see was that mound presence, the Fu Manchu mustache, the scowl, two hundred pounds of body and 100 miles-an-hour of fastball flying at defenseless hitters. I'm about to interview Samurai short man, I thought. So when Gossage picked up I was, like most guys who have faced him, a little bit nervous, afraid to dig in. But midway through my introduction, there was a knock at Gossage's apartment door. He excused himself and what I overheard was this:

"Hello? No, I'm sorry. I don't speak Japanese. No, I speak English. Sorry. No, I'm sorry, I don't speak your language!" He returned to the phone, "They're very nice people over here! I'm enjoying the experience!"

I'm thinking, this is Goose Gossage? How long has this man been

in Japan? Relaxed now, I cut the boy-who-wants-to-be-bullpen-guy business short and dig right in. And the Goose? He spoke my language just great.

Yes, they scream, "Goose!" "Goose!" when I come in from the pen. The baseball over here is basically the same. The players aren't as strong and the ball parks aren't as big, but frankly, it's a challenge to get these guys out. And the strike zones? I really find the strike zone a little bigger over here. The strike zone in the States has diminished so much.

I'm still strictly short, basically the stopper like I was in the States. The bullpens are the same, usually down the lines or along the lines, like in St. Louis. And then maybe some of them are like in Shea, way down the lines. Characters in the pen in Japan? Well, no, there are no practical jokers. The Japanese are very serious people. There isn't any practical joking and there's no real laughter in the bullpen or dugout. Serious business, like going to the ball park, being on time. If you're supposed to leave on the team bus at five o'clock with the New York Yankees to go to the ball park, it leaves at five o'clock or a few minutes after. Here you're almost on time if you made it one minute until five, because the bus would be pulling away if you got there right at five. They're very punctual. The fact that they're all there early is supposed to show their enthusiasm for the game.

They exercise their players a lot—calisthenics—yes, it's a lot of hard work. I don't do it! They usually let their American players do their own program. I've had some really good outings. I've got seven saves. The press coverage you get over here is unbelievable. Oh God, when I first came over, I mean there were photographers, I had to watch where I went to the bathroom. The fans follow you. I stick out like a sore thumb over here. I don't find it tiresome. I've never let the attention get to me as a negative thing, I just think that it goes with the territory. I've got a Japanese interpreter, an ex-player, over here. I think I've built up a pretty good rapport with these guys right now. I think that there is a lot of mutual respect. It's been a real positive thing for me and for the Japanese players. I'd heard a lot of horror stories about playing in Japan, but I think that all depends on the attitude that you bring with you.

I grew up throwing the ball awfully hard, being very competitive, had it from Day One! We lived in Colorado Springs, and my older brother, he was grown, a good bit older than I am. He used to play catch with me out in front of his house. He used to bring me to the point of tears because he said that I wasn't throwing hard. And I'd rare

314

back and throw it as hard as I could. My father was a big influence too, of course. I mean his attitude was, if you were going to do anything you did it right. I remember a practice that I missed because I was out screwing around. I was just at that age, oh I think that I might have been a sophomore, in tenth grade in high school. And I missed a baseball practice. And my dad, boy, did he jump all over me! He said, "Look, either you're going to do it, or don't do it at all! Don't do it half-assed." Oh boy, he got on me, and from then on I never missed another practice.

Chuck Tanner is the man who is responsible for putting me in the pen. When I came up to the White Sox, 1972, he just made that decision. He'd done the same thing with Forster. It wasn't like he came to me on a particular day and said, "You're going to be in the bullpen." The writing was just on the wall. I think it was taken for granted that Terry [Forster] was going to be the left-hander and I was going to be the right-hander out there. We were the youngest two, supposedly ever, and that's what Tanner had in mind, two hard throwers. I hit the White Sox at a time when they were going with some young arms and also some veteran pitchers. It just was real good timing for Terry and myself. And I guess at the time it was pretty impressive to have two guys who threw smoke, you know?

But it wasn't all smooth sailing at first. I had some problems early. Chuck and I kind of had it out, over me not pitching enough. I was getting work about every ten or twelve days and I just couldn't pitch like that. And this is a funny story. This is the spring of 1975 when we had our little showdown in spring training. He shows me a list of people, pitchers who were going north with the club. And my name is on the list but crossed out. And I say, "Why aren't I going north?" And he says, "Because you haven't improved!" Chuck has a way of firing you up. And so I say, "Well I'll tell you what. If you pitch me, I will improve! I can't sit for ten to twelve days and be effective. I have to pitch and I have to pitch a lot." Oh man, he stood up and we got into the damnedest screaming match. Johnny Sain [White Sox pitching coach] kinda got in between us. To this day I can see Sain and Tanner and we'll still laugh about that day. I'll tell you what. I thought Tanner's veins were just going to explode. The veins in his neck and his head and I'm going, "Oh no!" I was mad myself. It was really something. And he said, "Okay, get out of my office!" The next time I pitched I gave up, I think, three runs. And that was 1975, the year Forster got hurt and I took over as the short man.

In 1975 I had a good year [Gossage was Fireman of the Year with twenty-six saves, and a 1.84 ERA. He pitched 141 innings, gave up

70 walks, 99 hits, and struck out 130]. I know that my walk-strikeout ratio was really good that year. I'd worked with Johnny Sain and Sain gave me my breaking ball. He got me to throw it, taught me the breaking ball. When I first came to the majors I had no idea about a breaking ball. I had a straight change and that was it. I called it a "slurve." Yeah, it's a slurve. And Sain taught me that and I think that's where I went backwards for a couple of years. I would throw with him every day in the bullpen before the game. I stopped working on my fastball and consequently I think I lost a little bit off of my fastball. I've come to the conclusion that you have to work as much on your fastball as you do your other pitches. You have to have your mechanics on the fastball down just like you do on your breaking balls. It's a touch thing. I had a big stride, came flying in at the hitter and that's just the way I've always pitched. That's my natural way. I have such a crazy wild delivery that it doesn't take me a lot of pitching and a lot of use to be effective.

In 1976 [Gossage went 9–17, 3.94 ERA and one save] Paul Richards took over as the Sox manager and he made me a starter. I was willing to do anything they wanted, but I really hated to leave the bullpen. Here I'd just come off of having a great year in the pen and I wasn't really a starter. I hadn't been a starter in five years and why start now? They needed arms. I don't think I got more than one game saved out of the bullpen that year. We needed help in the pen. That team, the 1976 White Sox, was probably the worst team that I ever played for in my whole career, or in professional baseball for that matter. I mean, we couldn't *catch* the ball. The pitching staff didn't have a chance. I think I had fourteen complete games that year. I don't feel like my record was indicative of the way I pitched. And was I unhappy? I was doing what they wanted me to do, but I really did want to be in the bullpen. I missed it.

Then in 1977 Chuck Tanner—he was with the Pirates then—and he traded for me. I was very happy when he called and said that they traded for me and that I was going back in the bullpen. I went, "Oh, all right!" I loved Pittsburgh. I wanted to stay and we were asking for a three-year contract for something like $125,000, $135,000 and $150,000, somewhere in that ball park. But [Pirates General Manager Pete] Peterson wouldn't give it to me. At that time, that wasn't really asking for that much money, not really. Then George Steinbrenner offered the long-term contract for $2.7 million or whatever. I've had people say that that was a real breakthrough, at least money-wise for bullpen guys. I've always looked at Fingers and Lyle as the pitchers who really took the modern day relief pitchers to a new level, how we're thought of, how we were used. Relief has become such a big part of the game. I look at myself as being there. I think I was one of the first to really put power pitching on the map as far as bullpen closers were concerned. I guess Allie Reynolds and Ryne Duren were there early but . . .

The Steinbrenner years? It started with tough negotiations, which of course they always are. There are never any easy negotiations. He basically wanted me and I wanted to come over and work with Sparky [Lyle]. Be the righty-lefty best ever, you know? I remembered the Forster-Gossage combination. That's the kind of vision I had. I never ever thought of coming over and taking Sparky's job because I always idolized Sparky. I always thought that he was one of the greatest, which he was. Hell, he'd just won the Cy Young Award the year before [1977]. And here I come over and they give me the job. I couldn't believe it. Sparky and I got along great, but it was only because Sparky was Sparky. He'd tell me, "Well shit, Goose, you throw a hundred miles an hour. Who are they gonna play, me or you?" And I'd say, "Yeah, but I didn't come over here for that. I came over here to work with you!" And he said, "Well, there's just not enough work for two short men in the bullpen." Which I disagreed with but . . . I guess that you have to have a stopper. But there are certainly lots of times where you know there's gonna be a lot of games.

As to why I took over the short role from Sparky, well, I'm not positive, because Martin never talked to me at all. I think it was coming from George [Steinbrenner] that I was going to be the guy. I was the big gun out of the National League. The year that I'd had the year before—I was going to set the whole world on fire. We were going to win another championship with Goose Gossage. Great beginning. We went to Tampa, George's home town, in that first spring to play an exhibition game against the Reds and I think I gave up something like five or six runs. George was pissed! You know, in front of his hometown fans and him bragging about how good I am. Here I give up five runs. That was my big Tampa debut for George. Then I proceeded to go downhill from there. I couldn't get anybody out for two months.

I've always said that 1978 would have never been the greatest comeback in [Yankee] history had it not been for me, because we would have never been that far out. I lost like three games the first week of the 1978 season on the road, two on homers. Then we came back to Yankee Stadium for the opener and Kenny Holtzman got introduced before me and they booed the shit out of him. And I run out to the first base line and oh, the house comes down. Big-time boos. When I get to Holtzman he says, "Hey, they ain't yellin' 'Goose,' motherfucker!"

317

So I stood there and I took my cap off. I was so pissed off, I wanted to kill these people, all the fans, you know. I took my hat off and I said to myself, I'm going to turn all those boos to cheers. They'll be cheering me by the end of this year. I was pissed. I had tears in my eyes, you know. And the funny thing, I stunk it up for quite a while. But surprisingly, nothing much was being said in the papers. I couldn't believe with Sparky there that they stuck with me. For two months I stunk. I'd come onto the mound and Munson would say, "Hey fuckhead, how are we gonna lose this one?" And I'd say, "I don't know, can I get back to you? I have a feelin' we're gonna find out! You just catch!" It was unbelievable. One time I'm having trouble and I'm getting the sign from Munson. He calls time out and walks out there and says, "Hey, shithead, check Rivers out!" I turned around and look out at center field and here's Rivers in a three-point sprint stance, facing the wall getting ready to run down the next pitch. All I could see was his ass, sticking up in the air. I said, "That son of a bitch!" But they had the greatest senses of humor on that team. Shit happened like that all the time.

Finally Billy was fired and Lemon took over. That was in like August. Billy and I never really got along. I think the reason was that he wanted to pitch Sparky. I don't know this for sure, but my gut feeling was that he liked Sparky and I think he was gettin' word from up above that I was going to pitch. If it hadn't of been for that, shit, I'd a been put on the bench.

I guess the memory of that 1978 season in New York that I'll never forget is one that probably won't surprise too many people. We came down to one game with Boston for the pennant in Fenway that year. It was the most beautiful day. It was one of those crisp fall days, clear as a bell and just gorgeous. Just one of the most beautiful days you could ever ask for. I went to bed the night before thinking that I could see me facing Yastrzemski for the final out. And I was really kind of—well the attitude was, who needs that, you know? But Sparky just kept telling me all that season, when I'd be having trouble he'd always be there telling me, "Hey, pressure is something that you put on yourself and that other people put you on. Take it as a game and go out and have fun and let the cards fall." But that day broke and it was beautiful. I woke up with that same Yastrzemski thought, and sure as hell, it happened.

I remember in most games, I used to get going in the fourth or fifth inning. The adrenaline started to pump. But in this game, hell, it was pumping from the time I got up that morning. When Dent hit the home run we were out there in the pen watching it. I never really thought that much at the time, it was like, "Home run, great!" Your mind is so geared and so intent on what you're doing. We've got a lead now and that's what it's all about. And you don't get too giddy out there. It's all business. Your intensity and your concentration is like, you know, it's your game now, it's getting into your innings, coming your way.

So when the phone rang to get me up in the pen, Lemon saying, "Get Gossage up!" I'll tell you what, I was shaking in my shoes. My legs were Jello. We were out there in that right field pen. And I just remember my legs shaking like jelly, they were just jelly. And I didn't even know how I'd get out there if they called me. The cart picked me up and brought me when they signaled for me. [In a sense, history had already been made that day. Bucky Dent had hit his now famous net shot to put New York ahead 3–2. Munson would then drive in Rivers, 4–2, and Reggie Jackson would hit one into Fenway's center field bleachers, making it New York 5, Boston 2. One on, two out, bottom of the seventh inning—enter Gossage.] I did get Bailey, three fastballs, to get out of that inning. But then they started.

In the eighth, Remy doubled and Yaz singled him in. Then Fisk and Lynn singled, to make it 5–4. I just got to the point where I was giving up base hits and line drives but finally got Hobson and Scott to get out of the eighth. In the bottom of the ninth, Piniella made the game-saving catch, one of the greatest plays I've ever seen. With one out, I walked Burleson and then Remy hit a fastball to right center field. This was just one hell of a play. Piniella lost it in the sun and the ball hit to his right. It landed so that it just took off and he just dove over to his right and backhanded the ball. And I mean, it was a great, great play. That froze Burleson at second. So I've got Remy at first and Burleson at second. Okay, now Rice is up. He nails a long fly ball to deep center. Burleson tags up and goes to third. So I've got two outs now, a man on third, and Remy had to hold at first, I think! I was so scared that I didn't know which end was up. I learned later that Lemon was thinking about bringing Sparky in and then he goes, "Hell, we lived with Gossage this year and we're gonna die with him!" And had he taken me out of that game, who knows what that would have done to my confidence or what course my career would have taken. Who knows?

Well now, here I am. Just like the stuff I went to bed thinking about. Me and Yaz. I just stepped off the mound and I thought, I've never felt like this. This is bullshit, you know. I've always had a great time playing the game. And I just stepped off the mound and I backed off and I thought, I'm talking to myself now. I mean, I'm really talking to myself. And I thought, this is stupid. What's the worst thing that could happen to you? Well, you lose! And if that happens you'll be home tomorrow in the mountains of Colorado elk hunting. I actually had that thought. I'll tell you—it was like the weight of the world had been lifted off my shoulders. I probably put another foot on that fastball that I threw Yastrzemski. And it moved, went in on him and . . . pop up to third! And I remember running right over there by Nettles, watched him make that catch, thinking, "God, we've done it!" Then Munson was there, on me, and then all hell broke loose. It was ironic because we had so much respect for the Red Sox that it was kinda like, "Damn, it's too bad that somebody had to lose this ball game." That's how I felt.

That is the moment of my career, and if you want to call it scared or fright or whatever you want to call it, that was it. That was the first time that I'd ever really faced pressure like that. I'd really never been in a pennant race. You don't know how you're going to handle it until you handle it. I think the whole secret to success is the fear of failure, getting that out of your system and not being afraid to fail. Because once you have it in your mind that you might fail, then you're going to fail. We can't be afraid to throw the Yastrzemskis of the world strikes, you know!

People ask me about those years with the Yankees and I haven't really had time to think back but I know the bus rides, those were the funniest. Oh God, we had some funny characters. Catfish [Hunter] and Lou [Piniella] getting on one another, those two were classics, great friends. Lou busting Cat about being a redneck and Cat getting on Lou about being beat out at Kansas City by a guy named Jim Wohlford. *Jim Wohlford!* Cat would scream that at Lou from the back of the bus. And of course Rivers, Mickey was a piece of work. During that time, the early part of 1978 when everything I touched turned to shit, Billy is bringing me into a game, and I'd just come off a couple of bad outings. So I'm riding in in the car and there are like 50,000 people in Yankee Stadium. Rivers runs over from center field and throws himself on the hood of the bullpen car and starts screaming, "No, don't bring him in again, don't bring him in!" And he's holding the game up because he doesn't want me to come in. I lean out of the window and say, "Get your ass off of this car and get ready to chase down line drives!" The first pitch was a shot into right center and he makes one of the greatest plays I've ever seen. And he comes in the dugout going, "You weren't shitting, were you?" I mean, you had to have Rivers. Rivers was one of the funniest guys I've ever been around. And Oscar Gamble—I mean these guys were hilarious people.

Nettles, oh God yeah, he was funny. He's the one that told Sparky in 1978, when they're using me instead of him and Sparky has just won the Cy Young Award the year before, Nettles is the one that said, "Hey Spark, it looks like you've gone from Cy Young to sayonara!" Nettles was great.

It was just a great team, full of characters and a lot of fun. And no real pressure, always light and everybody had a good time. Yes, a lot of that goes with winning but these guys would have been the same if we'd have been losing. Let's put it this way. You could never tell whether we'd won or lost. We were fourteen games out in August in 1978. And then we cranked it up. We weren't winning early that year, and I sure as hell wasn't pitching well, but everybody still had the same attitude. When you're going horseshit and your center fielder jumps on the bullpen car to keep you out of the game . . . that says it all.

Munson was a hell of a guy, his own man, but you know, that's the way that whole team was. There were a lot of those guys. Everybody was a man's man, did what they wanted to do and said what they wanted to say. If they felt like saying "Fuck you!" they'd tell you, "Fuck you!" Munson was probably even more outspoken than everybody else, except Reggie. Munson was smart. Sometimes when I was pitching he'd just throw his hand out and wave for the ball, show me and the hitter exactly where he wanted it, "Come on, bring it up, bring it right here, fastball!" And I'd say, "Damn Munce, at least do that down so they can't see it!" And he'd say, "Why? You're not gonna trick anybody!" It wasn't an argument, it was just a fun thing between us. And I'd say, "At least give me a fuckin' sign or something." But he'd just wave it so the whole world could see, here comes the fastball.

The whole image I portrayed, the anger or whatever people thought it was, that was real, just the way I felt when I came into a game. The way I got ready out there was all natural. The adrenaline, the killer in me was unbelievable. I'm like that in other games, but not at things like cards for instance. I don't like to play cards because I don't like to gamble. I like to have things in my power. Playing basketball I'm very competitive, and anything else that I do I'm competitive, only I like to be in charge of it. I don't like to play cards because of the luck of the draw. But the relief pitcher, sure I'm in total control. Things happen—bad hops and things like that are out of your control, the errors, you can't let those things upset you. They're just a part of the game. But when the ball's in your hand, it's you and the hitter.

There were some hitters that just wore me out. It wasn't that I hated to see them coming up, it was more like, "Damn, I can't get this fucker out." It was always a challenge. I never ever said, oh I'm afraid of this guy, nobody that I was afraid of. Zisk—Zisk used to hit me great. I couldn't get that fucker out. We still laugh about it today whenever I see him. The guy that used to piss me off too—I'd walk him and I'd always wished that I'd hit him on the first pitch—was Hargrove. He used to come up there for those twenty-minute at-bats. Ball one, foul ball, foul ball, foul ball. I used to say that if everybody was like him there wouldn't be any big league baseball—nobody'd come to watch. It was always 3–2 and I'd always throw him at least ten or twelve pitches. Then I'd end up walking him. It took him five minutes to get into the box. He'd be trotting along to first with his walk, and I'd say, Why didn't I just hit the fucking guy? When he'd come up I'd want to hit him. Just get it over with, save me and the fans a lot of agony. But I wanted to get him out too, you know?

The thing with Cliff Johnson in 1979, that was just a bunch of locker room bullshit. Cliff was pissed off because he wasn't playing. After a game I wadded up the tape that held my socks up and I threw it across the room at Cliff. He was walking by and it went by Cliff's head and Reggie [Jackson] said, "Hey, how did Cliff do against you in the National League?" And I said, "Well, he couldn't hit what he couldn't see!" Which was not badmouthing him, I mean, it was just in fun. So I went to the bathroom and I'm naked. I'm in my shower shoes and I'm standing up there going to the bathroom before I go into the shower. And I look over there next to me at the next urinal and there's Cliff. And all of a sudden he's right in my face screaming, "Do you think you can back that shit up?" And I said, "What are you talking about?" So he takes my head and slaps it real hard. And I hauled off and we started fightin'. And we were separated. I told him he was a worthless piece of shit. Then it starts all over again and I fall against the wall. He falls on me and we fall down the wall and fall on the bathroom floor. I put my hand out to break my fall and that's when I tore the ligaments in my thumb. But that's basically what happened there. That hurt us. I was out about three months of the season there.

That was news, but the New York press [is] so aggressive there. Everybody's out to get the scoop and everybody wants to be the first. There's a lot of aggressiveness in the press there. New York is aggressive, I don't care what you're doing—crossing the street! The newspaper business is probably one of the worst. And there's so many of them. How can you have a close-knit group of journalists when they're working against each other? You don't get that feeling in any other city except New York. Some of those guys are good friends, but I'd say that the majority aren't. Then there was Dick Young. He was probably the worst. Oh, he was too much.

The day that I lost it with them was, well here's what happened. We'd come back to New York and I'd lost the day before in Chicago. There was a fly ball that the general consensus was should have been caught. I get the loss—blown save, blown game, and so fine. Now we're back in Yankee Stadium. Kansas City is following us right in. I save both games of a doubleheader and the first question out of this one guy's mouth is, "What happened yesterday in Chicago!" Oh, fuck! I went off on this motherfucker. I mean I wanted to kill him, I wanted to kill him. And instead of killing him I just went off. Called them negative fuckin' sons-a-bitches and told them to stick their pads and pencils.

It wasn't like I'd dodged the press. I'd stayed at my locker and answered all the questions in Chicago. It's not like no one got to talk to me. But it was a stupid question. And oh boy! Did I go off on that! I wanted to kill him! I was so furious I had tears in my eyes I was so mad. I really don't get that mad, thank God, very often. He hit the nerve. I mean, he hit a good one.

Yes, I did tell them they could take it to the little fat man upstairs. And George was George. But the one I remember with him—I had blown a save and he comes into the locker room the next night with this big shiny red apple. I don't know where he got this apple. This son of a bitch is the biggest red apple I've ever seen. And polished—he must have stayed up all night polishing it. I'd blown the save the night before and so he strolls in before the next night's game and presents me this big apple, gives it to me in front of the team, wants to reward me for my work, he says. He was just being sarcastic.

There was never a dull moment. And the Pine Tar Game was almost typical. I gave up the home run to Brett and they [Kansas City] went up 5–4. This was 1983, Yankee Stadium. And the thing about that was we were waiting for Brett. Nettles had noticed it a week or so before in Kansas City. We'd agreed that we'd wait until he got a hit to call it. [Pine tar can't be used higher than eighteen inches from the knobbed end of the bat.] There are a lot of publications that credit Billy with telling us to get the bat, but it was Nettles. He came to the mound and he said, "Hey, if he gets a hit in this at-bat, we're gonna get his bat. He's got pine tar all over that fucker." Brett hit a fastball, and hell, it wasn't even a strike. It was out of the strike zone, up. And I figured, I know he's going to try to pull the ball so I'm going to try to stay away from him. And he hits a foul ball that, if it had been fair, it would have been a home run, down the left field line. So I figure this next one, I'm going to come way in and up. But I came in and up and he—shit—lined it into the right field seats. But the idea was

Nettles's all along. It was his idea to get his bat. See, he had been called out on the same thing. And it was a bullshit thing. All the umpires had to do was lay the bat across the plate and measure, seventeen inches. It was way over that. It wasn't even close. Brett had it all over the barrel. I'm not saying that had anything to do with the home run. But it's just like a pitcher using pine tar or something. But Mac-Phail [the American League president] just didn't have any . . . well, they hated Billy, they hated George. We never got a break on anything.

Brett being the hitter, I'm sure that had a lot to do with it. Gaylord Perry [K.C. pitcher] grabbed the bat and started running through the stands and then we got it back. There was that big fracas. Then the umpires ruled in our favor and then the commissioner overruled them. We had to play the last inning and eventually lost the game. So they stuck it up our ass really. It was just a bunch of shit. First, they didn't stick behind the umpires. The rule in the book states . . . it was a rule. What pisses you off is that they can change the rules as they go along. Basically what it means is that the rules don't mean a thing. It's just like spitting on the ball, just like putting Vaseline on the ball. It wasn't even close.

I spent eighteen years in the big leagues and I think one of the things that I'll always appreciate is the players. I've had a chance to see some guys do some unbelievable things. The greatest catch I ever saw was Kevin Mitchell and I was sittin' right by him last year there in San Diego. I was in the bullpen down the left field line right by him. The ball's hit about fifteen or twenty yards past me, right on the line and it was like you couldn't believe your eyes. He's tear-assing toward the ball and you're lookin' for his glove. But his glove isn't anywhere around. It's on his left hand of course. He ran forever and the ball kinda came back on him a little. So he reaches over and just snatches it with his bare hand. I mean, he snatches it bare-handed like he's playing catch in his living room with his kid. Bare-handed you know? I've seen the replay a hundred times and still get a thrill out of it.

I have played on some great teams and played with some of the best players in baseball history. But I'll tell you this. The best player I ever played with was in a league of his own, and that's Dick Allen. Nobody else is even close. I played with him in 1972 in Chicago when he was MVP. I saw him do the most incredible things with the bat, the glove. He hit more balls hard. I could take you to any ball park we played in and show you balls that he hit so hard, balls that looked like rockets. You can kinda listen to stories about the old guys but it doesn't sink in because you don't have any recollection of them at all. You can't imagine how good they were. Mays, Mantle, and Maris . . . but I saw Dick Allen—he was the best, just unbelievable.

There's so much to remember, a lot of it I haven't really had time to sort out. I remember my first outing was in Kansas City. We opened the season there in 1972. Wilbur Wood got in trouble and they called down and got me up. This was like in the fifth inning and I was the middle man. And they said, "Okay, Wilbur got out of it, you can sit down!" When I went to sit back down, I missed the top step and fell all the way down into the dugout, right on my butt. And oh, man, did they get all over me. This was back when a rookie . . . now rookies come up and they act like they've got ten years in. That was my debut and boy, they really let my ass have it.

The first time I walked into Yankee Stadium, that was the old stadium, in 1972. I was with the White Sox and, no pun intended, but I got goose bumps. I did, I had goose bumps all over me. To be there and being a Yankee fan all my life. Growing up in Colorado we didn't get that much exposure to baseball but the Yankees were like America's team. It was just such a fantastic feeling. All of a sudden all kinds of things came to me, Babe Ruth and Whitey Ford, Mickey Mantle and Roger Maris and Moose Skowron and Bobby Richardson, Clete Boyer, all the great players and here I am. I got into that game and I got to the mound and I took a minute longer than I normally would. I was just in complete awe. For a kid, it was dream come true. I thought of my dad. He had died and he never saw me get to the big leagues. He always told me that I was going to play in the big leagues. I just took a minute and looked all around. Up at the flags, out toward the monuments. That was a long way from Colorado. A kid who'd dreamed of the big leagues and all of a sudden here you are! Really—Yankee Stadium. You stand there and think about where you are. Nothing set in with me that first year until Yankee Stadium. That moment did it. Hey, you're a big league ballplayer now!

Bill and Louise's restaurant, a breakfast barn just off Route 41 North near Kennesaw Mountain, Georgia—you make a right at the four-wheel place—comes highly recommended—serving up country ham and eggs, smoked sausage and eggs, pork chops and eggs. "The best country breakfast in the area" reads the sign in the beanery's window. "Not fancy but great food. My kinda place," says a pretty fair country ballplayer, one Howard Bruce Sutter.

On a cool gray October morning I met the man who made the split-finger fastball famous at Bill and Louise's. Bruce had the country ham and eggs and I went with something the menu calls "Streak O'Lean." Sutter is bearded, dressed country casual—blue jeans and an orange and white Nike sweatshirt. The guy looks like he could throw one of Louise's hams from Kennesaw to Fulton County Stadium if he had a mind to. I ask what Sutter has been hearing about two great relief pitchers—Fingers and Sutter—being inducted into the Hall of Fame. "I don't hear much about anything," he laughs. "I'm a hard man to find these days."

I follow up with a question about Terry Cooney's historic launching of Roger "The Rocket." Clemens had been ejected from the Boston/Oakland play-off game earlier that week. "Well, it should never have happened. Catchers go at it like that with umpires all the time. But see, they're looking at the pitcher. They've got the mask on and nobody knows. Usually the umpire will stand up, walk around, dust off the plate and get his two cents worth in. But it's kept kinda private. Nobody in the stands or watching TV knows. Let me tell you a story about Ted Simmons," he says, nodding at the catsup. I pass the bottle and click on my tape recorder.

Now this is when Ted is catching for the Cardinals and I'm pitching for the Cubs. Simmons, and [Paul] Runge, the home plate umpire are going at it the whole game. But hell, I don't know this, I just got in the game. We're in Wrigley, there are two outs in the top of the ninth inning and Simmons comes up to hit. The first pitch that I throw Ted, I mean that thing's gotta be a foot outside. Umpire—"Strike one!" So I throw another one and it's like six inches off the plate. Runge—"Strike two!" Well now I know. This is some kinda payback. So if I can just get it anywhere where the catcher can catch it, he's going to call Simmons out just to stick it up his ass. And what do I do? I hang a splitter and Simmons hits the damned ball out. Tie game. Ted comes all the way around the bases and when he gets to home plate he stops and tips his hat to the umpire. Ted trots to the dugout and doesn't see what's behind him. Runge is right on his ass waving his right arm. Threw him out of the ball game. Maybe the only time in baseball history that a guy gets run for hitting a home run or tipping his hat to an umpire.

That was one of my first years up. The Cubs were my first major league team. The first professional team? Hippey's Raiders, a semi-pro team near my home in Lancaster, Pennsylvania. I was a wild kid with a pretty good fastball and the Chicago Cubs saw me and signed me as a free agent.

I started throwing the breaking pitch when I was nine years old, so yes, I threw it in Little League. I think if you throw it incorrectly, it can hurt your arm. But boys are going to try to throw curveballs. I mean, they watch TV. They're gonna try to throw knuckleballs, screwballs, split-finger fastballs when they play catch. I think a curveball, when shown properly, is all right to throw. I had some good games as a kid. I threw some no-hitters when I was little but I didn't throw any when I was in high school or playing Legion ball. I threw a lot of one-hitters. I was wild then. I'd strike out seventeen or eighteen a game and I might walk nine or ten too. I went through spurts where I just couldn't throw the ball over the plate. But I'll tell you what I did, I just tried to throw it as hard as I could. I was aiming to be a big leaguer, that's what I was hoping for. I went to Old Dominion College out of high school but I dropped out. I wasn't going there to go to college, I was going there to play baseball. I figured my best way to get back into baseball was to drop out and play on some semi-pro teams and hope that the scouts would pick me up. The Cubs signed me as a free agent when I was playing semi-pro. A guy named Bob Hippey had a meat packing plant in Lancaster and he sponsored this semi-pro team.

I pitched well when the scouts were there. I could throw real hard and I had a good curveball, but nobody talked about velocity much back then. They didn't come in with the speed guns like they do today. There just wasn't that kind of stuff. I signed in 1971, but they signed me in October so I reported to spring training in 1972. I was a minor league pitching instructor last year with the Cardinals. This [minor league pitching] has changed somewhat today, but not as much as I'd have thought. What I'm getting at is this. When I came up, the high draft picks in the minor leagues were automatically made the starting pitchers. Everybody else pitched out of the bullpen. That's just the way it was. And in the seventies there were some guys doing a real good job relief pitching in the major leagues, but it still wasn't as prominent as it is today. That came about four or five years after I signed and then it changed. I wasn't a high pick and I was in the bullpen, right from the get-go. I only ever started maybe two games in my life and they were both in the minor leagues.

The first year in the minors I popped my elbow and I hadda go get an elbow operation. It turned out to be something that may have changed my whole career. I didn't pitch much that year. I think that I only pitched maybe five, six innings that whole season. When I started I was property of the Chicago Cubs but I played for a co-op team of the Boston Red Sox. We played in Bradenton, Florida—Pirate City. And we didn't even have enough guys. We had to wait until the June draft to put a team together. I hurt my elbow, and I tried pitching off and on that year and I couldn't. I waited and I finally went and had my elbow operated on on my own. My elbow was killing me and the doctor went in and straightened it out. I had it done back in Pennsylvania. It was an easy decision. I couldn't throw. I went down to spring training the following March and I pitched. Eventually they found out. When I went back after that first surgery, I was basically afraid to throw the curveball. That's when a Cubs pitching coach, a great guy named Fred Martin, showed me how to spread my fingers. I thought that the elbow problem would maybe end my career. Here it turned out to be something that started it, because I know I'd have never gone to the split-finger, if I hadn't been afraid to throw the curveball. So I started throwin' the split-finger and as soon as I did I started moving up the ladder. And the amazing thing is that it worked right off the bat. Fred started me out throwing it with a slightly different grip and then we made a slight adjustment and baby, that was it.

That second year I was playing A-ball in Quincy, Illinois, the Quincy Cubs, and like I said, I'd just had my elbow operated on. But I started throwing it and I was pretty consistent with it. I could make it break five out of ten times. Sometimes when it broke, I didn't know where it was going but it broke real big. And the hitters would commit themselves and a lot of the time they'd end up swinging at balls that bounced in the dirt. So something was there.

That year I started out slowly then started getting it together at the end of the season. The next year I went to another A-ball team—Key West, Florida. I was still young, I was only nineteen. And I did real well. Always the short man, always coming out of the pen. But down there I blew my knee out. I've had eleven operations. I've spent my whole adult life playing baseball and laying in hospital beds. My first year up, 1976, the major league season opened like on April 8 and I got called up May 8. I was down for a month and then spent the rest of the year with Chicago. I had like ten saves and a 2.71 ERA, a good year. When I first came up Darold Knowles and Mike Garman were the relief pitchers. They were the combination in the Chicago pen. They were the lefty-righty team, a theory that I don't really believe in anyhow. If you can pitch, you can get either guy out and if you can hit, you can hit either guy. It doesn't make a shit. It's what somebody forces you to believe when you were younger, that's what you end up doing. But those two were the Cubs relief pitchers and I was kinda the setup man. The one day that it finally turned, I was pitchin' pretty good and Darold Knowles, a left-hander, and I were both warming up and Joe Morgan was coming up to hit for Cincinnati. And the manager brought me in to face Morgan, the left-handed hitter. And I got him. So that was that, from then on I was the save guy.

The split-finger made me so successful at it. I keep hearing Roger Craig's name associated with the pitch. He has become the guru of the pitch, but I'll tell you what pisses me off about that. I taught Roger Craig the split-finger. That still doesn't set right with me. I understand that he's teaching it and he's doing a good job with it. Some of the guys that he's taught have been very successful. I don't think that just because Fred Martin and I started throwing it that we should have a patent on it or that anybody that wants to learn has got to come to me. Roger is a very qualified coach but here's how Roger Craig learned the split-finger fastball. He was the pitching coach of the San Diego Padres. In fact, this happened one of those times when the Cubs had Fred [Martin], who was a minor league pitching coach in the Cubs organization, up in the major leagues working with me. I happened to be struggling a little bit so he was with me. We were in San Diego playing and Roger called us over by the batting cage and wanted to know all about the split-finger fastball, how to hold the ball and all that crap. So now, when the split-finger is mentioned, all you ever hear is Roger Craig. This was during batting practice. He just wanted to know how to hold the ball and we told him. When people start talking about the split-finger, Fred Martin should get the credit. Roger is doing a good job and he deserves everything he can get as a major league coach and manager, that's his job. But as far as being the guru of the split-finger, that doesn't sit right with me.

Freddie Martin? A great guy. He was an older guy when he was with us, died in 1979. He played with the Cardinals back in the late forties and was in the scandal. He jumped to the Mexican League [with] Max Lanier and all those guys. Freddie said that he used to throw the pitch down there but he was in a time and place where he wasn't getting any recognition. Freddie was from the old school where you'd load 'em up, scuff 'em up, do whatever it took to get a guy out. The way Martin taught it and the way I threw it, the pitch wasn't the same as a forkball. You threw it a lot harder. And the ball has spin on it. When you're throwing it as hard as you can and it only has to travel sixty feet, the hitter's depth perception isn't real good. When that pitcher looks like he's throwin' it as hard as he can, that's half of the changeup effects of the splitter. It's like a changeup except harder. It looks like it's really coming hard and that's what gets them out in front. The changeup you want them to hit because you've got them fooled. They'll maybe make contact but just be off a little, pop fly or something. But with the split-finger they swing and it goes down. It's just not there. Where I threw it in the strike zone depended on a lot of different things. If I was throwing it for a strike I'd start it up higher. If I wanted to bury it in front of the plate, just trying to get them to swing at a bad pitch, then I'd start it lower. A lot of it depended on the count and a lot of it depended on the hitter. And hitters aren't dumb either. Some guys I had to throw strikes to and some I never had to throw strikes. Catchers really didn't have a problem with the pitch, it's not like the knuckleball. With the split-finger you know that most of the time that the ball's going to go down, and a lot of the time it's going to go straight down and away to the left-handed hitter. But it got me into problems with right-handed low-ball hitters like Jack Clark, Pedro Guerrero, and Gary Carter. It would come down and in to them and those guys hurt me over the years.

I know that 1979 was the Cy Young year and I had a nice string of years. But the best I ever threw in my whole career was the first half of 1977. And yes, they used me a lot. We were up there fighting for first place and this was Chicago, the Cubs. I had seventy-five innings in at the All-Star break. I went on the DL after the break with a pulled muscle and didn't get a save for like five weeks. But I still ended up with thirty-one saves which I think was a record at the time. Hell, I had like twenty-six saves by the All-Star break and I was really all but unhittable. I knew when they put me in that I was going to strike at least two or three people out. Chicago was a fun city to play in. The fans were so close to you. You'd get to see the same people almost every day. Cubs fans are pretty much the same people, especially the ones hanging out in the bleachers and along the lines by the bullpens. So we really got to know them and they'd get on your ass. But we'd give it back to them. I remember I left passes for one of my best buddies one time. About the fourth inning, I'm sitting along the line in the pen. And I look up and I see them taking him out in handcuffs. He's in there on my passes and they're taking him out. He'd crawled up into the scoreboard, said he wanted to see what it was like. Wrigley Field will do that kind of thing to you.

The Cy Young wasn't something that relief pitchers were winning at the time [1979] so it wasn't something that I thought about. Actually the year that I thought I should have won it was 1984 when I had forty-five saves. But I didn't. And you know, the Niekro brothers are the guys I beat in 1979 and they both won twenty-one games that year. I'm still not so sure that the Cy Young Award should be given to a relief pitcher. We have our Rolaids award. I don't get all hepped up about awards where you get voted on. Somebody doesn't like you and you're screwed.

In 1982, I was with St. Louis then, and we won it all that year. The biggest game as far as I was concerned came during the regular season. We were fighting Philly, going right neck and neck for the pennant. Anyway in this particular game, right at the end of the season, we had a one-run lead when I came in. The bases are loaded and there's one out and Mike Schmidt is hittin'. It's the bottom of the ninth inning and I got him on a splitter. He hit a ground ball back to me, home to first, double play and we win the game. And now we go to New York and we've got five games in three days. We went in to play the Mets and just blew them away and won with three days left in the season.

And if you don't think New York is a tough town, here's one from Shea Stadium. I don't think it was in that series but I used to enjoy going into New York to play, a big rivalry. The fans would get on you.

Here's an example of what it's like for a relief pitcher to pitch in New York. If you know where the bullpens are in Shea Stadium, they're down the foul lines and they have the bleachers right out there where they can watch you. And one day I get up and start heating up and the whole crowd stands up—everybody in those bleachers—and starts singing, "Sutter takes it up the ass! Doo-dah! Doo-dah! Sutter takes it up the ass, all the live-long day!" And I was laughing so goddamned hard that I couldn't warm up. That's Shea. Tough crowd!

What I remember best from the World Series that year was Willie McGee's catch. But the play-offs. We had to win the pennant first. We beat Atlanta three straight in the National League play-offs. And I believe I got the win in Game Two and then in the final game I came in in the seventh and got something like six or seven straight hitters. That was my first pennant and so there was a special feeling. In that last game Willie McGee had a hell of a day, a triple and a home run. I remember being . . . well, anytime you win a pennant it's exciting. But we had to play the Brewers in the Series. They were awesome, a great hitting team—Cooper, Molitor, Simmons, Yount, Thomas, Og-livie—and I'm still not so sure. That Series might have been a lot different if Rollie had pitched. Fingers was out hurt. We came back and beat them two games in the end and I don't know if we would have if Fingers had been there.

In the Series I got the win in Game Two and saved Game Three. That's one that I'll always remember because a pitch I threw to Gorman Thomas ended up being the tail end of one of the best catches I ever saw. Willie McGee dove over the fence and got that one. Saved my ass! And Game Four of that Series is known as the one that I "wasn't available" for. It wasn't that I wasn't available, it was Whitey. Herzog was the best manager I ever played for. I'd pitched in and won Game Two and then came back in Game Three and got the save. So Whitey refused to bring me in in Game Four. He knows pitching and he knows his pen. Even though we're in the World Series, we're up a game and if we lose Game Four all we are is tied, but if he over-uses me. . . . He wasn't going to hurt me to where he wasn't going to be able to use me for the rest of the games. That's what stands Herzog above all the rest. He's not going to hurt anybody and he's not going to play the game in a panic. Who's to say that these other guys can't do it is the way he looks at his bullpen. But as it turned out in Game Four we [the bullpen] didn't do it. An error in the seventh, a ground ball to first and LaPoint comes off the mound to cover the bag. Her-nandez's toss hits him right in the glove. LaPoint drops the damned ball. The son of a bitch weighs 240 pounds. If it had been a cheeseburger he'd a caught it. [Laughs.] That would have been the third out and they proceed to score four runs. They got six in all that inning and end up beating us 7–5. Good teams, you can't give them that extra out.

If there was a most memorable game for me, that one against Philly during the season was a big one. But Game Seven in 1982 was the one I guess. Andujar had been hurt by that line drive in Game Three and Whitey knew that he wasn't going to be able to go the whole way. I hired a limousine to take Gene Tenace and me and our wives to the ball park because I knew that I was going to either throw the pitch to win it or lose it. I didn't want to come out and fight the crowd either way. Once we had the one-run lead after seven innings—we were up 4–3—Herzog said, "You're the pitcher!" There was no fooling around. An uneventful two innings, no great plays or anything, which is what you want, but what a thrill! The crowd in Busch Stadium, the noise just kept building and building. And my stuff, I had real good stuff. I went in there and got them. I do remember one ball that Simmons hit back to me that I ran almost all the way to first base. I was afraid if I threw it over there I might throw it away. I've been known to do that. My boy did that in a game the other day and his mom turned around and said, "Chip off the old block!" But we picked up two more runs in the eighth, which was nice, and that was it. World Series. Big, big thrill.

I can't really say that I was nervous that night. I was always fine when they gave me the ball and I can't say that I was really nervous before any game. I think if I'd have been a starting pitcher that I'd have gotten too nervous. I mean, if you had to plan your whole day around pitching that night, well, I never did that. I didn't do this before Game Seven of the 1982 Series but I'd go fishing at four in the mornin' [during the season] and go home, get a couple of hours sleep and head out to the park and be ready to go when the seventh, eighth or ninth rolled around. Relief pitchin's what's great. You're screwin' around all the time during battin' practice, you're goofing around in the locker room before the game. The first five innings you can sit there on the bench and relax. The bullpen's too far down and you maybe can't see what the hell's going on. So then about the sixth or seventh inning I'd go on down to the bullpen because I knew that I needed to get ready to pitch. One of the biggest tricks is to try to control yourself. You don't want to get too juiced up. I didn't like spring training games because I knew that I was going to pitch that day. I didn't like that. I liked the idea of that call coming and somebody saying, "Sutter!" I'd turn the switch on and say, "Let's go!"

The first All-Star game that I pitched in was 1978 at San Diego. I came in in the eighth when the game was tied. We scored four runs in the bottom of that inning and I got the win. In the ninth I get two men out and here comes Lasorda, who's managing the National League. And Tommy says, "We're gonna take you out. This might be Niekro's last chance to pitch in an All-Star game so I gotta take you out!" So he hooks me and Niekro comes in and gets the last out. And that's in 1978. Goddamn Niekro pitched nine more years! Tommy and I still laugh about that. I like Tommy Lasorda. He's full of shit but I'll tell you what, he knows how to run a ball club. He don't get caught with his pants down very often. He knows how to run a team, he really does.

And the All-Star [experience] was fun because those years that I played it was like just about the same guys on our team every year. It almost got to be like a reunion. We looked forward to going. We knew that we were going to beat them. Parker and those guys used to yell at the American League players. Guys like Yaz, Murray, Rice—wait until you get Sutter. Because I think that they had never really seen the splitter. Hey, a relief pitcher should go five years in the National League and then five in the American and then come back. I never got to pitch in both leagues. But it was really a definite advantage, [to pitch to] a guy who had never seen me. The first time they batted against me, boy, they were in trouble, unless I just out and out hung one.

Managers—Herzog was the best and a real piece of work. Herzog is crazy. I remember the first time that I ever went fishing with him. We had a game that night. We meet to go fishing at about four or five o'clock in the morning. And at about eight o'clock we're out on the water and he hands me a liver, sausage, onion and mustard sandwich with a Budweiser. That was breakfast. We've gotta game that night and here I am drinking beer with the manager at eight o'clock in the morning. "Ah, one beer won't hurt you!" I'll tell you something else I saw Whitey do that was down right amazing. You just can't stand up in a jon boat. But he and this buddy of his both decide that they have to take a leak at the same time. So now we're in the middle of a lake and they get up together and pull off this unbelievable balancing act. You just can't do that in a jon boat. But they did. Both of them. And the boat never rocked.

Playin' for Whitey was great. And he was a bullpen manager, the best. He gets the most out of everybody he's got down there. He's not afraid to use everybody. You get some managers and they get to panicking. They don't want to use the five guys they've got down there. But

Whitey knows that you're playing 162 games and he's not afraid to lose a game. One game, like to save me so he'd have me for the next three or four. I pitched six days in a row one time and he told me to get dressed and sit up in the stands. You know he knew he wasn't going to use me.

Managers and pitching coaches that aren't very secure will always go to their relief pitchers, especially the short man and ask, "Can you go again today?" What kind of a pitcher would you be if you said, "No, I can't pitch today." Your arm could be hanging half off but you're going to say, "Yeah, I can pitch." I got that all the time. And finally I just told them to stay the fuck away. If you want me to pitch, you're the manager, you know where I am. Just give me a call and I'll pitch. But don't ask me whether I can pitch. I won't name names but I will say that Herzog never pulled that. He never asked. Whitey had the balls to rest his pitchers.

The Hall of Fame? It would be something that would really cap off a wonderful career, a great honor. I would very much like to be in the Hall of Fame. But on the other side, if I don't get in, it won't be the end of the world, won't ruin anything. Like I said, when people vote for stuff!

As far as my career ending? I know that a lot of ballplayers, maybe relievers in particular, have had trouble adjusting to retirement. But in my case it wasn't that I got bad or that I started losing my talent, I just got hurt. I couldn't play. I went through three shoulder operations trying to fix it. Two years of rehab, all the weight things. And it just didn't work out. Some guys just can't give it up. Maybe I'm just different, attitude-wise. I know that I did everything I could to try to keep playing. I could still use another shoulder operation and maybe someday I'll get it. But as long as I can play catch with the kids and throw batting practice to them, I'm not getting it. Let's just say I'm enjoying watching my kids grow up, and hunting and fishing, knowing that I had a nice career and that I gave it my best shot.

Mach III with Their Hair on Fire

WANTED

Man willing to work odd hours for great pay. Must be fearless, have great control, resilient arm (preferably left-handed), 95-mile-an-hour fastball or freak pitch of some description. Offbeat sense of humor and very short memory a must. Type B personalities need not apply.

Who, over the years, best fits our job description? All of the great ones meet most qualifications. Some are stronger in one area than others, of course. Mike Marshall's sense of humor was suspect but then you're not going to find too many Rodney Dangerfields out there who can give you 100-plus game seasons. Duren, Radatz, Gossage, Smith, Plesac and Dibble all had the 95-MPH fastball. And then there were the great specialty pitch guys: Wilhelm had the knuckler, Miller the change, Sutter the splitter, McGraw the screwjie, Face the forkball. Guys like Dick Hall and Dennis Eckersley never quite knew how to throw anything out of the strike zone. Funny motions? Dick Hyde threw from down under while Kent Tekulve came at hitters with that slingshot motion from behind third base.

The resume of a Roger McDowell or a Moe Drabowsky certainly would get any prospective boss's attention. Moe still carries his own bag of snakes into Orioles Fantasy Camps and Roger doesn't leave home without a well-packed mischief kit—stink bombs, fright masks, M-80s. The scary persona? Hugh Casey, Al Hrabosky, Rob Dibble are all excellent candidates. As to the forgetfulness that you need in relief, flakes like Loes, Stanhouse, and Anderson would fill the bill. However, most relievers have the ability to "turn the page after a loss," as Mitch Williams aptly put it.

But if you're taking about the prime candidate, the man who over the years had all the right stuff, the name is Rollie Fingers. He had the outstanding fastball, the great slider, and then late in his career when his heater began to leak gas, he developed a hellacious forkball. But according to Milwaukee Brewers pitching coach Larry Haney, what Fingers had most of was "the essential ingredient of relief."

Fingers had no fear. There was no situation that bothered him. I think that you could have put a man on each base and one in between each base and it wouldn't have fazed him a bit. He would still know that he was in total command.

Sparky Anderson takes the praise for this quintessential relief man further.

I don't believe that we'll ever see, in our time, a relief pitcher that can go the distance for seventeen years the way Rollie did. And I know his theory because I asked him. His theory was, "Shithouse or castle!" He never worried about it. He came in and was going to throw strikes. If you get him, fine. If you don't, fine. He never worried either way.

And it isn't just Fingers who thinks like that, he simply set the standard. "Outhouse or castle" is the attitude of short relief. Lee Smith, bowed to and called "Kahuna" by Red Sox fans, takes a kingly approach to his work on the mound.

When I come into a game, it's mine. I call my own game. I don't like to let anybody know what I'm thinking. And I don't want my pitching coach calling the pitches because pretty soon you're second-guessing them and then yourself. If somebody hits a home run off of Lee Smith, well, it was off the pitch I wanted to throw. I live with the call!

Jeff Reardon, the Rolaids all-time point leader, has that perfect "give me the ball" attitude, the mind-set of relief.

I want to get into every game I can. And that is why I've been successful. Physically I can do it and mentally I want to do it!

But we're not talking about robots here. A couple of blown saves and even the toughest of these mental muscle men can break. Those who have lived through the experience often come out with clearer understandings of what expectations and success are all about. Others never recover. Reliever Donnie Moore was one strike away from eliminating Boston in the 1986 American League Championship Series when he gave up a dramatic two-out home run to Dave Henderson, sending the series back to Boston. The Sox won Games Six and Seven and the right to play the Mets in the World Series. Moore took his own life several years later and many believe that it was because he'd been unable to let go of that pitch. Brian Downing, Moore's teammate, believed the hounding of the press helped push the Angels pitcher to suicide. Gene Mauch, Moore's manager, talking to Roy Firestone on ESPN's "Up Close," disagreed.

> I knew Donnie Moore very well. He was a fine, fine man but very unstable. He lived a long time after he threw that home run. And I don't like to point a finger at the press and say, hey, you're responsible for this guy doing whatever he did. And I don't believe it [the pitch caused Moore to take his own life]. He had a long time before he pulled that trigger.

Whether that one pitch ruined Moore's career and ultimately drove him to suicide will never be documented. What we do know is this. Relief pitchers who succeed can't afford the luxury of obsessing. There are too many big pitches, too many big games. As Dr. House pointed out, the great relievers all learn to practice the art of positive denial. And the survivors, guys like Dan Plesac of the Milwaukee Brewers, are quick to make this case in point.

> It takes a lot of ups and downs and a lot of being knocked on your can to deal with the pressures of this job. Finally you get to the point where you can just go out there and do it again. That's when you are effective in relief.

Tug McGraw, Rollie Fingers, Mitch Williams, Bruce Sutter: they're all classic examples of why God made some men to be starters but created others especially adapted to the day-to-day pressure you find in the pen. Most relief men are blessed with nervous systems that cry out for a daily pump of adrenaline. Tug McGraw discusses the difference between starting and relieving.

The whole difference is the waiting process. I couldn't deal with it. Didn't know what to do with my energy. "*Aaaaah!*" [He yells and pulls at his hair.] I was always playing catch between starts. I just wasn't cut out for that pace that a starter has.

Dennis Eckersley's secret? Fear! Not fear of one of those guys with the bats in their hands. What Eckersley fears is failure. And what Dennis does is this: He takes fear, turns it around in his head and fires it for strikes past hitters.

I've said that I pitch out of fear more than anything else and that's true. It would be different if I had one or two years' big league experience and I say I'm pitching out of fear. People would say, "Jesus, he's scared to death!" But that's not it, it's a fear of failure. I think you can use that to your advantage. You can use the emotions that you have and the adrenaline that you have when you go out there.

There's another fear, a close relative to the kind that Eckersley is talking about. These men may never blush when they're jacking around out there in the pen, but when they take their egos for a stroll across the white lines there's no greater fear than that of *embarrassment*. The reason Roger McDowell pitched so well against the Astros in the 1986 National League play-offs was the thought of hearing some post-game interviewer say, "What did he hit, Rog?" Mitch Williams has had the same kind of nightmare. "You don't want some guy coming up after the game and asking you how you held that homer," he said.

This is the mental stuff of relief, the persona that motored the specialty into 1990, the record-breaking season for the pen. Relievers earned an all-time high of 1,113 saves. A record number of pitchers had thirty or more saves. Twenty had twenty or more. And the individual medalist for that single season was Dennis Eckersley. "The Eck" again put up staggering numbers, saving forty-eight and only blowing two save opportunities.

But the man who took relief into a higher league in 1990 was Jeff Reardon. Among the active he is the pen's top gun. The hirsute right-hander worked the eighties with quiet magnificence in New York, Montreal, Minnesota and then Boston. Reardon has saved twenty or more games for eleven straight seasons, and thirty or more for six consecutive years. In the 1990 season he passed Bruce Sutter to become the all-time Rolaids scoring leader with 664 points. The following year Reardon joined Rich Gossage, Rollie Fingers, and Bruce Sutter in the 300-save club, a number that many believe to be a reliever's ticket to the Hall of Fame. And, in 1992, Reardon became baseball's all-time save leader.

There have been many big games and many opportunities since he picked up that first save with the Mets in the summer of 1979. Reardon barely remembers his three hundredth. "It was in Fenway, I know that. I was pleased to get it at home," he said. But there's one moment that he'll never forget. It began with "a surprise phone call" to the Minnesota pen and ended with the weight of the world resting right where it belonged, squarely on the shoulders of the game's premier relief pitcher.

Game Seven, the 1987 World Series. Top of the ninth inning, we're leading the Cardinals 4–2. Without a doubt the biggest moment in my career. We're in the Homer Dome, all those white hankies are waving. It's deafening. Viola is going and he is dealing. He had retired nineteen of twenty-one hitters when the phone rang in the pen. This was the bottom of the eighth when they called, just as Frank was starting to walk off the mound. I started getting loose, thinking I'm not going in. But if he gets in trouble in the ninth I'll get the call. And then it's the top of the ninth and Rick Stelmaszek, our bullpen coach, suddenly just turns, looks at me and says, "It's yours!"

And that was as nervous as I've ever been. I've been in some big games. But the seventh game of the Series and Frank had retired seventeen in a row. The top of the St. Louis order is coming up. Tommy Herr, Curt Flood, and Willie McGee. And I'm not known for holding runners on. I got Herr and Curt and now I'm facing McGee. I threw him two good fastballs for strikes and then I wanted to sort of back-door him with a curveball. You always want to end it on a strikeout. So I tried to fool him, get him on the back-door curve but he almost didn't swing. He just threw the bat at the ball and hit a little weak ground ball to Gaetti at third. I was actually hoping it would go foul because I wanted to come back with a high fastball and strike him out. But Gaetti threw him out and here's what I really remember. *They almost crushed me!* We had some weight on that team—Hrbek, Gaetti, Brunansky, Laudner, Puckett, a bunch of 230-pounders and I remember being on the bottom of that pile and I was screaming at Gaetti, "You're crushing me!" They kept piling on top and Gary was trying to do a little pushup on top and I was screaming, "I can't breathe." I remember the cover of *Sports Illustrated*. My big moment and all you could see was my beard, just crushed. I saved the game and I thought someone was going to have to save *me*!

Eckersley, Righetti, Reardon, top guns of the 1990s, thoroughbreds all, relievers with long and well-documented pedigrees. But as history has proven, there's nothing like a little pennant chase to heat up the spotlight. Especially when you've got a group like Cincinnati's Nasty Boys, that pen load of controversy who fastballed and bizarred the Reds to a World Championship in 1990. Randy Myers, Norm Charlton, and Rob Dibble—two typical left-handers, and a third who isn't but behaves like one. Myers is the quiet one, the guy who doesn't converse with the press. However his locker, decorated in "Early Desert Storm," says it all. Myers has his cubby stocked with grenades, ammo boxes, fatigues and a "Death to Mankind" knife. Charlton is the smart one, the penner that the "boys" call genius. Charlton distinguished himself in June of 1990 by putting his pitching shoulder up for grabs. Norm ran through a stop sign at third and then rather than sliding, opted to knock Dodgers hulk Mike Scioscia, cup over teacups at home plate.

Then there's Dibble, the Nastiest of the Nasties. Oh, that Dibble! He's a 6'4", 230-pounder, with an arsenal of 100-MPH fastballs that have a way of buzzing behind the heads of batsmen. Rob is also the league leader in fines and suspensions. Dibble on Dibble: "Being Hungarian, sometimes you just lose your mind." There's an entire trophy room of bagged prey out there, who if asked, would readily testify—ask Willie Randolph, Eric Yelding, Doug Dascenzo. It isn't just hitters who've felt Dibble's sting. Meg Porter, a first-grade teacher from Batavia, Ohio, once took a Dibble fastball on the elbow. Rob cranked this inadvertent heater into the stands after a disappointing outing in relief. Maybe he thought Meg was crowding the railing—it's hard to figure out what goes on in his Hungarian head.

Charlton, the triple major from Rice University, characterized the pen's Triplets of Terror for *The Show Magazine* like this: "I'd like people to think of us as nasty boys because we're aggressive. Not because we're assholes."

We'll make that one the reader's call. But the real deal on the Boys of Nasty is this. In 1990, the Reds championship season, they established themselves as the best three-man bullpen in the history of relief. Stan Williams, the Reds pitching coach, describes his overexposed penners with classic understatement.

When you have a lefty, righty, lefty combination like that, you gotta like your chances, every time you send them out.

And Stan sent them out. By the All-Star break they were 13–7, had 141 Ks in 141 innings, and had nailed down twenty-six saves of the Reds fifty wins. Their combined league-leading ERA of 2.93 at the season's end had the fans in Riverfront thinking back to the seventies and the pens of Captain Hook. And in the stretch run? Well the "Bad" got better. In post-season play, they posted a microscopic ERA of 0.29, giving up only one run in thirty-three and one-third innings. Their record four saves and 0.40 ERA in the National League Championship Series earned Dibble and Myers the first-ever co-MVP honors in a LCS.

The World Series wound down to Game Seven and the Nasty Boys had not given up a single earned run in thirteen innings of relief. Then Lou Piniella marched out there the way he did and not only made a statement about the Nasties, but reminded millions of fans just how much the game has changed. Why would a manager yank Jose Rijo, who has just gotten nineteen straight Oakland hitters to stick in Myers to get the last two, if baseball hadn't become a game of relief?

So 1990 proved to be milestone mania for the bullpen: "The Eck"; the Nasties' great season; Reardon's final leap to the top of the Rolaids heap; Righetti firing past all left-handers with 224 saves, surpassing Sparky Lyle's 222. Then there was the icing, that Bobby Thigpen thing. Thiggy was involved in a greater percentage of his team's wins than any other reliever since 1969, the year the save became official. And Thigpen didn't just break Righetti's season save record of forty-six, he went him eleven better. Thigpen yanked the shelf right out from under the trophy. His 151 Rolaids points marked the highest total earned in a single season, breaking Mark Davis's 1989 record of 126. And who knows what would have happened if Thigpen had been hot from the start? Barry Foote, the White Sox bullpen coach, recalls the April night in Texas when "Thiggy got it going." An unintended tip from a Rangers hitter ignited one of the greatest single seasons in the history of relief.

I think the turning point for Thigpen who set a record of fifty-seven saves, a record that won't be broken for a number of years, came in April. We're in Texas and we've got a three-run lead in the ninth inning. Texas has one out and Thigpen threw eight or nine pitches and we lost. He gave up four runs. It happened in like five minutes. The game was over. And after the game they do a thing for TV there. The big left fielder, Incaviglia, had hit a home run to end the game for Texas. He was talking on TV and he said, "All I've gotta do with Thigpen is sit on gas. Because I know he's going to come after me with the heater." Thigpen heard this. And he's got two other pitches, a slider and a changeup. The very next day he came in, bases loaded, no outs, eighth inning. And he got out of that inning, got Incaviglia on a ground ball. Then he went back out there and got them again in the ninth. That really turned his season around. He mixed them up more, fastball, slider, change, he became more of a pitcher than a thrower and then just had that unbelievable year.

Let's listen to one of the game's great pen-shaping managers and the top guns of that "unbelievable year"—Eckersley, Plesac, Olson, Williams, Righetti, and McDowell—those Mach III guys who raced out there with their hair on fire.

VOICES FROM THE PEN

I baited my note to the White Rat with quotes from two old friends of his. "Bruce Sutter suggested that I ask you about those four A.M. game-day fishing trips and the liver, onion and mustard sandwiches and cold Budweisers that you served him for breakfast." And then there was Captain Hook's message. Sparky says, "No one shaped the bullpen better than Herzog in the 1980s."

The return post card was direct and to the point:

"Bob, I don't know more than anybody else!"

—Whitey

I reached Herzog by phone a few days later. Sparky was right, of course. It's hard to find a more knowledgeable pen man than the man they call the White Rat.

I don't think that this has ever been mentioned. After the 1984 season, after we lost Bruce Sutter, the Cardinals were picked to finish last. I was picked to be the first manager fired in 1985. You know Sutter had saved forty-five games for us in 1984. You lose a guy like that and you don't replace him. We'd finished so far behind the Cubs, and we had Sutter. That Cardinal bullpen in 1985 may have been the best bullpen in history. I think going in, the only guy in that pen who had ever had a save was Ken Dayley. We had a bullpen that never lost but one game all year when we led in the seventh inning. And that game, the one we lost, wasn't tied until the ninth inning. Ken Dayley threw a high fastball to Van Gorder, the Cincinnati catcher, and he got a base hit to tie the game. We eventually lost in the twelfth. And that's the only game we lost when we had a lead in the seventh inning until the 175th game of the year.

That was the sixth game of the 1985 World Series. It took a bad call from an umpire [Don Denkinger's controversial call at first base] to get that done, or we woulda won the World Series in that game. But when you talk about bullpens, that was one hell of a bullpen. Jeff Lahti got nineteen saves that year and he hasn't gotten a save since, he got a bad arm. Bill Campbell we picked up in the Philly deal with DeJesus when we didn't think we were going to be able to sign Ozzie [Smith]. We brought up Worrell on August 30 so he'd be eligible for the play-offs. So we didn't have him until then but we got some kind of mileage out of Horton, Dayley, Campbell and Lahti. Forsch picked up a couple of saves, he was my fifth starter or spot starter. And a lot of times I'd middle-relief him. If he had a lead in the sixth inning, you know he'd pitch four innings and get a save. I imagine that's what happened [Forsch's two saves]. But the big key there was that we just flipflopped them, used left and right. And I don't see how the hell clubs expect to win when they don't have that left and right balance.

To me, Sutter was the best of all times. The nine years he put together consecutively were probably the top nine years in the history of the game. Those years that he had with the Cubs and with us, that was amazing what he did. And any time you have a fake pitcher, a screwballer or split-finger guy, it negates a lot of the lefty-righty business. And nobody's had the split-finger like Sutter had. What they're throwin' now is a forkball. Sutter was a big-handed guy and he popped that thing out of there with his thumb. His split-finger was different than what they're throwin' now.

One of the big relief performances for us was in Game Three of the 1982 National League Championship Series. We beat Atlanta three straight in that series but that third one was a more important game than everybody thought. We won 3-0, but if we lose that game I've gotta pitch LaPoint and Forsch in Games Four and Five, and they didn't pitch very well in Atlanta. I was really worried about winning that third game. So naturally I was really glad when Bruce put the damned thing away. He got seven straight hitters to close that one out. He also nailed down the seventh game of the World Series to beat Milwaukee that year. But you know that's what he wanted. He wanted to be there in the eighth and ninth inning. Bruce was a guy who could get you six outs but he couldn't go over forty pitches. The days he

348

went over forty pitches I made damned sure that I didn't use him the next day. He'd say he could pitch but his fingers used to get sorer than hell after he went over forty pitches and he really couldn't put the pressure on the ball where he wanted to.

In the third game of the 1982 World Series against the Brewers—that was the game that Andujar got hit with a line drive on the leg—I had to bring Sutter in to get me seven outs. He threw forty-four pitches and he got the save. Then the next day we had a 5–1 lead in the seventh inning and LaPoint dropped a ball at first base with nobody on. I brought in Bair and I brought in Kaat, then Lahti. Nobody got anybody out and we ended up losing the game. The press questioned why I wouldn't bring in Sutter to pitch an inning. And I said, "That's the trouble with you guys. You watch us play three days and you know more about my ball club than I do." But Sutter came back the next day, we lost that fifth game. I really didn't need him until the seventh game and then he came in and nailed it down for us.

I won't knock anybody, but there were some [managers] who would do anything to win a ball game. Some guys will pitch a guy twenty days in a row if they think they can win that twentieth game. And I think that you can ruin good bullpen guys pitching them like that, just pitching their asses off. When you see guys' arms blow out that are hard throwers, blown out at an early age, then I think they may have been overworked.

And no, artificial surface has nothing to do with the kinds of people that you want in your bullpen. I read that and I hear that, but I'd venture to say that between 1982 and 1987 our record on grass in St. Louis was as good as anybody in the league. I never thought about the surface when I was shaping my bullpen. If it's a fastball pitcher, you want the power guy, if it's a freak pitcher you didn't care. But most of the relief pitchers are power guys or freak pitchers or guys that can only hold their stuff for three innings. I think makeup has got something to do with it in the pen too. I don't think a hyper guy can be a starting pitcher because he worries himself to a frazzle waiting for his turn.

Memories? Well I lost some tough games to the Yankees in those play-offs three years in a row [from 1976 to 1978]. I guess the thing I remember most was in 1977, that Kansas City Royals team. That was the best team I'd ever managed and we won 102 games. In the fifth game of the play-offs we had the Yankees down 3–1. We got those three runs in the first three innings of that deciding game and we had chances and chances to score more and we never did. Mickey Rivers made a great catch on Porter to rob him of a triple. But as that goes, if you score in the first few innings and don't score again, you get beat eighty percent of the time. I went to the bullpen and brought in Leonard, my best pitcher. I didn't bring him in in a jam, I brought him in to start the inning to get me three outs. He hadn't pitched since the third game. But he gave up two quick hits. There wasn't a hell of a lot you could do about that, just bloops in to the outfield and then he walked Roy White on a 3–2 pitch. We ended up losing the ball game and the pennant, but every bullpen guy I brought in to that game did their job—Bird, Mingori, Gura, Littell and Leonard—and the Yankees got five bloop hits and one base on balls in the last two innings to beat us. They didn't hit one damned ball good. So all you can say is the pen did what I wanted them to do but we got our asses beat. I really couldn't criticize or fault any of them because they all pitched the guys the way I wanted them to. The Yankees had Sparky Lyle then and he shut us down. Sparky didn't blow you away, he just slidered you to death. You knew what you were going to get. He just kept throwing that slider down and in to the right-handed hitters and they kept trying to hit it in the hole and they kept hitting it to the shortstop. He just had a great slider and I think he was in just about every game in that series, throwing that thing at us.

But I made the moves that I thought were right. It just didn't work out. That's the big thing about managing. When you're going to your bullpen I always say I've gotta make the decision that I can live with. If so-and-so beats me I can live with that, but if he gets a base hit off this guy that's out there now, well I'm not going to be able to sleep tonight. So I make my move. And that's what I do. Pitchers will tell you that they're like that too. They can't look themselves in the mirror after the game if they throw their number two or number three pitch when the game's on the line. But they still do it!

DENNIS ECKERSLEY
Right-Handed Pitcher

CLEVELAND INDIANS, 1975–1977
BOSTON RED SOX, 1978–1984
CHICAGO CUBS, 1984–1986
OAKLAND ATHLETICS, 1987–Present

- **Struck Out Two Hundred Hitters In 1976**
- **Threw A No-Hitter In 1977**
- **Gave Up Historic Home Run To Kirk Gibson In 1988 World Series**
- **Threw The Final And Winning Pitch In The 1989 World Series**
- **1992 Cy Young Award Winner**
- **1992 American League MVP**

Dennis Eckersley, former wild man, sits on the Oakland bench in Baltimore's Memorial Stadium and talks about control. Tanned, handsome, sober, remarried. The new Eck is a gentleman to a fault, except with opposing hitters. Nobody hits, nobody walks. "The one thing I'll never show them out there is weakness," he said. "I may not have it every time out. But there's no way I'm going to give in. You never let them see weakness," he said.

I try to have a presence on the mound. I am big on that. Sometimes I may not be throwing very well. But I make-believe. I make-believe a lot when I'm not right. To try to convince myself. I think that hitters can sense weakness. They can smell it or see it when a guy's not right. I've had a lot of people tell me that. I try to create this presence whether it's real or not. I don't think that I necessarily visualize an out, see each pitch and how one will lead to another, but I know this. When I'm out there I try to convey one thing, and that's this, "I'm going to get you out."

The toughest part of becoming a relief pitcher for me was the accepting part of it. You didn't want to accept going to the bullpen because it wasn't that glorious. It wasn't like I went straight to the closer role with Oakland. So I kind of fought that mentally for a while. I think once I accepted that fact and had some success, and realized that it would further my career, after all, I had to be realistic. Me going seven or eight innings just wasn't happening anymore. So it was the best thing for me.

Tony LaRussa had asked me at the end of my first season with Oakland what I wanted to do. I'd been working out of the pen. I told him that I wanted to start. And then over the winter when we got Bobby Welch I said, "See ya, I'm back in the pen." But that's how we won the National League championship in 1988, so it worked out.

Here is the way I feel about relief pitching today. I feel important every day, not just one out of every four or five. As a reliever, when I get to the ball park I'm getting ready to pitch. It's kind of a neat feelin', you know. I may not pitch but I'm getting prepared mentally and physically to pitch. And I feel like an everyday player almost. Not that I'm more respected than somebody else, but I think the role has made the game more exciting for me, at least on a daily basis.

Drinking early in my career caused me so much trouble professionally and in my personal life. But fortunately I was able to deal with that. I do think that if I weren't sober that I wouldn't be here today. I was lucky because I bottomed out. I turned it around. I got my life together and that was in January of 1987. Then the trade came about that time to the A's so it was a crossroads. But the drinking was . . . I just couldn't stop. It was a constant up and down battle. I had some personal problems. I know this sounds funny but if there was any one thing that it came down to it was a videotape. I watched this tape of myself the following day. A relative of mine taped me while I was drunk. It was tough to take then but it was probably the best thing that could have happened to me.

It's funny because I'd had some success before the drinking became a problem. I think that the hunger [for success] is here now more than it's ever been. And that's a terrific feeling. I want it [success] bad. And I don't know why, I can't explain it but I want it. It's come along with sobriety.

One of the things I get a kick out of is all those handshakes. You get so many more when you're a reliever, especially a short man. Luckily I started long enough to complete a hundred ball games or so. That's a lot of complete games, but that's over a twelve-year span. So that's what, a hundred or so handshakes? But as a reliever, on a good year, I shake something like forty-five hands and that's like forty-five complete games. Whether it be one out or one inning, two innings, it doesn't matter. Whooo boy! You did it all, and it's kind of funny really. This is a very glorious situation but at the same time it can be a terrible, terrible experience. Losing is brutal.

I like the fact that I can come back and change everything the next day, the next outing, but it still sticks with me. I can't just walk away from it. I guess being hard on yourself is how you become good at something. I don't accept losing, ever. I remember being a starter and watching a reliever blowing my game for me too. And I never was really mad at the guy but I take it personally. I guess that's the only way to take it.

I guess I made the relief pitchers' highlight film and lowlight film in two consecutive World Series. In 1989, the last play to win it all—that was really kind of neat because usually the pitcher doesn't get the ball. I had the ball, which was unique. A ground ball to first and the toss to me for the final out. Quite a feeling. And of course, the year before when Gibson hit the home run that played in American homes for months to come. You talk about low points in your career! Gibson was hurt at the time, terrible physically. A horrible moment but it wasn't really that low . . . considering my career. I'd come from so far down, I've had a lot of ups and downs, really. People thought that I was going to dwell on that and it would come back to haunt me later but it didn't. Fortunately, we had an opportunity to play for a championship the following year and that took a lot of the heat off. Not that everybody was saying that I had to come back from that. Some things are just destined to happen. The Gibson home run was one of them. Too bad it was me!

After what happened with the 1988 Series, and then to have another opportunity in 1989, to me it just doubled the desire to win. I wanted that World Series ring bad and I looked at it as perhaps my only chance. And I wanted that memory. The earthquake had a lot to do with putting a damper on the championship, but to be able to have the ball, to get the last out meant a lot. I have nothing to compare that to. But then again, when you finally reach something, it's never what you expect it to be. That's what I found out. I thought because I was old enough that it would be special. Maybe later it will mean more. It's not that I don't appreciate winning a World Series, it just wasn't what I expected it to be. Maybe this one will be, the next one.

When I was younger I was brash but a lot of the stories get messed up. Especially the one about me screaming at the guys on deck during the late innings of my no-hitter. [Eckersley, with Cleveland, no-hit California, 1–0, on May 30, 1977.] What happened was this. In the ninth inning of that game everybody knew that the no-hitter was happening. And these guys were taking their time getting into the box. They were trying to throw my timing off. The last guy up—ninth inning, last out—was Gil Flores, who didn't have a great career. Nothing against him. There are about fifteen cameramen all lined up and I'm yelling, "Get in there! These guys aren't lined up to take your picture, pal!" At that time I was pretty brash. I was a kid, I had a good excuse.

I had a tough time with umpires when I was a kid. I just didn't know how to work 'em. You can't start yelling in the first inning because if you do, you're not going to get anything all night. But I was so intense, I just didn't know how to control that. But I got better as the years went on.

In the pen I'm not a big clown or anything. I may have been had I been in the pen when I was younger. But now I'm pretty serious out there. The part of the game when I really start paying attention is the sixth inning. Because if you find yourself being totally intense the whole game you'll . . . it's just like when I used to watch the play-off games, I'd be into every pitch but man, pretty soon I'd be exhausted. So I try to have as much fun as possible out there. Fun is success, fun is after, fun is doing the job. Fun is not before that.

I've said that I pitch more out of fear than anything else and that's true. If you can't control that or channel that, for your benefit, then you're in trouble. I think fear is a big motivator. Fear of blowing this game. And I have no problem with that. That fear is always there.

DAVE RIGHETTI
Left-Handed Pitcher

NEW YORK YANKEES, 1979, 1981–1990
SAN FRANCISCO GIANTS, 1991–Present

- **Rookie Of The Year In 1981**
- **Threw A No-Hitter In 1983**
- **Set Save Record With Forty-Six Saves In 1986**
- **After Giving Up A Game-Tying Grand Slam Showed His Displeasure By Throwing A Ball Over The Right Field Fence**

A roar goes up in the TV lounge in the visitors' locker room in Baltimore's Memorial Stadium. I stick my head in, then jump back. Yankees breaking away from the set, whooping and shouting over the results of the Belmont Stakes. "Anyone seen Dave Righetti?" I ask. Bad timing. The horses have just crossed the finish line. I'm caught in a doorway stampede of another kind. Half-dressed Yankees all around me, pulling on jerseys and caps, pushing past. They thunder by, cut across the big, well-lit room, make the turn and disappear into the dugout runway. "Summer Squall wins," a reporter says. The accent is New York.

"Seen Dave Righetti?" I ask again. The reporter shoves a micro-mini recorder in his rear pocket and waves his notebook at the far side of the room where Number 19 is facing his locker, methodically going through a little stack of Yankee caps, trying them on, one by one. Righetti remembers my letter and graciously pulls up two chairs. As we talk I note a rhythmic beat behind us. Don Mattingly is banging a bat into the side of a big brown plastic garbage can. Pop, pop, pop. Nice background I think. Righetti talking bullpen, Mattingly punctuating the conversation, grooving his swing.

I know that a lot of starting pitchers have had to make the same decision that I did. Stay a starter or go to the pen. Guys like Allie

Reynolds—but in those days relieving wasn't very well thought of. I had to follow Goose [Gossage] and Goose is an icon in New York City. To be quite honest, Sammy Ellis, the Yankees pitching coach, and Jeff Torborg were the ones behind the decision to send me to the pen. Especially Sammy. He always thought that I'd work well in relief. Sammy thought that I should be in the bullpen even before I had that good year in 1983 [14–8, 3.44 ERA] because of the way my arm action was. He didn't like the way I wore myself out as a starter. At the end of 1983 I couldn't pitch the last couple of ball games because of my shoulder. So Yogi, Sammy Ellis and Jeff Torborg asked me if I'd do it. I didn't give them an answer right away. I had a really rotten winter thinking about it. Here I was just getting my feet on the ground and I was determined to win twenty ball games the next year. All of a sudden the rug's pulled out from under you and you've gotta follow Goose. I wasn't scared but relief pitching was such a new dimension. I wasn't shocked because my father had told me, "Hey, if they lose Goose and they can't sign anybody. . . ." Bruce Sutter was the guy that they wanted but he wasn't a free agent that year. So anyway my dad said, "They are going to ask you!" And I said, "Yeah, oh right, Dad!" It was one of those things. And sure enough he was right. A few days later Yogi called. Then Guidry called and he said, "Listen, I think that you can do it too, and I think that you can be one of the best." That kind of got me really thinking seriously about it. I decided that when I talked to Yogi that I would tell him, "If we're going to do this, let's not do a trial. Let's do this for a whole year—this was 1984—and let's go for it. I'll be the best damned reliever that I can be for you!" And he handled me well. It turned out to be a godsend. [Righetti had thirty-one saves and a 2.34 ERA in his first year out of the pen.]

Basically I got started going through the ranks, so to speak, as a kid—Little League and then you play a little summer ball. I went into high school baseball young, and I had a good arm and I had good instincts. [But] I was playing with a lot of eighteen-year-olds and I was only sixteen. I wasn't very strong and I didn't hit the ball very well. So my job was to play defense in left field. Throw people out when I had a chance. I got tall all of a sudden and I think right after my junior year in high school I got up to about six feet. And I was still very thin but I had these long arms and these big hands. And all of a sudden I started throwing the ball pretty hard. I still wanted to be an outfielder so I kind of fought the opportunities to pitch every chance that I could. But then after my junior year in high school, I went into summer league with American Legion ball and that's when I found out that I might be a pretty good pitcher.

Paddy Cottrell, a Rangers scout, was a family friend for years. He had known my dad since the war. He was one of the first people to say, "Move him out of the outfield and pitch him. This kid's got too good an arm to waste out there." My dad, Leo Righetti, was in the Yankee system, and my brother Steve was an excellent player who signed a professional contract with Texas. But my dad stayed out of our baseball affairs when we were young kids and he didn't think at that time that I was anywhere near being a prospect or anything like that. And he just left me alone to enjoy playing ball. If I'd come to him he'd be helpful, otherwise he'd stay clear. He was a shortstop and he had a tremendous arm and he pitched some. And he did say that he made a mistake, that he should have pitched when he was in the minor leagues. He felt that he could have gotten to the big leagues quicker that way. And I heard him say things like that but he never told me that I had to pitch.

After high school I went to junior college in San Jose, California, didn't get drafted or anything like that. I grew to almost 6'3" and I was trying to catch up body-wise and strength-wise, but the arm kept growing stronger. I threw a lot that winter and I started throwing the ball hard. They came to me—Paddy Cottrell said, "Hey, we'd like to draft you." All of a sudden now I kind of liked pitching a little better, but I was still wondering if I could do it. That's how it evolved basically. It wasn't like I was a high school star or anything like that. I went to junior college just because my friends were going there, and I tried out for the team as an outfielder. They said, "No, you are going to pitch." And I'm glad I did. I went to the Yankees later, in 1978, one of those multi-players deals of George's. The one where Sparky went to Texas.

My brother played in the Rangers chain for a number of years. He could always hit and still can, for that matter. In fact he took some BP off of me as recently as last year and he did good. He's a big strong guy and a good athlete, and he could always hit. Especially when I'm just throwing BP to him he's going to rake me. He's a coach now for a high school team. And he's doing well. In junior college we played on the same ball club. This was 1977 and we were playing an inter-squad ball game. This was the first time that I ever pitched against my brother. We'd always been on the same team. I threw him a curveball, which I should have never thrown. I was working on it. At that time he was a good fastball hitter but wasn't that great of a breaking ball hitter. But I hung him a curveball and he hit a home run. And believe me, I never lived that one down. To this day he always says, "I only had the one at-bat against Dave and. . . ." But I'd like to strangle him for it but to be quite honest, I'm glad he had that moment against me

357

now. That's the only time I ever faced him, one at-bat and he takes me long. All those times with the tennis balls and the whiffle balls, of course. But the one time on a field where everybody could see and. . . .

My first year in the major leagues started off tough. I had a great spring training but they didn't bring me up to the big leagues at the time. Gene Nelson was a young kid in the Yankee organization. Gene was twenty years old and out of A-ball. He was a great story—he had a great spring and they brought him north instead of me. I went down to Columbus and pitched very well, well enough to make them finally decide to give me a shot at it. This was 1981. They traded Tom Underwood and Jim Spencer to Oakland for Dave Revering and it opened up a pitching spot. They needed a left-hander. I got off to a good start with a good ball club and that's what really made it work. I was in a groove from Columbus already and so when I got to New York they kind of let me alone, didn't want to mess with my head too much. They thought just being in the big leagues was enough on me, so I pitched well that year. [Righetti was 8–4 with a 2.06 ERA and won Rookie of the Year in the AL.] I know that left-handers are supposed to have control problems but I always had good control, up until my second year in the big leagues, that is. That first year winning Rookie of the Year and all and then being sent down the second year, that was really hard.

Psychological? Yes, I think so, I was trying to do too much. To be quite honest, I was trying to keep myself out of the minor leagues instead of just pitching and trying to stay in the big leagues. I was overdoing it, overthrowing, and I ended up leading the league in walks, I think. I had over a hundred walks. I've always been a four-pitch pitcher, always was. And when I got here they kept saying that I was going to be the next Ron Guidry and all this. They just wanted me to throw hard. Actually I wasn't that kind of a pitcher. I had a good fastball but I also had pretty good breaking pitches. I got away from them that year, just kind of got screwed up. And in 1983 I vowed to throw my changeup and curve, my whole thing. In 1983 it worked out well. I just had a whole lot of luck that year and won fourteen games. Throwing the no-hitter in the middle of the season was really a great feeling. Some great moments in that game, July 4th, I remember that, hot as hell. But when you're young I don't think it registers with you the way it does later. I've been here with the Yankees now and involved in some games and seen some games that were really historic. I was there for the Pine Tar Game, I saw Phil Niekro's three-hundredth win, saw the game that took Joe and Phil into the record books with most wins for brothers. I think I saved the game that tied that record. I saw Tom Seaver's three-hundredth win. I saw Winfield and Mattingly go down to the last game for the batting title in 1984. I saw Mattingly win the MVP with 145 RBIs, and those great home runs by Reggie, things like that.

Here's what I remember about the Pine Tar Game. It turned out to be a huge distraction to the ball club for a month and I think it hurt us quite a bit. After they ruled that we would have to replay the inning we had to go through with that. We were going to boycott the game and just give them the damned win, but losing those two outs we would have been two-and-a-half games back, or something like that to Baltimore, the eventual winner. So we played it out and lost. At the time of the Pine Tar Game we were playing well, real well. The replay was kind of a farce.

Fun in the bullpen. Well I've gotta be honest. Being in New York [with the Yankees] there's a lot of pressure not to do anything out of the ordinary because it can cost people jobs around here. There's not a lot of humor. We lost a coach in 1984, when I cut my finger on the water fountain out in the bullpen. It was a total accident but they fired a bullpen coach over that, Jerry McNertney. They didn't say it was over that, but that was it. So that put a lot of pressure on me, because here I was down there, I got hurt and I was on the DL for a couple of weeks, screwing around supposedly, which I wasn't. I just flailed my hand back during a conversation and cut myself. It just put pressure on me not to get anybody in trouble. So fun? I'm basically kind of quiet down there. Don't stay to myself, but we don't do a lot of screwing around. But when Bob Shirley was down there things tended to happen. I guess the most memorable one was the last day of the 1984 season when Mattingly and Winfield were going for the batting title. We're playing Detroit in the Stadium and Willie Hernandez is warming up in the Tigers pen getting ready to go in. It's the bottom of the ninth and he's getting ready to face Donny. And if Donny gets a hit he wins the batting title. If he doesn't and Winfield gets a hit behind him, [Winfield] wins the batting title. So this is a pressure moment and the Stadium is all excited about it. Willie Hernandez, I believe, is the MVP and the Cy Young that year. So Willie gets in the bullpen van to ride into the stadium and the driver's asleep. Normally the bullpen driver is a bullpen grounds crew guy, not a player. But Willie, not speaking English that well, doesn't know what the hell he's doing. So he just shakes the guy and wakes him up. Well it's [Yankees pitcher] Bob Shirley, not the grounds crew guy. He kind of woke him up and said, "Hey, I'm in the game." So Shirls slips behind the wheel and drives him into the ball game. At this historic moment in baseball history here somes Shirls, one of our own players, driving Hernandez, the Cy Young and MVP winner, in to face Shirley's own teammates, two great Yankees hitters going for the batting championship. Our dugout knows he's coming because we got on the phone and warned them. When the van came by they threw shit all over the car and everything. Shirley motoring the guy in to take one of our guys out of the batting title race. But it didn't bother Donny. He got the base hit and won the batting title [Mattingly hit .343, Winfield .340].

I know that there are a lot of stories about carrying on in the bullpen. But as to how I watch a game and what I do in the pen, I go down in the first inning. Here I was a starter the year before and so I felt that all eyes were on me because I followed Goose as the short man in the Yankee pen. I decided not to play that old prima donna role and walk out there in the seventh inning, so everybody can see you going out there and say, "Oh, there he goes!" Goose used to always go out there, I think, after the first half inning. I remember he'd go out there. I like that. He thought that the bullpen was the place for the bullpen pitcher and he didn't want any starters down there. So I like that. That was Goose's pen. You used to have to ask Goose for permission to sit in the bullpen. He ran it. An unchartered fraternity is a good description of the bullpen guys. You take a lot of pride in the role you play, and that's what's kept me in the bullpen all these years.

The start from the pen in 1984 was basically slow in terms of saves. I think I only had ten save chances the whole first half. I think I had nine chances or something at the time. They weren't running guys out there like they do now. It's almost automatic—if you've got a three-run lead now, it seems like you pitch the reliever. But in 1984 it started slowly. In the second half, Jay Howell came down to pitch in front of me and we made this like, little pact. He goes, "Listen, you've got ten or eleven saves now and we're gonna go for thirty!" I said, "Thirty, wow! No way, let's get twenty, twenty-five!" He says, "No, we're gonna go for thirty!" I think Jay won about six or seven games in the second half and I ended up saving thirty-one. I got twenty-one in the second half and that was nice, you know. We had that great rapport and it was a team within a team. Then Jay got traded and went on to the A's and then the Dodgers and went off on his own and has done so well, which is great. I've been blessed with great people in front of me—Tim Stoddard, Brian Fisher had a good year for me. Lee Guetterman, plenty of guys—these setup guys always willing to take the ball, you know, it means a lot to the short man. Somebody's gotta get you there.

That's another great thing about the bullpen guys that are willing to take the ball, knowing that the game might be in jeopardy.

Billy Martin was something else. I threw my glove one night in the dugout at him and it hit right next to his head. Billy would normally take all the pitchers out of the game, but when he got mad at you, he'd send Art [Fowler] out to get you. Art had this T-shirt he used to wear that said "Babe Ruth is dead—throw strikes!" Anyway this particular night I said, "Hey, Art, where's Billy?" "Oh, Billy's not feeling so good!" And so when I got in the dugout I fired the glove at him, I was ticked off. But you could do that with Billy. I wasn't being disrespectful or anything. Of course, he'd be the first guy to throw it back at me. So we got over it soon.

With Yogi, nothing really funny. He's very professional and quiet. That one year he was the manager, when I was in the bullpen, he handled me well. One thing I liked about him was that when you had a bad outing he'd use you again. He definitely didn't bury anybody. Billy had a habit of burying people. I remember Bob Shirley being buried for, gosh, well over twenty-five days. One year Billy got mad at me, it was 1985 and I ended up being Fireman of the Year that year, but I remember sitting in the pen without being used for twenty-five days. He was approachable, but I didn't talk to him during that time. I was wondering what the hell was going on. It turned out that he was worried about my arm. My arm had a little soreness in it and there was a lot of problems going on with the press. "Why isn't Righetti pitching in these situations?" Blah, blah, blah. Billy says, "Well, I'm protecting his arm." And they'd come to me and I'd say, "Listen, I've got my uniform on and I'm ready to pitch, you know!" So there were a lot of little problems there and he just didn't use me during that time. We went through a love-hate relationship, but other than that, I always got along well with Billy. Good manager. Every time he got fired we were either in first place or we'd won a lot of ball games. That's all I know and that's all I ever cared about too.

The one night that I'll never forget, and I guess one of the biggest home runs that I remember, was the one Reggie hit in Game Five of the 1981 American League division play-offs. We were all tied in games with Milwaukee, two and two and I was a starter at the time, but they put me in the bullpen that night for the fifth and deciding game. Guidry went the first four and I was supposed to pitch the next three. Goose was supposed to come in and close it. The inning before I came in Reggie had hit a two-run home run. Then Oscar [Gamble] followed with a dinger right behind him. That was big because we were down 2–0. I was just coming into the game and I ended up

361

getting the win. That was the biggest one that I ever remember. Then we went on to beat Oakland 3–0 in the championship series and eventually lost the World Series to the Dodgers four games to two.

When I think about memories, two things come to mind. A lot of guys can tell you about the day they got brought up to the big leagues, their first major league win was against this team or that. I really don't remember those things. I remember the score of the first game I pitched, the team and all. But I couldn't tell you the day, maybe not even the month. The things I remember the most are probably the Championship Series in 1981 for the pennant. We're playing Oakland in Oakland, my home town. And that was the first time my parents ever got a chance to see me pitch. I ended up winning the ball game, a shutout. It was Game Three, the one that clinched it for us. I went six innings, gave up five hits. And Willie Randolph broke it open, a scoreless game with a two-out home run in the sixth. Davis and Goose came in to finish it like they did so often that year. A real great combination. They came in for the final three innings and I don't believe they gave up a hit. Winning that game in my home town to send us to the World Series, that was my biggest thrill. I remember I got Tony Armas, that was the last hitter I faced. Then in came Davis and Goose. Randolph hit the home run and Nettles broke it open with a bases-loaded triple. Nettles drove in nine runs in three games. He was the MVP of that series.

After that I guess the next memory would be 1986, the forty-six-save season—that whole season, not just a moment. I was proud of that because it takes a season to really make a contribution. It was the strangest season. There I was in the middle of it. I think I had about sixteen or seventeen saves, a couple of weeks before the All-Star game, and I'm either leading the league in saves or right there. George [Steinbrenner] was ripping me in the papers, saying that I was the reason we weren't doing better. I think at the time we were about twenty games over five hundred. We had a hell of a ball club. He just ripped me to pieces in the paper in Toronto. I proceeded the next night to give up a grand slam to George Bell, and lost it out there on the mound and threw the baseball over the right field fence. What happened as a result of that, me throwing the ball in the seats, it took a lot of the interest away from what George had said because the press made quite a lot out of that. I ended up going to the All-Star game. He came out in the paper saying that I shouldn't be there. And I had like nineteen saves at the All-Star break and George didn't think that I should be there. It really fueled me, gave me incentive, because I pitched the whole second half mad. Boston stayed ahead of us and we just couldn't

362

catch them for whatever reason. But we won a lot of ball games and I ended up getting the record. But here's what I remember—I remember not enjoying it at all. Later, George said he just did it to get me fired up. He's done that to other guys and he used to test me every once in a while. He's actually been good to me at certain times and he's given me the benefit of the doubt. I guess maybe because he knows me well now. He likes to do that with young people. I think he wants to find out about them. That was tough. And actually I didn't enjoy it. When I got the save that broke the record, I didn't get excited or anything. It was a shame. It took a lot of the sting and excitement out of it. I was very proud of it and expect it to be broken and probably soon. I didn't enjoy it then but I'm enjoying it now, while it lasts. [Thigpen, the Chicago White Sox reliever, had fifty-seven saves in 1990, breaking Righetti's record of forty-six.]

I feel like I've had a lot of success out of the pen. There was an article in *Sports Illustrated* where I said that I wished that the New York fans would be more supportive of me as a relief pitcher. That quote meant supportive, being supportive of me as a relief pitcher. And I think a lot of fans read that kind of wrong. I wasn't upset by the quote because that's what I said. I felt that. The Yankees weren't behind it [Righetti staying in the bullpen] and everywhere I went someone was coming up to me talking about me being a starter again. That's how the fans felt. They didn't think of me as a reliever and every time I'd meet somebody, they'd say, "Righetti, when are you going to start again, throw another no-hitter?" I think the reason for that was because, all these years the Yankees never got behind me and said, he's a reliever, he's a great one, we love him in the bullpen. But every year they keep bringing up starting and we're going to move him back into the starting rotation. What I meant about being appreciated was, hey, I've been a reliever for seven years now and let's forget this starting thing, you know.

The manager changes have accelerated this problem because every time a new regime comes in, they all have their own ideas. They're gonna do this with me and that with me. The first question that the reporters like to ask the new people is, "What are you going to do about Righetti's situation. What are you going to do with him?" And then they've gotta go into the "Oh, we're gonna talk to Dave," and you know, it's the same thing every year and it's crazy. The only constant person that's been around is George [Steinbrenner] and he's the only person that I'd answer to when it came down to a change. We've talked about it periodically. I read that in the *Sports Illustrated* article where George called me the most loyal Yankee. No matter what team

I played for, that's what I'd do. I sign my name on a contract, I feel that you have to live up to that. And when that day ends, like at the end of this season, then there will be a difference. There will be loyalty there sure, but. . . . You know when you put your name down and decide to play pro ball, I think that you owe the organization everything that you've got and you don't try to undermine it. That's the way I feel about it. You honor your contract.

Dave Righetti became a free agent and changed his loyalty to the San Francisco Giants in 1991.

Mark Cresse is one of those guys that I wanted to be—bullpen catcher for the Los Angeles Dodgers. Cresse, a huge wedge of a man, sat along the first base line in Dodgertown's Holman Field and watched a diamond full of young Dodgers hopefuls work out. While pitchers ran the palm-lined outfield and bats cracked in the nearby cage, Cresse talked candidly about his years in the L.A. pen: about the temperament of a Mike Marshall, the Charlie Hough knuckleball, and about the day they discovered that Steve Howe had a problem. And of course, there was another name that came up. "Tommy?" Cresse said. "Well, he's the reason that I've got the best job in the world, the reason that I'm in the pen."

I tell people, often kids, when I go out and talk at schools, when you grow up you hope that you'll be able to do something that you love. And ever since I was a little pup, a Little Leaguer, I loved the game of baseball. My mom used to say that the only time I smiled was when I had a baseball in my hand. I wanted to be a major leaguer so bad. When I got released by the St. Louis Cardinals, it was like a crush, like my life was over. And this job gave me an opportunity to stay in a business that I loved. The thing that I think really helped was Tommy Lasorda. Tommy is a lot like me except he was a pitcher and had much more success in the minor leagues than I did. He played Triple-A ball for Montreal and won a lot of games for them. As far as his major league career, even though he didn't make it big in the majors, his reputation was made as a worker. Tommy is probably the hardest worker that I've ever seen. When I came up as the bullpen catcher, and when they write things about me in the media guide, they say that I'm a workaholic, but I can speak for Tommy here too. People will look at us and say, look at how hard they work. But when it's something that you enjoy, it isn't work. We're having fun. That's one of my big messages to kids. Whether it's baseball or medicine, if that's what interests you, then you work hard at it and enjoy doing it. For me being a bullpen catcher and now coach was the second best thing. If I couldn't play, then coaching, and who knows, maybe someday managing. . . .

I got started in the bullpen after I got released by the St. Louis Cardinals. I wanted to stay in baseball. When I got an opportunity to be a bullpen catcher with the Dodgers, I took it. Three years later Tommy [Lasorda] made me a bullpen coach. Since 1977 I've been the bullpen coach of the Dodgers. And I've seen a lot of great pitchers in our pen. We've gone through two different pitching coaches in the seventeen years that I've been there. Red Adams was our first pitching coach and now Ron Perranoski. Both of them have their own style.

Being the bullpen coach, I work with the pitching coach hand in hand. It's a relationship where Ron stands behind the pitcher and I'm the catcher. And the catcher is the one that can see the spin the best, see certain things that you can't pick up when you're not actually receiving the pitch. So we work very closely together. But Ron's definitely the brains behind the outfit and he's an outstanding pitching coach.

Now as to how Ron and Red differ. Well, Red Adams was a real player's pitching coach. Not to say that Ron isn't—it's just that Red would have a drink or two with them and they thought of him as a father. He was a great technician of the game, he coached them well. For example, the starting pitcher warms up in the bullpen. In the old days when Red was around, there was just me and the starting pitcher. Red wouldn't come out to watch him warm up. Whenever the pitcher is warming up, Ron is always there. I think that Ron might have taken it a step farther as far as the coaching aspect. Red's theory was that if they didn't know it by game time that they weren't going to learn it. But we've corrected a lot of guys before a game. Even a guy that's a professional pitcher can have certain flaws in his delivery that you can detect and make an adjustment. So why wait until they're out in a ball game and it hurts them. We can make the adjustment while they're warming up. So I kind of like the way that Ron Perranoski works with the pitchers. I think he's the best pitching coach that I've ever seen.

As far as the life in the bullpen, I think that the best way to correlate is that it's kind of like a fireman. They're almost exactly the same. You

sit in the firehouse, which in our case is the bullpen
as everything is going smoothly, you're just like a
TV. And it's the same with us. We just sit there and
We have our scouting reports and we go over the p
about how we're going to pitch those guys. But if t
is going good, we've got the best seat in the house
there's a fire or rally, then the relief pitcher's got to ь_ _
when our day really starts.

I've caught some great ones out there. My first year with the Dodgers
was 1974, so the first great one that I caught was Mike Marshall. We
acquired him from the Expos. He broke a record that year for most
appearances in relief and had twenty-one saves. He was a phenomenon
as far as his conditioning was concerned. He was a kinesiologist and
he knew exactly how to use his body and how it should perform.

The only thing for me when I joined the Dodgers, I was really proud
of the Dodgers. The team plays a significant role in [the] community.
Mike believed that a ballplayer shouldn't be a role model for a kid. He
thought that role models should be doctors, lawyers and presidents of
the United States. He didn't think that kids should look up to ballplayers. Which I don't agree with. But that was Mike's theory. Because he
had that belief, he didn't sign autographs for kids and wasn't real nice
to them. I kind of held that against Mike, not as a professional but my
personal opinion toward the man. To me, baseball is the American
pastime and kids do look up to players. We have a responsibility because of that. Mike didn't accept that responsibility, so I was kind of
upset with him for that reason. But as far as a pitcher goes, nobody
was in any better physical condition. He was real strong and he knew
exactly what he had to do to bounce back. He had to pitch every day.
And that was just Mike Marshall. He had a great screwball. He was a
good pitcher. Unfortunately, I just remember him best because of his
attitude. As great a pitcher as he was, he ruined it all for me because
of his attitude toward the game of baseball.

My next memory of a great bullpen guy would be of Jim Brewer, a
left-hander who pitched forever with the Dodgers and the Cubs. Jim
got killed several years ago in an automobile accident. He was as fine
a guy as anybody you'd want to meet. He was everything that I'd look
for in a major league pitcher. A pro to begin with, he had a great
screwball and threw real hard.

Then let's see, Charlie Hough was perhaps the next relief pitcher
that came along. That was a real nightmare as far as I was concerned,
because with that knuckleball, I can't tell you how many sacks of ice
I've had on Charlie Hough bruises. I'd just try to block balls instead

_ to catch them. Tommy [Lasorda] called him his Hope Dia-
, and every time we got into trouble Charlie would come in and
ᴄhe job.

The next guy to come along is one of the most tragic stories that I
can think of in baseball as far as abilities were concerned—Steve
Howe. As far as I was concerned, he had unlimited abilities, could
have been anything he wanted. He threw it all away because of co-
caine. It's a tragic story. The biggest story, as far as kids are concerned,
is the lesson that can be learned from it. Here's a guy that had a great
family, a beautiful wife, a beautiful little daughter. He had everything
as far as baseball is concerned, a great arm, a great attitude as far as
challenging hitters.

One time when he was playing in Los Angeles, we were ahead by
one run in the top of the ninth. I'd just warmed him up. I opened the
gate and was standing there ready to pat him on the tail, like I always
do and say "Go get 'em." But when I opened the gate there was no
Steve Howe. He had walked over to the phone. Usually I'm the only
guy that goes to the phone. It's the one that links the dugout, so I walk
over and listen and I hear him asking for Tommy Lasorda. When he
went to the phone I thought he was going to ask someone to get him
a new jock or he'd broken his belt or something. But I hear him asking
for Lasorda. I'd just warmed him up and he was throwing great. So I
think, is there something wrong with him? And then I hear him go,
"Tommy, this is the Howser. Tell them to pack our bats, I'm on my
way in!" That's the kind of confidence he had, to tell Tommy to tell
the bat boys to pack up our bats, the game was over.

This was a guy who pitched in a World Series for us. He was an
outstanding player. An interesting, not funny, story—we were in a
Sunday day game in Los Angeles and that's when we kind of [realized]
that there might be a problem. We were all in the bullpen. In the pen,
let's say we play a late Saturday night game. Instead of making the
players come out at nine o'clock in the morning and take batting practice, Tommy will call batting practice off so the players can go to
church or sleep a little bit later. So it was a day where batting practice
had been called off. In that situation I'm the first one, the first guy,
I'm always the first guy at the ball park. I'm out there warming up the
starting pitcher while most of the guys are still arriving. In this case I
don't see most of the players. The game started and we're getting into
it. There are five starters and five relievers on our staff and the five
relievers start moseying down to the bullpen. I'm sitting there and I
start counting heads. There's only four guys, and I'm thinking god-
dang, something's wrong here. So I thought, Steve Howe's not here.

I let it slide for a while because you know that Steve isn't going to pitch until the eighth or ninth inning anyhow. I figured he was in taking a shower or something or had gotten a late start. Now it's about the fourth inning. I thought he's cutting it a little slim, so I go to the phone and call Perranoski. I say, "Perry, is Howser in the dugout? You ought to send him down here pretty quick." Perry says, "He isn't here, must be in the clubhouse, I'll go check." So he goes in the clubhouse, and there's no Howser. About the sixth inning Howser shows up. And everybody goes, "Where in the hell have you been?" He says, "I locked my keys in my car and I didn't have an extra set and my wife was shopping." That was kind of shaky, you know, but it could happen. He went into that game in the eighth inning and did his job and everything and they didn't fine him or anything.

The next thing that happened, we were going on a road trip and we were going to Atlanta. The door closed on the plane and there was no Steve Howe. He'd missed the plane. So that's when we first realized that something was really wrong. We learned in drug education that one of the first signs [of drug abuse] is the inability to cope with time. People who are dependent on drugs are late a lot and can't understand or relate to time. We started testing and sure enough, we detected his problem for the first time. Steve ended up going to rehab. But the tragedy of the whole thing in his situation was that his earned run average was zero, zero, zero. Three months into the season he had to go to rehab. So Steve Howe's story was a real tragedy as far as I'm concerned.

After Steve Howe we sort of had a lull in the bullpen. That sort of became a weakness of the Dodgers. We didn't have a closer. We were counting on Steve Howe so we didn't draft any left-handed relievers. We ended up going through a lot of guys. Last year, probably our biggest asset was our relief pitching. Jay Howell came along through the free agent market. If we had had a good season last year, Jay would have probably had a shot at the Cy Young Award. He had a fantastic year. Jay Howell had one of the best years you'll ever see and it was kind of strange because he'd had a great year the year before too. It was marred by the play-offs when he had his glove checked for pine tar. Which was too bad because about ninety percent of the pitchers in the major leagues use pine tar and for him to get checked for pine tar was just crazy. As far as I'm concerned, pine tar should be legal anyway. The hitter can use it so he doesn't slip on his bat. Why shouldn't a pitcher be able to use it so he doesn't slip on the ball? Pine tar doesn't make the ball dip or move. All it does is give you a better grip. I'm not saying that pitchers should be able to use K-Y jelly or rosin on anything that will give them an advantage. I thought that Jay got hammered as far as what he did. People were calling him cheater and everything, when in reality he wasn't doing anything that the rest of the guys in the league weren't doing. But it affected him kind of mentally, the reputation of being a cheater. I thought it might hurt him, it was a highly visible game. But he came back in the World Series and pitched well. He gave up a home run to Dwyer to lose a ball game, our only loss, but other than that he pitched outstanding baseball in the play-offs and Series. He carried it over in 1989, and Jay and Mark Davis of the Padres were the very best, by far.

There have been some funny stories from the bullpen. One involves a fight that we got into with Montreal. They had a real big guy named Ken Singleton. Ken came running out. That was my first year with the team and I didn't know all the rules. This fight breaks out and I see this big guy Singleton so I said, "Shit. I'm big. I'll go over and get him!" So we tackle and roll around a little bit and now the fight gets broken up and we all go to the dugout. About a week later Montreal comes out to L.A. and I'm catching batting practice. Singleton comes over by the batting cage and he leans down and looks at my face and he says, "You're the guy!" I guess for about a week it was killing him. He'd gone down the Dodger lineup and couldn't figure out who the hell the big guy was he'd been battling with. Now he finds out it was the bullpen catcher. This leads into the real story. After the fight in Montreal, Walter Alston had seen me out on the field wrestling around and fighting and so he called me in and said, "Cresse, did you know that as the bullpen catcher you're not allowed to go out on the field during a game. That they could have forfeited that ball game." I said, "Oh God. . . ." I mean I was new at the job and didn't want to do anything to hurt the ball club. About a week later, after this stern comment from Walt warning me what will happen if I get out on the field, I'm sitting in the pen in Dodger Stadium on a Sunday day game. We have this shed in Dodger Stadium that we sit in to watch the game from the pen. It keeps the fans off of us. I'm sitting out there and I hear these two guys jump on the roof right above me. It sounded like someone had jumped on a drum. I hear that noise and I look up and they've sprung from the roof right out onto the field. There they are right in front of me, these two dark-skinned guys. I didn't know what nationality they were, but they looked like Arabs. They have something in their hands and they pull it out. One of them's got a can of lighter fluid and the other one has an American flag and all of a sudden they're dousing the flag with lighter fluid. I see this guy pull out this book of matches and I go, "God!" and I'm up and ready to run out there and kill them when I hear, in the back of my mind, Walt Alston's warning—"Forfeit the game, forfeit the game! You go on the field, we lose by forfeit." All of a sudden, Rick Monday comes running over from his outfield position and snatches the flag. This story becomes national news. Monday is an All-American hero for saving the flag. My flag. It was Mark Cresse's play! It was right in front of me, but all I could hear was Walt Alston's "Don't go on the field! Don't go on the field!" To this day, every time people mention Rick Monday, they don't talk about the great home runs, they remember the flag. That could have been and should have been Mark Cresse.

Here's another one, typical bullpen behavior. We were playing the Cincinnati Reds one year and we were right in the middle of a hot pennant race. One of their guys started a fight or something, and it wasn't really a fist fight. It was one of those typical baseball deals where everybody squares off and looks mean, you know. The next day, it was a Sunday day game and everybody thought that there would be another fight. The tension was really in the air. So we were taking batting practice and Ken Brett gets this idea. He loads up Don [Stan the Man Unusual] Stanhouse and Jerry Reuss on the bullpen cart. It's like a little flatbed truck that they drag the infield with. They load up this cart. It's about ten minutes before the Reds are going to take batting practice, so Cincinnati players are all in the dugout. It's early, about ten o'clock in the morning, so they're just sitting in there waiting to hit, trying to wake up. Here comes this little cart trolling by. It looks like a float in a parade. One of our guys is driving and we've got Stan the Man, Brett and Reuss in the back, just sitting there. They come tooting down the warning track and all of a sudden they get to the first base bag. All three of them pull their pants down and moon the Cincinnati Reds dugout, just drive right by with these three big asses sticking out right at the Reds. That broke the tension. I mean you could see guys crying in the dugout, laughing so hard that they were falling off the bench. End of fight potential, buddies again, after our guys moon them.

And of course there have been moments that I've experienced out in the pen, not always funny, like the Gibson home run in the 1988 Series. [Kirk Gibson hit a last inning home run to win Game One for the Los Angeles Dodgers.] That's kind of an interesting story there, certainly not funny because it brought tears to my eyes. I was in the bullpen and I was warming up Jay Howell. If it had gone extra innings he would have gone in. Gibson was hitting for the pitcher and Davis was on second base. In case it was a tie game he needed to get ready. I'm warming up Howell but my heart was really into watching the game. I was catching and looking over my shoulder at my son. Tommy is Brad's godfather so he's always in the clubhouse. He's like the sixth coach on the team. When it's the ninth inning in just about every game he comes down by the bullpen and finds a seat where somebody has left. Then we go over to the bullpen fence and bring him in with me after the game. So I saw him sitting there. He was getting ready to come in with me so I told him, "You sit right there and I'll come get you as soon as this is over." The way Kirk was swinging, I thought it was going to be over any second. And I wasn't thinking "Dodgers win!" I turned around, and Kirk fouled off about five or six pitches. It was a long at-bat. Real dramatic—he was hurt, swinging the bat like an old man, limping around, getting in and out. All of a sudden I see him swing the bat. From where I am, I could just see the swing. The bullpen shed was in the way so I couldn't see the outfielders. I saw him swing up on his front foot. I saw the trajectory of the ball in the air, so I thought, "Oh crap!" Then I heard the reaction of the fans. They were starting to roll. I went out like this to try to peek around the shed and I see Canseco turning. I thought, "God Almighty, that ball's out of here!" And then it hit me. I thought I was having a heart attack, a rush hit me so hard. I looked over at my son and he's up there yelling and screaming. I went over there to the fence and grabbed Brad, and ran into the clubhouse. The team was yelling and screaming and it was like an electric charge had hit our clubhouse. It was like nothing was going to stop us after that. The momentum just swung our way. And the feeling that I had, I've never had a rush like that, I really did think that I was having a heart attack. It hit me like no moment in baseball ever has. I hope that it hits me again some time.

As a matter of fact my first game in the pen with the Dodgers was the night that Hank Aaron hit the home run to break Babe Ruth's record. That was my very first game and I thought, "God, this is fantastic." Cannons were going off. And now I have these World Series rings. Like the man [Chico Escuela] says, "Baseball's been berry, berry good to me!"

DAN PLESAC
Left-Handed Pitcher

MILWAUKEE BREWERS, 1986–Present

- **Thirty-Three Saves In 1989, A Brewers Record For Left-Handers**
- **Struck Out Darryl Strawberry On Three Straight Pitches In 1988 All-Star Game**
- **Known For His 95-MPH Fastball, Great Control And Imitations Of Major League Hitters**

My visit with Danny Plesac in Baltimore's Memorial Stadium gave me a rare opportunity. I saw the playful side from the Orioles press box. Plesac was running down balls, making behind-the-back catches of batting practice flies. Then I saw the serious side as he nailed down a Milwaukee victory. I sat behind home plate with an advance scout from Cleveland and watched the 94s and 95s come up on the gun. The red flashing numbers were extremely impressive but the look on Plesac's face was the picture of short relief. It was nothing like the boyish face that I'd held my tape recorder to earlier that evening. In a game the following night, I saw Plesac right where some unfortunate short relievers will spend eternity. "Hell is walks and home runs." Plesac said that in the Milwaukee locker room earlier that night.

One of the toughest things to handle in this game is failure. And I went through it for three years, long before I ever got into professional baseball. I pitched for North Carolina State University and I came in there and frankly did not live up to expectations, mine or anybody else's. It bothers me to this day. I really wish I could go back to Raleigh and pitch against Carolina or Clemson. I lost some big ball games to those teams. There were just a number of teams that I didn't pitch well against. There was a lot of extra weight that I put in my own saddlebags because I was a second round draft choice out of high school and I wanted to come to N.C. State and dazzle. And things just didn't work out that way. When things started to turn sour then I ally started to press. I don't think that there was anybody there who wanted to win more than I did or anyone with more desire than I had. It's just that I was going through a difficult time, trying to deal with the pressures of being such a high draft pick. Believe me, it was a tough three years. Another thing, my brother Joe was pitching at N.C. State University and he happens to be one of the best pitchers who ever played there.

But 1983, my junior year, I was supposed to go high in the draft. Hard-throwing left-hander I guess. But I went out and had a miserable year. I was the last pick in the first round. The first two or three games in the minor leagues in the Brewers system, same old Danny. Just awful. Same as college, walking six or seven a game. But I was very fortunate. I got an excellent pitching coach, a guy named Mike Pazik, and we started from square one. "Try not to strike everybody out!" "Throw one pitch at a time!" "If you have a bad game, forget about it!" The same advice I'd been getting from Sam Esposito, my coach at N.C. State, but the time was right. I guess I was like an alcoholic who had hit rock-bottom. There was nowhere to go but up. And so I started to listen. I had really wanted to listen in college but there were always all those scouts in the stands, and I'm thinking, if I don't get this guy out there goes my chances at the majors. I don't know, when you're nineteen or twenty, you just see things differently. I wasn't very mature. Here's what I'd do. I'd pitch three innings and struggle and then I'd say, "Okay, I'm going to make up for this. I'm going to strike every guy out." I just couldn't get it through my head what it took to be a good pitcher at a high level.

In 1986 I went to the big league camp, when George Bamberger was managing the Milwaukee ball club. There were no lefties in the bullpen. It just so happened that I was in the right place at the right time and they were in such a need to keep a left-hander. Since I was the only one there I was really—although I didn't know it at the time—in a position to do only one thing, and that was play myself off the ball club. The first day of spring training I was throwing on the sidelines and George Bamberger was watching me. He walked up to me and said, just as I'd finished, "Mike, you looked real good. You were throwing the ball well." He didn't know who I was, he didn't even know my name. That was kind of a humbling experience to have the manager call you by the wrong name and then walk away. I thought, "Boy, this is going to be a long, long year." I was really disappointed at first about going to the bullpen. I'd never pitched out of the bullpen before and I didn't know how my arm would hold up or adjust to it. But it turned out to be a real blessing. At first I wasn't too happy about it, but then I started to do well and it became easier to accept the role. Now if I had struggled out of the pen I'm sure I wouldn't have been so happy.

The one thing I've learned about the relief pitching, no matter what anybody tells you, everybody out here is different. How they see themselves, how management sees them. I went through the first two or three months of the season pitching well but still doubting myself. Can I get Don Mattingly out? Can I get Cal Ripken out? Will I be able to handle Dave Winfield consistently? You see a lot of guys come up and do well for a couple of weeks, but the real question is can they do it with any consistency.

I started my career as a bullpen pitcher in the major leagues in 1986. We open in Chicago, three dates in Comiskey Park. Being born and raised in Indiana, that's only twenty-five miles from Chicago, so I was a nervous wreck. I was up all three games, didn't get in and George had told me that if we get you up all three games and don't get you in, then we're going to give you a day off and just let you get adjusted to the bullpen. So it's Friday night in Yankee Stadium. I still haven't pitched but I think I've got the day off. We're losing to the Yankees. It's the seventh inning, there's one out and the bases are loaded. The phone rings and they want me to get up. And I'm thinking, "Well there's no way I'm going to get in because I've got the day off, and secondly, this thing's too close to bring in Danny Plesac." It was real cold. I'll never forget Mark Clear [Milwaukee relief pitcher]—I remember this as plain as day. I told Mark, "It's so cold that I can't grip the ball." And he said, "Take this pine tar and put it on your sleeve." I said, "I can't do that. I don't want to get caught by an umpire with pine tar on my sleeve." It's my first game. But Mark said, "No sweat. Just take the pine tar rag and rub a little on the sleeve of your glove-hand side. When you catch the ball, just wipe your finger on the sleeve and it's sticky and you can grip it better." So I said, "Okay fine, how much do I put on?" So he took the pine tar rag, and we have the blue Brewers sleeve, and proceeds to put a strip about four inches wide across my forearm. I mean, I'm thinking an umpire would have to be blind not to see this! This is while I'm warming up. All of a sudden the phone is ringing and it's George saying that I'm in the game. I look at Clear and I say, "Mark, I can't go in there with this, what do I do now?" And he says, "Oh hell, just tell them it's your first game in the big leagues, you got nervous, shit your pants and wiped it on your sleeve!"

I was horrified. I ran out there and went through my warm-ups hiding my sleeve. I was doing anything I could so the umpire wouldn't see this four-inch streak across my sleeve. That was my introduction to the big leagues—Yankee Stadium's first Pine Tar Incident, I guess. It kind of loosened me up because I was really more concerned about the pine tar than I was about facing a bases-loaded situation in Yankee Stadium.

I've been through three stages in my career, up and down like a roller coaster, the exact opposite of that even keel business. I came into the big leagues in 1986 and every game to me seemed like it was life or death—I didn't want to get sent back to the minor leagues. I put so much pressure on myself to do well. When I didn't do well I couldn't sleep at night. As I started to do well I went into my second phase. The Dave Righetti phase! Everywhere I went, I was being compared to Dave Righetti. There I was in 1986, a nobody, and then all of a sudden, here I am in 1987 and I'm suddenly supposed to be the next Dave Righetti. And I got caught up in it. I read it in the papers, heard it from reporters and I wanted to be the next Righetti. Pressure! After a bad game I'd be thinking, Righetti doesn't blow games with three-run leads. Righetti would have gotten the job done. And then, it finally got to where I was in the third phase. I had some success and now I'm starting to read and hear how I'm supposed to be one of the best relief pitchers in all of baseball. Now I felt like I had to get the job done every time. I went through a phase, a two-week road trip on the west coast before the All-Star break where I was like at thirteen and fourteen save opportunities, having a great year and I blew three games in a row. I mean for five days and five nights I could not sleep. Righetti gets these saves, Eckersley nails down these wins. I got to the point where I got so low that I finally just told myself, "Look, I can't be Dave Righetti and I can't be Dennis Eckersley. I'm just going to be Dan Plesac. I'm going to go out there and do the best job I can." I hit such a low. But when I thought about it, at this low I was at sixteen saves and most guys would have loved to have been at sixteen at the All-Star break and have only blown four saves. But I wanted to be twenty for twenty. Now I'm finally at the point where I know that I go out there and do my best. After I blow one I can go home and sleep because I know that I'm going to come back the next day and come back hard. But until you've been up and down, it takes a lot of being upstairs and a lot of being knocked on your can to deal with the pressures of this job, to get to the point where you just shrug it off and go out there and do it again.

But the pressure, that's partially what they write your check for. It's going to be there to an extent, at home, in the pen, waiting to go in to a game. But as soon as that gate opens and I hit the grass, it all just leaves. I block everything out. I don't see the crowd, I don't know where I'm playing. I get tunnel vision with the catcher. I can't see the umpire, I don't see people walking behind the screen. It's just me and the catcher and that's quite a feeling. It's amazing, hard to describe. When you're in a streak and you're really hot, it's what the guys call "locked in." It could be the loudest stadium, Yankee Stadium, 50,000 screaming people with the bases loaded and you can almost hear the catcher, what he's saying to you. You can't hear it but it's crazy because you think you can. Really a special feeling.

But if you're going to go out there sixty games a year, hell, you're really only going to have great stuff maybe thirty-five or forty games. When you don't, you've got to make those hitters think that you've got it. In those twenty or twenty-five games when you're in that situation, you're really going to have to pitch and really concentrate. You know when you have it and when you don't. The only people who can tell as well as you are the guys with the bats on the other team. When they're hittin' rockets you know you don't have it. And the key is to be able to step back and say, "Now I can't pitch the way I normally do, because tonight I don't have the stuff. I don't have the 94-mile-per-hour fastball and I don't have the great slider." How you react in those twenty-five games, that's the key. As a relief pitcher this is always going on right in the middle of a jam. You're in there because there is some kind of trouble or the game needs to be closed out. So you have to constantly be talking to yourself, saying, "I'm just one pitch away from a ground ball, double play. I've been in these jams before and I'm going to get out of this one." Nine times out of ten you do. Of course, some nights you don't.

I can handle losing games. The sun still comes up the next day, but the ones that eat me up are the ones when I walk people. If I have a one-run lead and I give up three singles that win the game, then I can live with that, but a walk! Walking two guys, that tears you apart. That's something that you have control over. You can't defense a walk and you can't defense a home run. So if you can stay away from the walks and from the long ball, then you've got a chance to get people and win ball games.

The bullpen environment is perfect for me. A lot of going at it, busting each other. Constant death. If you can't take being ribbed or razzed, hang it up! You don't belong in the bullpen. And it doesn't matter how well you're doing or how badly, everyone and anything's fair game. You just can't take it personally. I've always worked on my imitations out there. Hitters, their stances, it's really something that I've done since high school. If there was a game on TV I'd be watching, I'd jump up out of my chair and start imitating the hitter. And when I was a kid playing in the back yard announcing the games, I'd be imitating the players, guys like Winfield and Reggie. And the funny thing is that some of the guys that my brother Joe and I used to imitate I've actually faced in real game situations. It was really quite an experience. How many times does a guy play a game in his back yard and look in at his brother who's in there imitating Reggie Jackson? You strike him out and then one day you're looking in and there's the real Reggie. Well you say, "Hey, this isn't my brother Joe. This Reggie's a little bit better hitter!"

That really makes you step back and think. And there haven't been many times that I've done that but the one that I'll never forget was in the 1988 All-Star game. We're playing in Cincinnati's Riverfront Stadium. I actually stepped back and said the words to myself. "Dan, this is a big moment!" I'd been in six straight games before the All-Star break and all of a sudden, there I am in there facing Strawberry. And you know it was the weirdest thing. I was talking to Mark McGwire before the game and he said, "You know, I think that you'll get in against Strawberry tonight." And we were laughing about it and I remember saying, "Oh, do you think so?" I remember just standing around before that game and watching guys like Saberhagen and Clemens throw and I'm thinking, how in the hell does anybody hit this stuff? So overpowering and yet guys go out there and hit rockets off of them. It says something about the athletic abilities of big league hitters. When I came into that game I had no idea who was on deck. All I did was get ready. I took my warm-ups and didn't even look in. And when I got the call and looked and saw Strawberry walking to the plate, I couldn't believe it. All you're thinking about is, don't humiliate yourself in front of fifty million people. Everybody that I ever knew was watching that moment. I remember thinking if this guy catches up with one of my fastballs he might hit it in the river. Three fastballs. The last one was clocked at 98 miles-per-hour. Probably the fastest I've ever been clocked by the gun. Yes, I'd say I was a little pumped up. It was weird because I threw the three pitches, struck him out and when I got back to the dugout I looked up and there in the stands was my wife, my mom and brother Joe. They were waving, a great moment, but it was like something from a B movie. I remember sitting down on the bench and realizing that I was scheduled to be the first hitter in the inning. I thought, "Great, that's it for me. I did my job, get me outta here. I can go home."

Of all the things that I've enjoyed in baseball, facing Strawberry in the 1988 All-Star game and so many more, but I think the one thing that I'll never forget really didn't involve me pitching or being in the game. It didn't happen to me, but I was there to see it. That was in the 1989 All-Star game in Anaheim Stadium. Nolan Ryan, now here's a guy that epitomizes pitching. This is a guy who everybody is compared to, every hard thrower, every great arm that ever comes up is compared to Nolan Ryan or Sandy Koufax. That's just the limit. To be sitting in the bullpen and sitting next to Nolan Ryan! As a kid, you watch him on TV. I think he was the second pitcher to come in to that game. I can remember watching him warm up and just sitting there thinking, "Boy, this guy in his forties, the greatest of all time, coming back to Anaheim where they love him." What will be in my memory forever is this picture of the pen gate opening and me sitting there. And the shade from the stadium was halfway across the field. I'm sitting there watching him take that slow walk across the outfield grass, that slow walk of his, you know how he leans to one side? Just him walking and the whole place—you couldn't even hear it was so deafening. And there it is, right in front of me. To see that from a player's perspective—it's something to enjoy as a fan, but to do it as a player . . . I thought this is something that I'll never forget. Just watching that slow walk through the shade, the coat over his arm, and him tipping his hat to those thousands of people. Money can't buy a moment like that.

Postscript: Baltimore. That evening (Tuesday, June 12, 1990) in the ninth inning the phone rang in the Brewers pen. Enter Plesac. Assignment: Protect Ron Robinson's 3–2 lead. Orioles pinch hitter Tim Hulett flies to left field. One down. Cal Ripken grounds sharply to short. Two down. Then Orioles catcher Mickey Tettleton takes a Plesac 90-MPH fastball and drives it into the night. Tie ball game! The Brewers make noises in the tenth—a hit, a walk—but Gregg Olson gives the door a gentle slam. Bottom of the tenth. Plesac vs. Orioles first baseman Randy Milligan. Plesac cranks and fires. Milligan swings, Plesac's head flies back, he wheels on the mound and watches the ball sail up and over the Brewers bullpen. Orioles 4–3. Blown game! Blown save!

The following evening I walk into the Brewers locker room. Plesac is sitting in front of his locker, working a pinch of Skoal into his lower lip. I'm sort of easing in his direction. It's the reluctant reporter, caught between compassion and the tough question. "Hey Bob!" It's Plesac! He's smiling. "I looked out my window this morning. The sun came up!" he said.

MITCH WILLIAMS
Left-Handed Pitcher

TEXAS RANGERS, 1986–1988
CHICAGO CUBS, 1989–1990
PHILADELPHIA PHILLIES,
1991–Present

- **Set Major League Record For A Rookie In 1986 With Eighty Appearances**
- **Cubs Fans Greeted Williams By Singing "Wild Thing"**
- **Takes Therapy At A Bowling Alley**
- **Had One Of The Most Auspicious Debuts In Relief Pitching History**

I'm standing in the visitors' dugout in Busch Stadium catching the heat of the late afternoon sun off the Cards new emerald green carpet. What time does a guy like Mitch Williams come to the ball park anyway? It's an hour before the Cubs take BP. He's probably still bowling, I think. A glove cracks down the left field line. Mitch the Pitch! It's "Wild Thing" and Phil Roof, the Cubs bullpen coach. They're the only two players in the ball park. The right leg kicks and Williams comes slingshotting in at the plate. Roof, a Frigidaire in Cubs gray, responds with a barrage of "atta boys." Williams chases sweat from his forehead with the back of his black glove, sets and comes in with another gunshot—a cracking loud fastball. "Not bad," I think. Williams has just gimped off the DL from six weeks of bad knee. I'm shocked by his velocity, impressed by the work ethic. Later he sat in the dugout with weights strapped to his ankles and talked about how one deals with rehab and the DL when you're captain of the pen's all-hyper team.

I'm too hyperactive to sit around for four days between starts. Tom House [psychologist and pitching coach for the Texas Rangers] was a big influence. He knew right away that my personality wasn't suited for a starter's role. He knew the more I could get out there, be on the mound and dealing with the adrenaline, that the better off I'd be. He was the only one that recognized it. They finally listened to him in the Texas organization. That was in the winter of 1985, so I went down and threw in relief in winter ball. That's where it all started. If I could have been a regular position player I'd have loved it. I'd have loved to have played first base and been in there every day. But realizing that my talent was as a pitcher, well, relief is as close to being a regular as you get. Like Tom pointed out, the more I went to the mound the more I could deal with the adrenaline. And that was me! They finally decided to make the change. They started bringing me out of the bullpen and I started having a lot more success.

The Wild Thing, the music, started in Chicago. I thought it was kinda neat. It was fun. But they only played it twice. Both times they played the song, I was all over the place, blew both saves, so Dick Pole, our pitching coach pulled the plug on that. I've been wild my whole life, my entire minor league career. In the minor leagues I threw only one game in relief. Ninety-one appearances in the minor leagues and ninety of them were starts. But I was some kind of wild. There was a game in A-ball when I walked seven straight guys and the manager kept me in. When he finally came out, and I said this in jest, but I'm standing on the mound and I said, "What, did it look like I was going to regroup here?" I don't know, maybe he saw something I didn't.

Opening Day with the Cubs, in 1989? That was wild, literally. I'd been traded over the winter for Palmeiro, my first appearance in Wrigley Field. It was real wild. We're playing the Phillies. I came in in the eighth and walked a couple of guys and got out of that. Then I went back out for the ninth and it was my first full inning in the National League. These guys got three hits in a row off of me, two broken bats and one looping line drive. I'm thinking, "This league ain't all that much fun." And then Mike Schmidt came up. This is a guy who has hit fifty-some career home runs in Wrigley. I'm sitting there with the bases loaded and nobody out, pitching to him. It's a situation you don't really love but there's nothing to lose. He's either going to hit it or he isn't. I ended up striking him out and I felt pretty good about that. I struck Schmidt out with the slider and the next two I got on all fast-balls. Load them up and then strike out the side. A nice way to start.

I've been on the DL for the last month and it was tough, the longest month I've ever spent. But I've had injuries before. I guess maybe my experience as a kid makes me know that I can deal with injuries. There have been some stories about me pitching in American Legion ball with a broken arm. What happened there was, I was pitching on a chilly night in Oregon, and I think it was like the second or third inning. Something popped in my elbow, and I tried to throw another pitch and it hit in the grass. I came off the field and went to the hospital. They told me that it had been strained and not to pitch for a week. So I played first base and in a week I started to pitch. I pitched for the whole rest of the summer, and this happened the second game of Legion ball. It was early and I finished up playing Legion ball that summer. I started playin' high school football and played two months at quarterback and started getting thoroughly annihilated. So I decided to hang it up and go see what was wrong with my arm because it had been bothering me. I went in and the doctor checked it, a quick exam. He felt around and said that he didn't think there was anything wrong but they X-rayed it. I had a break between the upper bone and the lower bone, between the bones there was about a half-inch break. I had pitched for two months and played football for two months with it. They finally operated, screwed it back together. I was in a cast for two months, and then I had another surgery. I had my last surgery that year on January 5. Opening Day in high school was, I think, the first week in March. When I got my arm out of a cast I couldn't lift a two-pound weight, so I had to spend about four hours a day in the weight room. But I got it ready. I played on Opening Day.

But the thing here [with his recent injury] was that the night that the knee went and they did the oral exam, the doctor said that it could be career-ending. He thought that I'd broken a bone behind my leg and torn the anterior cruciate ligament, which he said could be a career-ending injury. And that was kinda hard to accept, considering that after I'd done it I struck the next guy out, finished the inning and came in. It was a little hard to swallow. They went in and did the MRI exam. It confirmed that I didn't have a broken bone but I had torn the posterior cruciate ligament. There are four ligaments in your knee and that's the next-to-the-worst one to tear. It's the hardest one to tear. So they operated on it, but that was only to confirm what the MRI had shown. They flushed out all the blood. If they had fixed it, I'd have been out for the season. They'd have had to open it up good and reconstruct it. That's where I had to start from a month or so ago. I had to rebuild my leg. Build my quad up, make it strong enough to take the place of that ligament. It was every day, a lot of work, a lot of weight work, a lot of monotonous leg lifts. Walking around with weights on your ankles. I lift weights in the off season anyway so I didn't have any real problem with that. But sitting around and watching games was not something I enjoyed. I missed one road trip and that was it. When you want in there—I'm the hyper type anyway, so it was really rough, especially when you're wearing a uniform and you don't get to go out and pitch. I was optimistic, I thought it was getting better every day. I just don't believe that they're ever going to create an injury that will keep me out forever. Knock on wood. But I just don't think that I could do anything to myself that I couldn't rebuild and get back in there.

I've always been a competitor, I want the ball and everybody knows it. I don't know how big a problem it was, but there was a time early in my career in Texas when I was upset about not getting enough work. I was outspoken, but I don't think that is what you'd call a bad attitude. All I wanted to do was pitch more, get more work. It's tough when you're sittin' down there. I've known some guys that don't want to pitch. They're just content to sit there. I've never been content to just sit there, especially when you're on a team that's strugglin' and you know that you can get people out. You're not getting the opportunity—you feel helpless and worthless, and that's not a feeling that I enjoy. I'm experiencing the same thing right now because I'm not pitching much. I've been back for ten days and I've only pitched an inning and a third. That's a little hard to swallow too. But you just have to understand that that's part of the game. People are getting paid to make those decisions and they have to make them. I'm not afraid of anybody that walks to the plate. But there is a fear of failure, because when you come in as the short reliever, there's no excuse. You either win it or you lose it. But as far as being afraid of a situation or being afraid of a hitter, there aren't any that are going to walk up there that are going to scare me. But yes, there's a fear of failure. You don't want some reporter asking you, "How'd you hold that homer?"

Am I as intense in the bowling alley as I am on the mound? [Laughs.] Here's how that got started. *Sports Illustrated* wrote the article about me and brought attention to the bowling. The bowling started as an accident. I just went one night for fun. I went with my wife and some friends and we had fun doing it so we went back a couple of times. It was in the off season. And when I started throwing, I realized that I didn't have the pain I normally felt in my arm. After that operation I'd had in high school, every winter adhesions would build up in my elbow. I'd have to heal those up in spring training and that caused a lot of pain. That first time after the winter of bowling I went to spring training and had no pain at all. That winter, once I started throwing and found out it didn't hurt, I was bowling about one hundred games a week. I'm doing okay, I got my average to 207 last winter. It is like a weight lifting program because when you release a bowling ball right, your arm is fully extended. And you get the range of motion and it is a sixteen-pound ball. So it builds front and back on your shoulder, a natural motion, and you're throwing it underhand so there's no threat of injury. I haven't been able to bowl much now because of my knee, but it is something that I will continue to do. I used to hate spring training just due to the fact that I always had to break those adhesions up.

I enjoy the bullpen. And I can get pretty serious out there but there's a lot of laughs too. The funniest thing that I've seen happen this year is Phil Roof, our bullpen coach. Roof was a catcher for a long time. I was warming up in New York and it was the first time that he caught me. I started airing it out—I was feeling really good and I had a good fastball that night. He set up and I threw a fastball that was right down the middle and it just nicked the top of his glove and it hit him square in the chest and he didn't have on a chest protector. And I'm thinking, "Oh jeeze, this guy is dead!" All he did is stand up and go, "Shit!" Picked the ball up and threw it back. I was kind of embarrassed. I didn't know whether I wanted to go in the game or not. Here I've just hit a fifty-year-old guy right in the chest with my best heater and all he does is say, "Shit!" and throws it back.

You have to have the right attitude when you go into the game. Gossage had that. Goose was nuts! I got to spend some time with him in spring training once and he was pretty serious there. But I enjoyed my time with him. He was always one of my heroes, the guy that I admired the most. It was just the way he went about it, his way of taking the mound. The attitude has to be all or nothing. You have to remember that what you did last night doesn't mean nothin'. If you went out and stunk last night, big deal. You've gotta turn it on for tonight, handle the situation you're lookin' at. And if you were great last night, that doesn't mean nothin'. Everything in short relief is, "What can you do for me now?" You have to have a real short memory.

GREGG OLSON
Right-Handed Pitcher

BALTIMORE ORIOLES, 1988–Present

- **1989 Rookie Of The Year**
- **Set A Major League Rookie Record With Twenty-Seven Saves**
- **Pitched Forty-One Consecutive Scoreless Innings In 1989–1990—The Longest Run In The American League Since 1968**

Gregg Olson nervous? The 1989 Rookie of the Year, the guy who just threw forty-one consecutive scoreless innings at American League hitters? Olson nervous?

Brian Holton is on a tear—Olson's penmate has been pie-facing Orioles players for about a month now. He's pied three fellow bullpenners in three days!

In the Orioles locker room before a game with the Milwaukee Brewers, Olson is explaining his reluctance to give a pre-game TV interview to Home Team Sports host Tom Davis.

Olson: "Sorry, I'm not touching that, Tom, not with Brian Holton running loose!"

Davis: "It's not you he wants. He's waiting to get me."

Olson: "Maybe later. Let's give him a month!"

Olson is smiling now, sitting in a bright orange folding chair in front of his dressing cubicle. "Brian is dying to get me and so I'm kind of laying low, waiting for him to cool down," he laughs. Behind Olson, perched on a shelf in his locker cubby sit three fat green good luck charms—Michelangelo, Leonardo, and Raphael. I ask about the keeper of the bullpen's Ninja Turtles. "Yes, these are the famous turtles. I get more questions about them than I do my curveball," he said.

They're our good luck charms. Hey, if I didn't have them out there and things started going bad for us, it would be my head. I took the big ones on the road for one trip this summer and we came out real good. I took one on the road last trip and we went 9 and 4. So you gotta go with them, you know. Here's how it got started. Last year somebody gave us one of those little Ninja turtles and we kept it around and put it up in the pen for good luck. We won about two games in a row so it became our good luck charm. I started taking it out every game and sitting it up so it could see the game. And then it got stolen so somebody gave us another one and we won a couple more games. Then we added a second one. We went to Texas and I had them sitting next to me in the bullpen. It's a wide-open bullpen where the fans can lean in and you can shake hands with everybody in the stands. I had them sitting next to me, so some lady came up and gave me another one. Now we have three Ninja turtles sitting up in our bullpen for all the games.

And everybody looks at me like I'm strange. In Toronto's bullpen the stands are right overhead and the fans are leaning over watching me line them up. I think that one was on national TV, when we were playing for the division at the end of the season. I got a lot of calls from friends on that.

I don't know if all bullpen guys are superstitious, it's because of the way things go for relievers. If you're a position player if you have a bad night you can cut it off, go out and play the next day. But with us once you're going good you want everything to stay the same.

I do get a lot of questions about the curveball. Jack Buck and Tim McCarver were talking to me a few minutes ago [McCarver and Buck are in town preparing for the CBS "Game of the Week" telecast.] They were interested in seeing my grip on the curveball and the fastball. I hear a lot of comparisons from the media of my curve to Blyleven's breaking pitch. Do I grip my curveball differently than most pitchers? Well I think I do. I grip it with the four seams like most do, but I wrap my finger around one of the seams on the horseshoe. I wrap my finger a little bit around on that one so my middle finger is completely on the seam. And I never really lose my grip on it. I've got the curve and the fastball. Two pitches, no changeup. And that's the thing about being in relief too, you don't have the starter's repertoire.

I think with the big breaking pitch that you might get some calls in your favor. Anytime you throw the big breaking ball you will occasionally fool the umpires a little. One comes to mind—there was a game earlier this year in Texas where I kept getting into trouble and then battling my way out. Walks, then strikeouts. I had the bases loaded in the ninth. The score was tied, with two outs and a 2–2 count. I got a questionable curveball call for strike three. Boy I took it, just walked off the mound happy. The hitter is going [shakes his head] and everybody in the park knew what was coming. But that was my last chance to save that game. So when you get a call like that you get out of there fast.

I got one the other night. It was 3–2 and the hitter fouled like two fastballs off. Then I threw a curveball for strike three. Everybody in the park was fooled except for me and Mickey [Tettleton, the Orioles catcher]. It was ball four. It was close enough and it sure didn't hurt me. But if he [the umpire] hasn't seen it before or hasn't seen it enough, well . . . I've had a lot of mistakes called against me and a lot of mistakes given to me because of the sharp break.

Sometimes you go out there with nothing and get everybody out. Then there are other times. . . . I had great stuff Friday night against New York and blew the save. Everybody was saying, he's been up six out of the last seven days and this and that, but I got in the game and I thought, I can't believe I have this stuff. By all rights I should be dead. I had a great fastball and a great curveball and that was one of those nights where they [the Yankees] rose to the occasion and beat me. You're going to run into those nights, I made some mistakes and they took advantage of them. When I walked off the field there was nothing I could do to make myself feel any better. Sometimes you've got to give the hitter credit. He battled me the whole time. I locked him with a fastball that was out, I mean he didn't even move. It was close enough so you'd have to swing at it. So I'm thinking that I might have swung him over into thinking, "Well, he's going to come back with another fastball." And then when you get their thought process, halfway this, halfway that. Fastball? Curve? Curve? Fastball? So I threw the curveball assuming that he was going to swing at it. That's why I tried to throw it in the dirt. But I didn't get it down there. Base hit! When a guy guesses right, you better throw him the perfect pitch or else it's going to be a hit. And that pitch was the game. If he'd have let it go, it would have been a ball. It was down, but I wanted it way down. I wanted to bury it in front of the plate. I didn't do it. And when you've got to make the pitch and you don't . . . well, suddenly you're just standing there looking at a loss.

The Rookie of the Year award was really a big thrill. And I guess if I had to point to the real turning point for me last year [in 1989], it was a game early against Oakland. It was the first time Frank [Robinson] brought me in for a save chance. It was 2–1 and I got through the eighth all right. Then we went into the ninth and I had to face Dave Henderson, Dave Parker and Mark McGwire. And I struck all three of them out and we won. It was just one of those things where

387

everything was working right. I'd get the first strike on them and then I'd have them where I wanted them. That was a special moment, kind of a turning point, I guess.

The whole 1989 season was fun. We weren't expected to win and we did. And we had a lot of fun in the pen. And of course, you can't keep your head in the game all the time. Maybe just to stay loose, I'll go down and catch somebody napping and light a hotfoot, just to keep myself amused. But there were a lot of serious moments and great games in the season too. One game that really sticks out was the one we played in Boston. We were in a big slump and I think we were like 1–12 and on a road trip. We came into Boston and were down 6–0 in about the fourth. We roared back and it was just a great game, scored twice more and we beat them 9–8. And here's what was really funny about that game. During the game Frank called the bullpen and said he wanted Kevin Hickey to come into the bench—now there's a character, Kevin. So we're sitting there in the bullpen speculating about Kevin's fate. We're afraid that maybe someone in his family had died or that maybe he'd been traded. And then we come into the clubhouse after the big win all pumped up and we look at Kevin and all of a sudden we remember his situation. And I go, "Kevin, what happened?" He says, "Oh, Frank just called me into the bench to get the bench revved up, cheer the team on." And that's the team we had in 1989. That's the kind of guys we have in our pen. That game was a big win and Kevin was in there doing his thing.

The success I'm having now? [It's June 13, 1990, and Olson has allowed only two runs in his last forty-four appearances. His ERA is 0.29. When he allowed a run on May 7, at California, he had strung forty-one scoreless innings together, the longest chain of zeros in the league since 1968.] I can't explain it! The only thing that's different is that I'm walking fewer players. But I'll tell you what. I have nine more walks than Eckersley and I feel happy with the lack of walks, but he's something. Last year I had fifty walks and that's a lot of people to put on base in the late innings. That's fifty chances for the other team to win the game. I've cut that down quite a bit. And the answer was an adjustment of my foot on the rubber. I did that right after the All-Star break last year and from then on I went on my little streak [forty-one consecutive scoreless innings]. I let them hit their way on base instead of putting them on by myself. Al Jackson, our pitching coach, is the guy who noticed something. It had to do with my foot on the rubber. My foot was always half on the rubber and my heel was always hanging off. It would be hanging away from the rubber and it was causing me problems because the hole [in front of the slab] is different every night.

I was never consistently in the same motion. Because of this, I'd have to make an adjustment to get to the same point. And then after that it would become an adventure. So now that the foot's completely on the slab, I've got consistency, the same motion every time. Now I can concentrate on putting it in the zone.

I've been fortunate this season. [Mickey Tettleton, the Orioles massive catcher, gets up from his chair at the neighboring locker, takes Olson's hand, balls it up into a fist and raps his pitcher gently on the head. "Knock on wood!" he says. Olson thanks Tettleton for the reminder and continues talking.] But there have been times when I've gotten myself into positions where they just came back and beat me. And if I don't get a chance to come back the next night, then I'm really going to be all over myself mentally. I've gotta get back on the horse, but I'll have my nights where I'm not going to have anything, and I'm going to give it up. You can't go out and expect to save every game. I know that everything people are saying about me now will be turned around if I start to go bad. But the bad days can come, and when they do, it's really just a matter of how you come back, how you rebound the next night.

Speaking of rebounding. Moments later the early birds at Memorial Stadium who came to watch batting practice saw the following scene on the Orioles Diamondvision screen. Tom Davis and his pre-game guest, a redheaded Orioles player, sit in folding chairs along the third base line schmoozing, smiling to a TV camera.

Could it be? Yes, it's "The Pie Man," Brian Holton! Davis has found himself a substitute guest. Suddenly the big scoreboard picture flashes on. Olson carrying something flat and white, circling in from the outfield, he's behind Holton and . . . wham! Revenge for the Orioles pen!

As I watch Holton clean the cream from his face I can't help but feel for Olson. One doesn't take a penner like Brian Holton lightly. The keeper of the Ninjas will need all the luck that his turtles can muster.

ROGER McDOWELL
Right-Handed Pitcher

NEW YORK METS, 1985–1989
PHILADELPHIA PHILLIES, 1989–1991
LOS ANGELES DODGERS,
1991–Present

- Led The National League In 1986 With Fourteen Relief Wins
- One-Hit The Astros For Five Innings In Historic Sixteen-Inning NLCS Game In 1986
- Joined "Eddie The Eagle" As One Of Two Honorary Members Of Wrigley Field Bleacher Bums Club
- The Second Coming Of Moe Drabowsky

Roger McDowell, former stopper of the New York Mets and ace of the Philadelphia Phillies bullpen, met me for lunch at an Applebee's on U.S. 1, near his home in Stuart, Florida. Roger doesn't know it, but I've got the book on him from his fellow pensters. "Great kid but stay loose. Carries his own little mischief kit: cigarette loads, stink bombs, horror masks, hand buzzers, M-80s—a latter-day Moe Drabowsky."

Roger is decked out in Bermuda shorts, a surfing T-shirt, low-cut sneaks. He's smiling, ordering a beer. Instant likability. I mention his reputation for being . . . "Goofy?" he says. "It's true. Every once in a while I get the urge, just gotta do something off the wall." I check my notes and mention the Upside-Down Man. McDowell laughs. "You know about that, huh? That started in L.A. One of those days I just felt the urge to do something . . ." "Goofy?" I ask. He nods, takes a sip of beer and continues.

This was before a game, in 1986 in Los Angeles. They had a battle of the bands, three local bands competing for the bragging rights as best band in the L.A. area, something like that. They all come marching in through the center field fence and are getting ready for their pre-game show. It's right after batting practice. The first group comes in and they're in these Daniel Boone costumes, you know the ones with the coonskin caps. I'm thinking that it would be pretty awesome to get in that band, slip into one of those costumes and come marching by our dugout or bullpen with them playing an instrument. So I go over to the tuba player, and I'm thinking, this will work. I mean, how much can you screw up with a tuba? I say to the kid with the tuba, "Listen, I'll take you into the clubhouse to meet Darryl Strawberry, Gary Carter, Dwight Gooden, all you have to do is trade your uniform with me." And this kid, he goes, "Like really?" I say, "All you've gotta do is give me the uniform," And he says, "Yeah! It's a deal." And so we start sneaking away from the group. But all of a sudden the band leader comes over and wonders where I'm going with his tuba guy. I explain to him and he says, "No, you can't do that."

I'm really disappointed, because I'm like in this goofy stage now, the thing I was talking about and it's kinda like a nicotine habit. I really need to do something. Fortunately I'd bought some Halloween masks earlier in the day. L.A. is the best place to get great fright masks, tricks and stuff because of the movies. I've got these new masks and I don't know how I thought of it but I just decided to go in the locker room and turn my uniform around and go upside-down. I put my shirt on over my legs and put my pants on over my arms and head and eventually when I was done, my shoes were on my hands. It was really a production. I had to pack the mask with a towel, then get a sanitary sock and tape that to the towel and had it tied around my waist so that it would hand down and look like my head was coming out of my shirt, which is over my legs of course. And I just did it and I walked out in the dugout. Jesse Orosco and Steve Garland, our head trainer, and Charlie Samuels, our equipment manager, are helping and I can actually see through my pants leg. The concept is working, it looks like I'm walking on my hands.

And so I go walking out in the dugout and it's about ten minutes before game time. Everybody's laughing and having a good time and it looks funny. Then Bill Robinson, our first base coach, says, "You don't have a hair on your ass if you don't go out on the field." Well, I've got a hair on my ass. I walk up the steps of the dugout and the place is filled up. It's like five minutes before game time and now they catch it on Dodgervision and flash me up on the big screen up there. The next thing, WOR from New York is going on the air and they pick up on it and . . . the people in the stands, they actually think that I'm walking on my hands. I'm standing on my feet but it looks like my hands and I start doing these one-handed push-ups. And I go like this and then I lift up one of my "hands" and now it looks like I'm doing one-arm handstands. Then I go over to a step by the stands and just let my hands fall forward and it looks like I'm falling into the seats.

So that was the Upside-Down Man. Now the word's out around the league about it. When I go into places like Chicago, which is one of my favorite places, they have this cheer. Out in the bleachers they'll start asking for the Upside-Down Man, a chant—"Turn it around, Rog!"—"Turn it around, Rog!"—"Turn it around, Rog!" One of these days I'm going to do it for them. It's quite a production to get the costume made but I feel like I owe it to them. I shot a commercial in Philadelphia as the Upside-Down Man this winter. It's a Phillies promotion—very popular, very goofy.

In 1985 I was invited to spring training and was on the Mets forty-man roster. I came in knowing that their pitching staff was already established. They had the nine guys. Davey Johnson had gotten rid of Dick Tidrow, Craig Swan and all the older guys. And now it was Ron Darling, Sid Fernandez, Dwight Gooden. So realistically, I wasn't given a shot to make the team. He had two other guys—Bill Latham and Calvin Schiraldi were in the same boat that I was. [We] were selected to go to Tidewater [the Mets Triple-A farm team] and that was the whole intention, that I would be starting for Tidewater. Two weeks left in spring training, Brent Gaff got shoulder problems and he was their middle reliever. So there was kind of a contest between Latham, Schiraldi and myself, kind of like a tryout to see who would get to go north. And on April 1 Davey Johnson called me into his office and told me that I was going up with the big team. Of course, I asked if it was an April Fool's joke. This was April 1, and I didn't have the practical jokester reputation at that time because it was my first time in camp with the big boys. When I came out of the clubhouse everybody came up to me and congratulated me. But I was really nervous, because like two days before, Eddie Lynch had pasted this newspaper thing up on my locker, you know how *The Sporting News* runs headlines. At the same time I was trying to make the ball club with the Mets, Oddibe McDowell was trying to make the big club with the Rangers. He wasn't going to make that ball club and the headlines were, "McDowell To Be Sent To Minors." Lynch cut the headline up and pasted "McDowell To Be Sent To Minors" on my locker. And I came in and saw that headline and had tears. I really didn't want to go back to the minors. I'd had some good outings, especially against teams in our division when we played them in spring training. I pitched well against the Yankees and if you're a Met, you better do well against the Yankees. So it was a situation where I thought I'd done well enough to make it. I knew that I would be going up as a reliever. Davey told me, "You are going up as a middle man."

My rookie year was 1985. [McDowell won six, lost five, with seventeen saves, and an ERA of 2.83.] I was used early in middle relief. About a month into the season, someone got hurt so they decided to start me but that just didn't work. That ended in two outings. I didn't have the durability. About two months into the season Doug Sisk, who was the right-handed stopper, along with Jesse Orosco, the left-hander, whenever, sometime in there we switched roles. I was pitching well and Dougie wasn't. I became the right-handed platoon stopper, but in 1985 Jesse was still the main man, the force, whether it was a right-handed or left-handed hitter.

If there is one thing that sticks in my mind from that season it was the game I started in Cincinnati. I was really so afraid. I grew up there, had been a Pete Rose fan all of my life, so now I come in there and have to pitch to him. You know, I never got him out that first year. I think he got two hits, a walk, and I think I hit him once. How can a kid that grew up in Cincinnati, that grew up watching Pete Rose ever get him out?

Okay, my second start—hometown boy comes back to Cincinnati, it's the NBC "Game of the Week," on national TV. Riverfront Stadium, big family turnout, and this was when Marge Schott had taken over the Cincinnati Reds. Pete Rose was playing first base. My first time up is like the third inning. I hit a ground ball to third, and I'm like running. All of a sudden I find that the guy made an error on it and there I am standing at first next to my hero Pete Rose. And he goes, "Hi ya, Rog," and I didn't know whether I should say Mr. Rose or Pete or what. And then he goes, "You're a hometown boy, aren't you?" I nod and grin. He says, "How many people have you got here today?" I say, "Why?" and he says, "Oh I don't know, I was just wondering, you being from Cincinnati and all." Now I've gotten like everybody but the clubhouse boys to sign up for extra passes for me. And you only get six free tickets so you've gotta go to the other guys and get their passes. The word is that Mrs. Schott is a tough [freebie] ticket. So I say, "Oh I don't know, Pete, I put like fifty-three on the pass list!" And he goes, "Marge Schott will shit!" That was it. History. My first conversation with my hero Pete Rose.

Another thing from those first years is that Jesse and I became really good friends. And in 1986 we had this ritual when we got into a winning streak. The two of us would sit in the clubhouse and the game would start and we'd turn the TV on, watch the game, we'd play 500. Meanwhile we're eating cheeseburgers and french fries. We had this little [electronic] golf game. We had one of those and after we got done playing cards and eating, we'd play a round of golf. The winner would have to buy the cheeseburgers the next day. We had a running tab on the card game over the whole year. We did this every game, home and away. We were twenty games up by the All-Star break in the standings and it was like no matter what we'd do, we'd win. When you're up like twenty at the All-Star break, that's unheard of. There weren't any special rules about when we got to the pen, but we knew how Davey was using us. We'd be down there in the seventh inning. Just as long as when he called you were there . . . if he called and you weren't there, that was trouble.

I've always been active, so there's no way that I can sit through nine innings without doing something. I'd go nuts. It's not that I don't take the game seriously because I do. But when you don't pitch until the late innings you don't have to prepare for your job until about the seventh. And there was one time that I remember in Montreal—the pen used to be out beyond the fence in right field, and under the stands they've got this parking garage. It's all clean and smooth cement, shiny cement. So Jesse and I went out and bought these remote control cars. I got a cop car and Jesse got a Ferrari. They have the pylons—I would get my cop car and hide behind these cement pylons until his Ferrari goes by. I've got the siren going and I'm trying to catch him, with the siren going. "*Woooo, woooo!*" We had real fun there. We thought about taking a couple of sweatsuits out there because you could walk right up the steps from the pen and be in the crowd. The idea was to slip the sweatsuits over our unis and go on up and sit with the crowd and watch the game. But we never did do that.

I guess my favorite pen is the one in L.A. The bullpen is situated out in right field beyond the fence, kind of hidden. It's hard to explain but the field is here and the pen is here and they have stands here and here and the stands come around and circle the Pavilion. The bathroom is right here where you can look right down from the stands and see it. Jesse gets up to go to the bathroom and there are a bunch of Mexican people who are real Orosco fans who sit out here. They think that Jesse is Mexican. He isn't, but they think he is. There's always a big crowd of them out by the pen to cheer for Jesse. They're always looking over and asking Jesse for baseballs, autographs and all, so I get them all to stand up. If you open the bathroom door you can see right in. So they all stand up and I go, "Hey, who wants to see Jesse?" and of course there's a nice roar. So I walk over and open the door and there's Jesse, sitting there on the toilet reading a magazine. He looks up and there's the whole crowd, his fans looking down at him. I swear when he came out he didn't speak to me for three days. He threatened to get even, but he never did, nothing quite as good as that. I'll tell you one thing, when I went to the bathroom in the pen in L.A. from then on, I made sure that I didn't have to sit down.

My favorite ball park is Wrigley Field, I have so much fun there during and after batting practice. There's like forty-five minutes between BP and the start of the game. Last year I got one of my biggest honors there. I was inducted into the Wrigley Field Bleacher Bum Hall of Fame. There's only two people in it—Eddie the Eagle, the ski jumper from England who was in the Olympics, and myself. Here's how I got the nod. It started in 1985 or 1986. I got to be friends with this peanut vendor. The guy would come down to the bullpen and I'd say, "Give me some peanuts." He'd give me some peanuts and then the Coke guy would come down and I'd say, "Hey, give me a Coke!" I got to know these guys by sight. The second time we came into Chicago in 1986 they called me up at the hotel and asked me over to dinner. They were in their first year of college and their mom was going to cook. They pick me up, we drive out to their home, have dinner, and now I know who they are, know their families, leave tickets for their families. Later that year I found out that my buddy got fired as a peanut vendor but he was in the bleachers. He told his buddies out there that this McDowell is okay, he's a cool guy. Now I have an in with the bleacher people in Wrigley. After batting practice, I used to always get the hose out, pulled it all the way out to the bleachers and on hot days I'd hose them all down, all the people in the bleachers. This happened for two and a half years.

After I got done with that, well you know how if the opposing team hits a home run they'll throw it back? They'll get you out there. They got me a couple of times. They'll say give me a ball, and it will be like a kid twelve years old. You'll throw it to him and they'll say, "Hey, we don't want your Met ball!" and the kid will heave it back at you. Now it's gotten so that I know them out there and I can throw balls to them and they'll actually keep them. And we'll play games. I'll do pass patterns and they have to hit me with a down-and-out or a fly pattern. And I'd try to do whatever I have to, slow up or whatever, to make it into a diving catch. This entertains the hell out of them. I'd go all around the stands and play with the fans. I even got the center field cameraman to play quarterback. I'd go long, heading for home

395

plate and catch the ball over my shoulder and boy, they love that. They cheer it. Last year the Cubs front office told the grounds crew to take the hose out, no more hose, so I couldn't spray them down, heh! I found a bucket, and I'd have to fill it up and then I'd throw it up in the stands on everyone, but I still got the job done.

There's nothing like the bleachers at Wrigley. I'll tell you something—the bleacher crowd at a night game, it's nothing like the bleacher crowd for a day game at Wrigley. It's not the same. Not your hard-core degenerates. They're out there skipping work, the guys that don't have a job, guys that have nothing to do, they're wild. There's this one guy out there that they call the Bleacher Preacher. He wears one of these little beanies with a propeller on the top. I got to be good friends with him. One time he had a Frisbee and I asked him to throw it to me. I threw it back and we're playin' catch, me and this bleacher preacher, and he gets thrown out. I really felt bad about that. He wrote me a letter [explaining] that it was for throwing objects on the field, and I felt bad. I started it and he gets kicked out. Hell, I got to stay.

Baseball has always been such fun for me. And there are some great guys who aren't doers but love to see something going on. Magadan was like that with the Mets. He was very quiet but he liked to see things done. One time during spring training, we had a game in Miami in spring training against the Orioles. Me and Mags were sitting down there at the end of the bench and Billy [Williams] is umping first base. He signals over to Mags that he wants a cigarette between innings. So Mags goes, "Alright," and he goes, "Rog, go get your loads." I have this little mischief bag that I carry—the stink bombs, M-80s, cigarette loads—and so I run up to the clubhouse and I double-load the cigarette. This is my favorite load. You take the tobacco out and put one about halfway down in there, pack in some tobacco, and then put another right at the end. So between innings Billy comes running over and he lights it and all of a sudden *POW!* It goes off and he goes, "Goddamn it!" And now we're howling and he says, "I'm going to get you for this!" So he goes up in the tunnel and keeps smoking. We're waiting and he's smoking as fast as he can and *BAM!* Off it goes again, now we're rolling and he's, "You sons-a-bitches—the next time I'm behind the plate you better be swinging because I'm going to ring your asses up!" And Mags is going, "I didn't have anything to do with it."

Stink bombs—they're really great, they've gotten so sophisticated. They come in these little plastic vials. On commercial flights you ask the stewardesses for a Band-Aid. You get this stink bomb and tape it under the toilet lid. You set the toilet down gently so it doesn't break. When someone goes in there and sits down, it breaks and when the cabin starts smelling. It starts coming forward and they don't want to come out of there because when they do everybody's choking and carrying on. You can get the stewardess, it's like a stink bomb, stuff like a spray, and you can squirt a little on the stewardess. She does your work for you because she's like up and down the cabin. It only lasts about five or ten minutes, but they really do your work for you.

I guess my most embarrassing moment is the one that made all the blooper films. There were men on first and second, two outs and we're up by a run in the ninth inning against the Padres. Somebody hits a ground ball and it deflects off of my glove and I feel that I should have had it. It was a simple comebacker, and so now they're loaded up. I get the ball back and just out of frustration I go to throw the ball in my glove. I'm facing center field and what happens is, I miss my glove with the ball and it goes flying out between short and third base, like a nice little flare or something. Marvell Wynne is on third base and I don't know what he's thinking or whether this ball is going to go far enough for him to score, but I know what I'm thinking, "Holy shit, the ball didn't hit my glove!" And then I'm going, "Is there time-out? Let there be time-out." But all of a sudden I see HoJo [Howard Johnson] making a break into the hole toward short, reaching out and catching the ball. Man, he comes over and he says, "Are you okay?" I say, "Thanks for the save." Then here comes Davey Johnson out and I think, "Now I've done it. He's going to hook me." It's a left-handed hitter and Jesse's in the pen so I refuse to look at Davey because I don't want him to take me out. I know I'm gone, though, left-handed hitter and all, and I turn to HoJo and I go, "Has he made a move? [signaled the bullpen] Am I out of the game?" and HoJo says, "Yeah!" So I turn around and hand Davey the ball and start to walk past him. He grabs my arm and says, "Where are you going?" I said, "I'm out of the game!" He says "No, I just came to settle you down." Now I've gotta regroup. The bases are loaded and I've got a left-handed hitter coming up. I still gotta get HoJo for that. He got me on that one. But nice ending—I got the guy on a ground ball and we won the game.

I loved playing in New York. In 1985, my rookie year, we went down into the city and went to this club and saw Boy George in there walking around with another guy—Boy John, I guess. He didn't have quite as much makeup, but that's New York. I wasn't recognized there.

397

I used to ride the train from our house into the stadium. I got to know the conductors. Shea Stadium wasn't a regular stop, but they'd stop to let me off. There'd be like eight cars going to the city. They'd stop just for me. And all these people would be going, "What's wrong with the train?" And all of a sudden I'd pop out and walk off.

I guess the one game that I'll never forget, the most memorable game in my career, is the sixteen-inning job against Houston in the 1986 play-offs. Even more than the sixth and seventh games of the World Series that year. Because Knepper is throwing. Scott has already beaten us twice with an ERA like below one, and we can't hit him and we're figuring if this thing goes to seven games it's Scott again, and we can't beat him. Knepper is throwing outstanding in the sixth game and he's got a three-run lead in the ninth, and things don't look very hopeful.

Then Lenny [Dykstra] leads off in the ninth with a triple and we got one run. I'm getting up in the pen getting ready to go, trying to watch the rally which ends up being three runs to tie it. My heart is beating like ninety miles a minute. And I go in and end up throwing five innings. The only base runner, the only guy that gets on, is Kevin Bass. He hits a ball up the middle and two pitches later he tries to steal and Gary [Carter] throws him out. I got one at-bat, in like my third inning of work. I was the second guy up and Davey waves me back from the on-deck circle and says, "If he gets on, bunt him over." And I say, "What if he doesn't get on?" and he says, "Hit a double!" And the first guy, I think it was Ray Knight, gets out. I didn't get a double, I made an out. But I went out and I threw two more innings. The whole thing while I was out there pitching, I was thinking about me losing the ball game. I'd had some bad outings against the Astros that year, three losses I think, and all I could think was, I don't want to give this up. I don't want to be the one that looks up from his locker into about a hundred microphones and notepads and hear some reporter say, "What did you throw him, Rog?"

And I did pitch well. If I could ever pitch like that over a long haul. . . . I don't know what it was—things went right. It might have been the emotions, but I'll tell you that was a thrill. [I threw] fastballs and sliders, the stuff that I'd been using all year, but that day and that game were special. I made good pitches and then they did what I wanted them to do, like swing at a pitch in the dirt, hit a ball to second. Craig Reynolds, in those three losses I had to the Astros, he beat me twice. One was a single and the other one was a home run. I threw a sinker and he's pretty patient as a hitter. This ball just dove and he swung at it on a 3–2 count and I'm going, "This must be my day."

398

I pitch the ninth, tenth, eleventh, twelfth, and thirteenth. And then we score a run in the fourteenth. Jesse's already got two wins and has been outstanding, so they bring him in and there's no reason to think that he's not gonna get them. The first hitter up is Billy Doran and he strikes him out. The next guy up is Hatcher. It's funny, we used to kid with Jesse and call him the Mexican, and every time we went into L.A. it's like we claim he's leaving all these passes for his family. When he's walking in from the bullpen to the mound I'm sitting in the dugout screaming, "Come on, you Mexican!"

So Jesse strikes Doran out. The next hitter is Hatcher and his first fastball is hit like nine miles foul. He hits another one close down the line. And in our dugout it's like the Carlton Fisk thing in reverse—we're trying to wave that one foul. But that one hits the foul pole and that ties it up and now we're starting all over again. Tie game. Jesse gets out of that and later in the top of the sixteenth we score three. Then they come back in the bottom of the inning and have the tying run on second. I mean we're talking about some game here. Jesse later tells me this story about Kevin Bass, who is at the plate, a switch hitter. Keith Hernandez comes over from first. Carter's out there and they're talking about how to pitch Bass. Hernandez says, "If you throw this guy a fastball, I'm going to fucking kill you." So Jesse threw him all sliders and struck him out. And we won the pennant and that was the greatest game I've ever pitched in or watched.

Now in the 1986 World Series, I pitched in Games One, Three, Four, Six, and got the win in the Seventh. But I guess the most exciting moment was in Game Six. That's the one that will always be remembered as the turning point. The Series is three games to two in favor of Boston and twice we're a strike away from being eliminated. With two out and nobody on in the bottom of the tenth inning, we get three singles and the score's 5–3, Sox, and it looks like we're out of it. . . . But before I get to that, the Series itself. . . . Let me tell you, when a moment like that comes, you know it's different. You watch something like that, growing up as a kid watching the World Series on TV you think that the Series is such a big deal. But when I experienced it!

We lost the first two games in our place and now we've got to go up there and play. It's freezing in Boston. In the sixth inning Jesse and I had just come out to the pen from the clubhouse but these guys had been freezing out there for six innings. And the wind's howling, so we build this bonfire [out of] anything—sticks, straws, cups, paper napkins. We're putting our feet on it. But anyway Game Six, back at our place, when the ball went through Buckner's legs, I'll tell you where

I wasn't. I wasn't out there freezing my ass off in the bullpen. I had already pitched and I was in the clubhouse drinking beer, watching the game on TV. There were like four or five of us, in there watching it on the tube. When the inning started we were down a couple of runs and Charlie Samuels, our clubhouse manager, has this great collection of football helmets from every team in the NFL—real helmets—so each one of us in the clubhouse pick our favorite team and put the helmets on as rally hats. I'm wearing a Miami Dolphins helmet, Ronnie Darling is wearing a Patriots helmet, Heep's in a Oilers helmet, Samuels is wearing a Cleveland Browns helmet—he loves the Browns. Anyway there's four or five of us in there in these helmets trying to drink beer through the face masks. There's two outs and Carter, Mitchell, Knight get the hits. We're sitting there and like every time something good happens we take a drink of beer and bang heads. Pretty soon so much good is happening that we're not only getting a headache from the beer, we're getting a headache from banging heads. Now Mookie comes up with the tying run on third. I remember this very distinctly. I turned to Ronnie Darling and I said, "Wild pitch! He's going to throw a wild pitch. I call a wild pitch."

The first ball is inside and glances off of Gedman's glove and Mitch comes in and we score the tying run. And now we've got the winning run on second. This is a biggie for me because we call things all the time and then when it actually happens, it's a major, "I called it, I called it!" In a Series, it's a real biggie. So that ties the game. Now we're really getting wired and a couple of the guys have got to get out of their helmets and head out because they could be used for pinch runners or something. But then we had them all come back in and stay right there—me, Charlie Samuels, Danny Heep, Ronnie Darling, in our helmets, because we started the rally like this and you don't want to screw things up. Then Mookie hits the ground ball through Buckner's legs. We go wild and run out there in the tunnel and when the team comes running in there we are banging our helmets, unbelievable rally, hell of a finish.

Game Seven was, I guess, anti-climactic. I got the win, which was kind of deceptive because I really didn't pitch that well. Jesse was the guy. He came in and closed them out. But here's what was really great. After the game a major celebration, we partied all night. I don't think that we got any sleep at all. I think we went straight to the ticker tape parade in downtown New York. That's something that you never forget. They had these old cars that we rode in and I don't know how it happened, but there was an old fire truck behind us. There were so many people ganging around the parade that you couldn't see the car in front of you. The crowd would sort of open up and your old car would squirt through. People [were] waving and hanging on the *Do Not Walk* signs and hanging out windows, and our car overheated. So Karen, my wife, and I got up on the fire truck and were standing up there in the back and waving. We went to City Hall and it was like, I don't know, Ghostbusters—me in the fire truck waving at New York City!

EPILOGUE

Everybody's Got One

So what brought us to this day when a guy can go out and get his manager fifty-seven saves, a time when our starters complete less than ten percent of their games? How did the game that never changes end up talking in terms that sound like a cast of Dick Tracy characters—setup man, shortman, stopper, and middleman? Do we owe all this to the intuition of managers, the early men like Wright, McGraw, Griffith? Was it the pen shapers of the seventies and eighties—Anderson, Williams, Herzog, and Howser? The mound lowering and the dead ball–live ball controversy? They had to stop those pitchers somehow. Was it Duren's blinding speed, Fingers's fastball and slider, freak pitches from guys like Wilhelm, Miller and Sutter that made the pen what it is today? The great Davis/Gossage, setup/closer combo? Or was it simply the men who passed the ball along from decade to decade, one historic chain reaction—Manning to McGinnity to Brown to Russell to Marberry to Moore before the Second World War? Then Murphy to Casey to Page to Konstanty to Wilhelm to Duren to Face to Sherry for that 1959 World Series? Or was it the feats of the men during the Golden Age—Perranoski, Radatz, McGraw, Fingers, Sutter, Gossage, and Quisenberry? And how about the glamor of all these young millionaires—the kings of the hill out there today—Righetti, Reardon, Eckersley, Plesac, Olson and Thigpen?

All of the above, I suspect. But one thing is certain. The man who sums it up best is a pen man himself. So we'll close with the words of this manager, philosopher and Hall of Fame catcher.

"If a baseball team ain't got the big boy in the bullpen, it ain't got nothing!"

Yogi said that.

Index

Durocher, Leo, 20, 28–29, 41, 52–53, 69–70, 72–73, 77–78, 82, 89–92, 108, 139–140, 202, 254
Dyer, Duffy, 285
Dykstra, Lenny, 398

Easter, Luke, 146
Eastwick, Rawley, 261, 268
Ebbets Field (Brooklyn), bullpen of, 32, 72, 92
Eckersley, Dennis, 270–273, 339, 342
memories of, 351–354
Edwards, Bruce, 75–78
Egan, Wish, 96
Elliot, Claude, 17
Elliott, Bob, 61–62
Ellis, Sammy, 356
Elston, Don, 109–110
Ens, Jewel, 41–42, 44
Ermer, Cal, 222
Erskine, Carl, 69, 90, 201
Escuela, Chico, 372
Esposito, Sam, 108, 374
memories of, 125–137
Essegian, Chuck, 203
Estrada, Chuck, 99
Evers, Hoot, 96, 98
Expos. See Montreal Expos

Face, Elroy, 33, 109–110, 147, 203, 254–255, 258
memories of, 154–165
Fairly, Ron, 222
Farrell, Turk, 6–7, 108, 150, 209–210, 230
Faul, Bill, 210, 214–215
Feldman, Harry, 54
Feller, Bob, 61–62, 73
Fenway Park (Boston), bullpen of, 257
Fernandez, Sid, 392
Fingers, Rollie, 258–260, 270, 272, 316, 332, 337–338
memories of, 291–299
Finley, Charlie, 147, 189, 292, 297–298
Fisher, Brian, 360
Fisher, Cherokee, 16
Fisher, Eddie, 113, 120
Fisher, Jack, 99
Flanagan, Mike, 303
Flood, Curt, 340
Flores, Gil, 354
Foli, Tim, 13
Foote, Barry, 12–13, 342–343
Forbes Field (Pittsburgh), bullpen of, 32, 158
Ford, Whitey, 65–66, 111, 171–172, 177, 238, 243, 279
Fornieles, Mike, 109, 111, 250
Forsch, Bob, 348
Forster, Terry, 315, 317

Foster, Larry, 247
Fowler, Art, 83, 202, 361
Fox, Nellie, 130–131
Frick, Ford, 174
Friend, Bob, 156–157, 160
Frisch, Frankie, 29
Frisella, Danny, 288
Furillo, Carl, 121, 204

Gaetti, Gary, 340
Gamble, Oscar, 320, 361
Garagiola, Joe, 9, 33, 73–74, 97, 99, 146–147
Garber, Gene, 213
Garbey, Memo, 147
Gardner, Billy, 141, 251
Garland, Steve, 391
Garman, Mike, 329
Gee, Johnny, 70
Gehrig, Lou, 65, 68
Gelnar, John, 239, 243
Giants. See New York Giants
Gibson, Bob "Gibby," 212–213, 263
Gibson, Kirk, 353, 371–372
Gilbert, Larry, 58–59
Gilliam, Jim, 203
Ginsberg, Joe, 5
memories of, 95–106
Gionfriddo, G.I., 93
Gomez, Lefty, 19
Gonder, Jesse, 162
Gooden, Dwight, 392
Goosen, Greg, 240
Gorder, Van, 348
Gordon, Joe, 190–191
Gossage, Rich "Goose," 12–13, 214, 261–262, 270, 356, 360–362, 384
memories of, 313–325
Grabowski, Johnny, 19
Granger, Wayne, 267, 269
Grant, M. Donald, 288
Grant, Mark, 14
Gray, Ted, 96–98
Green, Dick, 294
Greenberg, Hank, 28–29, 54
Greenwade, Tom, 68
Gregg, Hal, 69
Gremp, Buddy, 59–60
Griffith, Calvin, 224
Griffith, Clark, 17
Grimes, Burleigh, 26
Grimm, Charlie, 41, 73
Groat, Dick, 156, 162–163, 221
Grote, Jerry, 274–276, 285
Groth, Johnny, 98
Guerrero, Pedro, 330
Guetterman, Lee, 360
Guidry, Ron, 304, 356, 358, 361

406

410

Westrum, Wes, 100, 282
Wheeler, Jack, 161
White, Bill, 221–222
White, Jo-Jo, 168, 202
White Sox. *See* Chicago White Sox
Wight, Bill, 99
Wilber, Del, 129–130
Wilhelm, Hoyt, 100–101, 108, 113,
    119–120, 129, 148, 257–258
  memories of, 138–142
Williams, Billy, 280, 396
Williams, Claude, 32
Williams, Dick, 259, 292, 294–295, 297
Williams, Mitch, 306–307, 310, 337–339
  memories of, 380–384
Williams, Stan, 203, 207–208, 221, 227,
    341–342
Williams, Ted, 43–45, 59–60, 149–150,
    214, 249, 253–254
Williams, Walt "No Neck," 120
Willis, Ron, 215

Wills, Maury, 226
Wilson, Earl, 65, 256
Winfield, Dave, 359, 375
Wohlford, Jim, 320
Wood, Wilbur, 113, 120, 325
Woodeshick, Hal, 213–214
Woodling, Gene, 96
Worrell, Todd, 348
Worthington, Al, 113, 130, 223
Wyatt, John, 254
Wynn, Early, 97, 130, 197
Wynne, Marvell, 397

Yankees. *See* New York Yankees
Yankee Stadium, bullpen of, 8–9, 173, 238
Yastrzemski, Carl, 114, 255, 318–320
Yelding, Eric, 341
York, Rudy, 39–40
Young, Cy, 17

Zimmer, Don, 96, 202, 219
Zisk, Richie, 322

413